Ethics and Values in Librarianship

Ethics and Values in Librarianship

A History

Wallace Koehler

ROWMAN & LITTLEFIELD
Lanham • Boulder • New York • London

Published by Rowman & Littlefield
A wholly owned subsidiary of The Rowman & Littlefield Publishing Group, Inc.
4501 Forbes Boulevard, Suite 200, Lanham, Maryland 20706
www.rowman.com

Unit A, Whitacre Mews, 26-34 Stannary Street, London SE11 4AB

British Library Cataloguing in Publication Information Available

Library of Congress Cataloging-in-Publication Data

Koehler, Wallace C., author.
Ethics and values in librarianship : a history / Wallace Koehler.
pages cm
Includes bibliographical references and index.
ISBN 978-1-4422-5426-8 (hardcover) — ISBN 978-1-4422-5427-5 (ebook)
1. Library science—Moral and ethical aspects—History. 2. Librarians—Professional ethics—History. 3. Libraries and society—History. I. Title.
Z665.K754 2015
020—dc23
2015013772

∞™ The paper used in this publication meets the minimum requirements of American National Standard for Information Sciences Permanence of Paper for Printed Library Materials, ANSI/NISO Z39.48-1992.

Printed in the United States of America

This work is dedicated to William:
My brother Bill
My son Will
My grandson Bill

Contents

Foreword   ix

Preface   xi

Acknowledgments   xv

1 Libraries and Ethics   1

2 Stewardship and Service   31

3 Classification   43

4 On Public Libraries   79

5 On the Freedom of Expression, Intellectual Freedom, and
Their Control   103

6 Libraries and Democracy   133

7 Intellectual Property, Copyright, and Fair Use   145

8 Qualifications of the Librarian   171

9 Love of Libraries and Advice on Library Formation 199

10 New Conditions and New Principles   213

11 Concluding Chapter   227

Bibliography   245

Index   269

About the Author   275

Foreword

As the field of information ethics expands globally and in ways that vastly transcend the longstanding profession of librarianship, it is harder to find specific new works dedicated to library communities. So this is a particularly valuable primer, as it offers fresh historical vantages on ethics and values in librarianship itself. Although the author, Wallace C. Koehler, is not a historian, and affirms that disclaimer, the work serves as a refreshing counter to the glaring ahistorical thrust in library and information studies education and scholarship. That said, there is both a time and place to this work, transparently delineated by the author. The almost exclusively (and not entirely) western emphasis is part of his proviso.

This book will be analyzed in the years to come by future library buffs and historians. And with Koehler's wholehearted support, it will be read alongside non-western and indigenized understandings of the field. The desire for this open reading is clear. Accordingly the storytelling elements of the narrative are warm and welcoming. They bring us into the reading library of the author, who has read extensively. We begin with Ranganathan's arguably global concept of Five Laws of Library Science (first published in the 1930s) and carry forward to present day in a much more tightly bound western tradition. Thus, the project extends over almost a century in scholarship and practice, certainly fitted into a western construal. But titles from long before are intermixed in this ethics and values trajectory, prompting the reader with critical pauses. For example, we encounter the documented reference to the public library in the time of Julius Caesar, the 1603 opening of the Bodleian library at Oxford, the formation of the Japan Library Association in 1892 (under the name of Nippon Bunko Kyokai), and India's first library training class held in 1915. By the time we catch up to the pioneering works of ethicists, such as the likes of Rafael Capurro (information ethics) and Martha M. Smith (global information justice), we have internalized a certain context for understandings of their contributions.

The structure of the book is built on a ten-chapter plan. Themes (e.g., stewardship, classification, intellectual property, privacy, the qualification of a librarian) comprise a layered text. For example, while Chapter 5 is primarily concerned with freedom of expression and intellectual freedom, Chapter 6 is concerned with democracy. The two chapters are of course inextricably linked. This approach makes for a purposeful slow read and non-reductive narrative. This is not an antiseptic account of ethics and values in librarianship; rather the solid text embraces complexity and context, built on a philosophical base. Moreover, the author assumes the reader values the literature of librarianship and relishes in meanderings through it. Indeed, we learn of "bibliophiles, bibliomanes, and bibliomaniacs" in this text. While Chapter 9 is said to "take an almost romantic path" on the love libraries, we would be hard-pressed today in North American library and information studies programmes to find students of library science so studied. And in truth, it shows in the amnesia prevalent in our field.

The author, professor emeritus at Valdosta State University and former director of its Master of Library and Information Studies Program, presents us with his account and it is naturally rooted in his wide-ranging interests and reflective of his long record of library and information scholarship. He encourages our interest in a more common project. He wisely affirms in the first sentence of the Introduction "the ethics of librarianship and its practice are not fixed or constant". But he does close the book with the firm expectation information workers have an obligation to the cultural record. No doubt, each generation will reframe the lens on the ethics and values of librarianship. The gift in this work is how the author documents something of his location and generation. It is up to others to extend the etiology, to counter and build up a matrix for it, and with any luck to continue to provide spaces for librarianship in the world of information ethics. For those reasons, this book belongs in many a library. And what becomes of the book, both its ideas and its physical artifact, forms another critical examination.

Toni Samek
Professor
School of Library and Information Studies
University of Alberta

Preface

The formal analysis of the ethics of library and information science is of recent etiology. S. R. Ranganathan is among the first to address the discipline and to provide us with guidance. First published in the 1930s, Ranganathan's *Five Laws of Library Science* (republished in 1963) provides a framework within which the ethics of the information professions can be assessed.

Ranganathan provided the first evidence of a shifting of ethical principles with his first and second laws. No longer is the stewardship of the collection to take primacy. Access and the needs of the end user are to be the first concern of the librarian. Ranganathan's fifth law, that libraries are organic entities, reminds us that the functions of libraries evolve and change as the needs and concerns of users change.

Throughout this work, the terms "library" and "book" are used in broad terms. "Book" is used as a generic term to denote an information container. "Libraries" are collections of information containers, be they physical, virtual, or both.

The underlying hypothesis is that the purpose of the library and its collection has undergone redefinition and will continue to do so. Each of the chapters addresses a facet of the changing environment and the implications of those changes for the library and the librarian.

THE PLAN OF THE BOOK

Ethics and Values in Librarianship: A History is organized by chapters that discuss in detail separate ethical themes. The introductory chapter addresses an overview of ethical issues and their development over the history of libraries and librarians.

Specific ethical precepts and concepts that have ethical implications and nuances are developed and examined in separate chapters. Chapter 2 addresses stewardship and service. Stewardship is concerned with the guardianship of the cultural heritage and records both as it is concerned with the preservation of artifacts as well as with the continuity of ideas. Stewardship is the defining library values; it describes the core functions of libraries in all of their varied contexts. It is the most enduring and the most unchanged of the values held by librarians. Stewardship, however, is challenged by service. Service has become the new first principle.

Chapter 3 explores library classification systems and their evolution. Some have incorporated classification as a function of stewardship, as indeed it is. Classification is sufficiently complex to require a separate treatment. Library classification began as a means to inventory the collection, to avoid redundancy, and to be able to locate and retrieve materials with relative ease. Classification has retained those characteristics but has added others, to include a mechanism to convey meaning through linguistic and encoded means. The first purposes of classification remain unchanged, but both cultural and technological changes have added to its "mandate." The classification function is second to and supportive of stewardship. It, like stewardship, dates to the beginnings of libraries. It is also critical to the provision of service.

Chapter 4 examines the concept of the public library. *Public* libraries have been an integral part of library history at least since the reign of Julius Caesar. Yet, as the record clearly demonstrates, our understanding of precisely what a public library is has changed significantly over time. The public library as it is understood in the West today is largely a mid-nineteenth-century development that underwent significant redefinition at the beginning and end of the twentieth century.

Chapter 5 addresses intellectual freedom, the freedom of expression, selection, and censorship. The history of censorship is probably as long as the history of libraries. Political, religious, and cultural authorities have always sought to limit discourse, either by prohibiting certain subjects or types of speech or by prescribing that which is acceptable and that which is not. Western concepts of intellectual freedom and the freedom of expression can be dated formally to the late eighteenth century when the First Amendment to the US Constitution and the French Declaration of the Rights of Man and the Citizen of 1789 were first promulgated. These concepts have since been reified as part of the organic documents of most countries, albeit often with exceptions and limitations. These concepts are also integral to the expressed beliefs of most library associations. For example, the International Federation of Library Associations and Institution's Statement on Libraries and Intellectual Freedom and the American Library Association's Library Bill of Rights mirror the provisions of the United Nations' Universal Declaration of Human Rights of 1948. Yet for all the organic and statutory support for freedom of expression and intellectual freedom, it has only been in the twentieth century that librarians have embraced them as core beliefs, and sometimes more in the breach than in the practice.

Chapter 5 is also concerned with freedom of expression, intellectual freedom, and related principles. While the terms "freedom of expression" and "intellectual freedom" were first used in the twentieth century, libraries have long been concerned with issues of intellectual balance and the development of appropriate collections. Explicit references to selection policies can be traced back to Richard de Bury's *Philobiblon*, written in the mid-fourteenth century.

Chapter 6 addresses the theory that libraries, ipso facto, are engines for democracy. There is an extensive literature to support the hypothesis that libraries are either a sufficient and perhaps necessary cause of democracy or that libraries undergird the democratic urge.

Libraries may help support the democratic ideals in societies already that are democratic. There is, however, nothing inherent to libraries that promotes either evolutionary or revolutionary change from less democratic to more democratic institutions. First, libraries existed long before the rise of the liberal democracies of the late eighteenth century forward. Second, libraries existed and were important institutions in the autocratic and totalitarian regimes of the twentieth century. Libraries, we suggest, are inherently conservative institutions that tend to support the regime in power. If anything, in times of social change, libraries will tend to support the status quo ante. That said, libraries that exist in liberal democratic societies and that are permitted to support liberal democratic ideals will do so. In that capacity and that capacity alone, libraries support and lend to democracy.

Chapter 7 addresses the development of intellectual property theory. Intellectual property has undergone a significant evolution in the West from an expression of the collective consciousness to individual ownership of the expression of ideas. The first effort to regulate intellectual property by government was the British Statute of Anne in 1710. By the end of the eighteenth century, the concept had been embedded in national constitutions (e.g., article I, section 8 of the US Constitution). The acceptable norms for the use of intellectual property (fair use) have undergone an almost 180-degree change since the eighteenth century. Once it was not only acceptable but common practice to "borrow" text verbatim from the work of others, incorporate that text into one's own work, and neglect to attribute the source of the work. Libraries, such as that at Alexandria, increased their holdings through the outright taking and copying of material that was found within their spheres of influence. Medieval monastic libraries perpetuated knowledge by copying and sometimes translating their holdings in order to protect and preserve their collections. Intellectual property practice underwent redefinition after the introduction of the printing press. It continues to be redefined in a digital environment.

Chapter 8 explores the qualifications of librarians. What qualifies an individual to be a librarian is not yet settled. Librarians in Rome were most likely educated Greek slaves. Medieval librarians were, for the most part, monks. Following the Renaissance, most librarians were educated men (never women) often trained in theology (many were priests or ministers of the cloth). By the seventeenth century, clergy were partly displaced by scientists, philosophers, physicians, and historians. It is not until the late nineteenth century that specific training regimes were established and that women were admitted into the profession. The twentieth century witnessed the development of educational curricula offered by schools to train professional librarians. The qualifications and depth and length of training for librarians are as yet not universally standardized. North America trains its librarians in professional schools and confers on them master's degrees. In most of the rest of the world, the bachelor's degree is considered the terminal degree. The certification or accreditation process also differs. Again, in North America programs are accredited, whereas elsewhere librarians are typically licensed based on education and perhaps examination.

Chapter 9 takes an almost romantic path. It concerns itself with book and library lovers. Bibliophiles and bibliomanes have been important contributors to the building of book cultures, and more specifically to the establishment of specific academic and public libraries. Major libraries were often the product of pleas to authority by bibliophiles. Juan Páez de Castro prevailed on his king, Felipe II of Spain, to establish a library at El Escorial. Justus Lipsius (1607, 91) extols his unnamed prince to promote library creation: "Consider, O Most Illustrious Prince, how the love of books brings favour and high renown,—such favour and renown as should be granted to great men like yourself." Gabriel Naudé addressed his library plea to the president of the Parlement of Paris. And Johann Christian Koch urged the elector of Saxony to build a library. Other bibliophiles, Sir Thomas Bodley and Thomas Jefferson among them, donated or sold collections to propagate major libraries. Andrew Carnegie and today the Bill and Melinda Gates Foundation have been major contributors to public library development through building programs or equipment grants.

Chapter 10 addresses the principles of confidentiality and privacy. These highly related concepts are very new to the ethics of librarianship. A survey of writing on librarianship suggests that these principles were not embraced as central to the core of librarianship until the mid-twentieth century. Once adopted, however, privacy and confidentiality have become important to library practice.

A final concluding chapter provides an overview and synthesis of the roots of the values and ethical practices of librarianship.

Acknowledgments

I owe a great debt of gratitude to those who reviewed earlier drafts of this work. Vera Blair, Dick Kawooya, Kathleen de la Peña McCook, and Paul Sturges provided excellent guidance and recommendations to improve this work. Charles Harmon and his staff helped me craft this work and to publish it. Toni Samek provided a thoughtful foreword. I thank you all.

Vera Blair encouraged my efforts. It would be wrong to say she assisted me with translations of German language materials. Without her very able help, I would have been lost.

I thank Lester Pourciau and Martha M. Smith, both of whom provided early inspiration to pursue information ethics. Also thanks to J. Michael Pemberton, who encouraged my initial forays.

ONE

Libraries and Ethics

Those of religion aside, the two most enduring institutions of civilization are libraries and universities.

—Alan Bundy (2001, 1)

What are the normative principles pointed to by the observed trends in library practices, and pointing to future trends now not quite visible?

—S. R. Ranganathan (1963, 20)

There is a golden thread of values and practices that runs through library work in all kinds of libraries—a golden thread that defines librarianship as a profession no matter where it is practiced.

—Michael Gorman (2003, 3)

INTRODUCTION

The thesis of this work is that the ethics of librarianship and its practice are not fixed and constant. Instead there are some few principles that have persisted with little change from the beginnings of libraries, but most are of much more recent etiology or have been significantly revised over time (see Budd 2001).

An examination of the historical library literature suggests that there are at least nine different classes of literature: (1) bibliographies, bibliographies of bibliographies, and historiographies; (2) catalogs of individual and sometimes several library collections; (3) histories of the library or of the book; (4) classification schema; (5) the "universal library" concept, to include the collection as well as the catalog; (6) theses on library management to include the duties and education of librarians; (7) expressions on the love of books; (8) advice on library creation; and (9) theoretical underpinnings of the library. Frequently elements of one or more of these concerns can be found in individual works.

At times the differences are clearly delineated, as is the case in Edward Edwards's (1859) *Memoirs of Libraries* or Pierre Le Gallois's *Traitté Historique des plus belles bibliothèques de l'Europe* (1680). Others, like James Kirkwood's (1669c) intertwines two or more classes in a single work. Still others, like S. R. Ranganathan, have produced several monographs, each of which addresses a specific concern.

There are prominent examples of shifts in ethics. Stewardship, defined broadly, has been the most "steadfast," yet is eclipsed by service. Others, like intellectual freedom and freedom of expression, are among the most recent and too often the most challenged. Still others—for example, access and the treatment of intellectual property—have undergone significant change from time to time and place to place (see Budd and Raber 1996).

Another very important set of changes has been the ethical perspectives of librarians toward women, minorities, the young, the old, and the poor. For most libraries, that history has been one of exclusion of almost all but men, usually elite males, from the use of or employment in libraries. It was not until the middle of the nineteenth century that women, the young, and the workingman were to be made welcome. It was not until the latter part of the nineteenth century that women could be librarians (see Hildenbrand 1996). It would be several decades later that people of color could be educated in the United States as librarians. It was not until the early part of the twentieth century that library collections welcomed the casual user. It was only after the middle of the twentieth century, at least in the United States, that minorities were to be admitted to most libraries. Libraries still grapple with access by "undesirables." At the onset of the twenty-first century, the role and therefore the ethics of library and information science have shifted. This book seeks to document many aspects of those shifts.

This work is placed in an interesting context. Michael Gorman (2000) suggests that library ethics are enduring. Jimmy Carter (2005) concludes that American values, broadly speaking, are endangered. These threats to American values are implicit threats to American libraries. This work is set largely within the Western tradition. European theory and practice dominated discussion until the beginning of the twentieth century. The work shifted more to the North American tradition thereafter. That said, the contributions of S. R. Ranganathan are at the heart of the book.

As is suggested throughout this work, information ethics and library ethics were not formally acknowledged until very recent years. Recent pioneers in the field, Robert Hauptman (1976, 1988, 1991), Thomas Froehlich (1992), and Martha M. Smith (1993, 1997a, 1997b) among them, were responsible for brining the concern to academic attention. Stephen Almagno, Johannes Britz and Tomas Lipinski (2001), Toni Carbo (2008),

Carbo and Smith (2008), Lester Pourciau (2001), Toni Samek (2007), and others soon began to contribute as well. Philosophers like Rafael Capurro (e.g., 1996 and 2006) and Luciano Floridi (e.g., 1999 and 2013) have taken information ethics to a new theoretical level.

Attention has also been turned to the introduction of ethics into library and information science education (e.g., Bearman 1987; M. M. Smith 1993; Koehler 2003; Carbo 2004; Jefferson and Contreras 2006; Samek 2012). The American Library Association, for example, considers knowledge of "the ethics, values, and foundational principles of the library and information profession" to be one of the core competencies for library and information science school graduates. The American Library Association (ALA) Core Competencies of Librarianship were adopted in 2009 (ALA Committee on Education 2008).

The rights of minorities and the promotion of diversity (e.g., Josey and Abdullahi 2002) in library and information science have long been of concern and have an important ethical component. These rights include the intellectual property rights of indigenous peoples (see, for example,JankeandIacovino 2012; Kawooya 2006; or Samek 2007). These rights include protection of indigenous knowledge and practices. There is also a dynamic literature that addresses rights of access and participation in the United States for African Americans (see e.g., E. J. Josey 1970), Hispanics (e.g., Ayala and Güereña 2012), Native Americans (e.g., Warrior 1995), and immigrants (see e.g., Burke 2008). The ethical perspective in librarianship is one of recognition, protection, and respect for indigenous peoples and knowledge. For minorities, the perspective is for respect, support, and inclusion.

In North America, a number of professional associations have been formed to support a variety of minorities and information diversity. These include the Black Caucus of the American Library Association, established 1970; the National Association to Promote Library and Information Services to Latinos and the Spanish-Speaking (REFORMA), established 1971; the Chinese American Librarians Association, established 1973; the American Indian Librarian Association, established 1979; the Asian Pacific American Librarians Association, established 1985; and the Gay, Lesbian, Bisexual, and Transgender ALA Round Table, established 1998. The very existence of these associations underscores the importance of the issues they represent.

LIBRARIES AS HUMAN INSTITUTIONS

Libraries are among the oldest of human institutions. Justus Lipsius (1607, 31–32), one of the great historians of the library, recognized that libraries followed soon after human beings began to write: "The art of writing must have arisen almost as soon as man began to learn and to think; and this art would not have been profitable if books had not been preserved and arranged for present and future use." Following soon after the creation of the first library, no doubt, so too arose rules and practices to manage those libraries and the information they contained.

Librarians and other information workers have long subscribed to standards of practice. These standards of practice have developed from the social norms that guide societies through the rule of law as well as its mores and values. In addition, librarians, like other professionals, have developed standards of practice that derive from the necessities and idiosyncrasies of the practice itself. Just as societies evolve and change, so do the principles that regulate librarians and libraries. Yet, despite their differences, different societies share similar structures and the functions those structures serve for those societies. Perhaps libraries are one of those structures common across societies and across time. François LaPélerie (1998, 68) puts the question thusly: "Is there an essential quality, a wisdom, a savoir-faire, that is universal, that transcends time and civilizations, and that defines the librarians' craft?"[1] [translation by the author]. There is a second dimension to the ethics of librarianship. Librarians must at times make decisions and apply their ethics at the point of delivery of services (Wilkinson 2014). The practical and the theoretical are not always congruent (e.g., Reinsfelde 2014).

One purpose of this work is to seek to address that question by drawing upon the work of library commentators across time and cultures. While librarianship is and has been a staple of most cultures, this book is limited for the most part to Western library culture. Where secondary sources point the way, both Western and other cultures are explored for their contributions to universal quality of the art and science of librarianship.

CHANGING IDEAS, CHANGING VALUES

A second purpose of this work is to chart the evolution of ethical practice in the information professions by focusing on library practice and the writings of library scholars across cultures and time. Isaiah Berlin (1991, 1996) has documented the flow, perhaps the torrent of ideas, of paradigms in Western culture. He does this by closely examining the philosophies as they are developed, challenged, modified, and replaced from the Greeks and Romans through contemporary thought. Berlin does not reference libraries or librarians. Yet through his explanations we can understand both why medieval scholastic librarians emphasized stewardship and the ancient philosophers (see Berlin 1991, 20–48), while the Bolshevik revolutionaries in the Soviet Union conceived of books and libraries as an extension of Marxism-Leninism and as tools of the revolution (see Berlin 1996, 77–115).

Perhaps Berlin's (2001) signal contribution has been his exploration of the more obscure as well as the better-known thinkers. He writes of Karl Marx and Niccolò Machiavelli as well as Georges Sorel and Moses Hess. Berlin makes clear that the history of Western thought advanced by both nuanced thought and revolutionary shifts. One can trace Western thought from the pre-Socratics (i.e., Thales, Anaximander, Pythagoras, and Heraclitus) who sought to understand the "world," its constituent parts, and the relationship of humans to that world. In the twentieth century, guiding paradigms have included political and economic models of capitalism, socialism, and fascism. Efforts to understand the modern and post-modern environment have included an essential tension between structuralism and existentialism. One of the most powerful forces has been the rise of nationalism. That force, nationalism, has bent and been bent by the Reformation, the Enlightenment, Romanticism, capitalism, and socialism (Berlin 1991, 238–261). Nationalism is now challenged by the new, essentially economic and sometimes cultural paradigm of globalism.

As we shall see, many of the foundational works of librarianship are by commentators more obscure still than those Isaiah Berlin illuminates. A few are well known for their contributions to other fields. Examples are Gottfried Wilhelm von Leibniz or H. G. Wells, who made contributions "tangential" to the discipline. Some like Juan Páez de Castro, Johann David Köhler, or Johann Christian Koch are almost unknown. Still others like Melvil Dewey, S. R. Ranganathan, or Anthony Panizzi are well recognized by the discipline.

The Library as Icon

We are defined in the way we perceive reality. Benjamin Belton (2003) provides an interesting analysis of the Orinoco River based on the perception of the river from philosophical and temporal perspectives. As basic social paradigms shift, so do the interpretations of societies' iconic symbols. The "library" as iconic symbol has shifted as the *topos-sphere*—defined as the sphere of cultural imagery—has evolved together with changes to the base social paradigm. These shifts in the topos-sphere expand or contract that which Jürgen Habermas (1991) has called the *public sphere*. As the public sphere is changed, so are the perceptions of the iconic focus and its place in society.

These changes in social definition and relationships have also been addressed by Umberto Eco (2004) in the more symbolic milieu of art and beauty (see also Budd 2001 and 2003). Beauty, for Eco (2004, 8–10), is not only in the eyes of the beholder; it is a socially defined quality that will adhere to an object or concept, whether the object or concept is possessed by the beholder on not: "A beautiful thing is something that would make us happy if it were ours, but remains beautiful if it belongs to someone else" (10). Just as beauty is a socially defined concept, and so are professional ethics. Beauty and ethics can be admired in the abstract as well as in the corpus. Ethics, like beauty, is a social concept to be redefined from time to time and place to place.

The Library and Ideas

The institution and the concept of library and of librarians have changed as Western society shifted from pre-modern to modern to postmodern. These have been a complex set of changes that serve to define the function of library and librarian in society. These changes have also affected the way in which the librarian perceives his or her (only most recently) role in practice and the ethics of practice.

To suggest that societies develop similar institutions to meet similar needs is not to say that these institutions necessarily bear much superficial resemblance to one another or that these institutions do not undergo marked change or restructuring over time. Nor is it to say that institutions in two or more societies that bear a superficial resemblance to one another are guided by similar principles. One need only look to changes in government in Europe from a prehistoric tribal structure to the Greek city-states, the heights of the Roman Republic and its devolution into empire and collapse, feudalism and divine right monarchy, to fascist dictatorships, to democratic republics and limited monarchies, and finally to the techno-bureaucracy of the European community. Each of these structures has served a regulative function, the governance of some defined population within some defined territory over some period of time. Similarly Soviet and American libraries in the 1930s shared a physiognomy and function, yet each had a very different social purpose.

Libraries: Modern Institutions in a Postmodern World?

Libraries—so Justus Lipsius (1607), Edward Edwards (1859), and Michael Harris (1995) inform us—are ancient institutions. Harris dates them from the end of the prehistoric era. Since the beginnings of writing, and therefore the beginnings of libraries, the concept "library" has grown and expanded. Yet it has not lost its first raison d'être. As Harris (1995) and others point out, libraries began as depositories of government and business records. In a more fundamental way, to quote Harris (1995, 3), "one of the purposes for the development of writing was to preserve human communication—to extend its duration beyond the sound of the human voice and beyond the memory of mortal persons, and it is probable that written communications were kept almost from the beginning of writing."

Jürgen Habermas (1991, 31) is perhaps the last of the modernists to address social institutions and their role as carriers of culture and enlightenment. Habermas is chiefly concerned with the idea of the "public sphere." By *public sphere* Habermas means an arena within which discourse can lead to democratization. Discourse, by its very definition, requires the exchange of information and social institutions that support that exchange. Libraries are among those institutions that contribute to discourse by serving as repositories of information and as mechanisms for the exchange process.

Habermas is a champion of a contemporary enlightenment thesis. The Enlightenment had its beginnings in the early eighteenth century. It is a belief of the autonomous self and the decoupling of the self from various dominating social institutions—the state, the church, the economic sector, and so on. The Enlightenment had as its basis science, technology, and learning; thus, in a sense, enlightenment theory transfers reliance from one set of institutions to another set. Science and the scientific method come to replace a more mystical interpretation, and hence a more rationalist and individualist one. In a "Habermasian" environment, the greater the number of information sources and the more widely disseminated they are, the greater their role in the public sphere and, therefore, the greater the democratization of society. In this Habermas echoes the analysis made by Alexis de Tocqueville (1835) a hundred years before. The expansion of libraries beginning in the nineteenth century coupled with nineteenth- and twentieth-century communications technology (telegraph, radio, telephone, television, Internet) produced an information sphere that reshaped social convention and political, social, and economic interaction.

Modernism and enlightenment are important concepts. As we shall see, libraries as we have come to understand them are very much of the eighteenth century. Without question, libraries have existed far longer than modernist thought. Perhaps libraries have participated in the public sphere from the first libraries of clay tablets to today's digital libraries. Yet, as any historian of philosophical thought can attest, our popular perception of the relationship of the individual to society and of the individual and of society to the supernatural and the metaphysical have changed and changed significantly from Hellenistic thought to existentialism and post-modernism. Thus information, rather than contributing to a growing autonomy of the individual in the public sphere, may very well, through the institutions that control and regulate information, contribute more to social control and collectivization of thought. The library, then, might be more of a mechanism for standardization and elite control than a liberalizing institution (see Harris 1973; Shera 1949).

Libraries in a Post-Modern Context

I suggest that the role of a library depends very much on the society in which it is found. Totalitarian and authoritarian societies will explicitly employ libraries to control and limit general access to information, just as they seek to control other social institutions (see Arendt 1951). More liberal societies employ both explicit and implicit means to regulate information institutions and transfers. Liberal and authoritarian societies differ both in the extent to which they seek to limit information transfers and the way in which they regulate information institutions.

The exercise of both positive (proscriptive) and negative (prescriptive) policies by liberal and authoritarian societies varies in degree and in kind. All societies, including those deemed to be liberal or democratic, will seek to control what information is available to the general public, to the public sphere. What is or is not acceptable varies from place to place and time to time. For example, in the United States (a liberal democracy) it was illegal to provide information on birth control in many jurisdictions until the middle of the twentieth century.[2] By the beginning of the twenty-first century that information was ubiquitous. Yet more than one twentieth-century US federal administration has sought to limit such information as part of its foreign policy. In the People's Republic of China (an authoritarian society) birth control and abortion are promoted as a matter of public policy. In the United States there are relatively limited efforts to regulate access to Internet content, particularly by minors in public institutions (libraries, schools). In China Internet access and use are far more tightly regulated.

Liz Greenhalgh and Ken Worpole (1995, 12–14) have defined public libraries as in the public sphere and have placed them as institutions in public space. The existence and use of public space, a concept related to the "commons," are integral parts of civil society. Much of the literature on civil society is concerned with the post-modern liberal democratic Western society and its institutions. The library—academic, public, and special—is an important civil institution to a greater or lesser degree of that society. That said, Western libraries came into existence in societies that were manifestly not liberal democracies. Moreover, libraries have functioned equally well in totalitarian and authoritarian societies of both the left and the right.

Existentialism and structuralism are two post-modern challenges to the Enlightenment and modern interpretations. Existentialism at its root is concerned with individual rationality in an irrational universe. Human beings are essentially powerless, no matter the degree to which we experience and understand the "reality" outside ourselves. While we experience "the world," the conclusions we may derive based on those experiences are as absurd as the information on which they are based. In his novel *La nausée* (1938) Jean-Paul Sartre was to argue that our ideas are derived from our experiences. Perhaps so, but our attempt to anthropomorphize that externality is meaningless. Indeed inanimate objects, inanimate as they are, are inherently indifferent to human beings.

In *Le mur*, set during the Spanish Civil War, Sartre (1939) painted word pictures of the impossibility of people trying to act rationally in response to the irrational. Albert Camus was to emphasize the absurdity and meaningless of life (*Le mythe de Sisyphe* 1942). For Camus, science was a futile exercise in an equally futile effort to seek the truth. Sisyphus was the anti-heroic figure of Greek mythology forever condemned to roll a rock up a hill, only to have the rock roll back before reaching the top. The myth is a metaphor for futility. For the existentialist, science imitates art imitates life. Our sources of information are varied, and all are equally incomprehensible despite our best efforts to comprehend them.

If existentialism is about the powerlessness of the individual in the face of irrationalism, structuralism is about the power of institutions in the face of rationalism. Structuralism contradicts the basic existentialist assumptions of human freedom and looks to the cultural determinates (structures) that dictate human behavior (e.g., Lévi-Strauss 1969). Structuralism grew out of Ferdinand de Saussure's (1972) *Cours de linguistique générale*, first published in 1916 and the work of subsequent scholars in the structures of linguistic analysis. Structuralists and linguistic structuralists seek to understand the symbolic and semiotic impact on human action by defined structures. Among these cultural structures are information, information packages, and the means by which information is communicated within a society. Structures, because they influence or direct human behavior, empower and are empowered by that behavior. Claude Lévi-Strauss was to argue that language and myth are the primary "carriers" of the collective conscience, the underlying structure of human behavior. If language and myth are among the determinants of human behavior, then information serves to fuel those determinants. Lévi-Strauss (1958) would argue later that "although they belong to another order of reality, kinship phenomena are of the same type as linguistic phenomena."

Recall that Alexis de Tocqueville argued that family (a kinship phenomenon) was one of several social institutions that intermediate between the individual and the state, thereby buffering the power of the state. At the same time, the press, books, and other information sources (linguistic phenomena, perhaps) are also strong intermediaries as well. If, however, the state can replace intermediating social structures with itself, the relationship between self and state is redefined in the worst case to totalitarianism. The state, where it is so predisposed and permitted to do so, manipulates information to overcome the power of intermediating social structures.

Michel Foucault might be described as a historian of the science of thought. Above all else Foucault was concerned with power. Power, for Foucault, is manifested in how society is structured. Power also lies in having knowledge, because that knowledge imparts authority, in both senses of the word, to the holder of knowledge.

How we choose to interpret power symbols may depend in part on our collective or individual interpretations of the symbols and how the use of those symbols affects our interpretations of self or collective interest. For example, Koehler (1981) describes the changes in Canadian federal fossil fuel policies in the 1970s from one supporting exports to the United States to one requiring exports from the Western producing provinces to the Eastern consuming provinces. What was perceived to be a national distributive policy by the Canadian federal government was seen as a rather costly redistributive policy by the oil companies and the Western provincial governments. In the end, the constitutionally relatively "weak" central government prevailed over the relatively "stronger" provincial governments and several very powerful international oil companies.

Michael Harris (1995, 4–5) posits that there are three societal factors that influenced the kinds of libraries found in the "ancient world." These are social conditions, economic conditions, and political conditions. Harris (1995, 5) argues that on the whole "libraries will flourish generally in those societies where economic prosperity reigns, where the population is literate and stable, where the government supports library growth, where large urban areas exist, and where book trade is well established."

Harris (1995, 6–7) further argues that a positive ideology supporting a book culture is critical. These ideologies can be addressed "under three broad headings: control, memory, and commodity. By *control*, Harris means that social elites utilize books (and other media) to control and form public opinion. Libraries are a necessary adjunct to that control. Libraries serve the memory function by contributing to the preservation of national identities, perhaps collection development with a purpose. They are also a mechanism through which researchers may clarify and sometimes redefine that national identity. The commodity value of libraries lies in their inherent ability to make markets for intellectual material. Libraries create a subsidy for "cultural commodities" by helping to underwrite scholarly enquiry as well as more pedestrian interests.

Harris bases his argument on the work of the sociologist Claude Lévi-Strauss. Lévi-Strauss was to argue that there is an inherent relationship between power and information, just as Tocqueville did a century before. For Tocqueville, one of the strengths of the American system of governance was the existence of competing mechanisms, including information channels, between the individual and government. Those mechanisms served to moderate the impact of state power on the individual.

What Is a Library?

What is a library? Before one can answer that question, perhaps one should ask first, "What is a document?"—as did Michael Buckland (1997)—and, "What is an author?"—as did Michel Foucault (1977). Buckland concerns himself with the thinking of the European documentalists of the first half of the twentieth century, particularly Paul Otlet and Suzanne Briet and their concern with the concept of "information as thing." The information management profession, as Buckland notes, was placed under increasing pressure as the number of scholarly publications exploded in the nineteenth and early twentieth centuries. The art of bibliography yielded to the science of documentation. Our understanding of *document* therefore underwent change. Paul Otlet (1934) argued that not only are written or graphic works documents, but so are the physical objects that serve to inform. Buckland (1997), interpreting Briet's writing, suggests that Briet offered four conditions for an object to become a document. These are:

1. There is materiality: Physical objects and physical signs only.
2. There is intentionality: It is intended that the object be treated as evidence.
3. The objects have to be processed: They have to be made into documents.
4. There is a phenomenological position: The object is perceived to be a document.

Suzanne Briet's (1951) famous argument is that the antelope in the wild is not a document, but that the same animal in the zoo is. Why? The purpose of antelope in the zoo is to inform and educate the observer, a function not fulfilled by the same animal in the wild. If we carry the Briet argument one step further, a document is in the eyes of the beholder. An antelope in the wild could be a document if the observer is observing with the express purpose to inform and educate him or herself.

Today we find the definition of document, book, or information container undergoing further change. S. R. Ranganathan (1963, 24–25) acknowledged, for example, this broadening of definition in the second edition of his *Five Laws of Library Science*: "Two fundamental changes have come [between 1931 and 1957]. One is the generalisation of the concept 'Book;' this has been emphasised in recent years by the term 'Documentation.' The second change is the generalisation of the term 'Growth.'" *Growth* refers both to an expansion in an understanding of librarianship but also to an expansion of the practice of librarianship "in many lands, including India."

The document has until recent years been an essentially static artifact. With the advent of the Internet, we "experience" documents that are not only not linear but also not static. Thus one can apply Ranganathan's concept of growth of librarianship as well as his fifth law: A library is a growing organism. According to Ranganathan (1963, 326):

> The Fifth Law tells us about the vital and lasting need for a constant adjustment to our outlook in dealing with it. . . . The Fifth Law enunci-

ates a fundamental principle that should govern the planning and organisation of libraries. While the first four laws embody maxims that
are nearly obvious, the Fifth Law is not perhaps so self-evident.

This book then is very much a test of Ranganathan's laws, particularly
the fifth law. A growing organism, according to Ranganathan (1963,
326–354), undergoes change in size, function, and purpose as it matures.
"The one thing that has been persisting through all those changes of form
has been the vital principle of life. So it is with the library" (Ranganathan
1963, 326).

Ranganathan speaks in terms of library changes as changes in books,
staff, patrons, and so on. His focus is on the physical institution, its management structures, and the people who populate it. He speaks eloquent-
ly in terms of the number of books and periodicals published and the
means to manage them. He is concerned with the library catalog and its
evolution. He addresses the increase in personnel and their specialization. And he speaks briefly to the evolution of library philosophy. Ranganathan (1963, 354) identifies the *vital principle*—the "spirit of the library" as "an instrument of universal education" that "assembles together and freely distributes all the tools of education and disseminates
knowledge with their aid."

While Ranganathan's concerns with *the library* were abstract, his arguments were largely particular and contemporary. He concerned himself
more, for example, with the specifics of library management or of classification and less with their philosophical justification. That said, Ranganathan did not ignore library theory. He added an eighth chapter, "Scientific Method," to the second edition of his *Five Laws of Library Science.* Ranganathan's (1963, 356) definition of science is critical to an understanding
of his work: "Science is thus not what it treats about, but what it achieves
in respect of what it treats about." Thus much of science is in its method.
The art lies in the application.

Any science, including library science, can be reduced to a set of axioms and assumptions. In a very real sense Ranganathan's fifth law is his
primary law, with the other four serving as commentary.

His first law, for example—*Books are for use*—immediately raises the
question, for use by whom? As we shall see, the use of books was once
restricted to the learned and the powerful. It has only been in the last
century and a half that the answer to "For use by whom?" has been
expanded in library theory to include virtually everyone in most places.
And as Ranganathan acknowledged, the very idea of a "book" has
changed.

LIBRARIAN INSTITUTIONS

Librarians have joined together to work toward their mutual interests. The American Librarian Association is the first national organization to form, followed by the library associations in the United Kingdom and in Japan. In 2002, Robert Vaagan edited an important volume for the International Federation of Library Association and Institutions (IFLA) titled *The Ethics of Librarianship: An International Survey.*

As Vaagan's (2002) work documents, many international and national library associations have addressed professional ethics. There are also many subnational and supranational organizations (provincial and state level organizations, for example). Librarians have also formed associations based on professional, social, and ethnic interests. Many have explicit and all have implicit ethical principles they represent and support. These include ethnicity and race, sexual orientation, and professional specialties.

Professional associations have become important for the recognition, development, and promulgation of ethical standards. Library associations have adopted codes of ethics as well as published positions on intellectual freedom and the freedom of expression. Many have taken strong positions on social and economic inclusion in the profession.

There have also been a number of conferences that focus on information ethics. Under the leadership of Lester Pourciau, the University of Memphis (Tennessee) convened a series of ethics conferences. Beginning in 1997, the conference series addressed key issues in library and information ethics (Pourciau 2001).

WORK IN MOVEMENT

Documents, of course, have never been completely "static." Umberto Eco (1989) speaks of *work in movement.* For Eco, there are three levels of openness for any work of art. The first level is interpretation. Eco posits that different observers can interpret any given work in essentially different ways. Legal language is inherently redundant, for example, in an often-vain attempt to reduce the degree to which it is ambiguous and the number of ways it can be interpreted.

The second is *openness.* Openness operates at the semantic level. Both William Shakespeare and James Joyce shared a proclivity for the pun. To fully appreciate either, one has to understand not only the "first" meaning but also the more subtle undercurrents of meanings.

The third level is the *work in movement.* A work in movement is by definition non-linear and open to interpretation. Eco provides as examples the Symbolist poet Stéphane Mallarmé, the electronic musician Karlheinz Stockhausen, and the avant-garde musician Pierre Boulez. Each experimented with the presentation of their work in non-linear format. The poetry of Mallarmé and the music of Stockhausen or Boulez can be served up in different order—that is, linear sections in non-linear structure by design. Mallarmé is particularly interesting in that he was concerned perhaps at the second level with the musicality of words, rather than with their meaning. Yet Mallarmé was inherently concerned with their various meanings, both modern and archaic.[3]

All graphic works are open to Eco's level one and level two openness, whether they are works of "fact" or of "fiction." While words on the page or notes on a score may remain fixed, those notes and words may be constantly reinterpreted. That reinterpretation may be culturally, intellectually, or temporally driven. Sometimes, as was the case with Mallarmé, meaning differences were intentional. More often a "static" text takes on new meaning as the meanings of words change, as cultures change.

The degree to which understanding may be changed is raised to a different power when non-linearity, Eco's third level, is added to the mix. In a digital environment, works in movement can be either structured or non-structured. The creator or the interpreter may apply rules to govern the non-linearity of a work (structured) or no such rules—the rule of no rules (unstructured). Michael Joyce (1996) suggests that the book, even as a single work in the digital age, is inherently chaotic. This sense of chaos is seen to extend across all genres of works to include non-fiction domains often traditionally treated as "non-linear" as well as the sometimes more linear fiction domains (Douglas 2001).

Michel Foucault (1977, 124–127) seeks to define the inter-relationship between the creation of discourse (the author) and the product of discourse (the work). He notes an evolution of Western thought:

> In our culture and undoubtedly in others as well discourse was not originally a thing, a product, or a possession, but an action situated in a bipolar field of sacred and profane, lawful and unlawful, religious and blasphemous. It was a gesture charged with risks before it became a possession caught in a circuit of property values. But it was at the moment when a system of ownership and strict copyright rules were established (toward the end of the eighteenth and beginning of the nineteenth century) that the transgressive properties always intrinsic to the act of writing became the forceful imperative of literature.

Thus author and discourse were not always so intrinsically mated in Western thought as they now are. Foucault (1977, 124–127) continues:

> These aspects of an individual, which we designate as an author (or which comprise an individual as an author), are projections, in terms always more or less psychological, of our way of handling texts: in the comparisons we make, the traits we extract as pertinent, the continuities we assign, or the exclusions we practice. In addition, all these operations vary according to the period and the form of discourse con-

cerned. A "philosopher" and a "poet" are not constructed in the same manner; and the author of an eighteenth-century novel was formed differently from the modern novelist.

Just as our concept of the document has undergone change, so has our concept of the author. The role and definition of author and artifact have been constructed, deconstructed, and reconstructed across the millennia.

If the definitions of *author* and *document* have been in flux, what then is the definition of library? Libraries have been well documented over time (see, for example, Buzás 1986; Carey 1972; Casson 2001; Christ 1984; Edwards 1859; Harris 1995; Lipsius 1607). Other scholars have provided us with insightful case studies into libraries in specific times and specific places (see, for example, Dix 1994; Houston 2002; Oliver 1999). These histories help us understand and define "library." The simplest definition might be that a library is an institution that utilizes librarians. What, then, are librarians, practitioners of librarianship, perhaps? Librarianship can be defined as a set of processes to study and manage recorded communication, the various roles that communication plays in society, information formats, and the development and application of characterization and classification schemes, as well as the study of and the use of information in society.

Librarians then may be "made" through both formal and informal processes. Anyone who owns and manages more than just a few books, documents, or what have you, is ipso facto an informal librarian. Other means and other experiences form the formal librarian. These means and experiences are further addressed in chapter 8.

A library, then, is an institution where a specific set of *informing* functions are undertaken. Throughout most of the history of libraries, the library has had to possess a large degree of physicality. It was a place with documents together with people to process and manage those documents. Given the digital revolution since the early 1960s, the physicality of libraries is not nearly so important as once it was. Digital archives and libraries abound. Physical libraries have been converted into hybrid libraries. Library functions are being redefined or refined. For example, where some libraries were once organized around the size of the book (e.g., Comerford 1999, 218), more complex classifications were developed to respond to the increasing complexity of libraries. As is shown in chapter 3, these schemes were based on a variety of organizing principles, from the institutional association of authors (Jesuit and non-Jesuit, orthodoxy and heterodoxy, etc.) to subject-oriented methodologies such as the Prussian Principles, the Dewey Decimal System (DDC), the Bibliotechnobibliograficheskaíà klassifikatsiíà (BBK), and the Library of Congress Classification System (LC) to MARC, AACR2, Dublin Core, and the various XML markup systems, including the Semantic Web.

Such a definition is overly broad. If we were to apply Briet's definition of a document, a library might include, for example, the modern definition of zoos and museums. While there is merit to that argument, it would have to include institutions not usually considered today to be libraries. If we limit the definition of library after Harris to an institution that collects graphic materials, the scope of the definition is further contracted.

> It is assumed that a library is a collection of graphic materials arranged for relatively easy use, cared for by an individual or individuals familiar with that arrangement, and accessible to at least a limited number of persons. (Harris 1995, 3)

Such a definition might include museums of fine arts, except that most such museums generally circumscribe greatly the "materials arranged for relatively easy use." Even that limitation may beg the question, as at least some museum patrons find "easy use" by studying and using displayed art for more than casual entertainment.

It is indisputable that libraries have existed in one form or another for more than three millennia in one place or another. The existence of libraries is evidence a priori that the culture in which those libraries are found values libraries. To go further, the existence of archival, public, professional, private, or academic libraries is evidence a priori that the cultures in which those libraries are found value archival, public, professional, private, or academic libraries.

Libraries and Society

Libraries have as part of their mission the preservation of historical memory and the edification of their users. They must also be understood within their social context. There are many writers who seek to place the library in its social space. A few representative examples include:

Basbanes, Nicholas, *A Gentle Madness* (1995)
Battles, Matthew, *Library: An Unquiet History* (2003)
Buzás, Ladislaus, *German Library History, 800–1945*, trans. William Boyd (1986)
Casson, Lionel, *Libraries of the Ancient World* (2001)
Christ, Karl, *The Handbook of Medieval Library History*, trans and ed. Theophil Otto (1984)
D'Angelo, Edward, *Barbarians at the Gates of the Public Library: How Postmodern Consumer Capitalisms Threatens Democracy* (2004)
Eaton, Thelma, ed., *Contributions to American Library History* (1962)
Edwards, Edward, *Libraries and Founders of Libraries* (1864, reprinted 1968)
Edwards, Edward, *Memoirs of Libraries*, 2 vols. (1859, reprinted 1964)

Fourie, Denise and David Dowell, *Libraries in the Information Age* (2009)

Gorman, Michael, *Our Enduring Values: Librarianship in the 21st Century* (2000)

Harris, Michael, *History of Libraries in the Western World*, 4th ed. (1995)

Irwin, Raymond, *Origins of the English Library* (1958, reprinted 1981)

Johnson, E. D., *History of Libraries in the Western World*, 2nd ed. (1970)

Lipsius, Justus, *A Brief Outline of the History of Libraries* (1607)

Le Roy-Ladurie, Emmanuel, *Les 1000 années de la bibliothèque et du livre* (1995)

Nunberg, Geoffrey, ed., *The Future of the Book* (1996)

Savages, E. A., *The Story of Libraries and Book-Collecting* (1909, reprinted 1969)

Schottenloher, K., *Books and the Western World* (1989)

Valentine, Patrick, *A Social History of Books and Libraries from Cuneiform to Bytes* (2012)

INFORMATION ETHICS AND VALUES

This book is "about" ethics and practice. Michael Gorman (2003, 3) informs us that "there is a golden thread of values and practices that runs through library work in all kinds of libraries—a golden thread that defines librarianship as a profession no matter where it is practiced." In a certain sense, this book is about tracing that thread to its origin. In an earlier work, Gorman (2000) informs us that the librarianship has a set of enduring values that will serve to carry us into the twenty-first century, if indeed we are wise enough to heed our history. We might suggest that Gorman could add that his golden thread extends beyond the "where" to the "when" as well.

This work purposefully examines both the "where" and the "when" of those values and practices. Michael Gorman would have us believe that the values of librarians are fairly homogenous over time and place. My own work with others agrees largely with the "where" part of the hypothesis (Koehler et al. 2000; Dole et al. 2000). Librarians of the late twentieth century tended to hold similar values no matter where or the type of library they were in, the position they held, or the country they lived in. That said, as we look to library practice and values across the ages, we find a very different picture. Library practice—explicitly—and library values—implicitly—can be shown to have undergone a significant metamorphosis over the recorded history of libraries and librarians. Some of those changes can be associated with technological changes, others with social and philosophical changes.

Time and Value Change

Some changes in values and practice are fairly recent; others are of long standing. Librarians, for example, have long agreed that their collections must be organized according to some logic. Just precisely what that logic should be has never been fully settled. Public library theory and practice as we know it today in the United States began to take form in the mid-nineteenth century, fairly recently in the history of libraries. The model we now accept—open to all, lending, open stacks, liberal collection development policies, focus on fiction for entertainment—can be shown to be an early twentieth-century development. Privacy and patron confidentiality are even more recent additions to library principles.

In a certain sense, Michael Gorman is right. Certainly libraries as human institutions have endured and will continue to endure in some form or another. Is he right about our enduring values? That perhaps depends on whether, first, we are willing to believe that the value set we now hold will persist essentially unchanged over some period long enough to be considered "enduring." Second, we must also accept that these enduring values have relatively shallow roots.

To understand the import of values and principles to librarianship, we must first seek to identify what these principles and values are. Ethics are generally perceived to derive from and serve as the application of moral principles. Morals represent a set of mores, customs, and traditions that may have been derived from social practice or from religious guidance. Information ethics are perceived to be a subset of applied ethics, or ethical principles that are both broad and theoretical but also have specific applications (M. M. Smith 1997b).

Ethics necessarily, at least in their applied form, undergo metamorphosis as underlying conditions change. Thus, for example, as technology changes the conditions of practice (e.g., Negroponte 1996), these change the ethics that guide the practice (e.g., Rudinow and Graybosch 2002; Lankes 2011; or Spinello and Tavani 2001).

Ranganathan's Five Laws

As is discussed later in this chapter, there is a long list of specific ethical principles that librarians recognize as important to their professionalism and practice. The great visionary and librarian S. R. Ranganathan (1963a) left us with an important charge, his five laws of library science. These five laws provide a general framework within which we can place the specific principles. The chapters that follow address recognized principles of practice and ethics by categories. These include access, classification, democracy, literacy, intellectual property, intellectual freedom, professionalism and training, social obligations, and stewardship and preservation of the historical record. The five laws are:

1. Books are for use.
2. For every reader, a book.
3. For every book, its reader.
4. Save the time of the reader.
5. A library is a growing organism.

Ranganathan's five laws set the stage for this work. The writings of others are to be weighed as they contribute to our understanding of the librarianship laws.

TECHNOLOGY CHANGES

Technology-caused changes may be possible to document given a rigorous analysis of historical documents. The world of libraries has undergone several major technological shifts. Paramount among these is necessarily the invention of writing that might be dated from cave paintings to the advent of stone tablets in about 3000 BCE.

The second is the adoption of the codex format in the second century CE. Lionel Casson (2001, 124; see also Valentine 2012) describes the transition from scroll to codex as "a change that profoundly affected all who dealt with books, from casual readers to professional librarians." The codex was found to be far more manageable than the scroll in a variety of ways. It was easier to store and retrieve, it was easier to use, and it was easier to carry. It was also easier to hide. There are some who attribute some of the success of early Christianity to the codex. Because the codex was relatively easier to use, hide, and to transport, it made the distribution of the message easier to transmit (Finegan 1974).

The third shift is the invention of relatively efficient and inexpensive means to manufacture paper. According to Michael Harris (1995, 77), economic technologies for the manufacture of paper passed from China through Central Asia to the Moslem Middle East beginning in the ninth century CE and finally into Spain in the tenth. Given its strong flax economy, Egypt became a major manufacturer of paper.

The fourth is moveable type printing technology. Elizabeth Eisenstein (1983) shows that printing brought dramatic changes to sixteenth-century Europe. Not a small part of that change was a redefinition of the role and relationship of the author/creator to his or her work. Elizabeth Eisenstein (1979, 121) refers to this process of individualizing intellectual output as "print-made immortality." Thus as Europe transitioned from an oral to a print culture, the idea of individual authorship emerged (Birkerts 1994, 159).

This change resulted in new demands on and by the state sector to intervene in matters of intellectual property. As John Feather (1994) points out, the state responded first by licensing printers and stationers. These licenses granted privileges to publishers who either held licenses to publish specific works to licenses to publish certain classes of materials (for example, government edicts). Licenses did protect certain materials and certain markets for certain publishers, but they were not primarily designed for that purpose. Licenses were a means by which government could regulate information content—in a word, censure it.

It was not until the early eighteenth century that copyright law came into existence to protect authors and to a degree the publishing monopoly of the owners of intellectual property. It was most often the publisher rather than the author who benefited. It was ungentlemanly, after all, to profit from one's labors. Copyright as a protection for authors in addition to other intellectual property holders was not to come fully into its own until the nineteenth century when popular authors (Charles Dickens, Victor Hugo, or Edgar Allen Poe, for example) could truly be enriched by the pen.

And fifth is the digital revolution of the twentieth century. Where does one begin to describe a revolution that is not yet settled? Much has been written on the impacts of the digital revolution and its impacts on society. Whether Michael Gorman (2003, 110) is right that the advent of digital information is not an "epochal transformation" remains to be seen. He is right when he states that "we are at an important point in the evolution of libraries."

The impact of the digital revolution can be divided into two major effects. The first is breadth, width, ease, and immediacy of digital media. Events occurring in one place can be known everywhere else almost immediately. Second and related to the first is the empowerment of individuals and communities of interests in a way that only communities of geography could once interrelate and communicate (Lester and Koehler 2007, 152–153). These empowerments may be counterbalanced by global commercial interests that are also making effective use of the digital environment (Thimbley 1998). The digital revolution has had and will continue to have an important if not pivotal role in shaping the future (Lester and Koehler 2007, 261–270). Responsibility for determining how that future will be shaped lies in us all. Theodore Roszak (1994, 244) leaves us with the following:

> The art of thinking is grounded in the mind's astonishing capacity to create beyond what it intends, beyond what it can foresee. We cannot begin to shape that capacity toward humane ends and to guard it from demonic misuse until we have first experienced the true size of the mind.

One cannot help but wonder whether there was speculation about the role of previous technologies and the ways they would shape the future as they emerged to help shape culture.

SOCIAL FACTORS

Technology is not the only factor that changes practice and modifies ethical precepts. Michael Harris (1995, 4–5) posits that there are three societal factors that influenced the kinds of libraries found in the "ancient world." It is not difficult to make the case that those self same conditions apply to medieval as well more contemporary libraries. These are social conditions, economic conditions, and political conditions. Harris (1995, 5) argues that on the whole "libraries will flourish generally in those societies where economic prosperity reigns, where the population is literate and stable, where the government supports library growth, where large urban areas exist, and where book trade is well established."

Harris (1995, 6–7) further argues that a positive ideology supporting a book culture is critical. These ideologies can be addressed "under three broad headings: control, memory, and commodity. By control, it is meant that political elites utilize books (and other media) to control and form public opinion. Libraries are a necessary adjunct to that control. Libraries serve the memory function by contributing to the preservation of national identities, perhaps collection development with a purpose. They are also a mechanism through which researchers may clarify and sometimes redefine that national identity. The commodity value of libraries lies in their inherent ability to make markets for intellectual material. Libraries create a subsidy for "cultural commodities" by helping to underwrite scholarly inquiry as well as more pedestrian interests.

In a somewhat different vein, Paul Otlet (1934, 3) would have us understand that any such analysis must be undertaken in an understood social context. Otlet distinguished between *livre* (book) and *document*, just as we seek to distinguish between print and electronic. Document is both a noun and a verb. Otlet (1934, 6) placed importance on the concept of *informations documentées*, or documented information. This concept of *informations documentées* lies at the heart of the library. There are uncounted ways to document information; but until it is, undocumented information is of little interest to us. Otlet (1934, 6–7) wrote that there are seven "parties" to documentation. The parties are the document itself, the library, the bibliography, document archives, administrative archives, ancient archives, non-bibliographic or non-graphic documents (e.g., music, film), museum collections, and *l'Encyclopédie*. The *Encyclopédie* is central to Otlet's thinking. It is a proposal for the centralization and systemization of knowledge.

In the concept of *Encyclopédie*, Otlet belonged to a long tradition of encyclopedist thought, beginning with Diderot in eighteenth-century France. H. G. Wells was equally intrigued with the encyclopedist notion, an idea he developed in a series of essays published together in 1938 as *World Brain*.

The web brings yet another opportunity to collectivize and centralize *informations documentées*. With the ongoing development of the Semantic Web, perhaps a twenty-first century variation on the *Encyclopédie* or *World Brain* will result. There will necessarily be differences. The Semantic Web will be more democratic than the World Brain. Both the *Encyclopédie* and *World Brain* were Platonic in concept. Intellectual elites were to process and publish the world's knowledge. The Semantic Web envisages no such filter, and many of its proposed applications are far more pedestrian.

Digitization of *informations documentées* together with the Semantic Web and coupled with Google Books (renamed from Google Book Search and Google Print), Project Gutenberg, and others, will lead to the marriage of the collectivization and the commodification of information.

SOURCES FOR LIBRARIANSHIP, PROFESSIONAL ETHICS, AND PRACTICE

It would be incorrect to assume that professional ethics in the information professions date from the first code of ethics to be promulgated by a professional association, that of the American Library Association in 1939, or from the first use of the term "information ethics" by Robert Hauptman (1988) in the mid-1980s.

While there were no ethicists developing explicit standards or codes of practice for librarians until the twentieth century, it is possible to identify practices and beliefs that may allow us to infer ethics that guided societies as well as librarians. These standards are implied from the writings of historians and bibliophiles and from actual practice. For example, Lionel Casson (2001, 88) describes Greek and Roman library architecture. The Roman library, he argues, was designed for readers; the Greek libraries were storage facilities, or, in Casson's words, "in essence, stacks." Architecture may therefore imply purpose and use, form and function. Ancient Greeks, we might conclude, valued libraries and their uses in different ways than did the Romans. This comparison of form and function suggests that the Romans emphasized library usage whereas the Greeks probably perceived them more as storage facilities.

A second approach looks to policy as an indicator of the way in which any given culture might perceive and value libraries. According to Lipsius (1607, 50), who cited A. Gellius, Pisistratus the Tyrant of Athens was among the first to establish a library of liberal arts for public use. Julius Caesar instructed the Roman polymath Marcus Terentius Varro (116–27 BCE) to establish a public library in Rome. That library was to have housed two separate collections of Greek and Roman materials. Varro did not live to see the library established, but he authored *De bibliothecis*. *De bibliothecis* has not survived, but it is reputed to have provided a blueprint for the establishment of public libraries. While it is unfortunate that *De bibliothecis* did not survive, it is significant that Julius Caesar directed that a public library be created and that Varro drew up plans for such a library. We can hypothesize that the Greeks and later the Romans valued the concept of a public library, that the Greeks and Romans valued not only libraries but also the provision of access to information by the Greek and Roman publics. We shall see, however, that the concept of "public library" has undergone significant redefinition over the ages.

A third approach considers the writings on libraries and books of scholars and philosophers. We can look to modern scholars like Lionel Casson or Elizabeth Eisenstein for their interpretations of the place of the book, the library, or library patrons at different periods. We can also analyze the writings of historians and bibliophiles at various points in time. While Varro's work on libraries has not survived, other important tracts are available to us for analysis. For example, Mathilde Rovelstad (2000) explores Claude Clément's (1596–1642) *Musei sive bibliothecae tam privatae quam publicae* and Gabriel Naudé's (1600–1653) *Avis pour dresser une bibliothèque*. She concludes that although Clément and Naudé were contemporaries, their interests were quite different. Clément was concerned with library iconography and its symbolic importance, while Naudé provided directions for library establishment, administration, and maintenance. Clément presents us with evidence of the importance of libraries as a seventeenth-century social institution. Naudé's work, considered by some as the first library science text, informs us on practice.

In addition to Clément and Naudé, there are a number of other library commentaries. These include Justus Lipsius's (1547–1606) *A Brief Outline of the History of Libraries*, first published in 1607; Johann David Köhler's (1684–1755) *Anweisung für reisende Gelerte, Bibliothecken, Műnz-Cabinette, Antiquitäten-Zimmer, Bilder-Saele, Naturalien-und Kunst-Kammern u.d.m mit Nutzen zu besehen*, first published in 1762; and Edward Edwards's (1812–1886) *Memoirs of Libraries*, first published in two volumes in 1859.

These works and others, as well as the writings and practice of such library giants as Melvil Dewey and Sir Anthony Panizzi (1797–1879), can be drawn on to reflect library practices from the perspective of the time in which the practice was implemented or the document was published—hence the inferential evidence for values and ethics.

Contemporary Ethics and Values

If values are a subset of morals (Rokeach 1973) and ethics are the application of values (Gorman 2000, 7), what are the values, morals, and ethics identified in the contemporary library and information professional practice?

We can discover contemporary information ethics and values in a variety of sources. These include such higher-order proclamations of rights that provide general social guidance like the *Magna Carta*, the *Universal Declaration of Human Rights*, the American *Bill of Rights*, and a wide variety of national constitutions. They serve to define the moral and legal bases for their societies. These documents usually guarantee intellectual freedom and often intellectual property rights. They represent the guidelines within which societies and the institutions that govern them *should* behave.

There have been several noteworthy papers that seek to enumerate core values and ethical precepts in the information professions. In 1996 Richard Rubin and Thomas Froehlich offered nine values and ethical principles: (1) privacy, (2) selection and censorship, (3) reference, (4) intellectual property rights, (5) administration, (6) access, (7) technology, (8) loyalties, and (9) social issues.

Again, Thomas Froehlich, in a very interesting paper in 2000, enumerates six professional values and five ethical principles. The six professional values he lists are (1) freedom and self-determination, (2) protection from injury, (3) equality of opportunity, (4) respect for patron privacy, (5) minimal well-being, and (6) recognition for one's work. The five ethical principles are (1) respect for the autonomy of the self and others, (2) seek justice or fairness, (3) be faithful to organizational, professional and public trust, (4) seek social harmony, and (5) act in such a way that the amount of harm is minimized.

Wallace Koehler and Michael Pemberton (2000) suggest the following: (1) patron or client needs, (2) skill and competence and the roles of the information practitioner, (3) support the profession, (4) responsiveness to social responsibilities, and (5) the rights of users, fellow professionals, the profession, and society.

They find that while there are many different and very specific provisions published by each of the organizations, they can essentially be reduced to six general categories.

Michael Gorman (2000) offers eight: (1) stewardship, (2) service, (3) intellectual freedom, (4) rationalism, (5) literacy and learning, (6) equity of access to recorded knowledge and information, (7) privacy, and (8) democracy.

Wanda Dole, Jitka M. Hurych, and Wallace Koehler (2000) and later Koehler, Hurych, Dole, and Joanna Wall (2000), drawing upon Katherine Branch's work (1998), surveyed librarians first in the United States, then worldwide. Librarians were asked to rank eleven values: (1) service, (2) equality of access, (3) information literacy, (4) intellectual freedom, (5) preservation of the intellectual record, (6) literacy, (7) professional neutrality, (8) diversity of opinion, (9) confidentiality, (10) cultural diversity, and (11) copyright issues.

Other commentators have identified and enumerated ethical principles within a specific context. Among them are Shiela Intner and Jorge Reina Schement (1998), Richard Stichler and Robert Hauptman (1988),

Robert Hauptman (1991), Richard Rubin (1991), Lester Asheim (1992), Sharon Baker (1992), Devlin and Miller (1995), W. G. Johnson (1994), Barbara Ford (1998), W. Lee Hisle (1998), and Ann Symons and Carla Stoffle (1998).

Walt Crawford and Michael Gorman (1995, 8) provided a more contemporary interpretation of Ranganathan's five laws:

1. Libraries serve humanity.
2. Respect all forms by which knowledge is communicated.
3. Use technology intelligently to enhance service.
4. Protect free access to knowledge.
5. Honor the past and create the future.

Based on these writings, a fairly comprehensive list of professional ethics and values can be developed:

- act to minimize harm
- confidentiality
- cultural diversity
- democracy
- diversity of opinion
- equality of opportunity
- equity of access
- faithfulness to organizational, professional, and public trust
- freedom and self-determination
- good professional practice
- information literacy
- intellectual freedom, selection, and censorship
- intellectual property rights and fair use
- literacy
- minimal well-being
- patron or client needs
- preservation of the cultural record/stewardship
- professional neutrality
- protecting library users' right to privacy/confidentiality
- protection from injury
- rationalism
- recognition for one's work
- respect for the autonomy of the self and others
- responsiveness to social responsibilities
- rights of users, fellow professionals, the profession, and society
- seek justice or fairness
- seek social harmony
- service
- skill and competence and the roles of the information practitioner
- support for the profession

ON LIBRARIANSHIP

Our concepts of libraries, documents, and authors have undergone significant change over the millennia. The history of libraries in the West has been well documented. Similarly, just as libraries have been redefined, they have also retained their essential functions over time; perhaps it is equally true that library ethics might be inferred from the theory, philosophy, and practice of librarians and libraries over time. Those essential functions define librarianship. A library might then be defined as a place (although not necessarily a *physical* place) where functions of librarianship are performed.

A list of contemporary ethical precepts is provided in the previous section. We explore these precepts and other library practices through the writings of library history scholars and key figures in Western library history. It is recognized that all the listed principles are open to interpretation in both theory and practice.

Library practice and library ethics are inextricably intertwined. The one helps define the other. We find few if any references to professional library ethics prior to the mid-1930s, and these are scarce until the last quarter of the twentieth century. By analyzing practice and ethics in historical and scholarly writing, we can derive dynamic definitions for practice, ethics, and librarianship.

It is a daunting task to select the most relevant works from the librarianship literature. It is in some ways more difficult to consider which works to include and which to exclude. There is a rich collection of library catalogs and other guides to library collections. That library collections were and are classified according to some sets of standards suggests underlying principles of information management. These are important documents, but for the most part they do not inform us on the "why" of collection classification but rather with the "how." This book is therefore not an analysis of catalogs; rather, it focuses on the reasoning underlying the cataloging as well as the reasoning underlying the development of other library principles.

As we have already seen, the concepts *information ethics* and *professional librarian ethics* are of relatively recent etiology. The first code of ethics developed by a professional library association was first promulgated in 1939. The first use of the term "information ethics" dates to the mid-1980s. This work seeks to explore the evolution of ethical and value principles. We now have fairly well-articulated concepts of those values. In order to ascertain and perhaps even date the emergence of librarianship principles, the book focuses primarily on those writing prior to the publication of the first code of library ethics by the American Library Association in 1939. Since 1939 and particularly since 1985, there have been a number of important works that address librarianship ethics and values. The works of the giants who predate our heightened concern with information ethics are explored to tease out those principles. Subsequent chapters address various specific areas of concern drawn from our understanding of twenty-first century principles.

The works of a number of authors of library- and book-related subjects provide the basis of the analysis. This book is not an exhaustive annotated bibliography of the historical literature. It is, rather, a survey of a selection of some of that literature in an attempt to identify professional values expressed implicitly or explicitly by a variety of commentators across time.

There have been both technological and sociological changes that have helped shape Western cultures as well as the practice of librarianship. These changes molded and continue to influence the ethical principles that guide the profession.

We explore the writings of the famous and not so famous in librarianship and related fields. Authors who have contributed were drawn to librarianship from a wide variety of backgrounds. Very early writers were usually Catholic priests and later Protestant ministers. Lawyers, engineers, physicians, philosophers, and scholars were also drawn in. Librarianship was, for some, like Gottfried Wilhelm von Leibniz, a minor byproduct of their interests in classification. For others, like Gabriel Naudé, it became a life's work.

As already noted, this work has a Western orientation. With the exception of S. R. Ranganathan, the authors are European or North American. Ranganathan is included in part because he trained in England but more importantly because of the impact of his scholarship both in his native India and the rest of the world.

In the following chapters we consider a range of ethical concerns of the contemporary profession. We are now coming from a place where a good university education to qualify as a "Librarie-Keeper" to a place where some might agree that there is no more to librarianship than can be achieved by a good post-doctorate education in the humanities and perhaps by extension to other meta-disciplines. The digital revolution, others would have it, has rendered the profession redundant (cf. Park 1992; Smith and Johnson 1993; Kent 2002). Indeed, as Michael Harris and Stan Hannah (1993, 106–107) prescribe, the profession must not only redefine itself, it must also leave behind several of its most "sacred" axioms: the humanities bias, information as public good, the dominance of physical media, and (that most recently achieved only in the twentieth century) the female-dominant workforce. Furthermore, as John Buschman (2003, 3) has suggested, librarianship is in crisis and "the crisis stems from the simple fact that we have been declaring crises in the field for more than thirty years. Further, we seem unable to clearly identify what we mean or effectively address the problems we identify." The heart of Buschman's (2003, 8) thesis is that libraries are falling victim to the "dismantling of the public sphere" in a market-oriented public arena. Buschman (2003, 9–10) identifies a strong link between libraries and educational institutions (yet another victim), a link we also recognize in a longer historical perspective.

The phenomena that John Buschman (2003), Michael Harris and Stan Hannah (1993), and others identify are not cases of claiming the "sky is falling." Indeed the public sphere is being privatized, for better or for worse. What we must recognize is that libraries have not always had a place in the public sphere and nor, for that matter, did educational institutions. Buschman asserts (2003, 47–48, emphasis in the original) that

> librarianship *has* historically extended the democratic public sphere within its walls: the flawed democratic bases on which librarianship was founded have been revised, extended, and more inclusive; the essential purpose of public enlightenment *was* reasonably well-supported by tax and tuition dollars for over 120 years; the Library Bill of Rights has been extended over the years; there have been conscious attempts to reach out to the poor, the disabled, and to better represent the historically underrepresented on our shelves and screens.

Buschman is perhaps correct in his assessment of the role of the public library and perhaps many academic libraries in the United States over the past century. What John Buschman and others decry is not the decline of the library but rather its redefinition into a form outside the public sphere—or perhaps as part of a very differently defined public sphere. As is argued in subsequent chapters, the public library as we understand it is the result of an evolution in librarianship theory articulated by the likes of John Cotton Dana (1906) at the beginning of the twentieth century. Dana's contemporary Melvil Dewey espoused a far less inclusive philosophy for the library. Consider also that Alexis de Tocqueville (1835), in his classic *Democracy in America*, identified various institutions that served to protect the public sphere, or rather the American democracy from the intrusions of the state. Educational institutions, book publishers, and newspapers were included among those institutions, but not the subscription or proprietary libraries of the 1830s.

The library in its various forms has been a resilient institution. While the base function of libraries, the storage of and access to information, has persisted from the very first Sumerian libraries to the present, their form and place in the public, private, and state spheres have depended not only on the information they guarded and the form in which the information was presented but also on the social paradigm under which they functioned. Indeed it might be suggested that libraries are essentially conservative institutions (see Harris 1973; Shera 1949). As the dominant social paradigm changes, library policy changes, but with an inherent conservative lag.

There is a final concern that should be retained while reading this work. Are libraries and librarians more marginalized as social institutions and actors than ever before? The debate over the past twenty years would suggest that it is so. Much of what the librarian has always done has been arrogated by other disciplines, other disciplines that have rediscovered much of the knowledge of the librarian without due recognition to the discipline. At the same time, the currency of the library, information, has undergone a commodification. This commodification has perhaps always been with us to one degree or another. The subscription libraries of the eighteenth and nineteenth centuries or the development of copyright in the early eighteenth century are early manifestations. But information gained new stature as a commodity as complex indexing algorithms were developed and as the digitization process proceeded in the late twentieth century. Libraries and librarians are seeking to redefine themselves as the social paradigm shifts. That redefinition, if (when) successful, will bring with it a change in practice and a change in professional ethics; just as previous changes have carried with them changes in practices and in ethics.

NOTES

1. "Y a-t-il une qualité essentielle, un savoir, un savoir-faire, qui seraient universels, qui traverseraient les âges et les civilisations et qui définiraient le métier de bibliothécaire."

2. The US Supreme Court decision *Griswold* v. *Connecticut*. 381 US 479 (1965) established a Constitutional right of privacy. It also struck down laws that prohibited the dissemination of birth control information.

3. I am struck by the first and last lines of Mallarmé's "Brise marine": "La chair est triste, hélas! et j'ai lu tous les livres. / . . . / Mais, Ô mon coeur, entends le chant des matelots." Literally translated, they are, "Sea Breeze": The flesh is sad, alas! And I have read all the books / . . . / But. Oh my heart, understand the sailor's song.

TWO

Stewardship and Service

Librarianship, thanks to centuries of effort, has a simple and clear goal. . . . Applying Ockham's Razor, that entities are not to be multiplied beyond necessity, the goal is information equity. Inherent in this goal is working for universal literacy; defending intellectual freedom; preserving and making accessible the human record; and ensuring that preschoolers have books to read.

—Kathleen de la Peña McCook (1999)

Amrou, the victorious general, was himself inclined to spare [the Alexandrine Library]; but the ignorant and fanatical caliph to whom he applied for instructions ordered it—according to the well-known story—to be destroyed "If," said he, "the writings of the Greeks agree with the Koran, or book of Allah, they are useless, and need not be preserved; if they disagree, they are pernicious and ought to be destroyed."

—Edward Edwards (1864, 8)

INTRODUCTION

Stewardship is the primal urge of the librarian. Service is the mantra. Both service and stewardship are embraced as essential librarianship functions. Yet there is an intrinsic tension between the two. Stewardship is an embracing, protective impulse. Service is an outreach. Use is an impulse.

Stewardship and service are treated together in this chapter as "magnetic opposites." Hernon and Altman (2010, 2) have made a useful observation. Libraries have long been assessed by what they possess (stewardship) but in recent years have shifted toward what they do (service). This

31

focus reorientation is in part a function of declining resources and of changing technology but also of a redefinition of library philosophy.

Perhaps this combination might be seen as an improbable pair, as both service and stewardship are crucial librarian values. They have been closely related in the minds of libraries since libraries were first conceived. The two, however, create a healthy tension, as the one plays off against the other.

Library doctrine has over time shifted to favor the one over the other. S. R. Ranganathan (1957, 351–353, §§ 76–765) provides a brief history of the evolution of libraries that illustrates that essential tension. His library history begins with an incarceration metaphor of "hiding place" or "book prison" prior to the seventeenth century to "limited freedom" in the seventeenth and eighteenth centuries. By *limited freedom* Ranganathan meant circulation solely *within* the library. The nineteenth century was a period of "stock-taking versus stock-use," or "a period grudgingly lending them out." Following World War I, libraries began liberalizing their lending policies.

Ranganathan speculated briefly about the future of libraries by citing H. G. Wells's novel *Men Like Gods*, first published in 1923. In *Men Like Gods* the protagonists, the Utopians, are able to communicate and learn through telepathy. We have not as yet achieved effective information transfer via osmosis, but the library as organism has evolved in the digital environment to something not unlike H. G. Wells's *World Brain* (1938) idea in some respects.

At each point in this history, librarians have preferred a more conservation-oriented or a more use-oriented philosophy. Greek libraries were more archive-like and Roman libraries more use oriented. Medieval monastic libraries were almost completely dominated by stewardship and conservation ideals. It was not until the nineteenth and even more so in the twentieth and twenty-first centuries that many libraries became user oriented. As a result, many of these libraries willingly sacrificed a certain degree of collection protection.

The digital library of the twenty-first century may provide even greater user access to collections. Project Gutenberg and most recently the Google Book initiative to scan the collections of major libraries offer unparalleled access to much of human knowledge. But unparalleled service may imply an unparalleled decline in stewardship. There are some who have identified digitization as a potential harbinger of a second Dark Age (Koehler 2006).

Stewardship is one of the enduring values Michael Gorman (2003) recognizes as inherent to librarianship. As is to be demonstrated, stewardship has long been defined as one of the primary functions of libraries and librarians. Interestingly, stewardship is not generally recognized in the codes of ethics of most professional associations. It is only most recently that stewardship has been included as one of the ethical principles recognized in a library association code of ethics, that of the Association des Bibliothécaires de France as "la tutelle."

RANGANATHAN'S LAWS, SERVICE, AND STEWARDSHIP

Both service and stewardship are intimately associated with all five of Ranganathan's library laws. Stewardship is important to the second and third laws (to every reader, his book; and to every book, its reader). A well-managed library contributes to save the time of the reader. Continuing stewardship contributes to library growth. In his *Five Laws of Library Science*, Ranganathan argued that while stewardship was and remained an important value, it had been yielded to other library values.

Ranganathan's first law is *books are for use*. Ranganathan (1957, 354, § 76) also holds that "the vital principle of the library . . . is that it is an instrument of universal education, and assembles together and freely distributes all the tools of education and disseminates knowledge with their aid." Ranganathan (1957, 26, § 111) further states:

> The first law of Library Science is: BOOKS ARE FOR USE. No one will question the correctness of this law. But, in actual practice, the story is different. The law has been seldom borne in mind by library authorities.

While perhaps no one would question that books are for use, Ranganathan (1957, 123, § 122) also recognized that society in general and librarians in particular are inclined to protect books and that book protection conflicts with use:

> Even as we are anxious to hand over our books to posterity, every succeeding generation may be actuated by an exactly similar altruistic motive; and in consequence books may have to be for ever in chains and may never be released for use. This aspect of the question seems to have escaped notice for a very long time and 'BOOKS ARE FOR PRESERVATION' had usurped the place of 'BOOKS ARE FOR USE' . . .

Ranganathan (1957, 78 § 18) further asserts:

> THE FIRST LAW would say "Plant your cheerfulness and perseverance in my words, BOOKS ARE FOR USE. Your duty is to serve with books. Service is your sphere."

Books are for use, as Ranganathan tells us. But even the first law is not immutable, as Ranganathan (1957, 123, § 122) also tells us. The Google Print initiative in 2005 and the many already existing digitization initiatives (such as Project Gutenberg) have the potential to obviate the inherent conflict between the ideas that "books are for preservation" and "books are for use." If and only if these digitization initiatives continue to provide access to the underlying collections to a global constituency under reasonable access conditions and without the need for "unusual technology" will "books are for use" be promoted.

However, these digital initiatives may undermine "books are for preservation." If we as a global society (or the more limited we as librarians) come to rely too extensively on digitized collections, the underlying print collections may well be deemphasized. If (and the probability is there) digitized collections are commercialized or censored and as some digital initiatives fail or are closed (the probability is almost certain), then their digital archives are imperiled. As digital collections fail, are censored, or are otherwise controlled, and as print collections are marginalized, the first responsibilities of librarians—stewardship and service through access (*books are for preservation* and *books are for use*)—may no longer be sustainable. These concerns are magnified for contemporary works that are created and published in digital format only. What becomes of those materials, "unprotected" as they are without an alternative and distributed print basis, when their publishers and collectors cease to publish and maintain the archives?

Stewardship is concerned with the preservation and maintenance of the cultural and intellectual record. Libraries are one of several institutions that participate in that preservation and cultural maintenance. Museums and schools are also part of the process. Many libraries contribute to and are contributed to by these other institutions. The recognition of the need for library stewardship has been increased in the digital age as librarians and others have come to appreciate the fragile nature of their digital collections. That fragile nature is even more pronounced for native web documents. Initiatives such as Brewster Kahle's Internet Archive (http://www.archive.org/) seek to preserve web page "snapshots" in the ever-changing Internet environment (see, for example, Koehler 1999a). The Internet Archive is also entering the digitization of out-of-copyright books as an additional means to preserve cultural heritage.

STEWARDSHIP DEFINED

Stewardship, as the quote from Edward Edwards at the beginning of this chapter suggests, has an inherent inner tension. The first is to preserve the cultural history of a society but, second, in a way consistent with the basic values of that society. If it is inherent in a society to promote diversity of information and beliefs, the tensions imposed on the librarian are minimal. If, on the other hand, social beliefs and values are narrowly defined by a specific orthodoxy, librarians may very well find their roles as stewards conflicted between social orthodoxy and informational heterodoxy.

The duties imposed on the librarian by stewardship can take several forms. In its most core meaning, stewardship means the guarding of the cultural, literary, historical, and scientific heritage of a culture. Not only are librarians directed to ensure that their collections adequately reflect their share of cultural beliefs; they are also charged with protecting the vehicles—the documents in their various formats—through which cultural manifestations are communicated. Thus librarians are charged with protecting these documents from disasters man-made and natural, as well as theft, vandalism, insect infestations, political pressures, and other threats known and unknown.

Important libraries have succumbed to disasters natural and man-made. The destruction of the Library of Alexandria has been decried perhaps from the very day it occurred (see Lipsius 1607, 42–45). That library disintegrated over time from the Roman defense at Alexandria in the first century BCE through challenges from flooding and fire until its final demise in 638 CE. In 1814 the British set fire to the US Capitol, which then housed the Library of Congress. The Iraqi National Library fell victim to war in 2003. In 2013 ancient manuscripts were destroyed in Timbuktu. The Pacific tsunami of 2004 significantly damaged libraries large and small from Sri Lanka to Indonesia. Almost every library everywhere and in every epoch has experienced vandalism and theft.

We have always been aware of threats to libraries, but it has only been in recent years that recovery plans for both man-made and natural disasters have been made more common. Lipsius (1607, 42–43) wrote of the ruin of the Alexandrian library: "A precious treasure! But, alas, though it was the offspring of man's immortal spirit it was not itself immortal. . . . Shame be to Caesar for having brought this about, even though without intent, this irreparable loss!" He also noted that historians before him were equally appalled at the destruction—Ammianus, Dion, Hirtius, Livy, Plutarch, Seneca, among them (Lipsius 1607, 44–45).

The US Library of Congress is one of many libraries that have developed stewardship initiatives. In its 1999 *Stewardship Report: Heritage Assets*, the Library of Congress described its digital collections policy (US Library of Congress 1999, 42–43). The Library of Congress's agenda is updated periodically (for example, the 2014 *National Agenda for Digital Stewardship*). The digital policy includes a requirement to "create a culture of technical and strategic innovation to ensure that the Library staff can provide traditional and expanded resources to readers. This vision grounded digital information services on the fundamental principles that librarians are the keepers, interpreters and mediators of information and knowledge, and that all citizens are entitled to equal access to information and knowledge." Lin Ming, Qui Weiquing, and Lian Zhang (2014) note further that stewardship and preservation not only preserve materials; they extend their useful life as well. Extending the useful life of materials enhances the service function of the library.

Many librarians until the mid-nineteenth century conceived of their role as one of collection protection rather than patron service. This tradition continues to a lesser or greater degree in some libraries, archives, and museums. Effective stewardship demands that materials be protected. Yet to promote knowledge of the cultural record, library materials must be used.

A Library of Congress symposium (Merrill 2003) found that stewardship has four key components: preservation and physical security and bibliographic and inventory control. While I agree that bibliographic and inventory control are important supports to stewardship; for the purposes of this book, these stewardship components are included under classification and are addressed in that chapter.

PRESERVATION AND PHYSICAL SECURITY

Preservation and physical security of library materials have often been accomplished through similar means. They are not synonymous. Preservation implies both the protection of the physical object against the ravages of time and use as well as the maintenance of the content and its cultural significance. Preservation therefore includes not only the great care taken to archive and protect an artifact but also the reproduction of the artifact to ensure the security of the content. Physical security includes the various means used to protect library materials from natural and human "disasters." These include theft, pillage, vandalism, fire, war, insect and rodent infestations, earthquakes, hurricanes, tsunamis, floods, and so on.

All too often efforts to preserve and secure library materials have meant limitations on access to those materials. Umberto Eco's novel *The Name of the Rose* provides a fictional yet reasonably accurate glimpse into the management of medieval monastic libraries. The novel is set in an Italian monastery and depicts life and mystery in 1327. Its sub-theme underscores the medieval belief that knowledge was dangerous but also the role the monasteries played in the copying and preservation of texts. Libraries, including Eco's *Rose* library, preserved texts in large part by prohibiting their use.

Generally policies that support the one support the other. When Sir Thomas Bodley prohibited flame (candles) in the Bodleian, he sought to protect the library from accidental fire. This prophylactic policy served to both preserve and protect the collection. Similarly, policies prohibiting the lending of books or of chaining books to the furniture protected the collection from theft, accidental losses, and to a certain extent from vandalism.

Preservation is now a complex science. The US Library of Congress (1999, 45–49) describes its more extensive initiatives to preserve library materials. These include binding and care, conservation, preservation reformatting, research and testing, the US Newspaper Program, deacidification, and preservation of audio/visual materials.

The preservation and conservation of digital materials require an additional set of skills and processes. Because standard digital hardware and software are constantly changing, it is necessary to migrate digital archives to newer formats on newer storage devices employing newer hardware and software. If these steps are not taken periodically, digital materials will not only deteriorate; they will become impossible to access and use. These sets of processes are analogous to the medieval practice of copying and recopying manuscripts and to translating those manuscripts from one language to another.

Kathleen de la Peña McCook (1999) offers a very interesting list of "library ancestors" to whom she acknowledges a particular debt. The list, as provided in her 1999 paper "Using Ockham's Razor: Cutting to the Center," is reproduced almost verbatim:

- Assurbanipal (668–627 BC) at Nineveh
- Eratosthenus (276–195 BC) at Alexandria
- Marcus Terentius Varro (116–127 BC) of Rome
- St. Jerome (342–420), patron saint of librarians
- Charlemagne (742–814) at Aachen, who established schools that included scriptoria
- Thomas Jefferson (1747–1826), father of the Library of Congress
- Anthony Panizzi (1797–1879), principal librarian, British Museum
- Cardinal Francisco Ehrle (1845–1934) at the Vatican Library
- José Toribio Medina (1852–1930), Spanish American bibliographer
- Nadezhda Konstantinovna Krupskîa (1869–1939), founder of the Soviet library system
- Ladies' Library Associations of the State of Michigan (1876)
- Jennie Maas Flexner (1882–1944), readers' advisor
- Vannevar Bush (1890–1974), "As We May Think"
- Jorge Luis Borges (1899–1986), director of Biblioteca Nacional of Argentina
- Major Owens (1936–), librarian in Congress
- St. Leibowitz (canonized 3174)

Some—like Eratosthenus of Alexandria, Anthony Panizzi of London, Francisco Cardinal Ehrle of the Vatican, or Nadezhda Konstantinovna Krupskaya of Moscow—were important librarians. Others—like Assurban-ipal, Charlemagne, or Thomas Jefferson—were political leaders. Still others—like St. Jerome, Marcus Terentius Varro, or Vannevar Bush—were scholars and visionaries.

If asked to choose sixteen "library ancestors," my list would differ somewhat from McCook's. But it would certainly include St. Leibowitz. "St. Leibowitz" is the fictional creation of Walter M. Miller, Jr., in his 1959 science fiction novel *A Canticle for Leibowitz*. In a post-atomic-apocalypse and well into the third millennium, the Order of St. Leibowitz maintained and copied the historical record remaining to them much in the same way the Carolingians promoted education and scriptoria and the Benedictines and other orders copied and cared for the historical record in medieval Europe. "St. Leibowitz" is iconic for me and perhaps for Professor McCook as a representation of the contribution made to stewardship by monastic orders from Charlemagne in the eighth century CE until the beginning of the seventeenth century.

The needs of preservation and use are not necessarily contradictory. Technology has served to accomplish both simultaneously. Antonio Durán Guardeño (2003, 6–7) contends that before the print revolution of the sixteenth century, five European libraries were responsible for the preservation of classical Greek mathematical holdings, particularly those of Archimedes. These five libraries were the Bibliothèque du Roy, founded by Charles V of France in Paris; the Laurentiana in Florence; the Marciana in Venice; the Vaticana in Rome; and the El Escorial near Madrid. With the invention of printing, many of the manuscripts were translated from Greek into Latin, printed, and distributed more widely throughout the public and private libraries of Europe.

The process described by Durán Guardeño in the sixteenth and seventeenth centuries is being repeated in the twentieth and twenty-first centuries, as library collections are being digitized and distributed globally across the web. The signal difference between the distribution of classical works in the seventeenth century and in the twenty-first century is not so much one of degree or of selection but with the structure of the distributions. The seventeenth century was largely decentralized, as works as physical objects were distributed to a wide variety of libraries. The twenty-first century distribution is more centralized. Although users throughout the world can access many of the digitized works, the works themselves are stored and managed on a limited number of servers. In a distributed model, library collections may be lost for any number of reasons, but copies will survive in libraries elsewhere. In a centralized system, should digital libraries fail for whatever reason, losses may be permanent.

To promote preservation and the dissemination of knowledge, advocates of national libraries argued vigorously for their cause. These advocates include Juan Páez de Castro (1512–1570), Gabriel Naudé (1600–1653), and Johann Christian Koch (1678–1738). Each of these advocates addressed their appeals to potential sponsors by appealing to their vanity and love of learning: Páez de Castro to the king of Spain Felipe II, Naudé to the president of the Paris Parlement de Thou, and Koch to the elector of Saxony. Páez de Castro's appeal resulted in the building of a university and library at El Escorial. Naudé was not immediately successful with his appeal, but he was to later participate in the building of one of France's great libraries, the Mazarine. Koch was unsuccessful.

Juan Páez de Castro's (1889) "Memorial" was addressed to Felipe II of Spain in the mid-sixteenth century. Felipe II ascended the throne in 1556 on the abdication of his father. Felipe II came to power at the beginning of the end of Spanish dominance and glory. Páez de Castro (1889, 12) proposed the library not only to glorify the name of his king but also to protect knowledge. He argued that unless the fruits of human arts and sciences were protected and stored in a safe place, they could be lost. Páez de Castro indicated that he had made the same argument to Carlos V, father of Felipe II: "Books contain the record of human arts and industry. There is danger that these could be lost if they are not put in a safe place."[1] (Páez de Castro 1889, 12).

The "Memorial," a document in four parts, describes a library of three major rooms and provides a brief history of books and libraries from Abraham and Moses to then contemporary Europe. The library's first room was to contain armoires, each with different classes of manuscripts and printed books: rare books, ancient books and their translations, books on canon and secular law, and books on philosophy. The first room was to be decorated with portraits of the writer of sacred works as well as Greek and Roman philosophers. The second room was to be the map room to contain maps and globes. It was to contain the genealogies of Spanish kings and related royal families. The third room was to serve as the state archive. As such, the third room needed to be the most secure and had to be maintained in secrecy.

Juan Páez de Castro was not the only supplicant of King Felipe II to found a central library at El Escorial. Bishop Juan Baptista Cardona wrote two documents in support of the library. In the first, "Traza de la Librería de San Lorenzo el Real," Cardona (1889b, 53) asserted that establishment of the library would bring benefits to Spain and all Christendom. The library would serve to preserve the best and most eminent of works. Part of the library's functions would be to transcribe, retranslate, and correct those texts (Cardona 1889b, 55–56). The library would also provide a defense of the faith against heretics. It would do so by providing clear texts that cleanly explained the truth (Cardona 1889b, 57). The library should also collect unpublished materials, including those that we now classify as "gray" (Cardona 1889b, 71).

Like Páez de Castro, Cardona outlined a plan for the library. Cardona prescribed library security to reduce vandalism and theft. He also advocated severe sanctions against those who abused their library privileges (Cardona 1889b, 70–71). Juan Baptista Cardona's second work, *De Regia S. Lavrentii Biblioteca, De la Real Biblioteca de San Lorenzo,* was published in both Latin and Spanish on facing pages. Cardona noted that scholars could use copies of major works. In so doing they would have access to those materials and implicitly help preserve the originals. But he stated that copied materials were often corrupted (Cardona 1587, 151).

Sir Thomas Bodley (1603) was concerned in the extreme with book preservation and security. Much of his statute for the library at Oxford consisted of rules to strictly limit use and access of the collection to reduce the risk of loss and damage. Open flame was prohibited. Books were not to be lent except to the very few and the trusted. Books were chained to desks. Only members of the Oxford community, and not all of them, as well as certain other scholars were permitted entrance into the library. Candidates for the post of librarian were to be carefully vetted.

John Dury (1596–1680) held a particularly dim view of the librarians of his day. Most, he argued, accepted their sinecures to enrich and advance themselves rather than to provide service to library patrons. These librarians were particularly protective of their collections, lest they be found negligent of their duties (Dury 1650b, 40), and practiced stewardship as self-interest.

Writing in 1762, Johann David Köhler (1973) noted the great lengths that the major libraries took to protect their collections. This care included the way in which books were stored and the limited access libraries provided for the use and copying of texts.

SERVICE

If stewardship is the oldest of library functions, service is now recognized as the librarian's primary responsibility (Koehler et al. 2000). There has always been a tension between service and stewardship, one giving way to the other as the essential function of the library underwent redefinition.

Sir Thomas Bodley (1603, 84–85) defined a very limited service role for his librarian at Oxford University. As already indicated, Bodley sought to protect the collection above its use by scholars. While he required the librarian to treat users/visitors according to their station as scholars, the courtesy of the library did not extend far beyond that courtesy.

Writing in 1699, the Presbyterian minister James Kirkwood saw the library as an extension of God's design, believing that mankind was inherently curious but unable to learn all things as an individual. To facilitate learning, "God hath endued Mankind with a Faculty of Speech, whereby they may Teach and Communicat to one another, all such Knowledges and Observations as shall be found out by any of them." (Kirkwood 1699c, 18–19). God, according to Kirkwood, may have provided mankind with the gift of speech, then with writing. Writing, to shorten Kirkwood's argument somewhat, led to printing, then to a proliferation of books. No one could read or acquire all books; hence, "Libraries are absolutely necessary for the Improvement of Arts and Sciences, and for Advancing of Learning amongst us" (Kirkwood 1967c, 27).

To bring about this universality of service and access to learning, Kirkwood proposed the establishment of libraries in every parish of Scotland.

John Dury (1650b, 42–45) defined the properly maintained and managed library to provide service to scholars and to have an impact on learning, but also to protect the collection:

> His work then is to bee a Factor and Trader for helps to Learning, and a Treasurer to keep them, and a dispenser to applie them to use, or to see them well used, or at least not abused.

In his second letter to Samuel Hartlib, Dury (1650, 61) was particularly critical of the library at the University of Heidelberg. He suggested that the very fact that the Heidelberg library did not open its collections for scholarship led to its decline as an important library.

Jean-Baptiste Cotton des Houssayes equated service with courtesy (1780, 36–41) toward visitors to the library, whether they were scholars or the merely curious. The librarian's responsibilities include making the faculties of the library open to its users. Indeed Cotton des Houssayes (1780, 41–2) asks:

> What . . . would be the object of these precious collections, gathered at so great an expense by fortune or by science, if they were not consecrated, according to the intentions of their generous founders, to the advancement, the glory, and the perfection of science and literature?

CONCLUSION

Libraries began primarily as document depositories. Greek libraries were primarily archives. Roman libraries provided somewhat more patron service. Medieval monastic libraries were for the most part storehouses and scriptoria. With the emergence of universities and university libraries, libraries became tools for scholars.

Slowly, libraries began to function less as archives and more as service institutions. By the mid-nineteenth century public libraries began providing service to the general public. In that capacity, public libraries increased their outreach and patron service responsibilities. Both public and academic libraries relaxed their regulations into the twentieth century, opening their stacks to their users, relaxing their lending policies, and increasing and expanding the nature of the collection.

The twenty-first-century public library has, to a very large degree, shed its responsibility as the repository of the cultural legacy of its society. This function has been relegated to national and academic libraries as well as to a limited number of major public libraries.

The digital revolution has had a significant impact on the cultural history maintenance role of libraries. First, many documents are created in native format as digital documents. These documents, by their very nature, cannot be part of the library's physical collection, although they may be included as part of the virtual collection. Many scholarly journals are published in digital format, some in both print and electronic, and while others have maintained a print-only format. Libraries may subscribe to journals in either format, but many have found electronic acquisition to be more efficient and economical.

By the mid 1990s, out-of-copyright books were being digitized and distributed over the web. Among the best known of these is Project Gutenberg, with an extensive library. By 2005 the potential commercial value of digital libraries spawned initiatives by Google and others to digitize the in- and out-of-copyright collections of major academic and public libraries. Other online libraries, for example the Digital Public Library of America (http://dp.la), the World Digital Library (http://www.wdl.org), and the International Children's Library (http://en.childrenslibrary.org) have been created.

While the digital revolution has resulted in a widespread distribution of popular and scholarly work, it has done little to ensure the stewardship of the cultural record. In fact, the digitization of information has raised threats to the continuity of the record. If anything, information digitization has created a renewed imperative for the library community to return to its first impulse, stewardship. Digitization permits, allows, and perhaps even demands the dispersion of collections. These disparate "sub-collections" can and are brought together as part of the catalog of physical and virtual libraries.

The virtual state of these collections, however, is their vulnerability. When digital publishers fail, and some will inevitably fail, their collections are at peril. From "time immemorial," content was protected because copies were distributed among several libraries—fewer when books were copied by hand, more after the advent of print. Should one library fail, others would remain to protect the cultural heritage. When a digital depositary fails, there is no longer any warranty that its slice of the cultural heritage will survive.

As Ranganathan has taught us, books are for use; but they cannot be used once they disappear. That said, users can often find the books they need more easily and efficiently in a virtual environment. The essential tension between service and stewardship continues. It is both deontological and utilitarian for librarians to find the essential balance between the two imperatives.

NOTE

1. "Mostré, como de los libros penden todos las artes, y industrías humanas; y en quánto pelligro están de perderse, si no se dá algum medio para que se guaradan en lugar seguro."

THREE

Classification

There are more things in heaven and earth, Horatio, than are dreamt of in your philosophy.

—Hamlet, act I, scene V

There is no matter connected to the administration of a Public Library which can vie, in point of importance, with the character and the condition of its catalogs.

—Edward Edwards (1859 ii, 749)

So even when people take classifications to be purely mental, or purely formal, they *also* mold their behavior to fit those conceptions.

—Bowker and Star (2000, 53)

CLASSIFICATION AS LANGUAGE

Classification is a variation on language. It is also a reflection of the socio-cultural milieu in which it is formed and of the materials it manages (Bowker and Star 1998 and 2000). It is a mechanism whereby seemingly abstract symbols convey meaning across time, place, and media from one person to another, however imperfect that transfer may be. Geoffrey Bowker and Susan Leigh Star (2000) make a strong case for classification as a social activity, an activity that reflects the perceived realities of the developer of the scheme. Classification systems also evolve as the subject of the classification changes or are perceived to change. They also change in concert with larger social shifts. In fact, according to Bowker and Star (2000, 1), our systems of classifications define our environments. Furthermore, as Bowker and Star argue (2000, 2), "these standards and classifications, however imbricated in our lives, are ordinarily invisible."

Bowker and Star (2000, 10–11) define classification as "a spatial, temporal, or spatio-temporal segmentation of the world," with "consistent, unique classificatory principles in operation." They further posit that the classificatory categories are self-exclusive, at least in ideal conditions. Thus classification is, in and of itself, a defining element in discourse and in social and institutional relationships.

Librarians strive to make classification as "noiseless" as possible so as to provide not only an accurate portrayal of information as possible without inordinately confusing the communication with over complexity. The concept of "noise" derives from information theory, first enunciated by Claude Shannon (1948) as a means to improve communication through the reduction or elimination of extraneous and unrelated interference. As collections grow and as media change, so to must the code change and grow. This chapter documents some of those changes in code and complexity from colophons on stone tablets to digital mark-up.

ETHICAL BASIS OF CLASSIFICATION

Classification is directly related to at least three of Ranganathan's Five Laws. Classification supports the first law—books are for use—by facilitating the "finding" of materials appropriate for specific applications or uses. Classification also serves the fourth law—save the time of the reader—again by providing a mechanism for a more efficient retrieval of information.

Classification essentially supports Ranganathan's fifth law—a library is a growing organism. As the library, the organism, grows more complex, the system(s) needed to describe that organism must necessarily become more complex. Moreover, as information systems become more interactive and inter-operable, the need for accepted standards to inter-link those systems becomes more intense.

Classification is not, of course, in and of itself an ethical impulse. It is a means to an ethical end, the provision of information in an articulated and logical way developed to facilitate the use of that information. As we shall see, classification qua classification performs an important ethical function. How information is classified, the terms used, also has ethical importance. Sanford Berman has been an important force to sensitize us to the importance of terms used in classification. For example, the term used to describe Americans of African descent in the Library of Congress Subject Headings has evolved from Negro to Colored to Black to African American. Similarly, the terms used to describe women in what was considered male-dominated professions or men in female-dominated professions have become more gender neutral. While these are socially driven changes, there is a strong ethical basis to the changes as well.

LIBRARIES AND CLASSIFICATION

Historically libraries have been organized in a wide variety of means. These include date of publication, date of acquisition, alphabetical order by author, alphabetical order by title; alphabetical order by subject, size, or shape; fiction and non-fiction; "good material and bad"; first argument and revisionist. Medieval library catalogs were relatively small, as the collections they reflected were small. Edward Edwards (1864, 45–50) described a number of eleventh- and twelfth-century libraries. The Library of Monte Cassino had eight hundred manuscripts; the Abbey of Corbie in Picardy fewer than two hundred.

Classification is one of the root functions of a library (see Taylor 1995 and 2004, Chan 2007). It can, in fact, be broadened to cover nearly all functions of the library (Zeng and Chan 2003). For example, acquisition constitutes the classification of materials deemed appropriate for the collection and the rejection of other materials not so deemed. Reference requires classification of user needs, however articulated, into an appropriate resource into matter form that fulfills that need. In so doing, a second classification function occurs—that is, the selection of one resource over another as more or less appropriate to meet the articulated and sometimes unarticulated needs of the end user. Additionally, acquisition constitutes the classification of materials deemed appropriate for the collection and the rejection of other materials not so deemed. Reference requires classification of user needs, however articulated, into an appropriate resource into a matter form that fulfills that need.

Libraries have been organized around some principle almost as soon as documents were first created. What matters most in this context is that libraries were and are organized according to some principle. It is possible of the library minder to retain an accurate mental catalog of his/her library so long as the collection remains extremely small. Once a collection exceeds some number of discrete documents, some other system is required. Edward Edwards (1859 ii, 749–760) described four major types of library catalogs of his day. The first might be described as encyclopedic. These catalogs array a list of topics in alphabetical order, without regard to the relationship of the topics. Under each topic, documents are listed that address that topic.

Second are catalogs based on general categories: theology, medicine, law, philosophy, history, literature, and so on. Books are then listed under each of the general categories. According to Edward Edwards (1859 ii, 762) the first such catalog of printed books were developed by printers. One such catalog of Greek works was provided by the elder

Aldus in 1498, classed as *Grammatica, Poetica, Logica, Philosophia,* and *Sacra Scriptura.* Conrad Gesner's *Bibliothèque universelle,* according to Edwards (1859 ii, 762) was the first book catalog designed not to promote sales but for use in libraries. Third catalogs may be a list of authors, in alphabetical order. And fourth are catalogs that combine two or more of the above.

Edwards (1859 ii, 758–760) alluded to a problem of subject catalogs. Too often, concepts may be described using more that one term (synonyms). They may also be sub-classes of a broader concept or they may be related in meaning to other concepts. I do not find where Edwards ever used the term "subject heading," but he clearly had it in mind.

Library science distinguishes several different yet highly related classificatory undertakings required for libraries to provide the information storage and retrieval services they are expected to perform. These functions include bibliography, descriptive and subject cataloging, indexing, and abstracting. In this work, classification is considered in its role as a core library function. The many ways information can be classified are not the subject of this work and we will not consider the relative merits of one classification scheme over another except insofar as the increasing complexity of information resources or the demands of technology require libraries to revise those schemes. Thus, for example, xml markup was meaningless, useless, and impossible to implement before the digital revolution. Whether one archival xml markup system is preferred to another is of little consequence except insofar as one can be objectively demonstrated to perform better as a classification method over another. Similarly one may ask whether Dewey Decimal Classification (DDC) is in some way superior to Library of Congress Classification (LC), faceted classification, or some other system. In the United States public libraries have long preferred DDC, while academic libraries generally employ LC. In the United Kingdom, and to a lesser degree in the United States, Bliss Classification gained some adherents (see Bliss 1935; Thomas 1997). Universal Decimal Classification (UDC) is an outgrowth of DDC in an attempt to address the multilingual nature of information as well as to expand the message conveyed by classification (see Mcilwaine 2000).

Classification has its cultural aspects. Colon classification has many adherents in India. And India is of course the birthplace and the home for most of the professional career of S. R. Ranganathan, creator of colon classification. Many classification systems, beginning in the fifteenth century, began with religious groupings. Catholic and Protestant catalogs would classify their "orthodoxies" first and follow with the "fallacies or heresies" second. The Dewey system moved "religion" to third place, but its critics have found it to be too Western in its orientation. Both the Library of Congress Classification System and the Library of Congress Subject Headings have been found to have cultural bias. Sanford Berman has identified implicit racist and sexist undertones in the Library of Congress Subject Headings. He has made it a personal imperative to identify and revise those headings.

Classification has its linguistic aspects. Germany for many years employed the Prussian Principles. German has a syntax and word construction that differs from many other European languages. German builds complex compound words by combining adjectives and adverbs with the subject noun to create a single word. The Prussian Principles, also known as the Prussian Instructions, employs a grammatical rather than an alphabetical order as a first step in catalog construction. Adjectives and adverbs are parsed from the central term. These are then regrouped on the target word (the subject noun) in order of descending modification of the target word. Take "Leihbibliothek" as a simple example. "Leihbibliothek" means "lending library." To properly index the term, Leih (lending) and Bibliothek (library) are parsed and then alphabetized as Bibliothek, Leih.

Classification has its political aspects. For example, the Soviet classification scheme, *Bibliotechno-Bibliograficheskaya Klassifikatsiya* (BBK) was developed beginning in the 1930s in consonance with Marxist-Leninist theory (Gurevich 1990). By the 1980s, most libraries in the Union of Soviet Socialist Republics had adapted or converted to BBK and its variants (Sukiasyan 1988). Libraries in the German Democratic Republic (Hohne 1978; Schultz 1984) employed BBK rather than a classification system of German etiology. It was also adopted for use in Bulgaria (Laskova 1984) as well as in other Socialist countries, including Mongolia. After the collapse of the Soviet Union in 1991, a number of libraries of countries formerly part of the Soviet sphere of influence—Bulgaria, the former DDR, and Viet Nam among them—began a retrospective conversion of their catalogs from BBK to other systems—UDC and LC among them. A number of libraries in these countries have cooperated among themselves to rationalize in the aftermath of what Nadia Caidi (2003, 103) has called their "socio-political transformation" beginning in the early 1990s. She also notes a shift in status among libraries in the four countries she studied (Caidi 2003, 115). During the era of Soviet domination, national libraries were norm setters ("mothers of all libraries") together with the scientific and technical libraries. After the early 1990s, university libraries' statuses increased as they launched automation programs and began cooperation among themselves.

Special libraries often build their classification systems on a specialized thesaurus. They do this because more generalized classifications systems are insufficiently precise to describe collections that cover a very limited number of subjects or disciplines. That many libraries have undertaken retrospective reclassification of their collections may reflect a belief that one system is better than another; but it may also imply a belief that the implementation of a common classification scheme is, for reasons of standardization, to be preferred.

In a way, then, this chapter offers something of a history of classification without recourse to extensive descriptions of their individual approaches. That said, we might argue that there are important underlying ethical concerns to how the classification schemes are constructed. It is important for us to remember as we evaluate these systems that they are dynamic, living representations of thought. As society changes, so does the way in which words are interpreted. Just as Mark Twain's *Huckleberry Finn* has been criticized from the day it was first published because the way in which slavery, and particularly Jim, was portrayed. it has also been targeted for its use of the "n" word. That racially loaded language has become the new obscenity, so too must classification systems reflect contemporary practice.

CLASSIFICATION AS LANGUAGE

In *The Search for the Perfect Language*, Umberto Eco (1995) has produced a historical tour de force describing Europe's quest to reconstruct the Tower of Babel. Eco (1995, 2–3), a twentieth-century polymath, imposed a fourfold limit to the work to focus on (1) the rediscovery of original or "perfect languages" (Hebrew, Egyptian, and Chinese), (2) the reconstruction of "mother tongues," (3) artificially constructed languages, and (4) "more or less magic languages." There has almost always been a common second language to permit communication between linked cultures. Among these are Greek, Latin, Mandarin Chinese, French, German, and today English. Specific languages have been identified with certain disciplines—Italian with music, Latin with medicine and the law, French with diplomacy, German with science. English is today's *lingua franca*. While there is no reason to believe that English will decline as the most important second language in the immediate future, there is no reason to believe that it will not be replaced at some point either by another "natural" language or by technology—a universal translator, perhaps.

Carl Linnaeus built his classification system with Latin, the common language of his day. There are some professions, aviation for example, where a very limited yet specific English vocabulary has been developed in order to facilitate communication and avoid confusion. Mathematic and music have, in their own way, come to form common communications pathways.

The multilingualism of the European Union has virtually forced European officials to create an official thesaurus of terms to provide maps across the many languages spoken across the continent.[1] According to Eco (1998, 88–89), both Meso-American and Chinese pictograms represent communication systems that carry messages across pronunciations. Pictograms or icons have again come into generalized use in the mid-twentieth century for standardized traffic signs, commercial logos, and a little later for personal computer desktops.

The mapping of languages provides an additional platform for information classification, one that incorporates an immense complication in definition. Classification schemes are artificial languages, in the way Umberto Eco means in *The Search for the Perfect Language*. A perfect language could give rise to a perfect classification scheme written in the perfect language. By perfect language, Eco does not mean the "best" or "premier" tongue; rather, he is addressing the search for either the root or basic source language or for an acceptable synthetic language. As Eco (1995, 18–19) puts it: "Some looked backwards, trying to rediscover the language spoken by Adam, a proto-Hebrew. Others looked ahead, aiming to fabricate a rational language possessing the perfections of the 'lost speech of Eden.'"

Eco documents a long list of efforts that include Leibniz's fascination with the *I Ching*, early Kabbalistic studies, Esperanto, and *latino sine flexione*. Thus in a classification scheme, artificial symbols synoptically represent content and meaning. In a perfect classification scheme, meaning would be translated to the appropriate symbols from one language and reinterpreted later without loss of meaning to another language or classification scheme. Ultimately, the perfect classification scheme could also be a perfect language.

As intriguing an idea as it is, we do not propose to recapitulate Umberto Eco's *Search* by replacing Eco's linguistic examples with catalog codes from other intellectual schema. Early library catalogers did not seek to ascertain how Adam and Eve arranged their books or how or why Adam named the beasts and the plants. They were seeking some logical (and sometimes illogical) means by which they could manage their manuscript collections once they surpassed three or more volumes. Nevertheless, the intellectual effort to discover or create a perfect language is not too dissimilar to the same effort to devise a classification scheme. And these classifications do, in fact, fall with the scope of artificial languages as Eco defined them.

THE BIRTH OF CLASSIFICATION

Classification Theory

The purpose of bibliographical classification is synoptical. Whatever its format, a classification system should convey some sense of the meaning of the underlying document. The catalog carries a second purpose as well. It is a location aid. Once a work is identified as appropriate to meet some need, the catalog provides the location or address of the storage point for that work. A third function is inventory control.

A library catalog can serve one, two, or all three of these functions simultaneously. The early library catalogs were non-stratified lists of manuscripts. As such, they were primarily inventories. Johann David Köhler (1728) demonstrated in his *Syllogie aliquot scriptorum de bene ordinanda et ornanda bibliotheca* that library catalogs not only were a finding tool, as they indicated whether a given library owned a specific work, but they could be used to categorize documents to their intended purpose. Köhler's *Syllogie* is a list of books of historiographical importance on European history and where they could be found.

By the fifteenth century librarians began to realize that catalogs could be used as a primary classification tool. At the same time, the catalog continued to have both inventory and address functions. As the number of books proliferated and as libraries grew larger, catalogs became mechanisms to provide placement addresses. Early catalogs were often organized according to date of accession and by document title. Before the sixteenth century authorship and individualism had not gained the status they were to later hold. Some libraries were organized along very broad lines: theology, philosophy, history, science, and the like. The catalog, sometimes alphabetical lists of titles and sometimes of authors, would give the shelf and shelf position of a given work. And sometimes a sense of content would be conveyed if the library were divided into sections.

Early Classification

If James Usher (1581–1656), archbishop of Armagh, Ireland, had his dates right, Adam became the first classifier in about 4004 BCE. According to Genesis 2:19:

> Now the LORD GOD had formed out of the ground all the beasts of the field and all the birds of the air. He brought them to the man to see what he would name them; and whatever the man called each living creature, that was its name. So the man gave names to all the livestock, the birds of the air and all the beasts of the field.

Nature, too, gives rise to classification. In a chapter aptly named "Classification," Charles Darwin (1859, 402), perhaps echoing Genesis, writes in *The Origin of Species*:

> From the most remote period in the history of the world, organic beings have been found to resemble each other in descending degrees, so that they may be classed in groups under groups. This classification is not arbitrary like the grouping of the stars in constellations. The existence of groups would have been of simple significance, if one group had been exclusively fitted to inhabit the land, and another the water; one to feed on flesh, another on vegetable matter, and so on; but the case is widely different, for it is notorious how commonly members of even the same sub-group have different habits.

The early philosophers were the first classifiers. Earth, air, fire, and water are, according to Empedocles of Acragas (495–435 BCE), the elemental building blocks of the universe. Love (good) and strife (evil) are the two forces that act on the four elements to bring forth motion. Stephen Hawking (1998) would most likely agree that there are elemental building blocks of the universe. He would most certainly differ on the elemental building blocks as well as the forces, now weak and strong rather than good and evil. For our purposes it is probably no more useful to classify most things by their basic elements, for first we would have to agree what those base elements are. Moreover, whatever the base elements and forces are, they are far too generally distributed to be of much use to differentiate among different classes of things.

Four elements and two forces may be a good beginning, but they are not sufficient to develop comprehensive taxonomies. Plato was among the first philosophers to recognize an order of nature, as he noted in the *Republic* and particularly in the *Statesman* (reporting the words of Socrates). Aristotle and Plato shared many points of classification theory but differed in a fundamental way. Plato believed in a knowledge based on fundamental principles, whereas Aristotle was more relativist. Knowledge for Plato was derived from a study of the divine. For Aristotle, it was derived from a study of the environment, human and natural. Aristotle recognized a greater complexity and wrote in terms of primary and secondary substances. In *The Categories*, Aristotle (350 BCE, § 1, part 1) tells us:

> Things are said to be named 'equivocally' when, though they have a common name, the definition corresponding with the name differs for each. Thus, a real man and a figure in a picture can both lay claim to the name 'animal'; yet these are equivocally so named, for, though they have a common name, the definition corresponding with the name differs for each. For should any one define in what sense each is an animal, his definition in the one case will be appropriate to that case only.

> On the other hand, things are said to be named 'univocally' which have both the name and the definition answering to the name in common. A man and an ox are both 'animal', and these are univocally so named, inasmuch as not only the name, but also the definition, is the same in both cases: for if a man should state in what sense each is an animal, the statement in the one case would be identical with that in the other.

> Things are said to be named 'derivatively,' which derive their name from some other name, but differ from it in termination. Thus the grammarian derives his name from the word 'grammar,' and the courageous man from the word 'courage.'

And:

when one thing is predicated of another, all that which is predicable of the predicate will be predicable also of the subject. Thus, 'man' is predicated of the individual man; but 'animal' is predicated of 'man'; it will, therefore, be predicable of the individual man also: for the individual man is both 'man' and 'animal.'

If genera are different and co-ordinate, their differentiae are themselves different in kind. Take as an instance the genus 'animal' and the genus 'knowledge'. 'With feet,' 'two-footed,' 'winged,' 'aquatic,' are differentiae of 'animal'; the species of knowledge are not distinguished by the same differentiae. One species of knowledge does not differ from another in being 'two-footed.'

But where one genus is subordinate to another, there is nothing to prevent their having the same differentiae: for the greater class is predicated of the lesser, so that all the differentiae of the predicate will be differentiae also of the subject. (§ 1, part 3)

The theory of classification in libraries has gained a great deal from contributions from many theoreticians who came to librarianship from a wide range of disciplines. Perhaps library classification can be dated to the reign of Ashur-bani-pal (or Ashurbanipal), king of Assyria at Nineveh in the seventh century BCE (Budge 1929, 17), and to Greek libraries in the sixth century BCE. Ashur-bani-pal and his scribes, according to Sir Ernest Wallis Budge (1929, 17), made "bilingual lists of signs and words and objects of all classes and kinds." Not only did the tablets have colophons, which in some cases indicated the library in which they were deposited, different document types were sized and shaped differently (Budge 1929, 21). Of equal interest, the Sumerian *Epic of Gilgamish* (or Gilgamesh) was found among the stone slabs of Ashur-bani-pal's library.

Justus Lipsius (1607, 49–50) informs us that Athenaeus parenthetically refers to the classification skills of Laurentius and asserts that Laurentius's skills eclipsed those of "Polycrates of Samos, Pisistratus the Tyrant, Euclid the Athenian, Nicocrates the Cyprian, Euripides the poet, and Aristotle the philosopher." Lipsius (1607, 50) cites A. Gellius's claim that Pisistratus was "the pioneer in this art in forming a library." Pisistratus, according to Gellius, was also among the first to establish a library of liberal arts for public use.

Sir Thomas Bodley specified that among the library keeper's duties was the obligation to arrange the collection by faculties and to provide catalogs for each faculty collection, listing authors alphabetically. In addition, each catalog entry was to provide the title of the work, volume number, and date and place of publication (Bodley 1603, 73)

Classification as applied in libraries and other information environments has also benefited from theoretical contributions to other fields. Four of the most important are the Swiss zoologist and polymath Conrad

Gessner (1516–1565), the English renaissance humanist and deductive logician Sir Francis Bacon (1561–1626), the German philosopher and scientist Gottfried Wilhelm von Leibniz (1646–1716), and the Swedish physician and scientist Carl Linnaeus (1707–1778).

After Gutenberg, the proliferation of books led to a demand for better bibliographical control of the written word. In 1545 Conrad Gessner, a physician and botanist, published *Bibliotheca universalis*, a catalog in Latin, Greek, and Hebrew of all books published in Europe, printed or manuscript. The *Pandeclarium sive partitionum universalium Conradi Gesneri Ligurini libri xxi* followed in 1548. This work arranged books across twenty-one general systematic tables. A second appendix followed in 1555. These works contained more than twelve thousand records for some three thousand authors. The work classified the entries by name.

Sir Francis Bacon, later Lord Verulam and the Viscount St. Albans, divided knowledge into three classes: history, poesy, and philosophy. These three classes are derived from the three "faculties of the mind": memory, imagination, and reason. Jesse Shera (1965, 79–80) credits Bacon as the foremost of the "precursors to science" and "bibliographic organization." Bacon is important to the classification science in that he developed the deductive hierarchy of the structure of knowledge, the foundation of modern classification methodologies.

Gottfried Wilhelm von Leibniz, a contemporary of Sir Isaac Newton, shares the credit with him for the development of differential calculus. Leibniz based his analysis of the physical world on the *monad*. The monad derives from atomist theory of the divisibility and granularity of physical structures. In effect any compound can be reduced to its basic parts and understood by those basic parts—atoms—and the combination of atoms into molecules, compounds, and so on. Leibniz also proposed that the universe could be described in organic, living terms. As a concatenation of living organisms, individual organisms cannot be differentiated one from another. This results from the fact that organisms are interdependent with one another. In understanding Leibniz, it is important to keep in mind that physics had yet to develop the concept of the atom as a fundamental building block of matter, not to mention the more fundamental particles that have been shown to be constituent parts of atoms (for an interesting discussion, see Hawking 1998, ch. 5).

Leibniz also argued that there is a connection between the mind and the form and content of language. To that end, some have suggested that Leibniz made early contributions to the development of artificial intelligence theory (e.g., Gates 1979; Churchland 1984; Pratt 1987). He posited that humans applied cognitively logical rules of universal classification. Logic and reasoning are based on the use of symbols. These symbol sets, we might suggest, might be used to classify information in an external context. To that end, Leibniz argued that a common and logical language could, through the application of a formal symbolic construct—perhaps mathematics—result in a more perfect communications system. For an interesting discussion of Leibniz's system, see http://homepages.which. net/~gk.sherman/gaaaaaaf.htm.

The Swedish scientist and physician Carl Linnaeus (Carl von Linné), 1707–1778, is known best for his development of a system of biological classification. That system remains the basis for the standardization of scientific nomenclature. In Linnaeus's view, he was recapitulating God's design through his taxonomy. Not only did Linnaeus offer a biological and botanical taxonomy, he also developed one for minerals as well. In addition and in collaboration with François Boissier de Sauvages, Linnaeus contributed to the development of systematic nosology: the arrangement of diseases by classes, orders, genera, and species. Linnaeus's taxonomy (class, order, genus, and species) has had an important impact on methodologies to classify information in a broader sense. It provides a format for Ranganathan's faceted/colon classification in the twentieth century.

Library Classification

According to Justus Lipsius (1607, 36), Aristotle can be credited with creating the first private library of which anything is known. Aristotle was also responsible for establishing a classification scheme. One Lipsius citing Strabo, Aristotle taught the Ptolemys of Egypt.

In 1556 Juan Páez de Castro advised his king, Felipe II of Spain, to create a library. The library, according to Páez de Castro's plan would be divided into rooms, each holding a different collection. The first room would be reserved for philosophical and theological works. The second room would hold cosmological, botanical, geographical, and astrological works as well as maps and related materials. The third room would house state and government papers, to include secret archives. The library, as proposed by Juan Páez de Castro, was incorporated into the El Escorial palace built by Felipe II near Madrid. The library at El Escorial is still maintained and was to serve as a "temple of science."

The Reverend James Kirkwood, a Scot, advised that when parish libraries were established, the various Presbyterian ministers within the parish contribute their books. Heritors would be appointed to receive and sort the books. The heritors were to be instructed to categorize the books alphabetically and the date and place printed. Kirkwood did not specify whether the books should be ordered alphabetically by title or author. We may infer he meant by the book's name or title as he later instructed library keepers "to rank the books according to name and number, in the general Catalogue" (Kirkwood 1967c, 37).

The catalogs resulting from the process were to be produced in four copies: one to reside with the minister, the second with the heritor, the third with the library keeper, and the fourth would be deposited at the principal library in Edinburgh. From the catalogs deposited at Edinburgh, a "general Catalogue" was to be produced. That general catalog was to include a value for each book. Finally, each parish library was to receive a copy of the general catalog.

Kirkwood advocated the creation of a union or general catalog primarily to place a monetary value on books, to avoid unnecessary duplication, and to provide a guide to scholars seeking specific books.

The Jesuit priest Claude Clément (1596–1642) allegedly was inspired to draft his *Musei sive bibliothecae* based on the catalog of the El Escorial library. Clément developed a pictorial catalog. Clément's work was elaborated by another Jesuit, Jean Garnier (1612–1681). Garnier was author of several religious works and edited others. In 1678 he published *Systema bibliothecae collegii Parisiensis S.J.*, a work that contributed to cataloging practice by describing the process used at the Jesuit library in Paris. Garnier developed a system of headings and subheadings by which the library was to be organized, based in part on religious and historical criteria.

The Abbé Jean-Baptiste Cotton des Houssayes, librarian of the Sorbonne, held that the librarian should employ a selection strategy based on "enlightened economy: guided by "the substantial merits of an able classification" (Cotton des Houssayes 1780, 43–44). He did not elaborate on the theme "able classification."

Gabriel Naudé (1627, 64) began his chapter "Arranging the Books" with a critique of classification systems proposed by Lacroix du Maine ("plan of a hundred cases"), Giulio Camillo ("dramatic works"), and Jean Mabun ("morals, sciences, and devotion"). He was also critical of the organization of the Ambrosian Library, where, according to Naudé (1627, 67–68), books were "stowed pell mell" by a number code and were accessed through an alphabetical catalog of authors and code numbers. Instead Naudé (1627, 65) proposed a subject classification based on "theology, medicine, jurisprudence, history, philosophy, mathematics, humanities, and so on." These were to be divided "under subheadings according to their several division" to be developed by the "librarian in charge." Naudé (1627, 69) rejected, however, the idea of classification based on an order of nature as an impossibility and rather embraced one of personal convenience:

> since the order of nature (which is always uniform and self-consistent) being incapable of application because of the wide range and diversity of books, there remains only the order of art, which every man usually wishes to establish to suit himself, according as he finds, by his own good sense and judgment, it will best suit his convenience, as much as to satisfy himself as from unwillingness to follow the examples and opinions of others.

The Danish bibliophile Frederic Rostgaard published *Project d'une nouvelle methode* [sic] *pour dresser le catalogue d'une bibliotheque* [sic] in 1697, followed by a second edition in 1698. Rostgaard (1698, 3–5) proposed a scheme dividing knowledge into twenty-four categories, each represented by a letter of the alphabet. The catalog itself would distinguish among volume sizes. In each class, the catalog would group and list books in order of size: folio, quarto, octavo, duodecimo, and so on.[2] Within each class, each book would be numbered, each class beginning with "1." A second catalog would list authors in alphabetical order with corresponding codes to the master list of works.

Library Classification in the Nineteenth Century

Until the nineteenth century the library catalog served largely as an inventory tool rather than as a search and retrieval system. Sir Antonio Panizzi is considered to be the pioneer of the catalog as a research tool (Battles 2003, 129–130). Before the publication explosion of the nineteenth century, library catalogs were relatively easier to search, but more often users knew of that which they sought. As library collections expanded almost exponentially, memory and book lists no longer would suffice to provide the needed bibliographic control to effectively use the collections.

The first library cataloging code of many was the British Museum Cataloging rules (BM), also called Panizzi's ninety-one rules, developed in 1839, after which later codes were developed. These rules were an important developmental step in classification, an author catalog with cross-reference guides (Fattahi 1997). The time was right, authorship was prolific, and catalog access to books by author alone was no longer enough. Book catalogs had to be updated constantly, and this system was outdated very rapidly. The British Museum code of 1841 was primarily developed as a cataloging system for the museum's holdings. It was a continuation of rules used heretofore in medieval monasteries, expanded and adapted for the needs of the museum. In 1853 Jewett's thirty-three rules were published, loosely based on Panizzi's rules, or more precisely, a continuation of these rules. This code is the earliest mentioned use of subject headings. Jewett's code was unique in that it used both author listings and alphabetized subjects (Fattahi 1997). Other libraries could also use his templates to create catalogs, facilitating inter-library cooperation.

Dewey Decimal Classification

Melvil Dewey's name is most often associated with library classification systems (see Wiegand 1968). Dewey was, as we have seen, neither the first nor the last but the most frequently recognized. Dewey's system, based on the classification of knowledge into a set of very general classes represented by numbers, further subdivided into sub-classes, and also represented by numbers, was by no means original to him. The top-level Dewey classes are arranged in ten groups:

000 Generalities

100 Philosophy; parapsychology and occultism; psychology

200 Religion

300 Social sciences

400 Language

500 Natural sciences and mathematics

600 Technology (applied sciences)

700 The fine arts and decorative arts

800 Literature (belles-lettres) and rhetoric

900 Geography; history; auxiliary disciplines

All "Dewey" numbers have three numbers to the left of the decimal point. Library and information science as a subject is classed under "Generalities" as 020. Greater specificity is indicated in the third digit to the right, such that 025 indicates "library operations." Further specificity is provided to the right of the decimal: 025.1 represents "library operations, administration."

DDC is a "decimal" system in part because of its use of the "point," and not "period" or "full-stop" [.] as a demarking symbol. DDC is an enumerative system in that it seeks to provide sufficient notation through numerical elaboration to cover general categories and all sub-categories to the point that an issue in hand can be sufficiently distinguished from other dissimilar and similar sub-classes.

There were numerous classification systems that predated Dewey's. Edward Edwards (1859 ii, 761–831) dedicated a single long chapter titled "Classificatory Systems" to their description and analysis.

Library Classification in the Twentieth Century

Library classification in the twentieth century is a much more complex undertaking than that of the nineteenth century. James Duff Brown was perhaps the more important of transitional theorists bridging the nineteenth and twentieth centuries (Beghtol 2004). Brown introduced into classification theory the concepts of "main classes" and "concrete" subjects. According to Begthol, Brown divided knowledge into less precise categories than had Panizzi or Dewey. Brown perceived "fuzzy" distinctions between classes, phenomena not recognized in earlier and many later classification schemes. Brown's categories are:

A	Generalia
B–D	Matter and force
E–I	Life
J–L	Mind
M–X	Record

The various systems developed in the second half of the twentieth century are standards built on standards built on standards. The twentieth century is marked by the increasing complexity of information and for managing information. Not only were there major innovations in communications, there were also major changes in the publication of information. These range from the introduction of offset printing, mimeograph, and xerography, to the Internet. No longer were classification systems named after individuals (Dewey, Cutter) but with descriptive terms or after corporate bodies (colon classification, Library of Congress, Dublin Core, Semantic Web).

Library of Congress

The Library of Congress Classification System is an elaboration on Cutter Expansive Classification with influences from DDC. Herbert Putman devised it in 1897. Putnam was Librarian of Congress from 1889 to 1939. He had assistance from Charles Ammi Cutter.

Library of Congress Classification (LC) is an alphanumeric-based cataloging system. The top-level categories are single letters:

A	General works
B	Philosophy. Psychology. Religion
C	Auxiliary sciences of history
D	History: general and old world
E	History: America
F	History: America
G	Geography. Anthropology. Recreation
H	Social sciences
J	Political science
K	Law
L	Education
M	Music and books on music

N   Fine arts

P   Language and literature

Q   Science

R   Medicine

S   Agriculture

T   Technology

U   Military science

V   Naval science

Z   Bibliography. Library science. Information resources

Second-level categories consist of the top-level character and a second alphanumeric. For example, "K Law" is subdivided as:

K	Law in general; comparative and uniform law; jurisprudence
KBM	Jewish law
KPB	Islamic law
KBR	History of canon law
KBU	Law of the Roman Catholic Church; The Holy See
KD to KDK	Law of the United Kingdom and Ireland
KDZ	America; North America
KE	Law of Canada
KF	Law of the United States
KG	Latin America—Mexico and Central America—West Indies; Caribbean area
KH	South America
KJ to KKZ	European Law
KL to KWX	Asia and Eurasia, Africa, Pacific Area, and Antarctica
KZ	Law of Nations[3]

Sub-classes are further subdivided using both letters and numbers. For example, KZ5510–6299 represents the international law of peace and peace enforcement. Values within the range represent further subdivisions of the subject. LC is an expansive system in that further subdivision can be and is attained by use of the decimal [.]. For example, KZD1002–6715 represents various aspects of the law of space.

KZD5648–5680.2 is set aside for the sub-class "un-peaceful uses of outer space" and its sub-class "disarmament and demilitarization regimes in outer space."

Universal Decimal Classification

One of the first classification systems developed in the twentieth century is Universal Decimal Classification (UDC), a system that grew out of Dewey's work. Like DDC, UDC is an enumerative system, but it also permits additional notation to provide greater description.

Paul Otlet and Henri de la Fontaine first developed UDC at the beginning of the twentieth century. Like DDC, UDC is based on a set of numbered categories and UDC maps well to DDC at the first level:

0   Generalities

1   Philosophy. Psychology

2   Religion. Theology

3   Social sciences

4   Vacant

5   Natural sciences

6   Technology

7   The arts

8   Language. Linguistics. Literature

9   Geography. Biography. History

The social sciences, for example, are further disaggregated as:

30   Theories and methods in social sciences

31   Demography. Statistics. Sociology

32   Politics

33   Economics

34   Law. Jurisprudence

35   Public administration

36   Social welfare

37   Education

38   Vacant

39   Ethnography. Customs. Manners. Traditions. Way of life. Folklore

Politics or 32, in turn is broken out as:

321   Forms of political organization. States as political power

322 Relation between church and states. Policy towards religion. Church policy

323 Home affairs. Internal policy

324 Elections. Plebiscites. Referendums. Election campaigns. Electoral corruption, malpractice. Election results

325 Opening up of territories. Colonization

326 Slavery

327 International relations. World, global politics. International affairs. Foreign policy

328 Parliaments. Representation of the people

329 Political parties and movements

In UDC, complex relationships can be described using its "punctuation":

+, plus: additive concepts (e.g., 321+636 indicates political organizations and animal breeding)

/, stroke: extension (e.g., 325/327 indicates a composite of 325, 326, and 327)

:, colon: relationship (e.g., 02:39 indicates the relationship of ethnography to librarianship)

[], brackets: sub-grouping (e.g., 35[636+327] indicates the public administration of the international relations of animal breeding)

=, equals: language (e.g., 35[636+327]=20 indicates the public administration of the international relations of animal breeding, written in English)

Librarianship (02) is found under Generalities (0).

Colon Classification

S. R. Ranganathan developed colon or faceted classification. It is primarily used in India. Like UDC, colon classification is an analytico-synthetic based system, in that meanings are analyzed and then combined as facets or terms to provide a wider description of the work at hand. A treatise on forensic medicine, for example, has to be cataloged as a work of medicine or of law in DDC and LC. In a faceted, synthesis-based system, both the medical and legal aspects can be represented as primary "meanings" of the work.

Ranganathan (1960, 2–4) divides "knowledge" into forty-two main classes, rather than ten for DDC or twenty-two for LC. He observed that these forty-two facets can be grouped into five groups: personality, matter, energy, space, and time, or PMEST. Each facet has "certain concreteness," and PMEST arranges them from most to least concrete. In addition, some facets are common to each of the classes, and these are called "common isolates." Punctuation is used to indicate the nature of the facet.

Ranganathan's book *Colon Classification* carries the colon classification

2 : 51N3

N60

The "2" is for "library science, 51N3 for "colon classification," N for 1900 to 1999, and 60 for the specific year, 1960.

Computerization of Records

In the mid- to late twentieth century the computer brought with it two significant impacts on library classification. The first was the computerization of existing catalogs using an electronic record template. The most important of these is the MARC movement. The MARC (aka Machine Readable Catalog) record is a complex set of metadata describing any given document. Metadata are "data about data." In a MARC record there are numerous metadata fields that are specifically defined to accept data of a specific type or sources. These would include a title field, an author field, a publisher field, and so on. The MARC record is constructed to accommodate variations in the bibliographic data it represents. Each record field is numbered and it is specific for one datum type. The 100 field, for example, is one of several "main entry fields." Its purpose is to accept the personal name, usually the name of the author (creator) of the cataloged item. Because naming conventions vary from place to place, the MARC 100 field is sufficiently flexible to accommodate most of the variations by using sub-field punctuation. Thus the 100 field for this book might be rendered: 100 1#$aKoehler, Wallace,$cDr,$d1945-. The "100" indicates a personal name field, the 1#$a indicates a surname; $c a title, $d dates associated with the $a field. Note that the punctuation ($a, for example) precedes rather than follows the associated string. The 200 range is reserved for the title of a work and its variations. The 300 range provides entries for physical description—type, size, length, and so on. The 400 range accommodates series statements—that is, is the work part of a larger group. The 500 range accepts notes and parenthetical information. The 600 range is for uncontrolled notes and parenthetical information. The 835 field is specific for electronic addresses.

There are many MARC flavors: MARC21, UNIMARC, UKMARC, DANMARC, and so on. Each has much in common, but all have variations to reflect local language and usage differences. All are Z39.50[4] compliant and can cross-populate records in each other's templates. They can perform the same functions with other Z39.50-compliant systems. But they tend not to perform the crosswalks with complete and absolute accuracy; inevitably some data are lost in the conversion.

It is important to remember that the MARC standards were developed to facilitate the bibliographic classification of non-digital materials (books, magazines, films, audio recording, etc.) in an electronic format. It can also be used to classify electronic documents. The MARC 865 field was developed specifically for that purpose.

The Classification of Digital Documents

The problem with most classifications, as it is with artificial languages, is that once one moves from simplistic concepts to the more complex, both the classification scheme and the language grow more ambiguous (c.f. Eco 1998, 88–89). These languages, and we include in these both classification schemes and contrived languages, begin to lose effectiveness as the concepts they are to portray become more complex. Both lack the lexical and syntactical flexibility to convey the intended message.

Digital classification has evolved rapidly since the 1960s. Digital data collections have been commercially available since 1965 when the Lockheed Corporation developed a machine-accessible database for the US Department of Defense. The databases were accessed through a telephone dialup linkage using an acoustical coupler running at three hundred baud between a rudimentary computer or proprietary "black box" and the database on a standard long-distance or telnet connection.

That database interface, long since commercialized as Dialog, is a for-profit subsidiary of the Thomson Corporation. Thomson along with a number of other companies, among them Reed Elsevier and OCLC (Online Computer Library Center), provide propriety interfaces to a wide range of bibliographic, numeric, audio, and full-text databases. Many of the proprietary interfaces are complex and require training for their best use. For example, Thomson's Westlaw and Reed Elsevier's Lexis are databases of legal documents, including legislation and court decisions. While the information underlying these databases does not belong to Thomson or Reed Elsevier, the interfaces to those databases are proprietary. Both Lexis and Westlaw have become so ingrained a part of the US legal system that the Lexis or Westlaw citation alphanumeric is considered an integral part of standard legal citation.

The connections and interface formats of the 1960s through the 1990s have for the most part been forgotten. Most are accessed from a desktop or smaller computer over an Internet connection (usually the web), to a web-based interface. There is still much value that remains in the proprietary interfaces, as they allow the expert user to efficiently retrieve extensive data. The databases themselves have evolved from almost exclusively bibliographic resources to full-text documents. The web has supported the addition of graphics to full-text documents as well. To repeat, while many of the databases provided by commercial vendors are created and maintained by the vendor or an associated company, many others have other beginnings. Almost all online database intermediaries offer access to the US Department of Education's ERIC (Education Resources Information Center) database. ERIC can be searched at no charge through the Department of Education website (http://www.eric.ed.gov/), but proprietary interfaces, some argue, facilitate the search.

These intermediary interfaces to databases are complex. Thomson, Reed Elsevier, OCLC, and others have also designed less complex interfaces for the "less sophisticated" database end user. The include Nexis's "Universe" products and OCLC's FirstSearch.

The Web Revolution

The World Wide Web is one of several applications that run on the Internet. The Internet was introduced in the early 1960s as ARPANET, then later as NSFNET. It was originally designed to be an electronic linkage between the US Department of Defense and a limited list of defense contractors in private companies and universities. In 1991 Tim Berners-Lee invented the World Wide Web by adding what has become an extraordinarily adaptive application to the Internet.

The proliferation of "native" web-based documents as well as the addition of other documents made accessible through the web has led to the requirement of additional HTML-based search and retrieval systems. Digital documents, web documents included, can be catalogued in the "old fashioned" way; and they are. These applications are revolutionary in that they not only are bibliographic utilities but also provide a direct and immediate linkage to the original "native" document. They are different in this regard from the earlier proprietary services that provided access to full-test representations of documents, but not to the original document itself. These catalogs require some to a great deal of human intermediation in their creation. Many of them can harvest metadata from websites and populate their data templates with that information. This is discussed further below. Almost all combine human judgment with metadata harvest. These catalogs to web-based libraries include the Social Science Information Gateway—SOSIG (http://www.sosig.ac.uk/) and Thomas, a gateway to US Congress information (http://thomas.loc.gov/). Anyone with a penchant for information classification can add one for herself or himself. Perhaps the best-known example of this type of resource is Yahoo!, which employs a traditional faceted classification methodology with web crawlers.

The second method is, for lack of another generic term, the web crawler or robot. These classification systems utilize a variety of technologies. Their primary function is to explore web documents and to retrieve keyword data. These data are placed in what classifiers have termed "inverted indices." Using a variety of criteria, search engines retrieve from their inverted indices document addresses (URLs) that meet the specified search criteria. The best-known of the search engines are Google, Yahoo! and Bing. AltaVista has been absorbed by Yahoo. HotBot has declined significantly in popularity. Others like Lycos and WebCrawler have been redefined.

Both the web-oriented bibliographical and search engine utilities have flaws. The bibliographical utilities are "unstable" in that their underlying documents are prone to change and extinction (see, for example, Koehler 1999b and McDonnell, Koehler, and Carroll 1999). These tendencies have created a maintenance problem hitherto unknown to bibliographical cataloging. The search engines, for their part, are primarily keyword utilities that capture a significant proportion of web documents with and without relevance for the searcher, as they frequently lack sensitivity to meaning and nuance. They lack sensitivity to meaning expressed in synonyms as well as in languages other than the language of the search term. They are insensitive to misspelling.

There are a number of initiatives to directly index web-based and other digital documents. They can be described in part based on the way in which they are encoded. Some carry index data between the HTML headers. The information placed between the headers is not seen directly by the viewer in a browser. The web browser will, however, interpret that data. For example, the following page source text is taken from a website I maintain:

[[[HTML]]]
[[[HEAD]]]
[[[TITLE]]]Home Page[[[/TITLE]]]
[[[META HTTP-EQUIV ="Content-Type" CONTENT ="text/html; charset=iso-8859-1"]]]
[[[script language ="JavaScript" type ="text/JavaScript"]]]
[[[!--
function MM_reloadPage(init) { //reloads the window if Nav4 resized
if (init==true) with (navigator) {if ((appName=="Netscape")&&(parseInt(appVersion)==4)) {
document.MM_pgW=innerWidth; document.MM_pgH=innerHeight; onresize=MM_reloadPage; }}
else if (innerWidth!=document.MM_pgW || innerHeight!=document.MM_pgH) location.reload();
}
MM_reloadPage(true);
//--]]]
[[[/script]]]
[[[link rel ="stylesheet" href ="nonline.css" type ="text/css"]]]
[[[/HEAD]]]

HTML is written using a special punctuation. The web page referenced above initiates with the following: [[[HTML]]]. This informs the browser that an HTML-based document is "coming." The second statement [[[HEAD]]] informs the browser that page interpretation data follow. The [[[/HEAD]]] statement informs the browser that the interpretation data are ended. The material that is presented through the browser to the viewer follows a [[[BODY]]] statement. The typical web page will end with [[[/BODY]]] [[[/HTML]]].

Many indexing systems place the index data between the [[[HEAD]]] and [[[/HEAD]]] statements. These data can be read by search engines and bibliographic utilities and harvested for inclusion in their databases. Dublin Core is perhaps the best known and most widely documented of the bibliographical systems.

Dublin Core

Dublin Core is an indexing utility developed by leading indexing and cataloging experts and major libraries and companies. Included among the participants are the Library of Congress and OCLC. The Dublin Core Metadata Initiative takes its name from the headquarters city of OCLC, Dublin, Ohio.

Dublin Core consists of fifteen elements: title, creator, subject, description, publisher, contributor, date, type, format, identifier, source, language, relation, coverage, and rights. These elements are reminiscent of the MARC format, and indeed Dublin Core data can be used to populate a MARC record.

[[[HEAD]]]

. . .

[[[link rel="schema.DC" href="http://purl.org/dc/elements/1.1/" /]]]
[[[link rel="schema.DCTERMS" href="http://purl.org/dc/terms/" /]]]
[[[meta name="DC.title" lang="en=us" content="Master of Library and Information Science Program—Valdosta State University" /]]]
[[[meta name="DC.creator" content="MLIS Faculty" /]]]
[[[meta name="DC.subject" lang="en=us" content="library science education MLIS" /]]]
[[[meta name="DC.description" lang="en=us" content="The homepage of a library science master's degree program" /]]]
[[[meta name="DC.publisher" content="MLIS Program, Valdosta State University" /]]]
[[[meta name="DC.type" scheme="DCTERMS.DCMIType" content="Text" /]]]
[[[meta name="DC.format" content="text/html" /]]]
[[[meta name="DC.format" content="34312 bytes" /]]]
[[[meta name="DC.identifier" scheme="DCTERMS.URI" content="http://books.valdosta.edu/mlis/" /]]]
[[[meta name="DC.language" scheme="DCTERMS.URI" content="en=us" /]]]
[[[meta name="DC.rights" scheme="DCTERMS.URI" content="Copyright MLIS Program 2005" /]]]

. . .
[[[/HEAD]]]

Archival Markup

There are a number of important SGML (XML) markup languages used in the archival community. These include, but are not limited to:

- CES (Corpus Encoding Standard)
- EAD DTD (Encoded Archival Description Document Type Definition)
- MEP (Model Editions Partnership)
- TEI (Text Encoding Initiative)

These markup systems were designed to meet the specific needs of a community managing digitized copies of historical documents and, as they come into existence, historical documents in "native" electronic formats. These programs consist of "tag sets." An HTML tag has, as we have seen, the following format [[[p]]] . . . [[[/p]]]. This particular set indicates the beginning and ending of a paragraph. We might partially mark up the following excerpt from the Gettysburg Address:

[[[p]]][[[title]]]The Gettysburg Address[[[/title]]]
[[[speakerfn]]]Abraham[[[/speakerfn]]][[[speakerln]]]Lincoln[[[/speakerln]]]
[[[date]]]November 19, 1863[[[/date]]][[[/p]]]
[[[p]]][[[time]]]Four score and seven years[[[/time]]] ago our [[[abstractperson]]]fathers[[[/abstractperson]]] brought forth on this [[[geo1]]]continent[[[/geo1]]], a new [[[geo2]]]nation[[[/geo2]]], conceived in [[[concept]]]Liberty[[[/concept]]], and dedicated to the proposition that all men are created equal. [[[/p]]]
[[[p]]]Now we are engaged in a great [[[event]]]civil war[[[/event]]], testing whether that [[[geo2]]]nation[[[/geo2]]], or any nation so conceived and so dedicated, can long endure. We are met on a great [[[event2]]]battle-field[[[/event2]]] of that [[[event]]]war[[[/event]]]. We have come to dedicate a portion of that field, as a final resting place for those who here gave their lives that that nation might live. It is altogether fitting and proper that we should do this.[[[/p]]]

The markup is largely made up. A computer program scanning the markup could populate a template with the keywords. Moreover, a search for "Abraham Lincoln" in the speaker-first name and speaker-last name fields would retrieve this and other similarly marked documents. A Boolean search for Lincoln (speaker) and November 19, 1863 (date), would retrieve this one document. The indexer might also add comments (in a [[[c]]] [[[/c]]] field perhaps) that might convey further meaning. If, finally, one sought to retrieve speeches by Abraham Lincoln and not about Abraham Lincoln, one could specify Lincoln as [[[speaker]]][[[/speaker]]].

Note that these markup systems differ from those like Dublin Core in that the markup is placed in the [[[body]]][[[/body]]] of the text rather than the headers. It is possible to include more than one markup system in a document. We might have used Dublin Core in our copy of the Gettysburg Address to provide even more description. There is a system—RDF—to facilitate multiple encoding.

Resource Description Framework (RDF)

According to the World Wide Web Consortium (W3C), "Resource Description Framework (RDF) is a foundation for processing metadata; it provides interoperability between applications that exchange machine-understandable information on the Web." RDF is *metametadata*. It permits the incorporation of various metadata schemes into a single format. RDF is written in XML and uses the HTML format. The purpose of RDF is for the "metamessage" to carry with it enough defining information about the metadata (hence, metametadata) for cross communication. It is therefore a crosswalk between various metadata systems in addition to a defining metadata scheme.

RDF is defined by "schema." Dublin Core is one such schema. It is conceivable that a second metascheme might use the same "rights" label. That second metadata language—let's call it ABCCore—might use the "rights" field not for a copyright statement but to define property easements. RDF would interpret the abc:rights and dc:rights statements as representing different metadata categories and would map them appropriately. The following gives an example of the RDF format:

[[[HEAD]]]
[[[TITLE]]]Ethics Links to Librarian and Information Manager Associations[[[/TITLE]]]
[[[META NAME=GENERATOR CONTENT="Claris Home Page 3.0"]]]
[[[X-CLARIS-WINDOW TOP=0 BOTTOM=435 LEFT=0 RIGHT=787]]]
[[[X-CLARIS-TAGVIEW MODE=minimal]]]
[[[META http-equiv="Content-Type" content="text/html; charset=ISO-8859–1"]]]
[[[META name="description" content="library and information science professional organization ethics statements and supporting material"]]]
[[[META name="keywords" content="professional ethics, standard of practice, librarian, information scientist"]]]
[[[META name="author" content="Wallace Koehler"]]]
[[[META name="distribution" content="global"]]]
[[[rdf:RDF

xmlns:biblink="http://biblink.ukoln.ac.uk/metadata/"
xmlns:rdf="http://www.w3.org/1999/02/22–rdf-syntax-ns#"
xmlns:dc="http://purl.org/dc/elements/1.0/"]]]|[[[rdf:Description
about="http://books/valosta.edu/mlis/ethics/EthicsBibOrg.htm"
    dc:title="Ethics Links to Librarian and Information Manager
    Associations"
    dc:creator="Wallace Koehler"
    dc:subject="professional ethics; standards of practice;
    librarian; information professional"
    dc:description="A catalog of library and information
    science professional associations and related ethics
    statements."
    dc:publisher="Valdosta State University"
    dc:contributor="Kara Whatley"
    dc:date="2000–01–25"
    dc:type="Text"
    dc:format="text/html"
    dc:language="en-us"dc:rights="copyright Wallace Koehler 2000 All
Rights
    Reserved"
    biblink:Extent="239400 bytes"
    /]]]|[[[/rdf:RDF]]]
    [[[/HEAD]]]

Semantic Web

This discussion does not begin to exhaust the range and variability of digital markup systems. No doubt even more complex systems will be developed. The Semantic Web is an ambitious initiative of the World Wide Web Consortium (W3C) under the leadership of Tim Berners-Lee (2001) to bring control to the web. The W3C defines it thusly:

> The Semantic Web provides a common framework that allows data to be shared and reused across application, enterprise, and community boundaries. It is a collaborative effort led by W3C with participation from a large number of researchers and industrial partners. It is based on the Resource Description Framework (RDF), which integrates a variety of applications using XML for syntax and URIs for naming.

In their *Scientific American* article on the Semantic Web, Tim Berners-Lee, James Hendler, and Ora Lassila (2001) assert that:

> the Semantic Web will bring structure to the meaningful content of Web pages, creating an environment where software agents roaming from page to page can readily carry out sophisticated tasks for users. . . . The Semantic Web is not a separate Web but an extension of the current one, in which information is given well-defined meaning, better enabling computers and people to work in cooperation.

Although the Semantic Web involves interrelating ontologies with translation tables and software, its Achilles heal lies in what its creators see as a strength: "XML lets everyone create their own tags—hidden labels such as or that annotate web pages or sections of text on a page" (Chugani, 2013). It is true that XML markup is relatively simple but tedious. That everyone creates his or her own tags creates a new post-Babel set of imperfect languages without an adequate set of enforceable standards to bring meaning to the chaos.

"Meaning is expressed by RDF, which encodes it in sets of triples, each triple being rather like the subject, verb and object of an elementary sentence" (Berners-Lee et al. 2003, 77). Well, no; RDF is not an expressive cross-linguistic perfect or root language in the sense that Eco means it. It is metametadata allowing for the interactivity of other defined metadata systems. RDF carries its own sets of definitions in its "triples." These definitions can be used to express relationships among people, places, things, and concepts, but only if the ontology writer does so using a generally accepted standard that can be translated through the RDF structure into another generally accepted standard. Letting each creator or author invent his or her own markup and define it in "pell mell" fashion does not confer meaning.

The good news of the Semantic Web is in its redefinition of the word "ontologies." An older dictionary[5] definition of ontology is "the science or study of being; that department of metaphysics which relates to the being or to being in the abstract." Tom Gruber (n.d.) provides an interesting definition of ontology, one he acknowledges is different from its meaning in philosophy:

> An ontology is a description (like a formal specification of a program) of the concepts and relationships that can exist for an agent or a community of agents. This definition is consistent with the usage of ontology as set-of-concept-definitions, but more general.

These differences are clearly recognized by Berners-Lee, Hendler, and Lassila (2001):

> In philosophy, an ontology is a theory about the nature of existence, of what types of things exist; ontology as a discipline studies such theories. Artificial-intelligence and Web researchers have co-opted the term for their own jargon, and for them an ontology is a document or file that formally defines the relations among terms.

The very underlying concept of the Semantic Web, the definition of ontology, lends confusion rather than meaning. Web-based ontologies are most likely taxonomies together with *inference rules*. Inference rules may offer guidance to the probability of meanings; but whatever the probability may be, even as it approaches 1.0 or 100 percent, any degree of imprecision multiplied across more than ten billion web pages adds up to misunderstanding. For example, exactly how many Mrs. Cooks were there at that trade show last year? And just exactly why were each of the Mrs. Cooks at that show?[6]

Finally, the definitions of the kinds of data the Semantic Web would function well with include specific data for which any authoritative source suffices: find a postal code, an address, a certain Mrs. Cook who attended a certain trade show last year. Searches for concepts and meaning, for the true definition of "ontology," or the answer to meaning of everything do not fare well in the Semantic Web structure. Berners-Lee, Hendler, and Lassila (2001) end their introduction to the Semantic Web with the following:

> An essential process is the joining together of subcultures when a wider common language is needed. Often two groups independently develop very similar concepts, and describing the relation between them brings great benefits. Like a Finnish-English dictionary, or a weights-and-measures conversion table, the relations allow communication and collaboration even when the commonality of concept has not (yet) led to a commonality of terms.

Finnish is an interesting language. Its pronouns do not carry gender. There is no "she" or "he," no "his" or "hers" in Finnish, only "it" and "its." Weights and measures offer some interesting definitional problems as well—the difference between weight (pounds) and mass (grams). Umberto Eco (1995, 349–350) informs us that in Italian there is no direct cognate for the English "to hop," as on one foot. Semantic ontologies must by necessity possess human intelligence and human ingenuity and perhaps a touch of the human soul.

Information classification is perhaps the most complex of information management functions. Classification includes several inter-related activities to include description, cataloging, indexing, thesaurus development, and abstracting. Therefore the term is being used in its widest definition.

Librarians have been classifying information since time immemorial. The need to classify has been driven by a variety of "forces." Perhaps the first of these is number or quantity. The larger the collection, the greater is the need to manage it. Diversity in the collection has also had a part in the impetus to classify.

Technology also drives information classification. As collections grow larger and more complex and as technology enhances both complexity and size, more complex classification systems have been developed. Technology changes are considered elsewhere in this work, but consider some of the more crucial. The transition from clay tablet to papyrus scroll not only created information containers easier to transport and to produce, but that transition prompted new information organization and storage processes. Scrolls could be and were stored in pigeonholes or cubbyholes. This shelving was frequently labeled according to subject matter and sometimes author. Scrolls and later books were often tagged with a colophon that also provided subject and authority data.

The advent of the codex changed not only shelving requirements; information labeling styles also changed. Over time, the metadata provided in the codex has increased to include tables of contents, indices, authority, and place and date of publication. The colophon has largely disappeared to be replaced by title and author imprinted on the spine.

Not all publishing traditions provide the same range of information. Non-fiction published in France, for example, differs from works published in Anglophone countries. English language material usually has a table of contents at the beginning of work. French publishers often place it at the end. English language books usually contain an index, often omitted from the French.

The advent of digital information and of digital catalogs has led to a proliferation of approaches and advances in information management and retrieval. The online public access catalog (OPAC) has replaced the card catalog in many libraries. Because OPACs are computer based, OPAC hardware and software are frequently developed and provided in the private sector. These technologies must be updated or replaced with some frequency and at some cost.

Library classification systems, it has been argued, are reflections of the belief systems of the societies where they are created and of the prejudices of their creators (Jens-Eric Mai 2013). Library classification in its various manifestations was fairly simple and straightforward before the middle of the nineteenth century. Before the sixteenth century, many libraries consisted of but a very few books. The manuscripts themselves carried metadata. The colophon, a tag attached to scrolls and later to codices, might indicate some combination of subject area, title, and author. As libraries became larger and as the collections became more eclectic, librarians proposed a variety of classification schemes. Juan Páez de Castro, a sixteenth-century Jesuit and confessor to King Felipe II of Spain, proposed a library at El Escorial. That library was to be divided into five rooms, the contents of each room based on subject, widely defined. The collection was to be further classified by author. One of the El Escorial rooms was dedicated to government documents. The nineteenth-century librarian Sir Anthony Panizzi is generally credited with the first fully articulated cataloging rules: *91 Rules for Compilation of the Catalogue*, published in 1841.

Panizzi's rules and rules developed subsequently were said to reflect social mores of their day. The Dewey Decimal System, the creation of Melvil Dewey, is said to have a Western Protestant orientation. The Soviet classification system, BBK, was developed to incorporate Marxist-Leninist principles into its classifications (Edwards 2013). As Chloë Edwards (2013, 40) argues, "Both [DDC and BBK] classifications are highly instructive as snapshots of thinking contemporary to their creation, and in the Soviet Union, library classification was construed as one more layer in the process of information control and indoctrination in Marxism-Leninism."

By contrast, Library of Congress Classification (LCC), developed in the late 1890s, is said to lack a theoretical basis. It is said to be driven by the needs of the Library of Congress. Universal Decimal Classification (UDC) was developed at about the same time as LCC by Paul Otlet and Henri La Fontaine. UDC, like LCC and DCC, undertook to provide a numeric or alphanumeric system to represent all aspects of human knowledge.

Other classification systems have been developed. Some have a basis in the language in which they were created. The Prussian Instructions were developed for Prussian-based and later and more widely German-based libraries at the end of the nineteenth century. An important aspect of the Prussian Instructions is German grammatical order. The Prussian Instructions were replaced first by *Regeln fur die alphabetische Katalogisierung* (RAK) and most recently by Resource Description and Access (RDA).

Resource Description and Access (RDA) is a recent initiative, launched in 2010. It is based on the Functional Requirements for Bibliographic Records (FRBR). It was developed to succeed a range of cataloging rules, among them the dominant Anglo-American Cataloging Rules (AACR, AACR2) and other systems. An important aspect of RDA is its international focus (Chandel and Prasad 2013) and the interest shown by the European RDA Interest Group (EURIG, 2011) and by IFLA's Paris Declaration (IFLA, 2009). Classification is moving away from more parochial systems to more international ones and from specific language bases.

Library catalogs are also evolving. Johann David Köhler (1973) observed that most libraries maintained catalogs and suggested that scholarly travelers familiarize themselves with those catalogs. The catalogs of the eighteenth century were printed and bound. Updating those catalogs was a complex undertaking. Where the card catalog made updating the catalog a far easier task, it did little to contribute to familiarizing others with the collection. Wider access to the various literatures became easier with the advent of dialup services like Dialog, OVID, and Chemical Abstracts. The precursor to the Dialog system was developed by Roger K. Summit in the mid-1960s for the US Department of Defense. In the 1970s Dialog was privatized and its databases were made searchable by paying subscribers. The search methodologies are complex, require skill to use, but provide highly relevant results. Dialog has changed ownership several times and is now held by ProQuest.

Union catalogs have become extremely important. In the United States, the public and academic libraries in many states have created union catalogs. These catalogs can be searched from a single point of entry. Patrons are often able to borrow and return materials from any member library. Global union catalogs have been formed. OCLC, an acronym for Online Computer Library Center, is the successor name to the Ohio College Library Center. At its founding, OCLC was designed as a union catalog of Ohio-wide academic libraries. OCLC created and now manages the world's largest union catalog: WorldCat. The catalog has 70,000 library members in about 170 countries. WorldCat is accessible online (www.world.cat.org) and points the searcher to the holdings of its member libraries. Union catalogs have become possible and accessible because of digitization and the Internet. Because union catalogs can be formed, they should be formed to "save the time of the reader."

The Internet and, in particular, the web contribute to the globalization of information access. The web brings new challenges to the many aspects of cataloging. Databases are accessible online. Search engines have created popular mechanisms for information access.

Indexers recognize that their art requires both professional and cultural value judgment. Hjørland (2011), for example, makes the case that one's epistemological approach to knowledge influences indexing decisions. Distinctions are made between manual and automated indexing (e.g., Tenopir 1999). Automated indexing has become more important with the advent of the computer and now the Internet. Nevertheless, Automated systems have human decision making in their design. How valuable are these functions? Bella Hass Weinberg (1988) has argued that indexing may not be sufficient to provide good "aboutness" for the expert information user. According to Weinberg, this is particularly true for indexed serials, as the depth of indexing for individual articles is at best limited.

Cultural biases can be identified in cataloging and indexing. One of the more important critics of indexing biases is Sanford Berman (1971). He demonstrated cultural and political impacts on the Library of Congress Subject Headings (LCSH). Many of the biases he recognized in the LCSH were gender and race based. Moreover, Berman recognized that while LCSH has an American etiology, it has acquired an international importance. For that reason, LCSH editors have an obligation to remain sensitive to languages' usages and connotations outside the United States. Berman and others also promoted updating terminology to reflect changes in language and cultural practices. He also raised the question of whether public libraries should include pornographic videos, particularly such classic titles like *Deep Throat* and *Behind the Green Door*, in their video collections.

ON DIGITAL INTELLIGENCE

The Semantic Web is not an ideal representation (in the philosophical sense of a virtually unattainable abstract representation of the "perfect") of digital markup. Perhaps W3C will succeed in developing a knowledge construct that attains those ends.

Digital markup, the Semantic Web included, is not an intellectual advance in the management of information. In many ways it is, in fact, a retreat to keyword or encyclopedic classification. Except where there has been human intervention (for example, Yahoo!), most markup languages and key term retrieval engines provide very little taxonomic structure. It is true that some retrieval engines attempt to group concepts using canonical approaches. The groupings are based on the degree to which any set of documents shares a set of like terms. The greater the agreement of terms, the greater the likelihood that the grouped documents share meaning. Sadly, these probabilities are reduced significantly when one sub-set of documents are in English and the other are in Finnish.

Neither the Semantic Web nor Google qualify as the "perfect" language. Library science and biblioéconomie are categorized as "Z" in LC, "02" in UDC, "020" in DDC, and "2" in colon classification. An RDF construct would require several ontologies to appreciate that, in one sense of the terms, they are synonyms but also that *biblioéconomie* when translated literally into English is library economy. Yet library economy in English is an archaic term that left the lexicon in the 1930s. A search of the two terms where there is a well-defined, controlled vocabulary—the cataloger's term for ontology in its computer science meaning—would result in a rich return set. Where there was no controlled vocabulary, the return set would indeed be small.

Digital Advantages

The computer has brought with it certain classification and cataloging advantages print and card catalogs could not support. Print catalogs evolved from simple subject cataloging combined often with placement and addressing based on physical characteristics, usually size to categorization based on subject, author, and title. While it is theoretically possible to expand the number of data points to a much wider list, it is in practice very cumbersome and complex to implement. Technological innovation has made it possible to expand the number of access points well beyond three to include date and place of publication, publisher, languages, and other descriptors and identifiers.

Computer algorithms also support other search strategies. Perhaps the most important of these is the keyword search. These technologies can be expanded to permit more complex information retrieval based on "meaning." These search sets can be presented to end users as graphical representations (GUIs, or graphical user interfaces) that are designed to carry intuitive interpretative power for the user. In addition, computer algorithms have been developed that permit associations based on less explicit associations. These "fuzzy" sets offer additional information-finding tools.

These recent informational innovations raise some very interesting ethical considerations. First, information professionals, as a professional responsibility, need to have proficiency in using and interpreting retrieval returns. Second, there is too often an assumption that the greater the technical sophistication of a given search algorithm, the greater its efficacy. Each search/retrieval system has its own idiosyncrasies, idiosyncrasies that may affect either favorably or unfavorably the return set. Third, the assumption is sometimes taken that digitized resources are superior to printed ones and that complex digital systems provide better research results than more traditional ones. While this is often true, it is not always so. Finally, librarians have served and continue to serve as intermediaries between information resources and information users. The greater the complexity of information resources and the retrieval systems, the greater the likelihood that information intermediaries will be required to assist the users and manage the databases.

CONCLUSION

Classification systems have evolved in an effort to convey the intended message in more accurate ways. In the beginning, most systems were limited to the shelf or pigeonhole address of a given work. The next step was to categorize key concepts according to simplistic then later more complex distinctions. The meanings of books were initially indicated along no more than ten categories, beginning with fire, water, air, and earth. Theological, ethical, philosophical, scientific, and nationalistic divisions were made. These distinctions arose as philosophy became more sophisticated but also as collections increased in depth and scope.

By the eighteenth century classification theorists had proposed enlarging the number of categories to twenty-two. Books were also distinguished by their size (folio, octavo, etc.). Libraries had long been arranging the placement of books by subject matter, then sometimes in order by title, and less often by author. In the nineteenth century classification systems became even more complex based on the work of the likes of Panizzi, Cutter, and Dewey. These systems, as admirable as they are, did not manage the classification of books with multiple subjects very well. How should a treatise on forensic medicine be cataloged—under law or under medicine? Of course these complex systems were expandable, the single most important contribution of the nineteenth century. Cataloging systems could be divided into an ever-more-complex array of sub-categories so that it would become possible to give a specific code for medicine-forensic.

The twentieth century brought analytico-synthetic systems such as colon classification, developed by S. R. Ranganathan. These faceted systems permitted the combination of codes to reflect documents with multiple subjects. They could be manipulated to permit subtleties of meanings to be reflected in the construction of the code.

It was always a given that various classification schemes would be applied by expert catalogers, preferably with expertise in the area in which they were working. There are exceptions to this rule—authors have often been asked to provide abstracts and sometimes key words to self-describe their work. Until the twentieth century the titles given monographs and journal articles were also generally long and descriptive. As scholarly work moved into the twentieth century, a new industry evolved. Indexing and abstracting services provided expert services, first in print, then later online. These services, to a certain degree, obviated the need for the complex title and partially replaced the linear printed catalog in codex format as a finding tool.

Interestingly, as we moved through the twentieth century into the twenty-first, the philosophical basis of some of our finding tools have regressed from the expert-applied classification to a keyword-based, machine-driven retrieval tool. The system has regressed because the classification of a knowledge product is based solely on the presence of searcher-provided terms (keywords) and not on a set of known index terms provided by an expert intermediary—or what library scientists have referred as pre- and post-coordinate terms. The intermediation role in computer-based systems falls to the ontologies. The structures of the ontologies and their cross mapping is, for the time being at least, the realm of the programmer. Clay tablets and papyrus scrolls carried identifying data on colophons and tags. Books in a library were given call numbers. What can we say for much of what is today found on the Internet? Some documents are well ornamented with metadata, and many others are not.

Search systems like Google and Bing—and before them, AltaVista, WebCrawler, HotBot, Lycos, and others—based their indices on words, actually not even words but character strings, found in the digital texts posted to the web. Like indexing systems for textual databases before them, they developed complex inverted indices to map multiple character strings and their proximity to one another within a specific text or document. While these are very sophisticated from a technical perspective, they are relatively simplistic from a "meaning" orientation. Moreover, these systems are language bound. Documents written in languages other than the search language are unlikely to be retrieved unless additional index terms are added to the documents to be retrieved. Those index terms must either be drawn from a pre-existing and agreed-on code or, at a minimum, be provided in a language likely to be employed in the search and retrieval process.

And finally Heroclitus (sixth century BCE) observed, "For it is impossible to step twice into the same river." Things change, and therefore no classification can ever be "perfect." This admonition is truer today than since human beings developed writing. Digital documents, particularly web documents, have been shown to be particularly transient in nature. Not only do they "come and go: fairly rapidly, their content also changes with great frequency" (Koehler 1999b). In such an information environment, changes to classification need also follow.

NOTES

1. See, for example, EUR-lex, a database of European Union legal documents at http://europa.eu.int/eur-lex/lex/en/index.htm

2. The terms folio, quarto, octavo, duodecimo, and so on, represent the number of folds for a printed sheet. A folio page is unfolded, a quarto in four parts, octavo in eight parts, and so on. A folio has the largest "footprint," which depends on the size of the sheet. A folio typically has dimensions greater than 30 x 40 centimeters.

3. JX was formerly used as the code for international law. Does the taxonomic change reflect a redefinition of international law as a concrete legal domain rather than the more imprecise social science implication?

4. Z39.50 (formally known as ANSI/NISO Z39.50-1995) is an American National Standards Institute (ANSI), National Information Standards Organization (NISO) standard that facilitates the exchange of data among databases. Database developers who adopt the Z39.50 do so to allow relatively seamless exchanges between otherwise independent databases.

5. *Oxford Universal Dictionary*, 3rd. ed., 1933.

6. What is he talking about? Unfortunately this is an un-marked-up linear document, and you will have to wait until the next paragraph to find out.

FOUR

On Public Libraries

In 1876 the modern library movement began. . . . The growth of libraries since 1876 has been very rapid.

—John Cotton Dana (1920, 2)

The history of the [American] public library is a record of a transition from a narrowly conservative function to a broad program directed toward the advancement of popular education.

—Jesse Shera (1949, v)

The public library in cities and towns and rural areas across the United States is a community center for books and information. . . . It is a commons, a vital part of the public sphere and a laboratory of ideas.

— Kathleen de la Peña McCook (2004,1)

PUBLIC LIBRARY INTRODUCED

The public library as an ideal has been with us for at least two millennia. The concept of public library as trope has carried a very different meaning from century to century. This chapter explores this idea in different societies and at different times.

The contemporary vision of the American public library is of an agency that offers free and relatively unfettered access to an ever-increasing array of media to the general public.

Jesse Shera (1949, v) distinguishes between social institutions and agencies. A social institution, he argues, is basic to society—examples he gives are the family and the state. A social agency, on the other hand, is a secondary and derivative social body, of which libraries and schools are examples. Institutions set the patterns of society; agencies result from the pattern. "Thus the distinction is more than a matter of degree; it involves a flow of power and authority." Drawing on the work of Émile Durkheim, Shera (1949, v) hereby places the public library squarely in the structuralist explanation of society as a secondary or derivative actor. This is not to say that libraries are unimportant; they simply are not as important as the family or the state.

The definition of general public is ambiguous and sometimes a synecdoche where some of the parts define the whole. "Public" can be taken to mean some proportion of the general population: adult men of means only, members of a specific organization, members of a specific culture or race, educated adults, residents of a given political region, and so on. As a matter of general practice, over the centuries the term "public" has tended to become more inclusive.

Public Library Defined

Public libraries are complex agencies. A number of definitions have been offered. Among the first is the definition offered in 1876 in *Public Libraries in the United States of America: Their History, Condition, and Management.* The US Department of the Interior, Bureau of Education Special Report (1876) defined public libraries as any library, however supported, open for public use. Many such libraries could be found at universities and government agencies. This definition is not inconsistent with practices reaching back to the founding of the Bodleian at Oxford in the seventeenth century.

The US Department of Education, Institute of Education Sciences (Chute et al. 2003, 4) in its report of public libraries employed the following:

> A public library is an entity that is established under state enabling laws or regulations to serve a community, district, or region, and that provides at least the following: (1) an organized collection of printed or other library materials, or a combination thereof; (2) paid staff; (3) an established schedule in which services of the staff are available to the public; (4) the facilities necessary to support such a collection, staff, and schedule; and (5) is supported in whole or in part with public funds.

Carleton Joeckel (1935, x) defined public libraries thusly:

> The only really essential requirement in the definition of a public library is that its use should be free to all residents of the community on equal terms . . . any library that has been officially charged with the responsibility, or has voluntarily assumed the responsibility, for providing free library service of a general nature to a particular community, or more or less definite portion of it [is] considered to be a public library.

In a chapter of his *Library Primer* titled "What Does a Public Library Do for a Community?" John Cotton Dana (1906, 12–14) offers six conditions for a public library and a definition. The six points are: (1) "it supplies the public with recreative reading"; (2) it supplies books "on every profession, art, or handicraft"; (3) it "helps in social and political education—in the training of citizens"; (4) culture; (5) "the free reading room connected with most of our public libraries, and the library proper as well . . . is a powerful agent for counteracting the attractions of saloons and low resorts"; and (6) the "library is the ever-ready helper of the school-teacher."

> The public library, then, is a means for elevating and refining the taste, for giving greater efficiency to every worker, for diffusing sound principles of social and political action, and for furnishing intellectual culture to all.

These are divergent and complex definitions for the public library. As Kathleen de la Peña McCook (2004, 3–8) makes clear, public libraries in the United States are complicated agencies, with multiple functions, resources, and staffs. Furthermore, public libraries are part of a larger complex of agencies and institutions bringing information in a variety of formats to the library patron.

The public library has not always been defined as a usually publicly funded institution open to all comers that provides general services including lending privileges. Moreover, the idea that public libraries should serve as entertainment centers as well as provide other information functions has not always been generally accepted. The notion that public libraries should, in fact, provide service to the public, widely defined, is a mid-nineteenth-century principle while the concept of the library as entertainment center came into its own in the twentieth century. Public libraries in the United States and in many other countries have also taken on the role as information gateways to the Internet. In some countries that function is highly regulated, and barely regulated in others.

Most public libraries serve a specific geographic or political constituency. As a matter of course, all persons residing in or who have some defined and legitimate participation in that defined constituency may, by right, have recourse to the full privileges offered by the library. Others may have a claim to privileges, but those privileges are typically more circumscribed than are those of the fully invested.

The rights and privileges of public library users typically include the ability to make use of library facilities during normal business hours, access to Internet-connected computers, the ability to query reference librarians, the use of the collection, and the right to check out books and other collected materials for some specifically designated period of time. Usually, but not always, materials may be checked out without charges.

For the most part, all members of the public may make use of the library collection without restriction. The rights of use of public access Internet computers may be or may not be circumscribed by policy and technology. Many public libraries install filters on their computers in an often-futile effort to limit access to objectionable material, usually of a pornographic or violent nature.

The idea of public library as physical space is also undergoing redefinition. Not only do many libraries, including many public libraries, offer distance reference and other services by telephone or Internet; many libraries (and others) have started to move into cyberspace by creating a digital presence. The digital library can and has begun to intrude into the information space occupied by the public library in its physical incarnation. William Arms (2000, 84–88) almost off-handedly describes some of the conflict that has occurred in the traditional library in transition into the digital environment. These include pressures to maintain traditional services as well as add the new ones, pressures on staff to add digital skills, salary differentials, and finite and limited budgets.

THE PUBLIC LIBRARY AND ITS CHALLENGES

Kathleen de la Peña McCook (2004, 1) refers to public libraries as "a commons, a vital part of the public sphere and a laboratory of ideas." That commons undergoes periodic challenges from political, economic, and cultural forces from a wide variety of sources. As we shall see described below, the post-modern, twenty-first-century concept of the public library is both changing and under attack. The public library has come to mean a publicly supported institution that provides information, education, and entertainment for its constituents.

Libraries and Culture

In the United States of the early twenty-first century we find ourselves re-engaged in what some are calling the "culture wars." This particular round of the culture wars results from the political resurgence of conservative and often religiously based interest groups seeking to restructure popular culture and public policy and to realign public practice to a standard more to their expressed beliefs. The culture wars focus on a wide range of concerns, including military conflict, political acts and speech, abortion, pornography, religious exercises in public spaces, immigration policy, evolution, and an activist judiciary.

If the public library is a carrier of culture, then it is necessarily one of a number of venues where the culture wars can be expected to be played out. One of the chief canons of librarianship is the belief that librarians and, through them, libraries should remain issue-neutral. The culture wars may well test that neutrality. Under the American Library Association's *Library Bill of Rights*, "a person's right to use a library should not be denied or abridged because of origin, age, background, or views." Further, "libraries should provide materials and information presenting all points of view on current or historical issues. Materials should not be proscribed or removed because of partisan or doctrinal disapproval."

Public Libraries and Competition

The idea that the public library might both educate and entertain has been, for the most part, accepted by most, although there remains a small yet vocal and sometimes persuasive minority arguing against entertainment. Two reasons are given for the opposition to entertainment. First, as a public institution, a public library ought not to compete with private-sector vendors. Booksellers and video stores provide ample access to popular fiction, and there is no need for libraries to participate in that practice. Moreover, for a public institution to compete with the private sector places the private-sector vendor at a competitive disadvantage. And finally, it is inappropriate for a public-sector actor to compete with the private sector in a market-driven economy.

Counter-arguments are both economic and philosophical. Libraries lend materials to people who cannot afford the same goods offered in the private sector. Libraries also retain materials in their collections long after they have disappeared from the private vendors' shelves. Third, as an educational institution, no library can fulfill its obligation without items representative of the changing literature and culture of its constituencies. And finally, if libraries do not offer what is asked of them, libraries will lose their patron base, and, in the end, they would then fail.

The second objection is that as a cultural and educational agency, libraries have no business "entertaining" their constituencies. The notion that public libraries should entertain is a relatively recent one and can be dated to the beginning of the twentieth century.

Libraries and the Internet

At the close of the twentieth century public libraries began a new redefinition of their purpose and function. Public libraries have become public access points to the World Wide Web and the wider Internet. Providing Internet access is a variation on the public library's function. For the most part, materials found on the web are not incorporated into a library's collection, and the library exercises little if any bibliographical control over the material that flows to those access points. Libraries and public libraries among them do incorporate some web content into their collections by subscribing to a variety of online databases as well as cataloging some number of web documents as part of the collection. But to restate the obvious, by far the majority of online content is not formally or informally incorporated as part of the collection.

Public libraries have been challenged as to their management of Internet-based materials. The US federal government has induced some public libraries to implement web monitoring and web filtering of content as a condition for grants. Some libraries have installed filters; others have chosen not to. Internet filtering was introduced under the guise of the protection of children from obscene and violent materials, materials that are openly and easily accessible online. Recent US legislation includes the Child Online Protection Act (COPA), the Neighborhood Children's Internet Protection Act (NCIPA), and the Children's Internet Protection Act (CIPA). CIPA and NCIPA, both passed in 2000, undertook to control e-rate (universal access) and LSTA (library services and technology) funds to libraries and schools. The e-rate program provides public institutions to preferential Internet rate access.

Not all legislation has withstood judicial scrutiny. We are not interested here in whether portions of NCIPA or CIPA are deemed constitutional. Our concern is with the implications of trends toward protecting children from undesirable material, however defined, changes in the definition of "public library" and thereby its place in society. If, to borrow from the medical profession's Hippocratic Oath, a librarian is first to do no harm, does the expansion of the library's mission to protect children substantially redefine the ethical obligations of the information profession?

Libraries and the Protection of Children

Protection of children and the place the public library has in that process raises many philosophical, ethical, and practical questions. This question is raised again in chapter 5, where matters of intellectual freedom and censorship are considered.

Is it the place of the public library, or of the state acting through the public library, to exercise *in loco parentis* privileges to regulate children's Internet use? Does Internet filtering censure the Internet for children and others? If so, does this represent a First Amendment violation? The Computer Science and Telecommunications Board of the National Academy of Sciences (NAS) concluded in 2002 (xi) that it was generally undesirable for children to have access to sexually explicit material. That said, how is "sexually explicit" defined and whose definition should guide policy? Even if a consistent definition can be arrived at, what is the role of the public library in that process? The NAS report (2002, 357–390) recognized that there are both social and technical dimensions. Some of these fall necessarily to librarians to manage. The NAS commission (2002, 379) provides some guidance to librarians to include management of browser

histories and filtered and non-filtered terminals for child and adult patrons. Libraries might also vary filtering according to the child's age.

If we accept that libraries (and other public institutions) should protect children from sexually explicit material because that material is
harmful to them, does it necessarily follow that libraries should protect
children from other harmful agents? How harmful to children do those
agents need to be before public institutions intervene? If libraries should
or must protect children, must they or should they seek to insulate other
protected classes from similar dangers? What constitutes harm? Who de-
cides what is harmful, and who defines the protected classes?

Others argue that it is not the place of the public library or other social
institutions to undertake to act *in loco parentis*. Decisions as to what information children should have access to are family decisions that libraries
ought not to preempt. Central governments, particularly the US federal
government, have sought to intervene in the decision process by mandat-
ing controls on access to information by specific groups in public libraries. This may represent a major shift in the guiding social paradigm defining the responsibilities of two of the major social institutions—family
and state, with the state exerting precedence over the family.

Public Libraries and Public Space

Public Forum Doctrine is a concept that has grown out of American
jurisprudence but has a human rights aspect that transcends national
boundaries. I will suggest that court decisions—at least in common law
countries like Australia, Canada, the United Kingdom, and the United
States—represent, if not in jurisprudence in the public forum, an extension of the public sphere. That expression of public sphere can be
changed through radical revisions of the interpretation of the law (and
sense of the public sphere) as the USSC did in reversing *Plessy v. Ferguson*
(1896) and replacing it with *Brown v. Board of Education of Topeka* (1954).
The Supreme Court held in *Plessy* that separate but equal segregation
based on race was constitutional; whereas in Brown, separate but equal
was found to be inherently unequal and therefore unconstitutional. The
Brown decision was not wholly accepted into the public sphere for
decades, but there seems to be little doubt that it is now part of the social
fabric of the country. Not all decisions are absorbed and accepted into the
social fabric so readily: witness the continued polarization in the wake of
the abortion decision *Roe v. Wade* (1973).

It is argued that under the public forum doctrine, the exercise of free
speech and thereby access to information is protected at a higher level
than in private forums. The guiding case law began with *Hague v. Congress of Industrial Organizations* (1939). In *Hague*, the Supreme Court
(USSC) held that labor union representatives had the right to distribute
literature, make speeches, and otherwise lawfully militate their cause on

property usually designated for public speech. Public forum doctrine was modified in 1983, when the USSC in *Perry Educational Association v. Perry Local Educators' Association* narrowed rights under the *Hague* standard. Three types of fora were identified by the USSC—two public fora and a non-public forum. Public fora include traditional and limited. The traditional forum is one where free and open communication is long established—a sort of Hyde Park. A non-public forum is government-owned property treated as if it were private property (e.g., the executive mansions of state government, the White House, military housing, and so on).

The limited public forum is a place designated by government as a public forum. The traditional forum has a long-standing and traditional history as such an arena. The limited arena may be so temporarily and may be withdrawn. But once privileges are extended to one group, privileges are extended to all groups. The doctrine can be applied using a "normal activities" test. In a public library, the normal environment might be said to support quiet reading and contemplation. Free speech is permitted so long as it does not exceed the normal activities test.

In *Kreimer v. Morristown* (1991), the US District Court, and on appeal in *Morristown v. Kreimer* (1992), the US Second Circuit Court of Appeals, brought public forum doctrine directly to the library. Richard Kreimer was deemed a nuisance by the management and patrons of the Morristown, New Jersey, public library and, as such, was removed from the library on occasion. Claiming his civil and First Amendment rights had been abridged, Kreimer filed suit in federal district court. The court found for Kreimer, arguing that the library rules were too vague. On appeal, the court of appeals held that public libraries are limited public fora and that the library's regulations were designed to minimize disruption of the library's purpose and function; in short, the rules met the "time, place, manner" rule for limited public fora.

Under the limited public fora rule, public libraries can to a certain degree determine the scope of the definition of *public*. Limited public fora ought not to implement policies that limit speech or access to information by regulating "annoyances." As Barbara Jones (1999, 11) argues, "appearance or behavior" is insufficient cause to bar use. Appearance and behavior must interfere with the "time, place, and manner" rule.

Barbara Jones (1999, 12–5) asserts that the *Kreimer* case is especially instructive for librarians. It incorporates professional values, intellectual freedom issues, and rights to access to information. Public libraries, she argues (1999, 13) do have the right in certain cases to limit speech and access to information. But libraries should tread carefully when they do so.

Public Libraries of the Twenty-First Century

As we have seen, public libraries in the twenty-first century are under pressure from cultural, political, economic, and technological forces. While the public library as an institution has been resilient, our definition of the public library has undergone change as the prevailing philosophical and technological paradigms have changed. Libraries and particularly public libraries have been modeled in the image of those paradigms. Thus, while it is impossible to predict what the twenty-second-century public library will look like, there undoubtedly will be some kind of institution to meet the needs of public edification, education, and entertainment.

HISTORICAL DEFINITIONS OF "PUBLIC LIBRARY"

The first-century-BCE definition of the public library differs in several important lights from that of the twenty-first-century library. By examining the thinking of various commentators on public libraries at different points in time, we can start to understand the perceptions that were held of libraries and how those perceptions have changed.

In so doing, we must appreciate that the defined philosophical relationship of mankind to God, to the state, and to one another has changed, just as the role of libraries has changed. When, as we see below, the eighteenth-century definition of a public library was different from that of the twenty-first century, the eighteenth-century definition of the qualified public library patron was also very different.

The first well-documented reference to the *public* library is Roman. In 44 BCE Julius Caesar directed Marcus Terentius Varro (116–27 BCE) to undertake construction of a public library in Rome. Lionel Casson (2001, 80) informs us that Asinius Pollio completed Varro's work. Pollio's library, according to accounts, was divided into two rooms—one for Greek manuscripts and another for those in Latin. Roman libraries (and this applies to Pollio's, one assumes) were open structures, built with reading rooms to accommodate the user (Casson: 2001, 82–83).

The Romans also placed libraries in their public baths. Casson (2001, 89–91) describes the Baths of Trajan, completed in 109 CE, as quite sumptuous, with rooms for both Greek and Latin books. If, as Casson states (2001, 91), Roman baths were frequented by all levels of society, their libraries were truly public as well. Casson (2001, 92) speculates that the bath libraries were more entertainment than education. They would have included both Greek and Roman classics.

According to Edward Edwards (1864, 12), there *may* have been a public library established in Greece by Pisistratus in the sixth century BCE. The Roman general Lucullus is also said to have established a library "open to all comers" (Edwards 1864, 15). Edwards (1864, 16) argued that however open the libraries of Lucullus or before him of Sylla, they were nevertheless *private* libraries. Although Julius Caesar aspired to found a truly public library, his assassination and the death of Varro postponed that library until the reign of Augustus. Augustus, according to Edwards (1864, 16–7), established two public libraries in Rome—the Octavian and the Palantine. Other public libraries were to be established throughout the Roman Empire, but each in its time fell victim to either human or natural disasters.

With the fall of Rome, the public library was to be eclipsed for one and a half millennia. It would not be until the late eighteenth century that subscription libraries would be established (Allen 2001), to be followed by government-supported libraries in the nineteenth century.

Fifteenth- and Sixteenth-Century Public Libraries

Libraries most certainly existed in Europe in the fifteenth and sixteenth centuries. Edward Edwards (1859 i, 83–84) described libraries of the Middle Ages as either monastic or palatial and that the monastic libraries were by far the more important of the two. Monasticism, Edwards (1859 i, 85–86) argued, was the dominant social force of a thousand years. The monk was a preserver of culture, a copier of texts, and very rarely an original author. Most monastic libraries were dominated by theological and ethical texts, with very little concern for literature as such. Edwards (1859 i, 100) informs us that the first English library, established in the seventh century by Pope Gregory the Great, consisted of but nine volumes. Pre-Gutenberg libraries were for the most part, and necessarily, quite limited.

Johannes Lomeier (Montgomery 1962) presented an extensive inventory of libraries extant in the seventeenth century, many of which had their beginnings in earlier times. These libraries, as Lomeier documented, were found at churches, monasteries, and universities. Richard de Bury (1287?–1345), for example, bequeathed his private library to Durham College, Oxford.

The fifteenth century was a time of major change for the library community. Johann Gutenberg, born about 1400, was to make a contribution of momentous importance to the world of books—the invention of the movable type printing press. By 1450 Gutenberg had printed his first Bible, the forty-two-line Bible.

The invention of printing has had consequences well beyond the fifteenth century. But one of its immediate impacts was the proliferation of published material. Improvements in printing technology and in paper manufacture increased the volume of output of books. By the eighteenth century there came a virtual flood of cheaply printed and produced books that had consequences for the book trade, libraries, authors, and readers not anticipated in the fifteenth century. Printing together with a growing literacy in Europe meant an increasing demand by various levels of society for reading material. These demands led to an increased output but also to a need for better and more public libraries for the reading public.

The proliferation of books led to a demand for better bibliographical control of the written word. In 1545 Conrad Gessner (1516–1565), a physician and botanist (his name also rendered as Konrad Gessner, Conrad von Gesner, and Conradus Gesnerus), published *Bibliotheca universalis*, a catalog in Latin, Greek, and Hebrew, of all books published in Europe, printed or manuscript. His *Pandeclarium sive partitionum universalium Conradi Gesneri Ligurini libri xxi* followed in 1548. This work arranged the books across twenty-one general systematic tables. A second appendix followed in 1555. The work contained more than twelve thousand records for some three thousand authors. The work classified the entries by name.

Gessner's *Bibliotheca universalis* is considered the first general bibliography ever published. Gessner was a great classifier. His primary contributions were in botany and biology. His contributions to bibliography provided a model for the many library catalogers to come as well as to the great classifiers to come: Gottfried Wilhelm von Leibniz (1646–1716) and Carl Linnaeus (1707–1784).

Seventeenth-Century Public Libraries

Public libraries begin to be mentioned again in the early seventeenth century. Sir Thomas Bodley (1603), through the gift of his library to Oxford University, undertook to establish there a "publick" library. The library that was to become known almost immediately as the Bodleian was "public" only insofar as the library was lodged in a public institution, Oxford University.

Access to the Bodleian library was very strictly circumscribed (Bodley 1603, 94). The library was strictly prohibited from lending its collection, except to particularly trusted members of the Oxford community (Bodley 1603, 84–86). The collection was limited to the best copies of the best books.

Gabriel Naudé (1627, 6–7) praised private book collectors who contributed their libraries to the use of the public. Naudé dedicated his life to the management of libraries, first for the president of the Paris Parlement, de Thou, then Cardinals Richelieu and Mazarin.

Public libraries should have general and balanced collections, Naudé (1627, 16) argued. That collection should focus on the arts and sciences. "It must also be said that there is nothing more to the credit of a library than that every man finds in it what he seeks" (Naudé 1627, 17). The public should be aided by a courteous yet knowledgeable librarian (Naudé 1627, 76).

Johannes Lomeier's (Montgomery 1962) *De bibliothecis liber singularis*, first published in 1669, is a discourse on European libraries and their history. John Warwick Montgomery (1962) provides a translation into English of chapter 10 of that work, a survey of the most famous libraries extant in seventeenth-century Europe. Lomeier did not provide us with a count of all European libraries, but he did suggest that there were many, as he asserted that it would have been an "infinite task. . . . Indeed, one may scarcely find any moderately famous city, scarcely any community, gymnasium, university, or monastery where a library has not been set apart for the public use of the studious" (Montgomery 1962, 12). On Lomeier's testimony, we learn that by the mid-seventeenth century there were many libraries available in Europe for serious study and that most of these libraries had their beginnings as private libraries bequeathed to public institutions by their owners.

Lomeier (Montgomery 1962, 12) also informs us on the difficulty of locating specific works of interest. He stated that he had sought the work of Louis Jacob,[1] a Carmelite brother who had written a survey of European libraries. But that he, Lomeier, had been unsuccessful in his searches.

Eighteenth-Century Public Libraries

Johannes Lomeier informed us of the ubiquity of public libraries in the major cities of Europe. James Kirkwood, a Scot and Presbyterian minister, proposed a plan to place libraries in every parish of Scotland. Kirkwood's ambitious plan, one that was in the end unsuccessful, included a system of libraries under the guidance of the Presbyterian Synod at Edinburgh. Kirkwood correctly noted the vast increase in the number of books available since the invention of printing. No student could possibly own all books of interest to him; "and therefore compleat and free Libraries are absolutely necessary for the Improving of Arts and Sciences, and for Advancing of Learning amongst us" (Kirkwood 1699c, 27).

Ministers and other church officials were to contribute their libraries to the project. In addition, Kirkwood proposed a plan to copy books bought throughout Europe and to republish them in Scotland. In that fashion, the parish libraries would have a constant supply of new material, but Scotland would develop a thriving publishing (or republishing) industry.

Kirkwood's libraries were to be used by students and ministers. The purpose of the libraries was to provide ministers with the means to instruct their parishioners, or, as Kirkwood (1699c, 56) put it, "Then certainly it must much more be our Duty, to provide [the ministers] with competent Libraries of the most useful Books, seeing without these they cannot study, nor be fitted sufficiently to Instructing their People in the Truths of their Religion."

In order to meet the needs of scholars and ministers, Kirkwood (1703, 62–63) proposed that the libraries collect diverse and perhaps eclectic books, so as to better "deal with the Adversary." Some books, he suggested popish books, were not "fit for the weaker sort of People," but were necessary in a proper library.

Johann David Köhler (1684–1755) came into scholarly prominence in a transitional period for European scholarship. From the Middle Ages and into the Enlightenment, European scholars were part of a "common culture of scholarship," a *respublica litteraria* (Eskildsen 2005, 421). That common culture of scholarship was subjected to a series of nationalistic and religious pressures across the eighteenth century so that as Köhler came into prominence in the eighteenth century there had been a shift from the Pan-European *imagined community* to a more parochial, nationalist one (Anderson 1991).

According to Köhler (1973, 9), *Die Substanz einer Bibliotheck sind die Bücher*, or books are the substance of a library. Johann David Köhler spent several pages describing different book types. Some are handwritten; others are printed. Some are in codex format; others are scrolls. Köhler warned his readers that handwritten books were relatively rare, that one is best prepared if one knows beforehand which library holds a specific item. One way to locate books is to consult library catalogs. Köhler listed several union catalogs as well as catalogs of individual libraries.

Köhler defined different kinds of libraries. He described these as public and private and open and closed. Open libraries might best be defined as those with open stacks, and closed libraries with closed stacks. Public libraries are those that permit the educated public access to their collections. Private libraries are those created by individuals and for the use of those individuals.

Most "public" libraries are associated with educational institutions — both universities and gymnasia or high schools. Most public libraries, as Köhler defined them, were open to very specific and limited constituencies. These constituencies usually included students, scholars, and gentlemen. For most public libraries, the rest of the general public were not included among those allowed access to the books.

Köhler distinguished between public and private libraries as well as open and closed library sections. He argued that private libraries were biased according to the interests of individual collectors, while open libraries sought a broader representation of thought on given subjects. Some libraries are public in that all learned persons might use them; others were closed to the general public.

Jesse Shera (1949) describes the evolution of libraries in the United States in great detail. The Puritans brought with them book collections.

Learned wealthy men built libraries. Naudé (1627, 5–8) went so far as to suggest that earthly immortality could be achieved by leaving one's name on a library. John Harvard left his four hundred books to what was to become Harvard Library (Shera 1949, 18). Shera also tells us that there was some sense of community ownership of books that contributed to the establishment of the Massachusetts Bay Library in the mid-seventeenth century.

The first Boston Public Library was created through a bequest by Captain Robert Keayne in 1655 or 1656 to dedicate a room for a library in a new public building (Shera 1949, 19).

Social libraries were begun in the 1780s (Shera 1949, 54). These were for the most part book clubs. Shera does not credit Benjamin Franklin with the creation of the social library, but Benjamin Franklin did play an important role.

In what was to become United States, the public library movement began as social or subscription libraries. In his autobiography, Benjamin Franklin (1944, 87–88) provided an account of the founding of the Philadelphia public library in 1730. He recounted that when he arrived in Philadelphia, there were no booksellers south of Boston. Most of Philadelphia's book lovers by necessity had to acquire their books from England. Franklin, noting that there were indeed books in Philadelphia in private hands, proposed that these readers band together in a "public" subscription library, a junto, to pool both money and books. Franklin (1944, 88) observed:

> So few were the readers at that time in Philadelphia, and the majority of us were so poor, that I was not able, with great industry, to find more than fifty persons, mostly young tradesmen, willing to pay down for this purpose forty shillings each, and ten per annum. On this little fund we began. The books were imported; the library was opened one day in the week lending to the subscribers, on their promissory notes to pay double the value if not duly returned.

The junto was, according to Franklin, eminently successful and copied by others in other cities. Franklin used the library to further his education and to provide what little diversion he would allow.

The open access movement of public libraries probably began in the United States in the mid- to late nineteenth century. Generally referred to as "reference libraries," these libraries had liberal entrance and lending policies. By the late nineteenth century open access reference libraries were also in existence in the United Kingdom.

Nineteenth-Century Public Libraries

Perhaps one of the forces fueling the development and growth of public libraries in the nineteenth century was the increased interest in reading and book access, first in the middle classes and then in the working or laboring classes. The upper class as well as the church maintained libraries, a practice the middle class began to engage in. Given the expense of books, libraries provided access for less affluent readers. Richard Altick (1957) describes the eighteenth century as an era of upper-class and, to a lesser degree, middle-class private libraries. The nineteenth century witnessed a greater demand for libraries both private and public among the working classes in England.

English libraries of the nineteenth century reflected both a demographic shift and also a philosophical shift. Again, according to Altick (1957, 24–26), library collections shifted from theology, literature, history, and the sciences to books purporting to aid in self-improvement, thrift, and conduct. This movement was driven by re-emergent Puritanism and a capitalist urge.

Circulating libraries replaced the social library as the primary form of "public" library in the late eighteenth and early nineteenth centuries (Shera 1949, 127). Circulating libraries rented books to the patron and did not require the payment of membership or subscription fees. They were established as for-profit enterprises. In these regards they resemble video rental stores of the twentieth century.

Mechanics' and miners' libraries were established by labor organizations to promote reading and educations among their memberships. In a sense, these libraries were financed much like the subscription libraries. The libraries were underwritten by the dues paid by the membership to the larger organization. These libraries and their membership not infrequently resisted municipalization of the library so as to retain their class character and interests.

Public lending libraries are a fairly recent phenomenon. In 1849 Edward Edwards (Select Committee 1849, 1) provided the following as a definition for public libraries:

> I would take it as embracing, first of all, libraries deriving their support
> from public funds, either wholly or in part; and I would further extend
> it to such libraries as are made accessible to the public to a greater or
> less degree.

The report from the Select Committee on Public Libraries in 1849 was particularly critical of London. England and the rest of Great Britain were found to be without libraries where the poor might read. Other countries, the report (Select Committee 1849, iv) continued, were far better endowed with public libraries. Many London coffeehouses served as libraries or reading rooms for the working classes.

In 1849 Edward Edwards surveyed European and South American libraries on the matter of public access. Public access was defined as the admission of members of the public into libraries, but did not incorporate whether that public had free and open use of library materials or whether lending privileges were extended to any or all. Edwards reported that some libraries, while fairly restrictive in the admissions policies, were nevertheless fairly liberal in their lending and usages policies and vice versa (Edwards 1859 ii, 988–1028). Edwards concluded that free access was the general rule within certain limitations. Patrons were generally expected to be appropriately attired. Others restricted access to "educated persons." In the mid-nineteenth century those requirements could well be used to limit library use to the middle and upper classes. Moreover, in order to qualify for library admission, patrons might have to be listed on town rolls. That could serve to further limit the pool of patrons.

Edwards (1859 ii, 1052; see also Hewitt 2000) informed us that the first lending library in the United Kingdom was the Manchester Free Library. The library consisted of the main facility and two branches. It opened its doors on September 6, 1852. In 1857 the library's collection stood at about 454,000 volumes. This library, or at least the reference section of the library, was open to the general public. Individuals, on appearing on Manchester's citizens roll or the list of burgesses for Salford, were required to sign a voucher pledging to observe the library's rules. They would then be issued a ticket that permitted them use of the facility (Edwards 1859 ii, 1053). The library would publicly display the names of "defaulters," those who had not promptly returned books. Defaulters were to be barred from further borrowing until their accounts were cleared. Readers were expected to have clean hands when using the books.

Nevertheless, by the mid-nineteenth century the concept was well accepted that public libraries were indeed for public use. Moreover, the idea that these libraries might also lend their collections was becoming accepted as well. To support this view, Edwards cited the report of the Commission of Inquiry into the Imperial Library at Paris (Edwards 1859 ii, 1026–1028). The commission concluded that lending should be continued, but with appropriate guarantees. Edwards did not provide a date for the commission but noted it was convened in "recent years."

In addition, the Manchester Free Library established rules for its use. No one under fourteen was to be admitted into the reference section. The public was otherwise prohibited from other parts of the library. Nor were the intoxicated or the unclean welcome. No one was allowed to remove books from the shelves except by permission of the reference librarian. On their return, the librarian was to examine all books for damage. If damage were found, the borrower was required to pay for the repair (Edwards 1859 ii, 1049–1050). From these rules, we can conclude the Manchester library did not limit its services to scholars and gentlemen. It tolerated adolescents and other not-quite-so-reputable patrons.

The public library at the University of Cambridge was not nearly so "enlightened." It would only lend books to those holding the "M.B., LL.B., M.A., LL.D., or D.D." degree and who were members of the various Cambridge colleges. Borrowing privileges were limited to ten books

(Edwards 1859 ii, 1060–1061). But then, Cambridge was an academic library by our lights.

At about the same time the Manchester library opened to the public, the first American public library, the Boston Public Library, opened under city control in 1854. Jesse Shera (1949, 158–159) is less interested in when the library opened but rather in the why. He describes various forms of experimentation, including the social and circulating libraries, that led to a perception of a need for public participation in library funding. Boston had developed a stable economy by the 1840s, a growing and literate population, as well as government participation in various public works (water, gas, sewage). The political culture of the city was amenable to public funding of libraries as well (Shera 1949, 172–173).

The public library was often seen as a panacea for society's problems. Daniel Goldstein (2003) finds, for example, that the Iowa library movement thrived beginning in the 1890s because the public library and reading were seen as replacements for gambling, drinking, and prostitution. Goldstein further argues that librarian values as they relate to the relevance of the library as a means to control social ills depend on the specific issue and the prevailing social mores. Ilkka Mäkinen (1996) shows that public libraries were thought to be a solution to similar social ills in the nineteenth-century Grand Duchy of Finland.

Or the public library might be seen as a waste of public resources. Barbara Myrvold (1986, 65) has described opposition to the Toronto public library following passage of the Ontario Free Libraries Act in 1882. Despite some public misgivings, Toronto's voters viewed libraries in a more favorable light.

Twentieth-Century Public Libraries

John Cotton Dana should perhaps be considered the great democratizer of the public library. Trained as a lawyer and as a civil engineer, John Cotton Dana began his library career in Denver, Colorado. Dana was author of numerous speeches, essays, and articles in support of liberalization of public library policies. His contributions to practice include broadening the user base of public libraries from subscribers to the general public, open stacks, separate children's collections, foreign language collections to meet the needs of diverse population bases, and branch libraries to support specific interests (e.g., a businessman's library).

Dana (1920, 2–3) stated that in 1876 there were few libraries in United States, except those in schools and colleges, but that it is then that "the modern library movement began." It began in part because of gifts from the wealthy for public library buildings. Dana did not specifically name Andrew Carnegie, certainly the greatest single private benefactor to library building programs in American history. In addition, "the growth of print has increased the reading habit" (Dana 1920, 4). Those two factors contributed to the need for libraries, which in turn gave rise to the need for skilled librarians.

Dana was one of the first major proponents of libraries as entertainment facilities. Libraries serve several purposes, among them entertainment and the provision of answers to complex questions (1920, 10). He (1920, 9) argued further that:

> Most of us lead rather humdrum lives. Novels open doors to an ideal life in the enjoyment of which one forgets the hardships or the tedium of the daily grind. The library can make this reading of more value and help to extend it.

Public library culture underwent significant change in the twentieth century. As we have seen, Melvil Dewey undertook to educate women in library economy. John Cotton Dana promoted the hiring of women as library workers and directors. Wadsworth and Wiegand (2012) point to the World's Columbian Exposition in 1893 and its women's library as a tipping point. McCook (2004, 44–45) argues that the injection of women into the library profession has contributed to the moderating of the library as an uplifter of culture to a nurturing and service based institution.

CONTEMPORARY PUBLIC LIBRARIES

Public libraries have undergone important shifts. They began as elite institutions and remained so for the better part of two millennia. It was not until the eighteenth century and particularly the nineteenth and early to mid twentieth centuries that the public library became truly a public institution, in the broadest senses of the word.

Libraries have for the most part been conservative institutions. Some have gone so far as to argue that public libraries serve as mechanisms for social control by the political elite (e.g., Wiegand 1989 and 1998; Robbins 2000). Michael Harris (1973) has suggested a revisionist interpretation of the public library as an agent for social control rather than the prevailing hypothesis that the public library, at least in the United States, is an outgrowth of and a primary engine of democracy. The library as an engine of political change is addressed in more depth in chapter 6.

Public libraries' philosophies may lag the dominant social paradigm, but they will come to reflect it in time. Many public libraries in the United States, for example, discriminated against peoples of color, particularly the African American (Josey 1970, Phinazee 1980, and McPheeters 1988). Other libraries embraced different ethnic groups as they arrived as immigrants (Drzewieniecki and Drzewieniecki-Abugattas 1974). Cheryl Knott Malone (2000) urges a careful review of libraries and the constituencies they serve. She wonders whether libraries can be shown to serve the interests of subordinate as well as super-ordinate social groups. Historians have begun to examine groups other than the dominant social classes and their domestic and international clashes to better understand social dynamics at various points in time. The same can and has been done for libraries.

The relatively recent support of public libraries and library associations for a multiculturalist approach is of very recent etiology (see Malone 2000; Robbins 2000). As the history presented here suggests, public libraries and library associations have at times resisted liberal trends, just as they are today resisting more conservative trends.

Many positive and some negative social effects have been attributed to the public library. Libraries brought culture (see Allen 2001) from the cultural, political, and economic center to the provincial periphery. Libraries might moderate social vices. Public libraries brought education and entertainment to their patrons. Libraries served as vehicles of social reform by bringing women into positions of prominence, acculturating immigrants, and serving as gateways to the wider world. Libraries, it is claimed, promote democratic institutions. Public libraries directly reinforce the information commons (Jochum 1998). They promote philanthropy.

The Library: Bread and Circus

The public library as we know it is a twentieth-century institution. Public libraries transitioned from elite institutions to populist ones in the mid-nineteenth century; this is to say the public library was redefined from a research facility to one more attuned to more pedestrian needs. Libraries opened reading, children's, and reference rooms. In the twentieth century women began to take positions in the library, bringing to the libraries what some have called a more nurturing environment. Public libraries began to redefine their acquisitions policies under the guidance of such reformers as John Cotton Dana.

Public libraries benefited from the philanthropic benevolence from the likes of Andrew Carnegie in the nineteenth century and the Bill and Melinda Gates Foundation in the twentieth. Public libraries were, for the most part, no longer created at the bequest of wealthy book collectors.

To re-quote Jesse Shera (1949, v), "The history of the [American] public library is a record of a transition from a narrowly conservative function to a broad program directed toward the advancement of popular education." The public library has also moved toward the advancement of popular entertainment. Douglas Raber (1997), in writing about the Public Library Inquiry of 1949, discusses the social climate of the day in general and of librarians in particular. Identifying librarianship as among the "pseudo-professions," Raber (1997, 9) notes that public librarians in the United States faced a crisis of identity in the mid-twentieth century, just as they do at its end. Raber (1997, 3) notes that public library ideology is established on a democratic sense of purpose in the United States, a sense of purpose threatened by the perceived excesses of World War II. Moreover and more importantly, the public library profession was largely left to define its own legitimacy, image, and values. This, we suggest, permitted the public librarian and other librarians to find their identities within an insulated public sphere, a public sphere only moderated indirectly by the other social identities they might hold (i.e., citizen, parent, religion, political allegiances, etc.). The mid-twentieth-century public library ideology was, as a consequence of the war and other social factors, redefining itself. Raber (1997, 140–141) finds that the public library was cast as one of the major bastions of democracy. The library, a middle-class "democratic middle-ground," would serve by providing an intermediating buffer between power and an "atomized mass society." Because of the social importance of this role, public library collections in the United States needed to consist of "serious materials," and through that "the public library [could] contribute to the process of defining the public good." Thus as late as the mid-twentieth century the Public Library Inquiry would propose collection development policies in support of democracy and the public good and a rejection of public libraries as repositories of popular fiction (Leigh 1950).

The public library can expand its popular educational and entertainment mandates because libraries have been differentiated and reified into distinct institutions with their own identities. The public library no longer is required to serve a research function, although some, like the Atlanta Fulton County, New York, or Boston Public Libraries, have maintained that tradition. Public libraries are also no longer required to meet the specific needs of various corporate entities. These are well served by special libraries, developed and maintained for the support of very specific constituencies.

And finally, as the underlying social system has undergone change, so has the public library. Recalling Jesse Shera's (1949, v) argument that although libraries are secondary social institutions, they help frame public opinion and social mores, they are in turn shaped by those same opinions and mores. As the role of the public library has changed, so has the role of the librarians who staff them. There has been a sometimes subtle and sometimes not-so-subtle shift in the values that guide public librarianship. Libraries are no longer the reserve of men of means. Public libraries now serve all genders, ages, races, and classes. Their mandate has always been to educate. In the nineteenth century that mandate was expanded to uplift their patrons; and in the twentieth century it was further expanded to entertain them as well.

New Threats

The public library may now be threatened from a variety of sources. As the political entities that fund them face economic challenges, libraries are sometimes seen as relatively painless sources for budget reductions. Public library closings and curtailments, once considered rare, have become more common.

There are political and social challenges to library autonomy. Various interest groups, of the left and of the right, conservative and liberal, have sought to force public libraries to acknowledge their agendas. The neutrality of the library and of librarians can thereby be compromised. These efforts can take the form of challenges to specific books that describe variants on sexual, gender, religious, and political concerns. Libraries may be challenged for their foreign language collections or their lack thereof.

And most recently public libraries have had to adjust to the implications of the Internet. As libraries have come to see themselves as public gateways to the web, they have had to accommodate changing technology and changing perceptions of the place of the public library as an information provider.

PUBLIC LIBRARIES, LIBRARIANS, AND THEIR ETHICS

Public librarian professional traditions have more shallow roots than other librarians. The public library as we know it today began in the middle of the nineteenth century in England and the United States. Academic and, in many senses of the word, special libraries can trace their traditions to Alexandria and Sumeria.

Public librarians are faced with all the requirements of other librarians and more. They have as their constituencies the populace as a whole. Public libraries have not always had the population as a whole as part of their constituencies; and even when they did, they have not always provided the same level of service. We might argue that discrimination based on race, creed, gender, sexual orientation, age, ethnicity or other criteria represents the exception rather than the rule; but we would then be wrong. As public libraries reflect the dominant social paradigm, where a society condones discrimination, so do its libraries. Where a society condemns discrimination, so do its libraries.

That US libraries' discrimination is social history. Louise Robbins (2000) has documented for us one set of consequences for librarians who engage the social paradigm: ostracism, threats, and loss of employment.

Public libraries are far less insulated from economic and political forces than their academic librarian siblings. In some jurisdictions, public librarians may be insulated to a degree by their trustees, but they are a part of the economic and political fabric of the community. Academic libraries are protected to a greater degree by their traditions as well as their participation in the academic paradigm. Special libraries serve a specific constituency. While they may suffer from economic forces, their function and their salvation lie in their very particular service to that specific constituency.

CONCLUSIONS

The idea, the concept of the public library has undergone significant redefinition from its first conception more than two millennia ago to the present. These changes result from changes in technology as well as library philosophy.

The ethics of public library practice have developed from provision of services to elites to special groups to a broad number of social and economic groups. Public libraries are no longer archives. To provide service to diverse communities, public libraries maintain limited archival collections. Those collections are often restricted to genealogical and local materials.

The development of public library ethics is not frozen. Public libraries are continuing to redefine their collection policies from non-fiction to electronic games, toys, and tools.

Public libraries are also expanding their definitions of appropriate clientele. The clientele ranges from infants to the disadvantaged. Others have significant outreach programs to patrons of varying social and linguistic backgrounds. Yet libraries are sometimes challenged because they either have or do not have collections in more than one (or an official) language.

These definitions of the appropriate patron pool vary. As public libraries seek to expand their patron pools in one direction, they sometimes lose patrons from other groups.

Technology and technology change have also impacted public library practice. The advent of the computer in the library has redefined how public libraries are used. Public access computers have also forced public libraries to reconsider their Internet access policies for adults and children.

The evolution of ethics in public libraries is not finished. Public library ethics, like library ethics in general, remains a work in progress. This work in progress nevertheless remains compliant with Ranganathan's five laws. As public libraries modify their service provisions, they retain the ability to provide books for users, users for books, and to save the user's time. The public library remains organic and dynamic.

NOTE

1. Louis Jacob de Saint-Charles, *Traicté des plus belles bibliothèques* (Paris: 1644).

FIVE

On the Freedom of Expression, Intellectual Freedom, and Their Control

As a matter of constitutional tradition, in the absence of evidence to the contrary, we presume that governmental regulation of the content of speech is more likely to interfere with the free exchange of ideas than to encourage it. The interest in encouraging freedom of expression in a democratic society outweighs any theoretical but unproven benefit of censorship.

—US Supreme Court Justice John Paul Stevens
(*Reno v. ACLU*, 117 S. Ct. 2329 [1997])

In short, intellectual freedom is the heart and soul of the [library] profession.

— American Library Association Office for Intellectual Freedom
(2006, 394)

The Commission [on Online Child Protection] concludes that the most effective current means of protecting children from content on the Internet harmful to minors include: aggressive efforts toward public education, consumer empowerment, increased resources for enforcement of existing laws, and greater use of existing technologies.

—Commission on Online Child Protection, *Final Report* (2000)

INTRODUCTION

There is a long history and concern with the question of intellectual freedom, freedom of expression, and the control and manipulation of information. Rights of intellectual freedom are integral parts of our publicly expressed culture. These rights are usually defined as both the right to freely express one's thoughts and beliefs and the right of access to information.

These rights are balanced by both social restraints as well as the freedom of others to object to those expressions of values and beliefs. Every society has placed limits on what it will or will not tolerate. Those limits may be policed through the specific application of both positive and negative state sanctions. Or they may be regulated through a more informal interpretation of social mores. Those standards and their targets are constantly changing. Libraries have never been, are not, and cannot be completely immune to these changes. To restate the obvious, what we consider to be "riff-raff" books, inappropriate for the library collection in one age; become the classical, "must-have" literature in another age. In the seventeenth century, for example, as Paul Keen (1999) demonstrates, the place of literature in the public sphere was being redefined. Old elites were concerned that new readers were being unduly influenced by a new literature.

Liz Greenhalgh and Ken Worpole (1995, 12) acknowledge that public libraries, at least those in the United Kingdom, are a manifestation, an application of the public sphere and are, as well, important "public spaces." Their definition of public space is derived from sociology. David Sudnow (1972) addresses the way in which public space is used for social interactions. Susan Shimanoff (1980) is concerned with the changes and impacts to public space by communications technology. Joshua Meyrowitz (1985) addresses the effect of electronic communications on social relations. Greenhalgh and Worpole (1995) address some of these changes in the context of the library. As public space is redefined by cultural and technological change, the public library has retained its place as a public space: "This, we feel, is one of the pre-eminent values of the public library, as neutral space, as democratic, non-sectarian territory" (Greenhalgh and Worpole 1995, 12).

"Public space" and "public sphere" serve to help define the library and most importantly its function in society. While all libraries are vulnerable or subject to changes in the social definitions of public space and public sphere, it is the public library that is most effected by those changes. We can point to the legal and critical acceptance of novels like Henry Miller's *Tropic of Cancer* or William Burroughs's *Naked Lunch*, both banned in the United States until the early 1960s. But, both were well accepted by the critics. The social environment therefore serves to qualify Ranganathan's third law: to each book, its reader. Because libraries are cultural institutions, their selection and de-selection policies are a reflection of prevailing social philosophy as well as the more parochial needs of the specific public the library serves. Each book may have its reader, but if the book is not included in the collection and is otherwise unavailable, the reader may never even be aware that the book exists.

As we well know, libraries, and public libraries in particular, do not and cannot collect all books. They do not, in part, include certain books in their collections for expedient reasons. They also exclude certain books on legal, social, philosophical, and moral grounds. Those grounds for excluding books from libraries or even for sale and distribution within a given society have undergone constant redefinition. Materials critical of government may be barred in some polities, while books descriptive of violence or "deviant" sexuality may be in others. What is acceptable in one community may be unacceptable in another. Reasons vary; the effect is the same.

And finally, while the principles of intellectual freedom and freedom of speech are among the most exalted in principle, they are often highly qualified in fact. It has only been recently in historical terms that librarians, through their professional associations and individually, have actively promoted these principles. For most of its history, the library profession promoted controls of one kind or another on the formation of their collections. The very earliest libraries were limited to records. Greek and Roman libraries focused on non-fiction and established classics, as did medieval monastic libraries. Libraries were to collect only the "best books" and to avoid fiction of all kinds through the seventeenth century. "Riff raff" and suggestive books ("French novels") were excluded from most libraries into the beginning of the twentieth century. Books were sometimes de-selected for political reasons; for example, most US public libraries removed pro-German materials from their collections during World War I (see Wiegand 1989). Similarly, many books were culled from libraries in occupied France on political grounds during World War II. Shirley Wiegand and Wayne Wiegand (2007) document the impact of the Cold War on library collections. Today in the United States the most effective challenge to information is based of the grounds of harm to children. Hence, I argue that the principles of intellectual freedom and of freedom of speech are held to be among the most important to the library community; but they have also been the most qualified by the library community.

DOCUMENTED RIGHTS

The Enlightenment into the late eighteenth century witnessed the introduction of human rights protected by constitution and by philosophy. Thomas Paine's 1791 *The Rights of Man* is among the first of treatises on the rights of the individual and that of government. In *The Rights of Man,* Paine defends a republican government over monarchy and the French Revolution from the critique of Edmond Burke. Men, Paine (1915, 42–43) reminds us, are born of *equal degree,* which is to say equal under law. Moreover, preceding generations are no more equal than the present generation. According to Paine (1915, 44–45) the natural rights of humanity include "all of the intellectual rights, or rights of the mind." These rights, however, must not be "injurious to the natural rights of others." All civil rights are derived from natural rights. "A man, by natural right, has a right to judge in his own cause; and so far as the right of the mind is concerned, he never surrenders it." Humans are both individuals and social beings. Natural rights are exchanged, Paine argued, for civil rights to accommodate the social being.

Rights Defined in Law

The Declaration of the Rights of Man and the Citizen of 1789 provides inter alia that

> 10. No one shall be disquieted on account of his opinions, including his religious views, provided their manifestation does not disturb the public order established by law.
> 11. The free communication of ideas and opinions is one of the most precious of the rights of man. Every citizen may, accordingly, speak, write, and print with freedom, but shall be responsible for such abuses of this freedom as shall be defined by law.

The ideas of Paine and of those arising out of the French Revolution are the culmination of the ideals of the Enlightenment. Law can nevertheless circumscribe these principles of the natural rights of individuals to opinion and communication. Thus those rights were never recognized as absolute either by philosopher or government.

The question has arisen more than once as to where the boundary between rights and regulation lies. Since mankind has been capable of communication and expressing ideas, there have been those who have sought to control and restrain that activity. The concepts of intellectual freedom are embedded in most political traditions and are reflected in many of our basic foundational documents. These fundamental documents include constitutions and basic or fundamental laws. The *Declaration of the Rights of Man and the Citizen* and the First Amendment to the US Constitution, both dating to the late eighteenth century, are among many such defenses of the freedom of expression. The constitutions of most countries contain clauses that implicitly or explicitly promise one or both of these rights to their citizens.

These rights are further defined by international intergovernmental organizations.

The most important of these international expressions of intellectual freedoms are found in Articles 18 and 19 of the United Nations Universal Declaration of Human Rights of 1948. They specify:

Article 18.
Everyone has the right to freedom of thought, conscience and religion; this right includes freedom to change his religion or belief, and freedom, either alone or in community with others and in public or private, to manifest his religion or belief in teaching, practice, worship and observance.

Article 19.
Everyone has the right to freedom of opinion and expression; this right includes freedom to hold opinions without interference and to seek, receive and impart information and ideas through any media and regardless of frontiers.

The Council of Europe's Convention for the Protection of Human Rights and Fundamental Freedoms of 1950 reaffirms the rights of human beings as specified in the United Nations Universal Declaration of Human Rights. Articles 9, 10, and 11 specify freedoms of thought, expression, and assembly. It should be noted that these rights, as specified in the convention, are not absolute. For example, Article 9(2) and Article 11(2) permit limitations in support of democratic society and to protect the "rights and freedoms of others." Article 10(1) acknowledges the right of the state to license "broadcasting, television or cinema enterprises." These can be, as we shall see, important limits on non-conventional speech.

Article 9—Freedom of thought, conscience and religion

1. Everyone has the right to freedom of thought, conscience and religion; this right includes freedom to change his religion or belief and freedom, either alone or in community with others and in public or private, to manifest his religion or belief, in worship, teaching, practice and observance.
2. Freedom to manifest one's religion or beliefs shall be subject only to such limitations as are prescribed by law and are necessary in a democratic society in the interests of public safety, for the protection of public order, health or morals, or for the protection of the rights and freedoms of others.

Article 10—Freedom of expression

1. Everyone has the right to freedom of expression. This right shall include freedom to hold opinions and to receive and impart information and ideas without interference by public authority and regardless of frontiers. This article shall not prevent States from requiring the licensing of broadcasting, television or cinema enterprises.

2. The exercise of these freedoms, since it carries with it duties and responsibilities, may be subject to such formalities, conditions, restrictions or penalties as are prescribed by law and are necessary in a democratic society, in the interests of national security, territorial integrity or public safety, for the prevention of disorder or crime, for the protection of health or morals, for the protection of the reputation or rights of others, for preventing the disclosure of information received in confidence, or for maintaining the authority and impartiality of the judiciary.

Article 11—Freedom of assembly and association

1. Everyone has the right to freedom of peaceful assembly and to freedom of association with others, including the right to form and to join trade unions for the protection of his interests.
2. No restrictions shall be placed on the exercise of these rights other than such as are prescribed by law and are necessary in a democratic society in the interests of national security or public safety, for the prevention of disorder or crime, for the protection of health or morals or for the protection of the rights and freedoms of others. This article shall not prevent the imposition of lawful restrictions on the exercise of these rights by members of the armed forces, of the police or of the administration of the State.

Non-governmental Organizations

The International Federation of Information Associations and Institutions (IFLA) has taken a strong position on intellectual freedom and freedom of expression. The IFLA Statement on Libraries and Intellectual Freedom was adopted in 1999 is a firm expression in support of intellectual freedom:

> IFLA (The International Federation of Library Associations and Institutions) supports, defends and promotes intellectual freedom as defined in the United Nations Universal Declaration of Human Rights.
> IFLA declares that human beings have a fundamental right to access to expressions of knowledge, creative thought and intellectual activity, and to express their views publicly.
> IFLA believes that the right to know and freedom of expression are two aspects of the same principle. The right to know is a requirement for freedom of thought and conscience; freedom of thought and freedom of expression are necessary conditions for freedom of access to information.
> IFLA asserts that a commitment to intellectual freedom is a core responsibility for the library and information profession.

IFLA therefore calls upon libraries and library staff to adhere to the principles of intellectual freedom, uninhibited access to information and freedom of expression and to recognize the privacy of library user.

IFLA urges its members actively to promote the acceptance and realization of these principles. In doing so, IFLA affirms that:

Libraries provide access to information, ideas and works of imagination. They serve as gateways to knowledge, thought and culture.

Libraries provide essential support for lifelong learning, independent decision-making and cultural development for both individuals and groups.

Libraries contribute to the development and maintenance of intellectual freedom and help to safeguard basic democratic values and universal civil rights.

Libraries have a responsibility both to guarantee and to facilitate access to expressions of knowledge and intellectual activity. To this end, libraries shall acquire, preserve and make available the widest variety of materials, reflecting the plurality and diversity of society.

Libraries shall ensure that the selection and availability of library materials and services is governed by professional considerations and not by political, moral and religious views.

Libraries shall acquire, organize and disseminate information freely and oppose any form of censorship.

Libraries shall make materials, facilities and services equally accessible to all users. There shall be no discrimination due to race, creed, gender, age or for any other reason.

Library users shall have the right to personal privacy and anonymity. Librarians and other library staff shall not disclose the identity of users or the materials they use to a third party.

Libraries funded from public sources and to which the public have access shall uphold the principles of intellectual freedom.

Librarians and other employees in such libraries have a duty to uphold those principles.

Librarians and other professional libraries staff shall fulfill their responsibilities both to their employer and to their users. In cases of conflict between those responsibilities, the duty towards the user shall take precedence.

The IFLA's Committee on Free Access to Information and Freedom of Expression (FAIFE) further interprets the IFLA's position:

The right to know

All human beings have the fundamental right to have access to all expressions of knowledge, creativity and intellectual activity, and to express their thoughts in public.

The right to know and the freedom to express are two aspects of the same principle. The freedom of expression is realized by the preservations of the right to know. The right to know is related inherently to the freedom of thought and conscience and all other fundamental human rights. Freedom of thought and freedom of expression are necessary conditions for the freedom of access to information.

The right of access to information and ideas is vital for any society. If citizens are to participate and make informed choices, they must have access to political, social, scientific and economic information and cultural expressions. They need access to the widest range of ideas, information and images. Freedom, prosperity and the development of society depend on education as well as on unrestricted access to knowledge, thought, culture and information.

This right to intellectual freedom is essential to the creation and development of a democratic society. The state of intellectual freedom in libraries is an important indication of the progress of democracy in a nation.

The IFLA's 2014 Lyon Declaration addressed to the United Nations, titled Access to Information and Development, reinforces the organization's position on intellectual freedom and access to information. The Lyon Declaration takes the import of freedom of access to information a step further. That access is seen as strongly interrelated with sustainable development and as a sine qua non to that development.

National library associations have also adopted statements on intellectual freedom (Koehler 2004). For example, the American Library Association's (ALA) Library Bill of Rights (1948), first adopted in the same year as the Universal Declaration of Human Rights, makes express those rights in the library context:

I. Books and other library resources should be provided for the interest, information, and enlightenment of all people of the community the library serves. Materials should not be excluded because of the origin, background, or views of those contributing to their creation.
II. Libraries should provide materials and information presenting all points of view on current and historical issues. Materials should not be proscribed or removed because of partisan or doctrinal disapproval.
III. Libraries should challenge censorship in the fulfillment of their responsibility to provide information and enlightenment.
IV. Libraries should cooperate with all persons and groups concerned with resisting abridgment of free expression and free access to ideas.
V. A person's right to use a library should not be denied or abridged because of origin, age, background, or views.
VI. Libraries which make exhibit spaces and meeting rooms available to the public they serve should make such facilities available on an equitable basis, regardless of the beliefs or affiliations of individuals or groups requesting their use.

The Canadian Library Association's Statement on Intellectual Freedom has taken a similar position:

> All persons in Canada have the fundamental right, as embodied in the nation's Bill of Rights and the Canadian Charter of Rights and Freedoms, to have access to all expressions of knowledge, creativity and intellectual activity, and to express their thoughts publicly. This right to intellectual freedom, under the law, is essential to the health and development of Canadian society.
>
> Libraries have a basic responsibility for the development and maintenance of intellectual freedom.
>
> It is the responsibility of libraries to guarantee and facilitate access to all expressions of knowledge and intellectual activity, including those which some elements of society may consider to be unconventional, unpopular or unacceptable. To this end, libraries shall acquire and make available the widest variety of materials.
>
> It is the responsibility of libraries to guarantee the right of free expression by making available all the library's public facilities and services to all individuals and groups who need them.
>
> Libraries should resist all efforts to limit the exercise of these responsibilities while recognizing the right of criticism by individuals and groups.
>
> Both employees and employers in libraries have a duty, in addition to their institutional responsibilities, to uphold these principles.

Given the strength of the Universal Declaration of Human Rights, national constitutions, and international and national library associations, freedom of expression and freedom of access to information would seem to be well established principles of long standing. In truth, these principles are neither of long standing nor fully accepted with their full implications by the library community. Moreover, these rights have been challenged and continue to be challenged by a variety of agencies, including governments, religious organizations, and civic groups.

Freedom of expression and absolute censorship are polar opposites on a continuum of control and practice. No society, at no time, however open and tolerant, has permitted unfettered communication, spoken, written, or portrayed. Freedom of expression therefore ranges from a state of complete control to one of no control. While the information professional is presumed to prefer less to more control over access to and the dissemination of information, the information professional is nevertheless delimited to legally and socially defined norms. Information professionals are not infrequently tested and sometimes sorely tried to establish the limits in which they function. For example, an Italian court in 2005 vindicated a librarian charged under obscenity laws when the librarian "granted access" of allegedly obscene materials to a minor. However, as Batambuze and Kawooya (2002) point out, principle must sometimes yield to common sense. They describe a Makerere University librarian who found it wise to flee Uganda under the Idi Amin dictatorship rather than to insist on displaying a copy of *Time* magazine containing an unfavorable story of the president for life. In such circumstances a librarian quite literally may not live to shelve another day.

If there is a continuum between complete censorship and complete freedom of expression, where do the limits lie? In some societies those limits have been broadly defined and in others very tightly defined. Classic liberal political theory holds that everything that is not expressly denied is permitted. We draw on social mores and practice and formal jurisprudence to set the limits. In the United States, for example, the First Amendment to the Constitution guarantees freedom of speech. While that may be true in principle, there are distinct limits in fact. Justice Oliver Wendell Holmes set one of those limits when he wrote that one was not permitted to yell, "Fire!" in a crowded theater. Limits have been imposed on what can and cannot be taught in American secondary schools. States, most recently Kansas, have sought to proscribe the teaching of the theory of evolution or intelligent design as it pertains to the human condition.

Censorship

There is an extensive literature on censorship. Censorship can take several forms, some quite subtle and others more blatant. The reasons given to justify or to attack censorship are equally as diverse. Self-censorship has been described in a variety of industries, including publishing, film, theater, book sellers, as well as libraries and schools. The following represent descriptions of self-censorship and codes in films, games, and comic books:

> Gregory Black, 1994, *Hollywood Censored: Morality Codes, Catholics, and the Movies*
>
> Lea Jacobs, 1991, *The Wages of Sin: Censorship and the Fallen Woman Film, 1928–1942*
>
> Eric Nuzum, 2001, *Parental Advisory: Music Censorship in America*
>
> Amy Kiste Nyberg, 1998, *Seal of Approval: The History of the Comics Code*
>
> Murray Schumach, 1964, *The Face on the Cutting Room Floor: The Story of Movie and Television Censorship*
>
> Matthew Spitzer, 1987, *Seven Dirty Words and Six Other Stories: Controlling the Content of Print and Broadcast*

This list is by no means definitive.

The film industry has for many years either applied their own codes that range from "G" for general audience through the official NC-17 (no one under seventeen admitted) and the marketing "XXX" for adult content usually of an explicit sexual nature. Film rating came rather late to the United States when in 1968 the motion picture industry imposed a rating system on its products.

The British Board of Film Classification (BBFC, see http:// www.bbfc.co.uk/) performs a similar function in the United Kingdom and has done so for films since 1913 and for videos since 1985. The BBFC provides ratings from U/Uc (universal, all viewers over age four) through 18 (for viewers over eighteen years of age). While the BBFC is a non-governmental organization, it has been accepted by local government and since 1984 (passage of the Video Recordings Act) by the national government as the de facto regulator of films and similar material. The board commissions research to help guide its policymaking. A recent example is the 2012 *A Review of Policy: Sexual and Sadistic Violence in Film, a Report for the British Board of Film Classification* (http://www.bbfc.co.uk/ sites/default/files/attachments/ BBFC%20sexual%20and%20sadistic%20violence%20report%20December %202012.pdf). On review, the board may make editorial recommendations to make a work acceptable or, in the end, find a given work unacceptable.

Australia regulates films through a federal government agency, the Classification Board (until 2006, the Office of Film and Literature Classification; for additional detail, see http://www.classification.gov.au/About/ Pages/Who-We-Are.aspx). Until 1984, film and publication classification fell to the customs service and later to the Attorney General's Office. Under the Commonwealth Classification Act of 1996, the Classification Board has competence to regulate films, computer games, and print materials. Its film classification system is similar to the British. The Classification Board also applies classifications to books. Books appropriate for all readers receive an unrestricted classification. An Unrestricted-M class applies to materials inappropriate for those under fifteen years of age (Australia Government 2005, 5–9). "Prohibited" categories include inappropriate descriptions of sexual activity, nudity, violence, drug use, and profanity. The Restricted-1 category is limited to persons over eighteen. Restricted-2 also limits sales to those over eighteen and is unavailable for sale in Queensland (Australia Government 2005, 10–15). Materials rated RC, or Refused Classification, may not be imported into or sold in Australia (Australia Government 2005, 16). For a contrarian perspective, see http://www.refused-classification.com/contact-about-help.html.

Its enabling legislation is the Classification (Publications, Films and Computer Games) Act of 1995. The office's regulations (Australia Government 2005) specify that adults should be permitted access to whatever literature they may desire. Children, however, should be protected "from material likely to harm or disturb them." And all should be protected from unsolicited material. Exceptions to adult freedom of access include materials "likely to condone or incite violence; particularly sexual violence" and material that demeans, where "demeaning" has a sexual definition.

In Canada, the provinces regulate film ratings. The regulatory boards include the Alberta Film Classification Services, the British Columbia Film Classification, the Film Review Board, the Manitoba Film Classification, the Quebec Film Classification, the Saskatchewan Film Classification, and the three-province Maritime Film Classification.

The Ontario Film Review Board (2012) (OFRB) regulates films and video games in the province. The OFRB states that it represents the various communities of opinion and geography within the province. Its objective, as specified in the Film Classification Act of 2005, "is to classify film and thereby provide the public with sufficient information to make informed viewing choices for themselves and for their children." It reports to the Ontario Minister of Consumer and Business Services. The OFRB was first established in 1911 as the Ontario Censor Board.

The OFRB applies a ratings code not dissimilar to the British and US models. It bases its decisions in part on "community standards":

> Throughout its history, the Board's policies have been shaped and influenced by external social forces. It continues to adapt and mirror the tastes and standards of the various societies it serves. (Ontario Film Review Board, 2011)

Women and Children First: Censorship and Pornography

Since time immemorial it has been observed that the "younger generation" is prone to all varieties of vices. Socrates was accused of corrupting youth with his teachings. In the eighteenth century it was thought that inappropriate literature could disorient the young and prompt them along inappropriate pathways (Lowenthal and Fiske 1957). H. G. Wells (1938) decried the dilution of education provided by English public schools, a process accompanied by the equally pernicious practice of grade inflation.

The common thread running through most contemporary censorship of films, the arts, and literature is the need to protect children from harm from sex, violence, racism, and other forms of "deviant" behavior. Marjorie Heins (2001), in her *Not in Front of the Children: "Indecency," Censorship, and the Innocence of Youth*, argues that not only is the argument of harm to children scientifically unproved; harm to children hides a much broader agenda for censorship and social control.

The clash of one culture with another can be destabilizing. Catharine MacKinnon and Andrea Dworkin (1998) militate for the rights of the sexually oppressed over those of the pornographer. Few of us would argue that within the cultural context of the United States in the third millennium that pornography is a social good. Still, attacks on pornography are at the same time attacks on the freedom of expression. For the time being, the line has been drawn against pornography that incorporates children or representations of children. Whether the line has been drawn correctly is a cultural and political question for societies to address. Indeed, as James Kincaid (1998) or Ronnie Carr et al. (2014) have shown, the concept of a child as child, an innocent being, rather than as a "small adult" or as an economic unit, is still in flux and dates from the mid-twentieth century.

Our perceptions of "child" represent a redefinition of the public sphere concept of children as economic assets or property, just as the social definition of women has undergone a parallel definitional change. Children are now clearly seen as different from adults, as women are equal to men in the new understanding in the Western public sphere.

Yet, as Kincaid (1998) also clearly demonstrates, Western culture has a mixed perception of the erotic nature of children, and by extension of that of women. Children and women are exploited in the popular culture; and so long as appropriate safeguards are taken to ensure that the exploitation is sufficiently subtle, it is not only tolerated but also largely acceptable. But as Kincaid (1998) demonstrates throughout his book, the line between acceptable and unacceptable is a thin one and one that continually moves.

John de St Jorre (1994) provides an extraordinary insight into the culture and politics of the censorship of the erotic in the first two-thirds of the twentieth century. As he points out: "Censorship of the printed word in the West these days is rare; to most people it appears ludicrous, even obscene. Yet, just over a generation ago, many books—some great, others less than great—were banned in much of Western Europe and in the United States. They were condemned as erotic, pornographic, corrupting—obscene" (St Jorre 1994, xi).

Herbert Foerstel (2002, 179–262) illustrates that censorship is clearly alive and well in US schools, in public libraries, in the media, and on the Internet. The number of titles challenged changes yet increases.

The US Department of Education has defined *harmful to minors* in section 2441 of its regulations defining the No Child Left Behind Act of 2001, PL 107–110, as:

> HARMFUL TO MINORS.—The term 'harmful to minors' means any picture, image, graphic image file, or other visual depiction that—
>
>   (i) taken as a whole and with respect to minors, appeals to a prurient interest in nudity, sex, or excretion;
>   (ii) depicts, describes, or represents, in a patently offensive way with respect to what is suitable for minors, an actual or simulated sexual act or sexual contact, actual or simulated normal or perverted sexual acts, or a lewd exhibition of the genitals; and
>   (iii) taken as a whole, lacks serious literary, artistic, political, or scientific value as to minors.

Libraries have options to respond to challenges to their materials. In her case study, Emily Knox (2014, 740–749) has found that in the United States public librarians have been offered three strategies by challengers to provide content control. These include the reclassification of works from one part of the collection to another, labeling for content, and the application of "commonsense" in selection and collection development. In so doing, libraries may be able to retain challenged materials in the collection. The use of one or more of these options may be an acceptable compromise. It is, nevertheless, a dilution of an ethical standard. The adoption of these and similar policies offers a useful segue to the next section, self-censorship.

Self-Censorship

Self-censorship occurs when an institution or an individual chooses either to not create or collect specific materials for cultural, moral, legal, or other reasons. In a library context, self-censorship differs from "normal" collection and removal in a number of ways. Libraries by necessity must manage their collections. Not only do libraries have space considerations; patron needs and wants must also be addressed. Special and academic libraries are equally constrained by their purposes and missions.

Self-censorship occurs when libraries are concerned with potential legal or moral threats or threats of violence. Marjorie Fiske (1959, 2), in a study of California school and public library selection policies, found that librarians in those institutions were strongly influenced by internal and external considerations. Librarians, according to Fiske (1959), were shown to implicitly or explicitly engage in self-censorship in order to avoid controversy. Other studies have found that libraries frequently engage in self-censorship in the selection or non-selection of lesbian, gay, bisexual, transgender, intersex, and questioning (LGBTIQ) materials. According to Gough and Greenblatt (2011), librarians frequently eschew LGBTIQ materials in their collection decisions because of the nature of the materials and perhaps because of the interested patron pool. Self-censorship may also be found in library education. Hill and Harrington (2014) suggest that sexual issues are often skirted or avoided in library and information science texts, and particularly in the sections on collection development.

We have seen instances of self-censorship in the news media, most recently in the fallout from the publication of the cartoons depicting the Prophet Mohammed by the Danish newspaper *Jyllands Posten* in 2005 and the French magazine *Charlie Hebdo* in 2015. Violence was threatened in the Danish instance, while twelve members of *Charlie Hebdo* editorial board died following an attack. An attack in Denmark in February 2015 was related. After each event, many news outlets, including major newspapers and television networks, declined to make copies of the cartoons public. Many were, however, quick to point out the decision not to publish was not censorship but editorial discretion. Many also rightly stated that the images are available on the Internet.

Controversial Art and Censorship

Controversial art sometimes sparks social change. D. W. Griffith's 1915 film *Birth of a Nation* generated intense controversy in the United States when it was first screened. The film depicts African Americans in very derogatory ways while extolling the virtues of the Ku Klux Klan. Its impact was twofold: it reinvigorated the Ku Klux Klan, but it also significantly strengthened anti-racist efforts to include the role of the National Association for the Advancement of Colored People and counter-responses to the film's message. The showing of *Birth of a Nation* led to major race riots, and it was banned from public viewing in a number of major American cities

Censorship and self-censorship are found in a number of countries. For example, in the United Kingdom the National Viewers and Listeners Association, and under its new name Mediawatch-UK, was founded by Mary Whitehouse in 1965. Its mandate is to address profanity and blasphemy, violence, sex, and homosexuality in the British entertainment media. Its stated mission is: "Mediawatch-UK campaigns for socially responsible media and against content which is potentially harmful." (http://www.mediawatchuk.com/who-we-are-and-what-we-do/). The mandate is broad.

Following the July 7, 2005, bombings in London, in September 2005 the Tate Britain Museum in London decided to withdraw a work of art titled *God is Great*, by John Latham, stating that it might be interpreted as offensive. The work is a sculpture that includes a copy of the Bible, the Koran, and the Torah imbedded in glass. According to a story by David Smith (2005) in the *Guardian*, the Tate's management feared a violent response from Islamic fundamentalists. The artist is quoted as saying that the Tate's decision was not censorship but rather an act of cowardice. He also requested the return of the piece.

France prohibits speech that contradicts the findings of the Nuremberg trials after World War II. The Fabius-Gayssot Law of 1990, amending the Press Law of 1981, has been applied to revisionist historians and at least one politician accused of denying or minimizing the historical record on Nazi atrocities. French reaction to artistic and political expression is not new. For example, novelists and their work have been challenged, among them Victor Hugo's *Les Misérables* first published in 1862 and Émile Zola's article "J'accuse," published in the journal *L'Aurore* on January 13, 1898. The Nobel laureate novelist Anatole France found his works placed on the Catholic Index of Forbidden Books in the 1920s. Among his best-known quotes is from his 1894 novel, *The Red Lily*: "The law, in its majestic equality, forbids the rich as well as the poor to sleep under bridges, to beg in the streets, and to steal bread."

Censorship and the Law

In the United States the Supreme Court is the one institution that represents the final reification of beliefs and changes of beliefs within the public sphere. That alone perhaps explains the intense politicizations of appointments to that bench. The Court's relaxation of censorship in the United States began first with its decision *United States v. One Book Named Ulysses by James Joyce*, which in 1934 overturned provisions of the Comstock Law of 1873.

The Comstock Law regulated pornography as well as birth control devices and educational materials on birth control. The first strike against the Comstock Law came with the 1936 decision of the Second Circuit Court of Appeals in *US v. One Package*, permitting the importation of birth control devices if provided by a physician. The final leg of the Comstock Law as it regulated birth control came in 1965 in the Supreme Court decision *Griswold v. Connecticut. Griswold* affirmed the right of privacy in seeking medical treatment and information concerning contraception. In so doing, it overturned a Connecticut statute prohibiting the dissemination of such information. The effect of the *Griswold* decision has been far reaching, as it established a right to privacy in marital relations, said to be implicit in the Constitution and in its amendments.

US Law

> *Hazelwood School District v. Kuhlmeier*, 108 StC. 562 (1988) expanded the authority of school officials to regulate student publications.
>
> The Communications Decency Act (7 U.S.C. 223; unconstitutional, Reno v. ACLU, 117 S. Ct. 2329 [1997]) was a first effort to regulate Internet pornography. The anti-indecency section of the law was declared unconstitutional by the Supreme Court of the United States in *Reno v. ACLU*.
>
> The Children's Internet Protection Act (PL 106–554), 2001 (CIPA), established school and library Internet e-rates to limit harm to children. The act mandated mechanisms to protect children from online pornography, which included Internet filtering or other technologies.
>
> The Neighborhood Children's Internet Protection Act (§ 1732, Communications Act of 1934, as amended) (NCIPA) established a requirement for public libraries to filter the Internet in the interest of protecting children from harmful materials. The focus is on e-mail and other technologies now referred to as social media.

UK Law

> The Obscene Publications Act (1959) liberalized publication regulation following the defense of D. H. Lawrence's *Lady Chatterley's Lover*. The 1970s represented a shift in regulatory attitudes from one banning a priori explicit sexual acts to one seeking to regulate the glorification of sex and violence. Special interest groups in the UK, among them the Festival of Light and the National Viewers and Listeners Association, later renamed Mediawatch-UK, sought to pressure government to deny licenses to a variety of films, including *Last Tango in Paris* and *The Exorcist*.
>
> The Protection of Children Act of 1978 bans child pornography. The act does not permit exceptions based on artistic merit.
>
> The Indecent Displays Act of 1981. The advisory group the Broadcasting Standards Council 1989 undertakes to insulate the unsuspecting public from displays of indecent material. Shops are required to shield the public by clearly identifying the business (e.g., sex shop) or placing materials behind counters or separate rooms.

Harmful to Minors

Protection or shielding of minors from sexual activity and from the use of minors in the production of sexually infused material is an important theme in the management of media. The use of minors in the production of sexually explicit material and representations of children either by actors in their majority or by others means is prohibited in a number of polities. As shown previously, legislation and court decisions in a number of countries have sought to address these issues.

Protecting children becomes, then, the justification to censor sexually explicit and other materials. These protections, in turn, have ramifications for libraries, particularly public libraries. For example, in order to qualify for funding under the Schools and Libraries Program of the Universal Service Fund, or E-rate, by schools and libraries, implementation of filtering software on public access computers is required. Filtering is designed to block objectionable material, particularly to minors.

To even suggest that persons under eighteen or sixteen years of age might benefit from erotic experiences has been considered controversial. The Judith Levine book *Harmful to Minors: The Perils of Protecting Children from Sex* (2002) is a case in point. Levine was critical of American legislation and court decisions that limit access to information to minors.

Whether sexual or violent content is or is not harmful to minors, a new standard has emerged. Sexual content, particularly material that portrays children, real or virtual, in sexualized situations, has become inappropriate. That conclusion is recent. The Vladimir Nabokov novel *Lolita*, first published in 1955, is a critically acclaimed work that features a sexual relationship between an adult man and an adolescent girl. The novel and the two film treatments in 1962 and 1997 were subjected to criticism because of the subject matter.

The 1970s was a decade of explicit sex as part of popular culture, exemplified by such films as *Deep Throat* (1972) or *The Devil in Miss Jones* (1973), neither of which undertook to represent actors as children. Perhaps the tipping point came with the 1978 release of *Pretty Baby*. The film is set in an early twentieth-century New Orleans bordello with strongly sexual scenes and frontal nudity, including the adolescent Brooke Shields. By 1980 Brooke Shields was no longer to be shown nude in the film *Blue Lagoon*. Popular culture has therefore shifted, so that by the beginning of the twenty-first century, images of nude children and to a certain degree similar "adult" content in written material is not as acceptable as once it was (see, for example, Altair 2011, 79).

Child pornography, however defined, is considered illegal in many jurisdictions. The US Government, for example, has promoted increased criminalization of child pornography. It provides extensive resources to help define and prosecute such pornography (see, for example, http://www.justice.gov/criminal/ceos/citizensguide/citizensguide_porn.html). The US Justice Department holds that child pornography is not protected under the First Amendment.

The Internet has contributed to the ease of distribution of child (and other) pornography. Therefore the Internet has also contributed to the proliferation of pornography. Librarians and other information professionals have been placed in ambiguous positions when managing potentially pornographic materials, especially those materials that incorporate children. Is the Nabokov novel *Lolita* appropriate in a public library collection? If so, where should it be placed in the collection? Would *Pretty Baby* or *Blue Lagoon* be included in the film collection of a public library in 1980 or 2015? Both technology and popular culture as well as the law have shifted to a point where information ethics may well have changed to permit a more careful consideration of child-related content.

INTELLECTUAL FREEDOM AND SELECTION

Librarians exercise a great deal of authority in determining what materials shall be brought into the library as well as shall remain in the library. Selection and de-selection (a.k.a. weeding) policies are, in the best of all worlds, based on some rational set of criteria developed to meet the needs of the library patron. In a perfect world, resources would be unlimited. Librarians would select everything within the defined scope of the library, as there would be no financial constraints. The perfect library would possess limitless shelf space for the limitless collection. In that perfect library, there would also be an unlimited staff to perform all necessary tasks managing the unlimited library.

In reality, there is no unlimited library. Librarians must make decisions, sometimes difficult decisions that form and maintain the collection. Let us first disabuse ourselves of the idea that the World Wide Web is or can become the unlimited library (Koehler 1999b). There have been a number of initiatives to bring some semblance of order to the web. These initiatives result in the establishment of very rudimentary to quite complex library structures on the web.

The following is but a short list of literature on selection philosophies. It is meant to be suggestive of the range of the literature, rather than be fully representative of that literature:

William Blades, 1881, *Enemies of Books* (London). This work addresses, for the most part, natural causes in the destruction of books. There is one chapter that addresses explicit human causes.

Etienne Gabriel Peignot, 1832, *Essai historique sur la liberté d'écrire chez les Anciens et au Moyen Age; sur la liberté de la presse depuis le quinzième siècle, et sur les moyens de répression dont ces libertés ont été l'objet dans tous les temps; avec beaucoup d'anecdotes et de notes; suivi d'un tableau synoptique de l'état des imprimeries en France, en 1704, 1739, 1810, 1830, et d'une chronologie des lois sur la presse, de 1789 à 1831* (Paris: Crapelet).

Etienne Gabriel Peignot, 1806, *Dictionnaire critique litteraire et bibliographique des principaux livres condamnes au feu, supprimes ou censures* (Paris: A.A. Renouard).

Fernand Drujon, 1879, *Catalogue des ouvrages, écrits et dessins de toute nature poursuivis, supprimès ou condamnès depuis le 21 octobre 1814 jusqu'au 31 juillet 1877* (París: Eduorard Rouveryre).

Fernand Drujon, 1889, *Essai bibliographique sur la destruction volontaire des livres ou Bibliolytie* (Paris: Maison Quantin).

William Henry Hart, (1872) 1969, *Index expurgatorius Anglicanus: Or, a Descriptive Catalogue of the Principal Books Printed or Published in England, Which Have Been Suppressed, or Burnt the Common Hangman, or Censured, or for Which the Authors, Printers, or Publishers Have Been Prosecuted* (New York: B. Franklin).

Diane Ravitch, 2004, *The Language Police: How Pressure Groups Restrict What Students Learn* (New York: Knopf).

Nicholas J. Karolides and Ken Wachsberger, 1999, *100 Banned Books: Censorship Histories of World Literature* (New York: Checkmark Books).

Marjorie Heins, 2001, *Not in Front of the Children: "Indecency," Censorship, and the Innocence of Youth* (New York: Hill and Wang).

Jonathan Rauch, 1993, *Kindly Inquisitors: The New Attacks on Free Thought*. Chicago: University of Chicago Press.

Henry Spencer Ashbee [pseudonym Speculator Morum], 1885, *Biblio-theca arcana seu catalogus librorum penetralium, Being Brief Notices of Books That Have Been Secretly Printed, Prohibited by Law, Seized, Anathematized, Burnt or Bowdlerized* (London: George Redway).

Peter McDonald, 2009, *The Literature Police: Apartheid Censorship and Its Cultural Consequences* (New York: Oxford University Press).

David Bradshaw and Rachael Potter, eds., 2013. *Prudes on the Prowl: Fiction and Obscenity in England, 1850 to the Present Day* (Oxford: Oxford University Press).

There is an equally long history of books published *sub rosa*, or in secret. In the Soviet Union there was a virtual industry, known as *samiz-dat*, engaged in writing, reproducing, and distributing a literature other-wise suppressed by the state.

Censorship in History

Examples of censorship have been found from the very beginning of library history. According to Frederick Kilgour (1998, 96), Pope Gelasius I (d. 497) issued the first list of books banned by the Catholic Church. Justus Lipsius (1607, 77–78), in his *History of Libraries*, quotes John Salis-bury, who wrote:

> The learned and most holy Gregory not only banished astrology from the court; but also as is reported by them of old times, gave to the flames those writings of approved merit, and whatever else the Pala-tine library in Apollo's temple possessed. Preëminent among those were some that seemed designed to reveal to men the will of the celes-tial beings and the oracle of the higher powers.

Lipsius (1607, 78) then adds, "This quotation is worthy of note." Fur-thermore, Lipsius supported translations of books from their original lan-guages to "the common tongue" to facilitate access; a practice Lipsius asserts was followed by Philadelphus, founder of the Library of Alexan-dria. Lipsius endorsed the practice in his day (Lipsius 1607, 39). He (1607, 96–97) also supported the idea that libraries should be appointed as to better support study for purposes of pure ornamentation. He notes Ro-man architectural design and decoration that supported what he felt was appropriate library use—study. For reasons not fully explained, Lipsius (1607, 104–105) would have had libraries decorated with the busts of the writers of the books ensconced in the library. The ability to look on the "counterfeit presentment" of each author somehow added to the experi-ence. He based his argument on Roman practices, where apparently, the admixture of books and busts was not only common but lent to the librar-ies' environment and to the users' enjoyment. Lipsius (1607, 116–7), in closing, notes that libraries should be so located, appointed, and stocked so as to attract scholars to their use as widely as possible.

The son of Henry VIII, Edward VI, sent commissioners to Oxford to root out remnants of Catholicism. One byproduct of that quest for Protestant purity was the destruction of illuminated manuscripts in Oxford University's library. These books were considered "necessarily Popish" (Granniss 1906, 15–16).

Etienne-Gabriel Peignot's (1823) *Manuel du bibliophile* describes itself as a treatise on the selection of books. Peignot also made something of a name for himself as a librarian by labeling pornographic works as immoral. He was also author of a work, published in 1806, of disapproved books: *Dictionnaire critique, littéraire et bibliographique des principeaux livres condamnés au feu, supprimés ou censurés, précédé d'un discours sur ces sortes d'ouvrages.*

Melvil Dewey (1898), perhaps the best known of American librarians held that

> science has as yet devised no instruments delicate enough to record the greater danger to the individual and the State from poison in the great current, which has one to be a mighty flood, of modern reading matter. The most hopeful, and perhaps the only practicable, method of guarding against this serious danger is through the public library, which must now in the last days of this eventful century recognise the gravity of the new responsibility which it cannot shirk.

Science may not have devised a sufficiently delicate instrument, but claims and counter-claims have been made for and against the influence of certain literatures on readers. Whether reading or viewing sexual or violent content predisposes one to antisocial beliefs and behavior has yet to be established or disestablished in the scientific literature. Thus Dewey and his successors must still wait. That said, librarians have in large part reversed the philosophy of a century ago in favor of guarding against the danger of public libraries not providing balanced and uncensored collections to its patrons. The American Library Association, a body Dewey helped found, argues today:

> Intellectual freedom can exist only where two essential conditions are met: first, that all individuals have the right to hold any belief on any subject and to convey their ideas in any form they deem appropriate, and second, that society makes an equal commitment to the right of unrestricted access to information and ideas regardless of the communication medium used, the content of the work, and the viewpoints of both the author and the receiver of information. (ALA Office for Intellectual Freedom 2006, xv)

Perhaps it is true, as the ALA's Office for Intellectual Freedom (2006, 394) holds, that "intellectual freedom is the heart and soul of the profession." Robert Hauptman (1991, 85) has expressed a similar but somewhat more limited sentiment: "In a democracy, intellectual freedom is the most basic of individual rights." Intellectual freedom has not been the heart of the profession for most of the history of libraries. It is only in the twentieth century that intellectual freedom has been equated with democracy and accepted as among the first principles of librarianship by librarians and library associations.

Selection

Selection policies are closely related to censorship and intellectual freedom concerns. We are generally of the belief that selection and its corollary de-selection are essentially positive actions, whereas censorship is generally a negative function. From the perspective of professional ethics, librarians have been given the charge to select and de-select according to the needs and requirements of the abstract concept of libraries as well as to meet the specific needs of their own institutions. At the same time, librarians have the moral imperative to resist pressures to exclude or remove materials based on criteria external to the profession and their specific circumstances.

Most library commentators going back to Richard de Bury (c. 1345) and Sir Thomas Bodley (1603) have addressed the question of which books should or ought to be included in libraries and which should be excluded for particular or general reasons. Censorship can take several forms. The first form is the outright prohibition of a given document by some authority, usually government or church. Expurgation and bowdlerization are less dramatic forms of censorship. Expurgation is the removal of "offending" material, while bowdlerization is the rewriting of that material in a more acceptable format. Less dramatic perhaps, but the ALA's Office for Intellectual Freedom (2006, 148–150) finds it as equally offensive as other forms of censorship.

It is legitimate to exclude or remove materials under certain circumstances, and libraries—particularly public libraries and certain special libraries—properly engage in de-selection or collection weeding as a matter of course. Librarians, then, are charged to ascertain which materials are most appropriate to meet the needs of their patron base and those materials necessary to meet the information demands placed on the institution. Different libraries necessarily have different patron bases and different requirements to meet specific needs.

The thesis that different libraries may have different information requirements is not unique to the twentieth and twenty-first centuries. Generally speaking, however, library theoreticians did not begin to differentiate among libraries as we speak of them today—public, academic, and special—until the beginning of the twentieth century. They did, however, differentiate among them as public and private libraries. Private libraries were privately held collections owned by an individual or small group to meet the library/information needs of that individual or group to the exclusion of others.

A public library, on the other hand, did not include individuals who did not have a proprietary interest in that library. Public libraries were frequently associated with a university, church, government, or other institution. Many public libraries were the result of gifts or bequests of private libraries by particularly benevolent bibliophiles. Richard de Bury and Sir Thomas Bodley willed their libraries to Oxford University. Thomas Jefferson sold his collection to repopulate the Library of Congress after the burning of Washington, DC, in the War of 1812. Gabriel Naudé (1652, 68–69), architect of the Mazarine Library in Paris, saw the purpose and constituency of a public library as "to make it a common comfort for all poor scholars, religious persons, strangers, and for whoever is learned or curious, here to find what is necessary or fit for them."

Access to public libraries could be strictly regulated, restricting the meaning of "public." Sir Thomas Bodley (1603, 93–94), for example, very strictly limited use of the Bodleian in the library's statute:

> Now because it is apparent, that Nothing makes more for the Ease of the Keeper, the Quietness of the Students, the Security of the Books, and the Honour and Dignity of the University, than that we should proceed with some choice Limitation, in the Admission of such Persons, as are to study in the Library; we do utterly reject the Opinion of those, that would have no Exception to no Man's Access: For that a Graunt of so much Scope would not minister Occasion of daily pestering all the Room, with their gazing; and babbling, and trampling up and down, may disturb out of Measure the Endeavours of those that are studious. And therefore not to give way to so great an Inconvenience, we do thus determine and decree; That no Man shall enjoy the Freedom there of Study, but only Doctors and Licentiats of the Three Faculties, Batchelors of Physick, and Law, Batchlors of Arts of two Years standing, and all other Batchelors; if they come thither in their Habits and Hoods, and there demean themselves with Reverence, in giving Place to their Superiors, and in seemly Performance of all other Duties.

The private library of Jules Cardinal Mazarin was developed under the guidance of Gabriel Naudé during the mid-seventeenth century. The collection was scattered during the Fronde but reassembled with support from the Paris Parlement following pleas from Naudé in 1652. The plea, published as *Avis à nosseigneurs de Parlement, sur la veint de la bibliothèque de M. le Cardinal Mazarin* and later republished in English and German, is provided to us from an early nineteenth-century retranslation and incorporated as one of the series edited by John Cotton Dana and Henry W. Kent, *Literature of Libraries in the Seventeenth and Eighteenth Centuries* (published individually by A.C. McClurg and Company in 1906 and republished as volume 6 in a collection by Scarecrow Reprint Corporation in 1967 under its 1652 title *News from France, or A Description of the Library of Cardinal Mazarin before It Was Utterly Ruined, Sent in a Letter from Monsieur*

G. Naudaeus, Keeper of the Publick Library). Naudé pleaded Parlement to reverse its policy to break up the library. He (1652, 66) described the collection and the means by which the library was built and argued that the intellectuals of "Paris, and not Paris only, of France and not France only, but all of Europe, are indebted for a library."

The Bibliothèque Mazarine was to become France's first public library. It was first housed at the Collège des Quatre-Nations. Since 1945 it has been a part of the Institut de France. Today, according to the library's website (http://www.bibliotheque-mazarine.fr/enghisto.htm):

> The Bibliothèque Mazarine's reading room, restored between 1968 and 1974, recreates the surroundings of an important XVIIth century library and, over three hundred and fifty years after its foundation, remains an institution accessible to all, to the merely curious or the learned, nationals and foreigners.

Naudé evidently had a sweeping acquisitions policy. According to Ruth Granniss, (1906, 24–25), Naudé would buy books in gross lots from booksellers without prior inspection and after aggressive bargaining. He would sort them later, remove books duplicated in the collections of his patrons, first Henri de Mesmes and later the Cardinals Richelieu and Mazarin. He would frequently purchase duplicates for his own library.

We can also derive insights into Naudé's acquisition policy by examination of his description of the collection of the Mazarine Library. Naudé (1652, 47–51) gave an inventory of the library when on February 14, 1651, he was required to hand over the library into receivership. That inventory includes:

> Small wing off the main building: theology, law, and philosophy
> First mezzanine: medicine, chemistry, and natural history
> Second mezzanine: "Bibles in all languages . . . Greek, Hebrew, and other Oriental tongues, Latin,—in old and recent editions,—French, Italian, Spanish, German, Flemish, English, Dutch, Polish, Hungarian, Swedish, Finnish, Welsh, Hibernian, and Rutenian" as well as *Bible* commentaries.
>
> Third mezzanine: Varied subjects, books and manuscripts in "Hebrew, Syriac, Samaritan, Ethiopian, Arabic, Greek, Spanish, Provençal, Italian, and Latin."
>
> Main Library, first room: Canon law, politics, miscellaneous subjects
>
> Main Library, second room: Heretical books—Lutheran, Calvanistic, Socinian, others, many in Hebrew, Syriac, Arabian, and Ethiopian.
>
> Gallery, two rooms: ecclesiastic and profane, universal and special history, mathematics, "the Fathers, Scholastics, controversies, sermons, books of the Louvre press, and almost all of the humanities" atlases, maps, charts, volumes of tariffs, travels and voyages.

Thomas Jefferson contributed his library to the United States following the burning of Washington, DC, by the British during the War of 1812. Jefferson's library formed the core of the Library of Congress.

In each century, advice on the selection of books has been offered by a variety of authors. The range of that advice and the target for that advice underwent a subtle change as libraries became more complex and as the types of libraries began to become more differentiated. Richard de Bury, writing in the fourteenth century, discussed his personal collection strategy.

Sir Thomas Bodley, born in 1543, was an avid collector of books and a benefactor of Oxford University. In his *Statutes*, endowing what was to become the Bodleian Library, Bodley did not specify a specific selection strategy. He did authorize the library trustees or overseers to draw on library income to procure better editions of books already in the library, to acquire new titles, and to repair books in the library (Bodley 1609, 85). It needs to be remembered that Bodley was born just as the Gutenberg revolution was unfolding. Many books in the library of Bodley's day were handwritten rather than printed. The quality and accuracy of various copies or editions varied widely.

Bodley's bequest to the Bodleian Library provided an endowment to fund the deposit in the library by the Stationers' Company of books published in England. It did not specify that only books on certain subjects or certain authors were to be acquired. The endowment established an early precedent for the legal deposit of books and other printed materials in national libraries. In his 1612 letter to Thomas James, first keeper of the Bodleian Library, Bodley (1926, 221–222) expressed reservations about the Bodleian collecting plays, almanacs, and other unworthy materials. The "harme the scandal will bring unto the Librarie, when it shal be given out, that we stuffe it full of baggage books." Moreover, "the more I thinke upon it, the more it doth distaste me, that suche kinde of bookes, should be vouchsafed a rowme, in so noble a Librarie." Some plays, but "no more than one in fortie," were worthy enough for the library. Perhaps Bodley's views were more extreme than were those of his peers (Hackel 1997, 121), but they are nevertheless an indicator of prevailing attitudes.

By 1640 the Bodleian's second keeper, John Rous, had relaxed the stringent selection criteria to permit a wider acquisition of what Bodley had termed "riff raff" books. These books, derived from another bequest to the Bodleian Library, did not, however, represent a major revision of the policy.

In the seventeenth century authors would suggest that libraries should restrict their collections to "good books" and avoid "bad books." It must be recalled that by the seventeenth century books had become a good deal more common following the advent of inexpensive papers and, more importantly, the printing press. Commentators and proto-critics had a far more varied list of books in a wider range of languages than they had had before the end of the sixteenth century.

Perhaps the best known of the seventeenth-century library advisors was Gabriel Naudé. Naudé's *Avis pour dresser une bibliothèque présenté à Monseigneur le Président de Mesmes* was first published in 1627, revised and reissued in 1644, and translated in several languages, including Latin, German, and English. The 1950 English translation is the source of the analysis for this book. Naudé, it should be recalled, had been the chief architect of libraries for Cardinals Richelieu and Mazarin. His *Avis* was not written to guide the creation of a minor private library but rather for the establishment of a library to bring glory to the name of Henri de Mesmes, a library that might attract and be used by scholars from throughout Europe.

Naudé (1950, 20–21) instructed that the works of ancient and modern "first and principal authors" be collected. First and "best editions" were preferred. Commentators and interpreters of these important texts should also be included in the collection. These "first and principal authors" should be collected in their original languages together with the best translations.

John Dury (1650b) provided limited advice on library selection policy in his "The Reformed Librarie-Keeper, or Two Copies of Letters Concerning the Place and Office of a Librarie-Keeper." Dury (1650b, 47) advised librarians to maintain correspondence and contacts with "those that are eminent in everie Science" in order to identify new materials and to facilitate trade with those at home and abroad. Dury's instruction to maintain contacts was for the most part limited to members of the academy. Learned doctors of the university were to be asked to meet annually in order to guide library acquisition and to edify librarians on the advances of their particular disciplines. "The Doctors are to declare what they think worthie to be added to the common stock of Learning, each in their Facultie" (Dury 1650b, 52).

Dury (1650b, 54–55) would also call on university faculties to scrutinize the lists of books deposited in the university library by publishers and stationers each year to determine which should be added to the university catalog and which should not. Dury did not advise that books not selected be discarded; rather "becaus there is seldom anie Books wherein there is not somthing useful" (Dury 1650b, 55), these books should be retained, separately cataloged, and placed in an ancillary library.

The 1974 reprint of Charles Sorel's 1671 *De la connoissance des bons livres ou examen de plusiers auteurs* offers four treatises on related library subjects. In the first, "De la connoissance des bons livres de nostre langue," perhaps anticipating the US Supreme Court ruling on obscenity, Sorel (1974, 5–66) argued that before one could recognize "good" books, one needed also to be familiar with "bad books" (Sorel 1974, 2). Sorel

(1974, 5–66) developed several criteria for book selection. The title of the first chapter of his first treatise can be translated as "On the Judgment of Books by Title, Author Name, Their Reputations, and Above All, First Appearances." By "first appearances," Sorel meant both first editions as well as the first time a treatment on a given subject appears in print. A successful book would often spawn the publication of other, inferior works with similar titles and similar subject matter. A successful book would be followed by similarly titled books. Examples Sorel (1974, 7–18) provided include a book partially titled *The Honest Man* (*L'honneste-homme*), which would be followed by others partially titled *The Honest Woman, The Honest Girl, The Honest Boy* (*L'honneste-femme, L'honneste-fille, L'honneste-garçon*), and so on.

Authority was important to Charles Sorel. Certain authors are more important than others, and, necessarily, important authors should be collected to the exclusion of the not-so-important. Sorel preferred classics to modern writers, but he felt that there was a place for modern books that met his stringent criteria in the library. That said, Sorel (1974, 30–31) advised that one ought not exclude unknown authors or unknown works from a library until after one had actually examined the work. Perhaps this sense of magnanimity resulted from the fact that Sorel was author of a number of works of fiction, some of which were comedies.

In a French library, books written in French should be preferred to books written in other languages. Both the originals as well as translations of major works have a place in the French library. Sorel was particularly sensitive to correct writing. Authors should take particular care with grammar and construction.

James Kirkwood, a Protestant clergyman, advocated the development of parochial libraries throughout Scotland. These libraries were needed because of the proliferation of books and the demands of students. Both "Old Books in any Art or Science" and "New Books, so soon as ever they are heard of or seen in the World" were appropriate for inclusion in the parochial libraries (Kirkwood 1699c, 29). These libraries, located in churches and managed by ministers, would create a network to meet the information needs, for:

> although a Student had all the Advantages that can be reasonably expected in one man, yet he cannot Acquire all the Books in the World, that may relate to the Subject he studies; and so he will still be uneasie and suspicious, that there may be something worth his Knowledge in these Books he wants. And it is not to be expected, that any man can advance or improve any Art or Science to a full Degree, till first he have a full and comprehensive Knowledge of that hath been written and discovered of that Subject before him: and therefore compleat and free Libraries are absolutely necessary for the Improving of Arts and Sciences, and for Advancing of Learning amongst us. (Kirkwood 1699c, 26–27)

Kirkwood was an early advocate of union catalogs in part so that each Presbytery could "endeavor to have on Copy at least, of every valuable Book extant in some one Bibliotheck or other within their bonds." (Kirkwood 1699c, 33–34). Further, Kirkwood (1699c, 39–40) advocated collecting "all" books from diverse sources, domestic and foreign, as well as reprinting books, old and new, deemed worthy. He defined it as a duty to provide complete libraries "of the most useful Books" for study and religious instruction (Kirkwood 1699c, 56). In fact, he (1699c, 57) contended that God ordered that knowledge be communicated from previous generations in large part through writings, that libraries by necessity be populated with a diversity of books. Hence library building and maintenance represent a deontological obligation on the Church and its members.

James Kirkwood did not specify what constituted "useful Books" in his first treatise, a failing he acknowledged in his 1703 work titled "A Copy of a Letter Anent a Project, for Erecting a Library in Every Presbytery, or at Least County, in the Highlands." He did so to guide those donors who preferred giving books rather than money (Kirkwood 1703, 62). "Popish" publications may have been dangerous for "the weaker sort of People"; but they were nevertheless needed, because "for the Library of a Divine they are convenient and necessary, that so they may be the more able to deal with the Adversary" (Kirkwood 1703, 63). Libraries and the books in them have as their primary charge proving the "Truth of the Christian Religion" (Kirkwood 1703, 74); and that must be read as Protestantism and more particularly Presbyterianism.

While James Kirkwood did not offer specific guidance on which books are useful and which are not, we may conclude that he supported a wide range of works in the arts and sciences. Moreover, he advocated that diverse perspectives and points of view be a necessary part of the selection process, including Roman Catholic materials to provide balance and depth in the collection. Thus by the end of the seventeenth century selection criteria shifted from an essentially orthodox to a heterodox strategy, if only to counter the misguided.

Selection theory in the eighteenth century underwent subtle change. Jean-Baptiste Cotton des Houssayes, librarian of the Sorbonne, held that the duties and responsibilities of the librarian should include the ability to discriminate between works of merit and those without and to avoid those that are unworthy and exclude those without "well-approved utility" (Cotton des Houssayes 1780, 43). The librarian should employ a selection strategy based on "enlightened economy," guided by "the substantial merits of an able classification" (Cotton des Houssayes 1780, 43–44). A librarian, according to Cotton de Houssayes (1780, 43), should be able "to distinguish, with equal taste and accuracy, original works that are worthy to be proposed as models, from those equivocal productions justly condemned to forgetfulness for their mediocrity."

Johann David Köhler was among the first to publish a bibliography specific for an academic discipline other than theology. Köhler, a historian, logician, and very briefly a university librarian, published the *Scriptorum de bene ordinanda et ornanda bibliotheca* in 1728. The *Scriptorum* is a historiography of key writings in European history. As such, it represents an assessment of major and minor works deemed essential for historical analysis. By implication it represents a list of important manuscripts that an academic library might have collected in the first third of the eighteenth century.

Köhler's (1973) *Anweisung für reisende Gelerte, Bibliothecken, Münz-Cabinette, Antiquitäten-Zimmer, Bilder-Sale, Naturalien-und Kunst-Kammern, u.m.b. mit Ruken zu befeben* is a travelogue for the educated. The first section describes libraries throughout Europe, to include the hours the libraries were open as well as the status of the libraries as "public" or "private." The work suggested that potential patrons familiarize themselves with the collections of those libraries by examination of their published catalogs.

The University of Göttingen, in Saxony, produced a number of eighteenth-century university librarians who advocated the *Universalbibliothek*, or the universal library. The *Universalbibliothek* was conceived as a central repository of the world's knowledge, organized and cataloged along an efficient and effective system to provide easy access to that information. Among those university librarians was Christian Gottlob Heyne. He is considered one of the leading proponents of the *Universalbibliothek* and its organizing and selection principles. He was largely responsible for the major expansion of the University of Göttingen's holdings, particularly of English language materials (Jefcoate 1998).

Drawing perhaps on Naudé's work before him, Heyne supported the collections of materials across all disciplines and, wherever possible, in the language in which they were originally written. According to Graham Jefcoate (1998, 116 [emphasis in the original]), "Heyne did *not* acquire as merely to confirm that his acquisition policy was effective." He eschewed foreign materials with purely local value. Moreover, Heyne acquired materials of scholarly merit and tended to avoid those of a more popular nature. Instead, he "was able to show how comprehensive coverage of subject fields of interest to eighteenth-century research institution could be attained." (Jefcoate 1998, 116).

In the late nineteenth century collection theory had shifted somewhat. Writing for the bibliophile and the private library maker, Jules Richard (1883, 50–51) noted in a chapter of his book *L'art de former une bibliothèque*, titled "Choix des livres," or the "Choice of Books," that a physician and a lawyer would collect books that reflect their respective professions. Beyond individual needs and tastes, certain books were essential for the bibliophile's collection. And he argued further that if certain books were incorporated in a library, that alone was an indicator of inappropriate

tastes. Given that, Richard held, bibliophiles and bibliomanes have varying tastes and interests

Melvil Dewey (1989, 5), writing in 1876, held that "only the best books
on the best subjects" are candidates for library collections. If only the best
books on the best subjects are to be collected, what are the "best subjects"
and what criteria should be used to determine the "best books"?

In the late nineteenth and early twentieth centuries American public
libraries were perceived to be bastions of middle-class morality and were
expected to provide edification and instruction on appropriate social
mores. While there was a growing attitude that public libraries should
reflect those values, specific collection strategies were centered on such
issues as the desirability of including romance novels in the collection
(Garrison 1972/1973). Earlier in their history, public libraries had to determine whether works of fiction, comedies, and poetry were appropriate
literary genres for collection.

CONCLUSION

The International Federation of Library Associations and Institutions
(IFLA) and a not insignificant number of national library associations,
among them the American Library Association (ALA) and the Canadian
Library Association (CLA), have taken strong positions in opposition to
various forms of censorship and information control as they apply to
libraries. As we have seen, the positions taken by these library associations are not necessarily consistent with national policies, at least as they
apply to specific areas of censorship and information control.

The librarian's concern with freedom of expression, censorship, and
other forms of information control are natural corollaries to S. R. Ranganathan's five laws. Freedom of expression provides the librarian and the
patron, through books and other vehicles, with the means to fulfill information needs. The control of information has inhibiting influences on the
first, second, and third laws. Yet there are restrictions on information
dissemination that are generally accepted or imbued in law and practice.
In recent years we have become more concerned with "speech that insults," particularly speech that insults racial, religious, and ethnic groups.
Some of these are considered in chapter 11. Thus what we consider protected speech may be undergoing redefinition, a redefinition reflected by
Ranganathan's fifth law.

SIX

Libraries and Democracy

Libraries, which are the quintessential manifestations of the common good, have always favored order and society over individualism.

—Michael Gorman (2003, 139)

In times of national stress, as at present, when the call is for national unity, the screws are turned tighter on freedom of thinking.

—Stanley Kunitz (1939, 209)

The modern public library in large measure represents the need of democracy for an enlightened electorate, and its history records its adaptation to changing social requirements.

—Jesse Shera (1949)

INTRODUCTION

Are libraries either necessary or sufficient causes of democracy? Do libraries promote or sustain democracy and democratic institutions? To put the question in a somewhat different way, can democracy arise in societies that either do not support a library tradition or fail to support what libraries they have? And can libraries prosper or even exist in non-democratic societies? Are libraries catalysts for democracy?

A second related question would be, if in fact libraries can and do exist in non-democratic societies, do the libraries in those societies help support or undermine non-democratic institutions? An easy and almost off-handed answer might be to note that libraries have been a part of the mix of social institutions for at least five thousand years. Yet perhaps with the exception of the Greek city-states, democratic institutions date only to the late eighteenth century.

The Enlightenment marked an important watershed for the development of libraries because of its focus on science and learning (Bivens-Tatum 2012). Adherents of the Enlightenment were not by any means democratic. Peter the Great and later Catherine the Great of Russia, for example, undertook to bring learning to Russia. To promote that end, Catherine purchased the libraries of Denis Diderot, Voltaire, and others (Gorbatov 2006). Autocrats though they were, both Peter I and Catherine II helped move Russia into the eighteenth and early nineteenth centuries.

Third, Liz Greenhalgh and Ken Worpole (1995, 22–23) express the concern that in the post-modern environment, representative democracy may be in decline. Political scientists have analyzed what we understand to be representative democracy. They have offered a wide range of descriptions and sometimes prescriptions for the preservation of democracy. These are discussed further below, but to echo Greenhalgh and Worpole, there is evidence that representative democracy may be threatened in a variety of ways, ranging from the domination of economic interests over executive and legislative branches to the replacement of democratic institutions with more autocratic ones. The library in the democratic society has been defined as one of many institutional impediments to the erosion of democracy.

The fact of the matter is that libraries are no more the catalysts of democracy than are any other conservative social institution: the family, the church, the state, the academy. Although I have taken Michael Gorman (2003, 139) out of context above, his statement that "libraries, which are the quintessential manifestations of the common good, have always favored order and society over individualism" suggests that libraries are inherently conservative institutions and that, in their "preference" for order over individualism, libraries are at best inherently a-democratic and at worst anti-democratic.

At the same time, as Nancy Kranich (2001) has argued, an informed citizenry is more likely to be a participatory citizenry. By creating an informed citizenry, the civic culture, and therefore democracy will be strengthened. Whitney Seymour (1981) argues for an interdependent relationship between libraries and emergent as well as mature democracies. According to Stephen Schechter (1990), in democratic societies libraries are vehicles for civic education. And public libraries are ubiquitous in democratic societies (Hafner and Sterling-Folker 1993). A recent UK report by the Department of Media, Culture and Sport (2014, 3) asserts: "The library does more than simply loan books. It underpins every community."

More accurately, libraries are mirrors of the societies in which they are found. A society that is democratic will support libraries that support democratic society. The more autocratic, authoritarian, or totalitarian the society, the more autocratic, authoritarian, or totalitarian are its libraries. Nadezhda K. Krupskaya, the architect of the Soviet library system, defined and designed libraries that supported socialism and the Soviet system. Indeed, the Soviet classification system (BBK) was drafted by communist librarians to support Marxism-Leninism. No doubt Krupskaya would have defined Marxist-Leninist libraries as the "quintessential manifestations of the common good." No doubt Nadezhda Krupskaya would have seen "the common good" in a very different light than does Michael Gorman.

PUBLIC SPACE, AND SOCIAL ROLE

If libraries support the common good, however defined, and if libraries are reflections of the society in which they arise, they may also become more or less catalysts for or guarantors of democracy as their missions are redefined. Colleen Alstad and Ann Curry (2003) assert:

> The traditional mission of the public library—supporting the self-education of the citizenry in order that they may become fully participating members in a democratic society—has been devalued of late in favour of popularizing the library to attract more users. This shift has led to an emphasis on entertainment and marketing, and an abandonment of what many feel is the true purpose of a library. Loss of democratic tradition has simultaneously occurred on another front: civic space which allows for public assembly and discourse has disappeared or been downgraded into places for leisure and recreation rather than politics, with a concomitant decline in the quality of public discourse as citizens increasingly depend on profit-driven mass media for their "opinions."

If we read Alstad and Curry correctly, the shift in emphasis from self-education to entertainment in public libraries undermines the traditional democratizing and socializing role of the library. Moreover, they perceive that North American civil authorities have begun to restrict civic spaces and increase private spaces along a broad spectrum of services and amenities, a process that can be illustrated by a constriction of the town square and the advance of the shopping mall. If Alstad and Curry are right, public libraries in democratic societies may well be abdicating their civic function to curry favor and build library traffic.

Andrew Ó Baoill (2000) analyzes the introduction of the web into the civic debate and expressly as a factor in defining public space. He accepts a definition of "public space" as that civic arena outside or beyond the control of other social institutions—government, church, and even the economy. Ó Baoill (2000) argues that cyberspace might once have been public space, but it can no longer so qualify. Ó Baoill's analysis of cyberspace could apply equally to library space.

The public library may continue to serve as "an arena of common or collective interest," but is it public space? For Jürgen Habermas (1995), the public sphere is an arena of common or collective interest. By the strictest definition of public library and public space, the public library ceased to be public space once it became a rate-based publicly governed institution. That process of "shifting" the subscription library to the state had its beginnings in the mid-nineteenth century in the United Kingdom and the United States and expanded throughout Europe and North America.

Nancy Kranich (2001) is representative of those who seek to protect and project the role of the public library in the public sphere. Alstad and Curry (2003) represent the view that public libraries no longer seek to occupy public space. Perhaps the public library has not entirely abdicated its civic functions. Recognizing the role of the state in the support and governance of public libraries, we can argue that the ideal public library should be "public space-like." Public libraries are not the sine qua non of democracy, but neither have they fully abdicated their place in the civic and public spaces.

In her biography of Ruth Brown, Louise Robbins (2000) explores structural discrimination in US public libraries before the *Brown v. Board of Education* Supreme Court decision. Libraries, schools, and other public institutions excluded individuals of color or shunted them to "separate but equal" facilities that were clearly separate but also clearly unequal. The *Brown* decision may have removed the formal legal justification for discrimination against minorities, but it did not erase with the same ease the informal social instruments of discrimination. The *Brown* decision was more than fifty years ago, yet vestiges of discrimination based on race still remain in American society.

To their credit, most US public libraries adapted to the new social and legal realities. And to their credit, most US public libraries have expanded their vision to include women, children, the disabled, as well as minorities as legitimate and welcomed patrons. That said, however, we must also remember that this tolerance and this acceptance is recent.

DEMOCRACY DEFINED

In a speech before the House of Commons on November 11, 1947, Winston Churchill offered these words: "Indeed, it has been said that democracy is the worst form of government except all those other forms that have been tried from time to time." Churchill's views of democracy followed those of an earlier statesman. Federalist Paper 51 is signed by Publius but is usually attributed to James Madison and sometimes to Alexander Hamilton. Writing in 1788, Publius asserted:

> But what is government itself, but the greatest of all reflections on human nature? If men were angels, no government would be necessary. If angels were to govern men, neither external nor internal controls on government would be necessary. In framing a government which is to be administered by men over men, the great difficulty lies in this: you must first enable the government to control the governed; and in the next place oblige it to control itself. A dependence on the people is, no doubt, the primary control on the government; but experience has taught mankind the necessity of auxiliary precautions.

A polity is considered democratic where a defined population group participates directly in the legislative process. How the population is defined may vary and has varied widely. The electorate may be defined by any number of characteristics. The criteria to include or exclude members of the electorate include some combination of citizenship, residency, age, gender, race, religion, ethnicity, wealth, hereditary status, and education.

Democracy is sometimes confused with government form. A republic is defined as a polity where the population selects both the legislative and executive/administrative elites, usually for fixed terms. A monarchy is a political system where the executive leadership has a de jure hereditary basis. A constitutional monarchy exists where the powers of the hereditary leadership are circumscribed to a greater or lesser degree and where the legislature has some basis of popular representation. An oligarchy exists where a specific class of the population selects the chief executive officers from within itself or from other classes. Thus both the United Kingdom and the United States are considered democracies; but one is a monarchy and the other a republic. That said, neither is a democracy in the purest sense of the concept. They are not democracies because the electorate does not usually participate directly in the decision-making and law-making processes. These responsibilities are reserved for legislatures and bureaucracies.

It might be argued that countries like the United States and the United Kingdom are democracy-like because the legislatures are elected directly by a widely defined electorate. Yet this is not or has not always been so. Until 1913 and passage of the Seventeenth Amendment to the Constitution, US senators were elected by state legislatures. The president is not elected directly by popular vote but by the Electoral College. In the United Kingdom, the House of Lords, a body of dwindling importance, has a hereditary basis for participation.

For a political system to function effectively, it is assumed that the electorate, however established, must be sufficiently knowledgeable to make informed and intelligent decisions. It is further assumed that political leadership, however chosen, must be sufficiently mature and knowledgeable to properly perform the duties of office. For example, in the United States for most of its history, twenty-one was accepted as the minimum age of voting, a requirement lowered to eighteen by the Twenty-Sixth Amendment to the Constitution, adopted in 1971. One must be twenty-five to be elected to the House of Representatives (article I, section 2); the Senate, thirty (article I, section 3); and president, thirty-five (article II, section 1). The Fifteenth Amendment, adopted in 1870, prohibits denial of rights of citizenship, including voting rights, based on race; while the Nineteenth Amendment, adopted in 1920, expands voting rights based on gender. Thus in the United States and in most other countries, there are structural limits on the exercise of the basic mechanism of democracy—the franchise.

The ability of some segment of the population to participate in the selection of political elites is a necessary but insufficient condition of democracy. Inherent in democracy is some degree of choice based on informed and unbiased decision making. Even, however, in the most open of societies, there has always been some degree of control exercised over the complete and open access to information. Openness can be considered as a matter of degrees. Some societies permit their citizens greater or lesser access to information and to that information interpreted by others. The ability to express opinion is also an important function, yet it too is regulated to one degree or another in all societies.

Democracy and the Individual

We recognize that the basis of Western society since the Renaissance has been an increasing emphasis of the place of the individual as the primary building block of society. The individual replaced the community, corporate bodies, the group, and the state in the theory of the liberal democracy. For the individual to become the center of civic order, other institutions had to recede. These include the state, the church, and even the family. In their extremes, both the fascist and communist impulses were reactions to the perceived chaotic nature of individualist democracy and a return to more autocratic forms of governance.

Even at the beginning of the twenty-first century there are vestiges of divine right monarchy, not to mention the remnants of class-based or caste-based society in otherwise democratic societies. To borrow terms of the ancien régime, we have moved from an elitism based on *noblesse de l'epée* and *de la robe* to a *noblesse de la bourse*. Our new elites are no longer barons and dukes but CEOs and CFOs. Thomas Friedman (2005, 46), in his popular analysis of the "flattening" of the world, alludes to changes to the role of the individual in a rapidly changing economic environment, an environment driven by information systems.

Political scientists recognize that, while we may maintain the individual as the essential building block of the democratic society, societies (democratic or otherwise) have their basis in group dynamics. Just how societies are organized along which groups is a matter of theoretical concern. Some have argued that liberal democracies are organized along pluralistic lines. Pluralism suggests society constructed in plastic and fluid configurations where individuals shift group allegiances according to their particular concerns, beliefs, and interests. A corporatist society is one in which individual and therefore group interests are unchanging. The group negotiates in the interests of its members. In pluralist and corporatist societies, government serves to negotiate among the competing interests. The primary difference between pluralist and corporatist structures is that in pluralist societies, group membership changes as individual interests change. In a corporatist society, individuals remain members of their defining group and accept group interests over their own.

John Rawls (1993) theorizes that government should serve as a neutral arbiter of the interests of various groups in society. Government serves to mediate interests and definitions of the "good" to establish the "common good." According to Rawls, justice can be prioritized along two principles: (1) all individuals have basic rights and the right to claim those rights; and (2) while social and economic inequalities exist, they are acceptable only when all have equal rights to compete for preferential status, and the underprivileged should be disproportionately benefited. Rawls's conception of the role of government—as arbiter—is a liberal democratic one, one that can function in either a pluralistic or corporatist environment.

Libraries and Rights

Can or have libraries excluded individuals from some or all library services based on membership in some class or group? Clearly the answer is yes; libraries have and continue to base access to their services in whole or in part on class or group membership. Is this anti-democratic? Here, the answer is less unequivocal. Most public libraries have a geographic criterion for full use of library services. Other types of libraries have very explicit criteria for inclusion on the authorized users list.

We accept as a general rule that academic and special libraries may narrow significantly the class or group of individuals who may have any access to their collections. Privilege is propriety. Whether public libraries can or should exclude individuals is all together another matter. Over the history of the United States, the criteria for access to public libraries have broadened. Only subscribers were permitted to use subscription libraries. With the introduction of the rate-based library movement in the 1850s, access was expanded to adult white males, including those of "lesser means." Libraries also began to open their doors to women and children. Almost all libraries in the United States were segregated on the basis of race. As Louise Robbins has demonstrated so well for us, segregation on the basis of race was to continue as an accepted practice well into the middle of the twentieth century.

Rights of access have been expanded in US public libraries, to include others considered undesirable. Most recently, courts have required public libraries to admit the homeless and those who are perceived to be "eccentric."

LIBRARIES IN SOCIETY

Public libraries now solicit the patronage of populations heretofore excluded or disenfranchised. Kathleen de la Peña McCook (2000, 5) writes that libraries build communities. Community, McCook acknowledges, is a broad term. She dedicates her first chapter to help us understand her use of the term. Her conception of community is congruent with the definition of *public sphere*, usually an extra-governmental definition of cooperative group activity. She notes concepts of the loss of social place, of a defined physical space for community in the United States as cities have been redefined. Of course, community needs to be defined solely as a physical space, as McCook acknowledges, citing Amitai Etzioni's (1993) work. We recognize that in the Internet environment, virtual community is virtual reality. It is now possible, perhaps even desirable, to find community within computer games while avoiding human contact in either physical or online space (Chako 2008, 10).

Libraries as Agents in a Democracy

Libraries in democratic societies are widely described as agents for the maintenance and, if you will, maintenance of democracy. Public libraries have been described as important resources of community information (Durrance et al. 2001, 49). Libraries have provided their patrons with local information, government information, employment resources, and assistance for immigrants. Furthermore, libraries help "incubate" community interaction (Durrance et al. 2001).

Libraries as Catalysts for Democracy

Many librarians want to believe that libraries are engines of democracy. Unfortunately, reality belies the belief. Libraries existed long before democracy was conceived. Libraries have existed in the most totalitarian and authoritarian of states as well as in the most democratic of states. Consider that Gabriel Naudé, said by many to be the father of library science, was a monarchist. Mao Zedong, architect of Chinese communism, was employed briefly as an assistant librarian. Nadezhda K. Krupskaya, architect of Soviet and children's librarianship, was as a Bolshevik far more collectivist than individualist in philosophy. She was also Lenin's wife. Her concern for children and the social utility of libraries is reflected in the following:

> Children spend the greater part of their time outside the school. Here they come under the influence of the street and frequently of hostile hooligan elements. Questions concerning the organisation of the children's out-of-school hours, the Young Pioneer movement, the provision of libraries and workshops and social work for the children, are of tremendous importance. (2002)

In arguing for a democratic role for libraries in 1938, the president of the California Library Association, Sydney Mitchell (1939, 209), noted in contrast that "in the totalitarian state the librarian becomes merely an agency for propaganda, for the dissemination of such information as the authorities care to pass on." Mitchell most certainly was not arguing that libraries are essentially totalitarian. He was responding in opposition to national efforts to censor and suppress John Steinbeck's *The Grapes of Wrath*.

E-DEMOCRACY

The Internet has brought opportunities to the public and political arenas not previously possible. Some commentators suggest that the Internet creates a new public sphere, one in which a more open and participatory political process becomes possible. In a work published just after the creation of the World Wide Web, John Hartley (1992) suggested that the news media, particularly in the use of pictures, encourages a widening of the public sphere. If photojournalism, television, and other forms of graphic news delivery contribute to the creation of a public sphere, then the web must have a further broadening effect. This impact might serve to reverse the decline of the public sphere. The decline is a process that, according to Jürgen Habermas (1989), began in the twentieth century after a beginning in the seventeenth century.

There is an interesting critique of the Habermas political sphere thesis that arises from feminist literature. Rather than the creation of a generalized public sphere, limited, partial, or counter-public spheres may exist or co-exist with other public spheres (Felski 1989, 167). Felski's argument can be expanded to imply an atomized e-structure to politics, one made up of competing virtual homogeneous groups or single-issue groups that give rise to a corporatist negotiation for social importance and power. These groups need not be originally organized as political entities. Yet their very existence, made cohesive across electronic networks, creates at a minimum the potential for influencing the political process. Indeed, as Paul Keen (1999) demonstrates, new forms of communication, whether they arise from an introduced technology or from changing public tastes, contribute to the definition and re-definitions of public discourse and therefore the public sphere.

Samantha Fleming (2002) concludes that information and communication technologies (ICTs) can contribute to the process of democratization in developing countries, more specifically in South Africa. Fleming (2002, 2), drawing on the work of Burt and Taylor (2001), argues that ICTs are not value-neutral and that they draw on the social conditions where they are applied. Given the political and social environment of South Africa, the use of ICTs is yet another means for the social and political activist to participate in the appropriate arenas. Fleming (2002, 2, emphasis in the original) very specifically states, *"technology is just a tool."*

Technology may be just a tool; but that tool, to be used effectively, must be available to a reasonable proportion of the population. Davison et al. (2000, 1) argue that ICTs play but a small role in the lives of most in developing countries: "The sad reality is that the participation of many developing countries in the global information society remains insignificant." By implication, the use of ICTs in developing societies less open than contemporary South Africa may not be tools for the development of democracy but more for social control.

There is ample evidence that polities like Cuba or the People's Republic of China utilize ICTs as mechanisms for social control. Moreover, "technological leapfrogging" is as yet not particularly well understood, and the implications for developing societies are unknown. Technological leapfrogging is the replacement of an old application with a completely new one (for example, shifting from a society with virtually no telephony to one that is cell phone saturated without passing through the intermediate "stage" of the use of landline-based telephony).

Mohsen Kahani (2005) discusses e-voting in Iran. While Iran could not be described as one of the most democratic of societies, an ICT application for e-voting has been adapted effectively in that society. It would seem, however, that in polities where choices are limited among candidates, it matters little at least in the short term what format the ballot takes. The United States may offer the counter-case to this argument. The ballot format and the interpretation of the votes cast in Florida during the presidential election in 2000 may have been the determining variable in the outcome of the national election where George W. Bush was determined to have won Florida's electoral votes and therefore the presidency by the very slimmest of margins.

Simon Rogerson and Robert Beckett (2003) argue that there are global individual rights based in large part on a reading of the United Nations Declaration of Human Rights. All too often these rights are observed in the breach. These rights support the development of democracy.

CONCLUSION

As compelling as the argument appears, libraries in and of themselves are not engines of democracy. Libraries are institutions that support the status quo, whatever that status quo might be. That said, in democratic societies libraries underpin the democratic character of that society. To support the status quo in democratic societies, it is important to support the institutions that support democracy. This includes libraries.

Therefore, insofar as supporting democratic society has an ethical imperative, supporting libraries in a democratic society also has an ethical imperative.

SEVEN

Intellectual Property, Copyright, and Fair Use

INTRODUCTION

Ideas and treatment of intellectual property differ over time and by country. These traditions and current approaches reflect both the legal and ethical environments in those countries and at the international level. Western notions of intellectual property and fair use have undergone an interesting and progressive change over the centuries. Three similar applications of intellectual property doctrine have resulted from a mix of judicial systems and cultural imperatives. There are important differences among the British, American, and European Continental practices. These three approaches together with the ethical and legal thinking elsewhere in the world have undergone something of a convergence in the latter part of the twentieth century. This convergence is based in part on the overwhelming dominance of American information industries, particularly in the entertainment segment and in larger part because of the Berne Convention,[1] the World Intellectual Property Organization (WIPO) and the Word Trade Organization (WTO).

Intellectual property doctrine is not an idée fixe. Definitions of intellectual property vary from culture to culture and from time to time. Despite efforts to codify and standardize intellectual property doctrine at the international (e.g., the Berne Convention or World Intellectual Property Organization) and at the national levels (e.g., UK Copyright Designs and Patents Act of 1988 or US Digital Millennium Copyright Act of 1998), national jurisprudence has varied and will continue to do so. Moreover, many in the informing professions are of the belief that the current state of intellectual property regulation is more restrictive than the history of intellectual property rights should allow simply on the grounds of precedent. Indeed, the rigidity of intellectual property regulation on the one hand may, in fact, serve as a damper for future creative processes and inhibit the distribution of important and sometimes life-saving technologies and know-how. Yet the very variability of intellectual property law from one jurisdiction to another creates an environment of uncertainty in practice and opinion for the library practitioner and ethicist. Peter Yu (2006) makes an interesting case that national intellectual property regimes may be less convergent than one might think. He documents five "disharmonizing trends" and argues for care in reaching "harmonizing" conclusions.

Recent developments in copyright law have been described as a commodification of information. These trends have raised concerns among those who are concerned with the historical development of intellectual rights, those concerned with comparative intellectual rights and legal practices, and those concerned with future trends in the development of intellectual property (e.g., Vaidhyanathan 2001; Bollier 2002; Lessig 2002; Wong and Dutfield 2010; Shah, Warsh, and Kesselheim 2013). These concerns are often expressed in terms of ethics or jurisprudence, cultural sociology, or the impact of intellectual property regimes on the development of new ideas in a social milieu.

The online and digital environments have brought to intellectual property issues greater focus and attention. These two interrelated technologies support a range of practices that may or may not be legal and/or ethical. Certainly the entrepreneurial and economic environments in which information is created, transmitted, consumed, transformed, retransmitted, and re-consumed has undergone changes since the advent of online information access and particularly since the advent of the World Wide Web in 1991. They have also created another arena of concern: digital rights (or restrictions) management (DRM). DRM has more to do with technical rather than legal or ethical intellectual property management, but it does raise important use and access concerns for information professionals.

Intellectual property covers three general areas of concern: copyright; patents; and trademarks, service marks, and the like. Intellectual property may also incorporate practices and processes as well as trade secrets (such as the famed original recipe for Coca-Cola). All intellectual property issues are of concern to informing professionals. Copyright and fair use and other exceptions to copyright are probably of greater day-to-day interest to librarians, but patents, service marks, and trade secrets are also matters of interest to the practice. Intellectual property practice is also concerned with the appropriate use by others—in a word, fair use. What are the rights and responsibilities of those who use or apply the intellectual property of others?

A more fundamental set of questions concerns what is precisely "intellectual property." If indeed, intellectual property exists, whose property is it? How does intellectual property come to be created? How should it be protected, and how strict should that protection be? When does the protection cease?

The short answers to these questions are: "It depends." It depends on the kind of intellectual property—copyrightable, patentable, or trade-mark-able. It depends on place and context. It depends on "when." And it depends on practice. When is a "knowledge product" protected and when is it not (see e.g., Drassinower 2003/2004)? And how has practice evolved over time?

The current practice, one that rather rigidly protects the rights of the intellectual property owner over those of the user and creator, is of recent etiology. Current practice, as defined by the Berne Convention and maintained by the World Intellectual Property Organization, is a North American and European twentieth-century phenomenon. A very different culture existed in Europe and North America before the beginning of the eighteenth century, one that persists to some degree in other parts of the world and is reflected in the writings of the proponents of the information common today.

These rather rigid interpretations of intellectual property rights may be balanced by other considerations. Just as the British House of Lords ruled in 1774, in *Donaldson v. Beckett*, statutory law may supersede common law, but it does not replace a common law over which the statute had no effect. While the Berne Convention, WIPO, WTO, and national intellectual property legislation have certainly changed the face of the law, there may be areas where this statutory and treaty blanket have not yet touched. Newman and Koehler (2004) assert, for example:

> We are concerned with an essentially European concept, that of the *Moral Rights of the Author*. These rights are contrasted with his or her legal rights. The "Moral Rights of the Author" are rights associated with but separate from copyright. The legal concept "copyright" is defined in international law by the Berne Convention on Copyright, and has its most recent incarnation in UK law as the Copyright Designs and Patents Act of 1988 and in US law as the Digital Millennium Copyright Act of 1998. The Moral Rights of the Author originate in French civil law's distinction between the author's inalienable moral rights over his work (*droits moraux d'auteur*) and his separate, saleable economic rights. While the economic rights correlate well to the Anglo-American common-law systems' concept of copyright, the moral rights are quite different.
>
> Where copyright is often justified as a fit reward for the authors' labors and an incentive to further creation, the moral rights are intended to protect the natural bond between an author and his artistic creation, a bond analogous to that between parent and child. In this vision the protection of the author's quasi-sacred connection to his work is of paramount importance: no public interest in free use of the work, or publishers' interest in its economic exploitation can challenge

it. Great works enrich the soul of mankind, but even a minor work is still the author's spiritual child, and thus worthy of respect.

A SHORT HISTORY

The history of intellectual property management is complex and has undergone change. The following sections provide a brief history of that process.

Before Gutenberg

Prior to the invention of printing, manuscript books could be reproduced only through the laborious process of copying text by hand. In the first centuries BCE and CE, library historians inform us that major libraries, including the Library at Alexandria, enhanced and expanded their collections through state-sponsored taking and copying of any text that fell within their sphere. Lionel Casson (2001, 77) writes that books were freely copied in Rome: "Once an author had sent out his gift and presentation copies, his book was, so to speak, in the public domain, anyone could make a copy of it." These same practices continued into the sixteenth century as monasteries copied and recopied the Greek, Roman, and church classics.

Before Copyright

Sixteenth- and seventeenth-century European intellectual property theory and practice differed greatly from the contemporary. Generally speaking, intellectual property was not nearly so closely guarded as an individual proprietary right but rather was seen as an expression of the collective social process (Hesse 1996). Outright borrowing of words without attribution was not uncommon; indeed, as Ann Blair (2003) reports, authors were not inhibited from literally cutting text from a work by another and literally pasting that material into their own.

The tale of Miguel de Cervantes Saavedra and his second volume of *Don Quixote de la Mancha* offers a fascinating look at an intellectual environment without copyright protection for authors. *Don Quixote* as written by Cervantes was published in two parts, volume one in 1605 and volume two in 1615. Cervantes is reputed to have written the *Quixote* sequel to counter the impact of an "unauthorized" sequel by perhaps Alonzo Fernández de Avellaneda writing under the pseudonym Jerónimo de Pasamonte (Percas de Ponseti 2002[2]). Cervantes and his intellectual property, the book as well as the character of Don Quixote, were unprotected in law. Cervantes's only recourse to counter the Avellaneda/Pasamonte "misappropriation" was to write his own second volume.

Copyright

The British Statute of Anne of 1710 is the first formal copyright law. The US Constitution, adopted in 1789, raises intellectual property protection to a higher plane. Under article I, section 8, Congress is empowered to legislate copyright and patent protection, "to promote the Progress of Science and useful Arts, by securing for limited Times to Authors and Inventors the exclusive Right to their respective Writings and Discoveries." Both in the United States and in other countries, the definitions of "limited Times" and "exclusive Right" have been extended and more restrictively defined from the eighteenth century to the present, often to the advantage of the rights holder and to the detriment of those seeking exception to those rights.

After the Press

In the mid-fifteenth century Gutenberg and those who followed radically changed that process by significantly easing the creation of copies and through printing copies that were for the most part exact. Printing reduced both the cost of reproduction and the errors inherent in hand reproduction.

Before copyright, license and copy-tax regulated the publication of books (Edwards 1859 ii, 577–602). License and copy-tax served two distinct purposes. The first was censorship. The second was to ensure the deposit of books published in a country in one or more designed depository libraries. According to William Patry (1994), Venice was perhaps the first jurisdiction to license printing. Johannes de Spira was granted a Venetian license in 1469 that gave him a monopoly to print certain works of Pliny and Cicero; both works would have then been well within our conception of public domain. By 1517 Venice began adopting a series of printing patents and licenses. Indeed Patry (1994, 12) points out that the 1545 Decree of the Council of Ten "prohibited publication of an author's work without proof of the author's permission." Patry (1994) also informs us that the German states had begun to protect intellectual property; in 1528 the widow of Albrecht Dürer received the right to the exclusive publication of Dürer's engravings, a right she had to protect in 1532. Patry (1994) quotes Dürer's warning to copyright pirates:

> Hold! You crafty ones, strangers to work, and pilferers of other men's brains. Think not rashly to lay your thievish hands upon my works. Beware! Know you not that I have a grant from the most glorious Emperor Maximillian, that not one throughout the imperial dominion shall be allowed to print or sell fictitious imitations of these engravings? Listen! And bear in mind that if you do so, through spite or through covetousness, not only will your goods be confiscated, but your bodies also placed in mortal danger.

Again according to Patry (1994), the first printing patent granted in England was to William Facques. Henry VII granted Facques the exclusive right to print official documents in 1504. A second patent was issued to Richard Pynson in 1518. In 1538 Henry VIII required that all new books seeking publication be approved by the Privy Council, a policy that persisted until 1694.

Book licenses were initiated in Aragon under Felipe II in 1558 (Moll 1994) and were extended throughout Spain. The Consejo de Castilla began licensing books in 1716 in all Spanish kingdoms except in Navarra during the reign of Felipe V (Garcia Cuadrado 2001, 100–102). In Spain as well as in the rest of Europe, licenses were a means of controlling publications and of imposing censorship. Licenses were withheld until offending and erroneous texts were corrected. Both the Crown and the Church participated in censorship and in the granting of "imprimatur" to publishers.

Sir Thomas Bodley introduced the informal book deposit in England in the early seventeenth century. Bodley provided funds for books published in England to be sent to Oxford University. Bodley's bequest was, of course, not a formal act of government but the wishes of a private individual. Before Bodley, Edwards (1859 ii, 584) informs us, books were sent to the licensing agency once they were published. It was in the reign of Charles II that English stationers were first formally required to make deposits with the "Keeper of His Majesty's Library" and at Oxford and Cambridge (Edwards 1859 ii, 584).

The Star Chamber Decrees of 1566, 1586, and 1637, and the Licensing Act of 1662 were the beginnings of English law to formally regulate publishing (Patterson 1968, 5). The Statute of Anne of 1710 first introduced copyright, but it also expanded the depositary obligations of book publishers to nine copies of books, of which one was to be placed in Scotland as well.

The Statute of Anne replaced a system of licenses and printing patents (Patterson 1968, 4–19). The term "copy right," according to Lyman Patterson (1968, 4), was not part of the publishers' lexicon until 1701. The legislated concept of copyright replaced common law "stationer's copy" beginning in 1710. The statute granted rights to authors and to those to whom authors assigned their right:

> Whereas Printers, Booksellers, and other Persons, have of late frequently taken the Liberty of Printing, Reprinting, and Publishing, or causing to be Printed, Reprinted, and Published Books, and other Writings, without the Consent of the Authors or Proprietors of such Books and Writings, to their very great Detriment, and too often to the Ruin of them and their Families: For Preventing therefore such Practices for the future, and for the Encouragement of Learned Men to Compose and Write useful Books . . .

. . . the Author of any Book or Books already Printed, who hath not Transferred to any other the Copy or Copies of such Book or Books, Share or Shares thereof, or the Bookseller or Booksellers, Printer or Printers, or other Person or Persons, who hath or have Purchased or Acquired the Copy or Copies of any Book or Books, in order to Print or Reprint the same, shall have the sole Right and Liberty of Printing such Book and Books for the Term of One and twenty Years, to Commence from the said Tenth Day of April, and no longer; and that the Author of any Book or Books already Composed and not Printed and Published, or that shall hereafter be Composed, and his Assignee, or Assigns, shall have the sole Liberty of Printing and Reprinting such Book and Books for the Term of fourteen Years, to Commence from the Day of the First Publishing the same, and no longer; And that if any other Bookseller, Printer, or other Person whatsoever, from and after the Tenth Day of April, One thousand seven hundred and ten, within the times Granted and Limited by this Act, as aforesaid, shall Print, Reprint, or Import, or cause to be Printed, Reprinted, or Imported any such Book or Books, without the Consent of the Proprietor or Proprietors thereof first had and obtained in Writing, Signed in the Presence of Two or more Credible Witnesses; or knowing the same to be so Printed or Reprinted, without the Consent of the Proprietors, shall Sell, Publish, or Expose to Sale, or cause to be Sold, Published, or Exposed to Sale, any such Book or Books, without such Consent first had and obtained, as aforesaid, Then such Offender or Offenders shall Forfeit such Book or Books, and all and every Sheet or Sheets, being part of such Book or Books, to the Proprietor or Proprietors of the Copy thereof, who shall forthwith Damask and make Waste-Paper of them: And further, That every such Offender or Offenders, shall Forfeit One Peny for every sheet which shall be found in his, her, or their Custody, either Printed or Printing, Published or Exposed to Sale, contrary to the true intent and meaning of this Act.

The printing patent also protected the stationer's rights to publish but had a broader scope. The patent was a grant from the executive (sovereign), whereas statutes were acts of the legislature. In early eighteenth-century England, sovereign privilege often trumped legislative authority; thus so did the patent over the copyright.

In 1775, the Copyright Act was amended to deny copyright protection to publishers and authors unless the appropriate book deposits were made (15 George III). These laws set the standard whereby books would be deposited with a national library as condition of copyright. In the late twentieth century that requirement was dropped. Intellectual property is now copyrighted as soon as it is created, and no depository requirement exists. These deposit laws were, as Edwards maintains (1859 ii, 598–600), an uncertain way for libraries to build their collections, as the laws were more often observed in the breach.

During the seventeenth century there appears to have been little regard for intellectual property. James Kirkwood, a Presbyterian minister writing on establishing libraries in the various parishes throughout Scotland, advised that a correspondence be maintained by a trusted "Printing House and Paper Manufactory" with printing houses throughout Europe.

Through this correspondence, the trusted publisher should acquire copies of books printed elsewhere "as soon as possible." The publisher was then charged to reprint books, new or old, and to distribute those books deemed "worthy" to each of the parish libraries. He makes no mention of compensation to the original publisher or authors for the reprinting of the books (Kirkwood 1699c, 39–40). Moreover he suggested that his plan would have a positive effect on Scotland's economy, as it "will keep all that Money in the Kingdom, which now goes out for buying of books and Paper" (Kirkwood 1699c, 53)—an argument now offered by developing countries to protect and promote their economies. Kirkwood identified other social and moral values that would accrue from the policy. Students would no longer need to go abroad to study, preserving those costs and preserving the monies in Scotland. Moreover, "Gentlemen" would prefer the reading of new books to gaming and drinking (Kirkwood 1699c, 54). He foresaw a glorious future for Scotland. In the near future, from his perspective, Scotland would become the publisher for Europe; in three to four hundred years all parish libraries would be the equal of the greatest libraries elsewhere (Kirkwood 1699c, 54–55).

The libraries Kirkwood envisioned would have been established around the churches in each parish. These parish libraries would provide students, including ministers of the church, with relatively easy access to an ever-expanding base of knowledge, to wit, books. To deny access to knowledge, even by neglecting to construct and furnish libraries with books would be to deny one of God's gifts to mankind. The libraries were to be used to the advantage of young men entering the ministry (Kirkwood 1699a, 75) and to support and propagate the Christian Religion (Kirkwood 1699b, 63–68). To that end, books would be used to counter "Popism," Deism, and Atheism. Finally, Kirkwood recognized that Scotland was in his time a very poor country and that the establishment of a printing and publishing industry could contribute to its economic development (Kirkwood 1699b, 70).

Western jurisprudence on intellectual property has undergone a significant metamorphosis since the eighteenth century. Many librarians today also recognize that a fair and reasonable approach to the intellectual property concept is an ethical consideration explicitly as an intellectual property concern or as a subset of the general obligation of observance of legal norms.

As John Feather (1994) points out, eighteenth-century legislation was focused on the protection of intellectual property held by publishers. Only slowly did the process begin to recognize the rights of authors and other intellectual property creators. Johann David Köhler (1973) clearly recognized that the preservation of texts often required their systematic copying and recopying. Indeed as Carla Hesse (1996) and Ann Blair (2003) have shown, the practices we now call plagiarism were both commonplace and acceptable practice. If we read Köhler correctly, however, we may conclude that he held at least one reservation against the copying of library materials. He admonished library users to adhere to the rules of the library and particularly to determine if and how library materials might be copied. This seems to imply that in the eighteenth-century German context, some rights of intellectual property lay with the owner of the artifact, the library, rather than with the author or publisher.

Richard Carey (1972, 236 n. 3) informs us that Felixe de Juvenal de Carlenças, author of *Bibliothéques*[3] [sic], published in 1740 in Lyons, borrowed heavily from Pierre Le Gallois's *Traitté historique des plus belles bibliothèques de l'Europe*, first published in 1680. According to Carey, Juvenal de Carlenças often copied large passages of the text. And Pierre le Gallois borrowed very heavily from Johannes Lomeier's *De bibliothecis liber singularis*, first published in 1669 (Montgomery 1962, 3).

According to John Montgomery (1962, 3), these two works describing contemporary European librarians were preceded by but one work— Louis Jacob's *Traicté des plus belles bibliothèques*, published in Paris in 1644. These works were followed by eighteenth-century contributions to guides to libraries, including *A Critical and Historical Account of All the Celebrated Libraries in Foreign Countries*, attributed to a "Gentleman of the Temple," published in London in 1739 (Montgomery 1962, 68 n. 21), and Johann David Köhler's (1943) *Anweisung für reisende Gelerte, Bibliothecken, Münz-Cabinette, Antiquitäten-Zimmer, Bilder-Sale, Naturalien-und Kunst-Kammern, u.m.b. mit Ruken zu befeben.*

We see no evidence to suggest it, but Köhler, Juvenal de Carlenças, and the Gentleman were perhaps familiar with the British Statute of Anne of 1710. The Statute of Anne extended copyright of then contemporary works to stationers, publishers, and authors for a period of twenty-one years, with a fourteen-year extension if the rights holder was still living (see Feather 1980). The statute would not have applied to noncontemporary material and therefore not to much of the material with which the three eighteenth-century authors were concerned. The residents of France and Saxony would not have been bound by the Statute of Anne, but the same cannot be said for the Gentleman. As European scholars, perhaps they would all have been influenced by it.

The practices do suggest that the late seventeenth and early eighteenth centuries were pivotal in the definition of intellectual property rights. Between the eighteenth and twentieth centuries, practice slowly evolved in Europe and North America toward a balance among the rights of creators, publishers, and users. Even so, there continue to be variations in practice. There are different traditions and current approaches to the protection of intellectual property in different countries (see e.g., Bently and Sherma 2014). The French emphasis is on fairness and originality, so that a work must show "a trace of the author's personality" (Vivant 1991). In addition, it is argued that norms-based (as opposed to law-based) practices have been developed within specific communities and professional groups. Fauchart and von Hippel (2008) offer a case study of French chefs and their intellectual property—recipes.

The highly formalistic German approach requires a high degree of creativity, one that is "particularly severe in computer related/created works" (Lea 1993, 63). These contrast with "the idiosyncratic United Kingdom copyright system," where "the standard of originality required of a would-be work is based more on labor expended (and costs incurred) than on questions of creativity" (Lea 1993, 127), and on the equally idiosyncratic American system that focuses more on legal title to a protected work than on originality, creativity, or labor inputs. It is commonly thought that British and American law primarily protect the interests of the investor and employer, while the civil law approach places somewhat more emphasis on the rights of individual authors (Bettig 1996).

> In France, the person who substantially contributed to the realisation of the final work and who marked it with his personality is the one who deserves protection (Delicostopolou 1992).

European continental, UK, and US practices share a distinctly *individualist* ethos. This focus on individualist rights is largely a trans-Atlantic jurisprudence and one of fairly recent etiology. African and Asian thought is more *collectivist* in orientation (Amegatcher 2002; Kuruk 2002; see also Britz and Lipinski 2001). And until the mid-nineteenth century much of Western thinking was also more collectivist than individualist. It has been shown (Hesse 1996) that Western thinking on the source and ownership of intellectual creativity has undergone a perhaps not-too-subtle metamorphosis from one still shared in Africa and Asia that the producer of intellectual property is a conduit creating a shared social good to one where the producer/owner holds a private, exploitable economic good. Whatever the merits of intellectual property as a private good, the swing of the pendulum today tends to trump fair use and other access rights of the information user to the benefit of the rights owner. In the twenty-first century European intellectual property harmonization across European Union countries may well be going though a two-prong change. According to Richard Arnold (2014) that change contains elements of holistic change, that is sweeping and immediate, and incremental change.

Copyright in common law countries and civil code countries can vary widely despite international measures to standardize practice. That said, copyright has generally been held as a statutory right, one created *de novo* by legislative act rather than an extension of common law. Courts have a more interpretative role in common law countries than in civil code countries and in some interesting ways open opportunities for differences in interpretation of even the same treaty law. In the United States, where copyright first came into statutory existence in 1790, full protection of copyright does not adhere to a work unless copies are registered and deposited with the Library of Congress.

The guiding US case law emanates from *Wheaton v. Peters* (1834). Henry Wheaton and Richard Peters, as reporters of the United States Supreme Court (USSC), were responsible for publishing USSC decisions. In this capacity, Peters had succeeded Wheaton in the late 1820s. Wheaton, as court reporter, had added significant indexing and organization of the cases. Peters undertook to publish cases to which Wheaton and his publisher claimed both statutory and common law copyrights. The presiding judge of the court of the first instance (circuit court), Judge Hopkinson, held that Wheaton had not met the statutory requirements of the Copyright Act in that Wheaton had not made the necessary deposits. Judge Hopkinson did not find a federal common law of copyright. The Supreme Court, splitting four to two, upheld Hopkinson. The entire bench agreed that an individual could not copyright Supreme Court decisions, but supporting material might well be copyrighted.

The implications of the *Wheaton v. Peters* decision continue to resonate in US practice. In 1985 in *West Publishing v. Mead Data*, Westlaw successfully sued Nexis/Lexis (US Federal Court of Appeals, Eighth Circuit 1986) over the misuse in Lexis of a Westlaw indexing system. Westlaw was successfully challenged in the mid-1990s by Mathew Bender of Hyperlaw (US Federal Court of Appeals, Second Circuit 1997). Both the *West Publishing* and *Bender and Hyperlaw* cases illustrate an inherent tension between rights of access and use of documents created in the public domain and the digital rights management interests of private entities who undertake to categorize and index those documents in the private sector. Certainly constitutions, statutes, and court decisions are not the property of Westlaw, Lexis, or Hyperlaw. However, the markup systems created by Westlaw or Lexis are as propriety to each of them as the Dewey Decimal System is to OCLC.

In the United Kingdom in 1774, *Donaldson v. Beckett*, decided in the House of Lords, offered a somewhat different interpretation of common law and statutory rights. According to Patterson (1968, 172–179), the House of Lords held that the Statute of Anne had indeed displaced any common law rights to copyright as they affect the stationers' rights as regulated by the statute. The statute did not disturb other rights of authors, under common law. The law lords also ruled that authors did once have perpetual rights in their works but that the Statute of Anne had limited such rights. As we shall see, the rights of authors and rights owners are again beginning to be re-expanded toward the common law perpetuity allegedly in place before the Statute of Anne.

The following recent cases illustrate some of the differences that do arise. For instance, the basis for copyright may vary as the courts interpret the law between "sweat of the brow" and originality as the basis for copyright. For example, the United States Supreme Court (1991) opted for an "originality" interpretation in its *Feist* decision. The Supreme Court held that Feist could copy data from telephone books published by others, as the publication of names, addresses, and telephone numbers listed in alphabetical order did not represent an original contribution or interpretation of data. In *Nautical Solutions Mktg. Inc. v. Boats.com*, a US federal district court (2004) ruled that the copying of photographs by Nautical Solutions from Boats.com and other advertising services was not a copyright infringement, at least so far as Boats.com was concerned. The court did suggest that if there were copyright violations, they were against the original photographer, not the second-party vendor. Canada's approach has evolved similarly. In *Tele-Direct (Publications) Inc. v. American Business Information Inc.* (1997), a Canadian federal trial court and the Canadian Federal Court of Appeals upheld an "originality" interpretation. In 1998, the Supreme Court of Canada declined review. Similarly, according to David Mirchin (2005), a Tel Aviv district court ruled in *Ma'arv-Modiin Publishers Ltd. v. All You Need Ltd.* that help-wanted notices were noncopyrightable. It further held that any rights to the ads belonged to the ad originator, not a newspaper.

Australian courts, on the other hand, have applied a "sweat of the brow" test. In a case reminiscent of *Feist*, the Federal Court of Australia (2002) held in *Desktop Marketing Systems Pty Ltd. v. Telstra Corporation Ltd.* that "sweat of the brow" did in fact convey copyright and that telephone books, lack of originality not withstanding, were protected.

Peer-to-peer (P2P) information transfers, primarily of music collections, became important in the early twenty-first century. Perhaps the most famous or infamous of these was the Napster case. Napster began supporting free P2P music transfers in 1999. The Recording Industry Association of America (RIAA) and other members of the music industry challenged the service. The court decided in *A&M Records Inc. v. Napster Inc.* (2001) that Napster facilitated the infringement of the rights of copyright holders. As a result, the free service was terminated in 2001. Napster resumed business and now offers music transfers for a fee, primarily in Europe.

The Canadian Federal Court of Appeals, in *BMG Canada Inc. v. John Doe* (2005), has taken an interesting position as far as P2P exchanges are concerned: "I cannot see a real difference between a library that places a photocopy machine in a room full of copyrighted material and a computer user that places a personal copy on a shared directory linked to a P2P service." In the United States the courts have taken a somewhat different approach. In *Sony Corp. of America v. Universal City Studios* (1984), the Supreme Court held that a technology that may be used to infringe copyright is not ipso facto illegal so long as that technology has legitimate applications. In *MGM v. Grokster* (2005), the Supreme Court revised *Sony*. In the *Grokster* decision, the USSC argued that, while technology may be held innocent, the defendants in *Grokster* actively promoted copyright infringement. Thus file sharing, as such, is not necessarily illegal, but certain P2P activities are. Technology may be held innocent; intentions are different.

Patent Law

Patents grant exclusive rights to the patent holder to a process, technology, or design for a specific but limited period of time. The fruits of those rights are largely economic. Patents can be divided into two types: *utility* patents and *design* patents. Utility patents have technology at their hearts; whereas design patents are primarily ornamental, rather than functional, in nature. Patents may cover certain business practices and processes, as has been tested in the *State Street Bank & Trust Co. v. Signature Financial Group* federal appeals court decision (1998). Patents do not have the same duration as copyright.

Patent law raises some very interesting questions. In the British case *In The Matter Of Patent Applications Gb 0226884.3 and 0419317.3 by Cfph L.L.C.* (2005), the judge, Peter Prescott, noted:

> We sense that we know "technology" when we see it. And no doubt that is correct, most of the time. . . . But it is not correct all of the time. Therein lies the delusion. You can prove that for yourself by trying to find a definition of "technology" that everybody can agree on. The more you try, the more you will discover what a horribly imprecise concept it is.

Judge Prescott argued further that British law did not specifically define "invention," the condition on which the grant of a patent is based. Instead the law specifies that which is not invention. Everyone agrees that innovation must be non-obvious and original in order to be patentable. Not everyone agrees as to what is "non-obvious" and "obvious." A patentable invention must contain elements of technology. Yet "most informed respondents agree that *trying to define the words 'technical' or 'technology' is a dead-end*" [emphasis in the original]. Judge Prescott cites article 52 of the European Patent Convention as to what an invention is not:

> (1) European patents shall be granted for any inventions which are susceptible of industrial application, which are new and which involve an inventive step.
> (2) The following in particular shall not be regarded as inventions within the meaning of paragraph 1:
> > (a) discoveries, scientific theories and mathematical methods;
> > (b) aesthetic creations;

(c) schemes, rules and methods for performing mental acts, playing games or doing business, and programs for computers;

(d) presentations of information.

(3) The provisions of paragraph 2 shall exclude patentability of the subject-matter or activities referred to in that provision only to the extent to which a European patent application or European patent relates to such subject-matter or activities as such.

(4) Methods for treatment of the human or animal body by surgery or therapy and diagnostic methods practised on the human or animal body shall not be regarded as inventions which are susceptible of industrial application within the meaning of paragraph 1. This provision shall not apply to products, in particular substances or compositions, for use in any of these methods.

According to article 56, "'inventive step' means not obvious to a person skilled in the art." He distinguishes between "hard" and "soft" exclusions. A "soft" exclusion follows from applications that follow discovery: "It is well-settled law that, although you cannot patent a discovery, you can patent a useful artefact or process that you were able to devise once you had made your discovery."

Judge Prescott also argued that British law and the European Patent Convention vary in their interpretations of patentable inventions in significant ways. The UK Patent Office looks for the "technical contribution" of the applicant. The European Patent Office first seeks to determine if there are any "technical features." "Or to put it a little more precisely, what the UK Patent Office does is to consider the exclusion under the description 'novelty', but the EPO does so under the description 'inventive step'."

The importance of patent law has a practical application as well as theoretical dimensions. The WTO and its trade-related aspects of intellectual property rights (TRIPS) provide a mechanism for the breaking or relaxation of patents under certain circumstances. It also provides for the manufacture and importation of generic drugs under specific circumstances. Perhaps drug patents and their ramifications for the treatment of life-threatening diseases for the poorest people in the world's poorest countries is the most important intellectual property challenge of our era. The WTO system under TRIPS's "compulsory licensing" provisions permits some relief to the poorest countries, but is in itself not a full-fledged rationalization of the process. Under compulsory licensing, poor countries could manufacture critical drugs for domestic consumption and export and can also import those drugs from other countries.

Fair Use

Fair use is an exception to the protections of copyright. It has been defined in statute. For example, the US Copyright Act of 1976 provided a four-part test for fair use. Under § 107:

> In determining whether the use made of a work in any particular case is a fair use the factors to be considered shall include
>
> 1. the purpose and character of the use, including whether such use is of a commercial nature or is for nonprofit educational purposes;
> 2. the nature of the copyrighted work;
> 3. the amount and substantiality of the portion used in relation to the copyrighted work as a whole; and
> 4. the effect of the use upon the potential market for or value of the copyrighted work.
>
> The fact that a work is unpublished shall not itself bar a finding of fair use if such finding is made upon consideration of all the above factors.

Fair use has also been a matter for courts to decide. In *CCH Canadian Ltd. v. Law Society of Upper Canada*, the Supreme Court of Canada (2004) upheld the rights of a library to make single copies of copyrighted materials for the research, professional, and scholarly use of its members and patrons.

In the United States, defining case law includes *Basic Books Inc. v. Kinko's Graphics Corp* (1991); *Maxtone-Graham v. Burtchaell*, (1987); *Encyclopaedia Britannica Educational Corp. v. Crooks* (1982); and *American Geophysical Union v. Texaco Inc.* (1994, 1995). The *Basic Books* case found that Kinko's infringed copyright when creating student course packs without appropriate payment of royalties. In *Burtchaell* the court found that extensive quotations from another work did not per se represent an unfair taking. The use of appropriately cited material was, in fact, a fair use of copyrighted material. In the *Encyclopaedia Britannica* case, the court held that wholesale copying and distribution of educational television programming, even for purely educational purposes, was beyond fair use and an illegal use of copyrighted material. In the *Texaco* case, the court found that the making of multiple copies of journal articles for distribution to Texaco researchers from a single subscription was an unfair taking of copyrighted materials.

Purpose and Character

Fair use countenances purpose and character of the challenged work as a defense to copyright infringement. Purpose and character justifications include criticism, parody, and artistic expression. In order to criticize a work (a legitimate intellectual undertaking), some portion of the critiqued work must be cited. Perhaps the greatest use of critiqued work is taken in parodies, a version of criticism. American courts have held that fair use as parody or criticism must have a transformative quality and that transformative quality must have a reasonable association with the parodied work (see *Mattel Inc. v. Walking Mountain Productions* 2003 as contrasted with *Art Rogers v. Jeff Koons* 1992).

The *Quixote* question discussed previously contrasts well with the outcome to sequels, authorized and unauthorized, to Margaret Mitchell's 1939 novel *Gone with the Wind*. In 2001 Alice Randall wrote and Houghton Mifflin published *The Wind Done Gone*, a parody from a slave's perspective of the original novel. In *Suntrust Bank v. Houghton Mifflin*, the court of first instance (US District Court for the Northern District of Georgia) found in 2001 that the *Wind Done Gone* infringed the rights of Mitchell's executor Suntrust Bank. In 2002 the Eleventh Circuit Court of Appeals lifted the publication injunction issued in the *Suntrust* decision. The parties to the case subsequently agreed to proceed with publication of the work as "an unauthorized parody." In 1991, it should be noted, Warner Books published *Scarlett*, Alexandra Ripley's "authorized" sequel to *Gone with the Wind*.

The US Supreme Court (1994) spoke definitively in favor of parody as a defense against copyright challenges and as at least an implicit cultural right in *Campbell v. Acuff-Rose Music Inc.* Perhaps better knows as the "Oh, Pretty Woman" case, it set the original Roy Orbison and William Dees song against the 2 Live Crew parody, "Pretty Woman."

Nature of the Copyrighted Work

The "nature" exception to copyright addresses the reason for the creation of the infringed work; that is, was it created for scholarly, entertainment, commercial, educational, or other purposes? Is the work fictional or non-fictional? Is it a statement of fact or idea (non-copyrightable), or does it represent interpretations or a specific expression of ideas or facts? A list in US law would usually not qualify for copyright (*Feist* rule). A restatement of the case law cited in this work would not qualify. In *Time Inc. v. Bernard Geis Associates* (1968), the historical value of still photographs from the film of John Kennedy's assassination was found to supersede the proprietary rights of the film's copyright holder.

Amount Taken

The amount of copyrighted work taken is an important consideration. In *Folsom v. Marsh* (1841), the US Supreme Court found that the taking of more than 350 pages of a work, even if for criticism, was an unfair taking. More recent court findings have further limited the scope of the "amounted taken" defense to virtually nothing taken. In *Harper & Row, Publishers Inc. v. Nation Enters* (1985), the Supreme Court found four hundred words to be too many.

Under the rule established by *Grand Upright Music, Ltd v. Warner Brothers Records Inc.* (1991) (see also *Bridgeport Music Inc. v. Dimension Films* 2004), any but the very minimum of music sampling was seen to be too much music sampling in the absence of a license.

A *de minimis* defense—amount taken—may still be a valid defense in the United States against copyright infringement. But clearly *de minimis* is very little indeed.

Market Impact

Under US law, market impact can be claimed as a fair use consideration. If a taking adversely impacts the value of the infringed work, then an unfair use may result. American law differentiates between commercial and non-commercial takings. In "noncommercial" actions, the plaintiff (copyright holder) must demonstrate the damage. But in "commercial" action, the burden lies on the defendant. The courts will look to determine whether a given infringing work substitutes for the original. If, for example, I make copies of a book, recording, film, or software application and sell those items without permission of the copyright owner, I would be in direct competition. If I were to re-record a song, for example, without pretense of parody, that too would be a copyright violation. The creation of collections of articles for sale to students without payment of royalties is a violation.

TEACH Act "Exception"

In the United States, the Technology, Education, and Copyright Harmonization Act (TEACH Act, 17 USC 101) of 2002 is a non–fair use exception to copyright protection. The TEACH Act permits, inter alia, the transmission of copyrighted material for educational purposes. The TEACH Act facilitates accredited not-for-profit institutions of higher education to provide educational materials in distance education courses. The TEACH Act is not a fair use exception to copyright but rather an educational exception.

Changes in technology necessarily effect copyright. As discussed earlier in this chapter, the Internet has led to new ways to transfer copyrighted material. P2P transfers are a case in point. The most recent legal response to technological innovation is the STELA Reauthorization Act of 2014. Originally enacted in 2010, the act regulates the retransmission of broadcast television signals by satellite re-transmitters like Dish or DirecTV.

INTERNATIONAL ORGANIZATIONS AND INTELLECTUAL PROPERTY

International organizations and multinational treaty regimes to manage intellectual property emerged and started to become important at the end of the nineteenth century. A number of countries, among them the United States, the Soviet Union, and the People's Republic of China were slow to adopt international norms. The following documents the trend toward internationalization of intellectual property regulation and management.

The World Intellectual Property Organization (WIPO) provides a searchable website as a resource to intellectual property regulation by country and international organizations, see http://www.wipo.int/tools/en/sitemap.html (accessed February 18, 2015).

Internationalizing Copyright

Intellectual property issues are defined at the international level in community law ("common" international law) and by treaty. Two centuries after Cervantes first suffered from a lack of copyright when in an environment of national copyright, the great English novelist Charles Dickens would campaign for an Anglo-American copyright treaty. In 1842, Dickens visited the United States for the first time. His books were immensely popular in the former British colony, but Dickens's intellectual property rights were little protected there. Many American publishers were taking his work with little or no payments of royalties. Dickens would campaign for a bilateral copyright agreement, but one was not entered into by the United Kingdom and the United States until 1891.

Similarly, Victor Hugo, the French novelist, worked for the adoption of an agreement to extend national copyright into the international sphere. Prior to the adoption of the Berne Convention for the Protection of Literary and Artistic Works in 1886, intellectual property published and copyrighted in one country was unprotected in another. The Berne Convention extended that protection for the nationals of the countries party to the convention.

A number of countries, the United States among them, were not party to the Berne Convention when it was first adopted. The United States was not to become a party to the Berne Convention, as amended, until 1989. The United States objected to several provisions of the Berne Convention, including the moral rights clause, removal of copyright office registration requirements, single copyright periods, and elimination of a mandatory copyright notice.

The Universal Copyright Convention of 1952 was adopted as a mechanism to incorporate the United States and other countries objecting to provisions of the Berne Convention into multilateral copyright and to accommodate the idiosyncrasies of American law. But in 1988 the United

States became party to the Berne Convention, and US copyright law was amended, consistent with the provisions of the convention. Russia and China also came late to the Berne Convention. China ratified it in 1992, and Russia in 1995. These and other countries have begun the process of revising domestic law to be consistent with the convention.

International Organizations and Copyright

The World International Property Organization and related international governmental organizations (IGO) regulate, implement, and (in the minds of some) create new law. WIPO is said to have concluded that copyright systems are better adapted to meet the challenge of technology than are *droit d'auteur* systems. The harmonization of European community intellectual property law may eventually result in laws not too dissimilar from those already on the statute books of the United Kingdom. The Berne Convention for the Protection of Literary and Artistic Works is recognized as guiding and defining international intellectual property issues. Article 6*bis* of the Berne Convention has been fundamental to the spread of explicit moral rights protection into the countries of the Anglo-Saxon or "common-law" tradition. It holds the following:

> (1) Independently of the author's economic rights, and even after the transfer of the said rights, the author shall have the right to claim authorship of the work and to object to any distortion, mutilation or other modification of, or other derogatory action in relation to, the said work, which would be prejudicial to his honor or reputation.
> (2) The rights granted to the author in accordance with the preceding paragraph shall, after his death, be maintained, at least until the expiry of the economic rights, and shall be exercisable by the persons or institutions authorized by the legislation of the country where protection is claimed. However, those countries whose legislation, at the moment of their ratification of or accession to this Act, does not provide for the protection after the death of the author of all the rights set out in the preceding paragraph may provide that some of these rights may, after his death, cease to be maintained.
> (3) The means of redress for safeguarding the rights granted by this Article shall be governed by the legislation of the country where protection is claimed.

Under the Berne Convention, the scope of moral rights protection for intellectual property has expanded worldwide.

The advent of international regulation under the Berne Convention, WIPO, and the requirements imposed on members of the World Trade Organization (WTO) has caused states members to restructure their intellectual property laws to be more consistent and to more strictly enforce existing legislation (see, for example, State Intellectual Property Office of the People's Republic of China 2003).

The likely outcome of creating parallel national intellectual property regulation will certainly be a greater conformity and homogenization of law consistent with the Berne Convention and WIPO and WTO requirements. When the United States became signatory to the Berne Convention in 1988, American law was slowly modified to take greater recognition of European continentalist practices, particularly in regard to the rights of authors.

COUNTERVAILING OPINION

The status quo is under challenge. This challenge is occurring along several fronts. These include national and international professional associations that find that current intellectual property regulations inhibit the free flow of ideas. It includes countries in development that tolerate the "one legal copy" regime. It includes scholarly analysis, the "creative commons," and open access initiatives. And it includes the unlawful and quasi-unlawful peer-to-peer services that try to ignore the intellectual property regulatory environment. The open access movement has two basic orientations. The first is to provide online access to scientific and scholarly literature as well as entertainment media at little or no cost to users. The second is concerned with computer hardware and software access, again with little or no cost to end users and modifiers.

These challenges and the history of intellectual property theory change suggest that the current "exclusivist" interpretation of intellectual property doctrine may well undergo an evolution. Given emergent practices, the doctrine as modified may be more tolerant of end user and information creator rights and privileges.

There are any number of "collectivist" or "commons" initiatives that have been proposed to provide a less controlled environment for access and use of information. A primary but by no means exclusive focus of the many open access initiatives concern access to and use of information provided over the Internet and the creation of code to present that information. Table 7.1 offers a short list of initiatives.

The open access argument often includes issues of equity and fair use. For example, in October 2003 the Conference on Open Access to Knowledge in the Sciences and Humanities in Berlin concluded:

> Our mission of disseminating knowledge is only half complete if the information is not made widely and readily available to society. New possibilities of knowledge dissemination not only through the classical form but also and increasingly through the open access paradigm via the Internet have to be supported. We define open access as a comprehensive source of human knowledge and cultural heritage that has been approved by the scientific community.

Table 7.1. Open Access Initiatives: A Small Sample

Licenses and Copyright

	Creative Commons	http://creativecommons.org
	BSD/ NetBSD/ FreeBSD	http://www.freebsd.org/ copyright/freebsd- license.html http://www.freebsd.org/ copyright/license.html
	GNU Copyleft	http://www.gnu.org/copyleft/ copyleft.html#WhatIsCopyleft

Digital Rights

	Electronic Frontier Foundation	http://eff.org/
	Digital Rights	http://www.digitalrights.dk/
	Campaign for Digital Rights	http://ukcdr.org/
	European Digital Rights	http://www.edri.org/

Open Access

	Open Archives Initiative	http://www.openarchives.org/
	Budapest Open Access Initiative	http://www.soros.org/ openaccess/
	Directory of Open Access Journals	http://www.doaj.org/
	Open Society Institute	http://www.soros.org/about
	Public Knowledge	http:// www.publicknowledge.org/

Publication

	Scholarly Publishing and Academic Resources Coalition (SPARC)	http://www.arl.org/sparc/core/ index.asp?page=a0

Public Library of Science	http:// www.publiclibraryofscience.o rg/
Archivx	http://arxiv.org/

In order to realize the vision of a global and accessible representation of knowledge, the future Web has to be sustainable, interactive, and transparent. Content and software tools must be openly accessible and compatible

Furthermore, the conference found:

Open access contributions must satisfy two conditions:

1. The author(s) and right holder(s) of such contributions grant(s) to all users a free, irrevocable, worldwide, right of access to, and a license to copy, use, distribute, transmit and display the work publicly and to make and distribute derivative works, in any digital medium for any responsible purpose, subject to proper attribution of authorship (community standards, will continue to provide the mechanism for enforcement of proper attribution and responsible use of the published work, as they do now), as well as the right to make small numbers of printed copies for their personal use.

2. A complete version of the work and all supplemental materials, including a copy of the permission as stated above, in an appropriate standard electronic format is deposited (and thus published) in at least one online repository using suitable technical standards (such as the Open Archive definitions) that is supported and maintained by an academic institution, scholarly society, government agency, or other well-established organization that seeks to enable open access, unrestricted distribution, inter operability, and long-term archiving. (Berlin Declaration 2003)

The Berlin Declaration is more individualistic than collectivist, for it recognizes the rights of "author(s) and right holder(s)" who grant access to digital works. And to a large degree the open access movement is concerned with access to and the use of digital works rather than all works, including print-based analog creations.

Recent commentators (e.g., Bollier 2002; Lessig 2002; and Vaidhyanathan 2001) have argued along an "information commons" metaphor. The bases of their arguments are derived from the concept that we all share an information commons (a collectivist traditionalist approach); that the more legalistic, individualistic, and pro–rights holder jurisprudence has significantly eroded the collectivist-traditional rights we all held—resulting in perhaps the inevitable loss of fair use and other information access and use rights.

CONCLUSION

Intellectual property, despite national and international efforts to define and rationalize it, is not consistently defined over time and place. Indeed Miguel de Cervantes had no copyright protection in the early seventeenth century. Yet there are those who would have it that we are strangled by it in the early twenty-first century. Moreover, the exceptions to intellectual property rights vary as well. We do not begin to argue that the major trend in the regulation of intellectual property—that of commercialized ownership of intellectual property and the concomitant reduction of the rights of consumers and users of information—are on the wane. The legal environment is buttressed by the Berne Convention, the World Intellectual Property Organization, and the World Trade Organization, and all are powerful explicitly legal constructs. Yet we do suggest that however distant the voices and however far in the wilderness they may be, there are intellectual forces that recognize an ethical wrong in the development of intellectual property rights management.

While the Berne Convention and WIPO have contributed significantly to a standardization of global intellectual property practice, that practice and the ethics associated with the treatment of intellectual property have not been and are as yet not uniform across regions and countries. Simon Newman and Wallace Koehler (2004) have pointed out, for example, that European intellectual property law has yet to be fully harmonized, despite the European Union and international agreements to the contrary.

These voices may have begun to have an effect in moderating the overall impact of intellectual property rights management. Contrast if you will the Digital Millennium Copyright Act of 1998 on the one hand and the Sonny Bono Copyright Term Extension Act of 1998 and the Technology, Education, and Copyright Harmonization Act (TEACH Act) of 2002 on the other. The TEACH Act defines certain guidelines for intellectual property in the teaching and research environment (see e.g., Lipinski 2003).

A second variant on exceptions to copyright and a furtherance of fair use is the Marrakesh Treaty to Facilitate Access to Published Works for Persons Who Are Blind, Visually Impaired or Otherwise Print Disabled adopted in 2013 (WIPO 2013, also known as the Marrakesh VIP Treaty). In keeping with article 30 of the United Nations Convention on the Rights of Persons with Disabilities (2006), the Marrakesh Treaty established exceptions to provide access to published materials for individuals with visual impairments. As of this writing, the Marrakesh Treaty is not yet in force.

Other voices may indicate a new shift in practice, a shift that could be a harbinger of changes to intellectual property practice to an earlier time. Baruchson-Arbib and Yaari (2005), for example, show that graduate students have attitudes at variance with "contemporary" practice. The students they surveyed have a more relaxed view of attribution and copy-ing—plagiarism—than do their "elders." Students tend to differentiate between "print" and online documents, treating Internet resources as subject to fewer protections and acknowledgments (Moeck 2002) or, as Baruchson-Arbib and Yaari (2005) put it, "bona-vacantia and free for use." These analysts typically prescribe instruction against plagiarism and inappropriate attribution of both print and online documents—for graduate students. Perhaps, but we should not also lose sight of the pos-sibility that we are witnessing a shift to the status quo ante, when, quite literally, cutting and pasting without attribution and other recognition was the accepted practice of the day.

We would also point out the obvious. For the most part the open access initiatives have been limited to the academic research and publica-tion environment. Without question, the scholarly publications industry has become very centralized and expensive. To a large degree, open ac-cess publications advocate a much freer environment for the distribution, use, and derivative utilization of scholarly materials. Some might see this as a mechanism to break the oligopoly of publishers; others see it as a natural extension of scholarly activity. But again, for the most part, the open access movement does not extend to the entertainment market. Whither goest scholarly publishing, the entertainment industry will like-ly continue to remain highly centralized and more controlled to the bene-fit of the rights holder and contrary to the interests of those who advocate freer environments (e.g., peer-to-peer transfers).

How, then, are the ethical responsibilities of the informing professions affected by intellectual property concerns? Without question, particularly in the twentieth and twenty-first centuries, the role, responsibilities, and ethics of the informing professions are highly defined and circumscribed by legislation and legal interpretation. From a purely legal perspective, informing professionals are bound to comply with the prevailing law; but are there exceptions that derive from moral and ethical considerations? An interesting exception to patent law has been implemented in the face of mounting opposition in African and Asian countries to prohibitions on copying anti-HIV, anti-malarial, and other patented medicines. Where quite literally lives may be saved at the expense of profit, ethical concerns may supersede legal ones and force changes in the law or concessions from the patent holder. The TEACH Act represents a needed, formal exception to intellectual property.

The strictness of intellectual property law together with its occasional ambiguity may create conflicts for informing professionals as they seek to interpret and obey the law but also to meet other professional ethical and moral responsibilities. It is certainly legitimate to militate against laws through appropriate judicial and legislative channels that are seen as overly constrictive. But do professional obligations extend beyond chang-ing the law?

Clearly intellectual property law, particularly copyright law, has changed as technology has changed. As it has become easier to copy the work of others—beginning with the printing press, xerography, and now digital reproduction—the legal protection of intellectual property has been more closely defined. The Digital Millennium Copyright Act is a direct response in both name and content to the digital revolution. The TEACH Act is itself an accommodation to the needs of distance education.

As we have seen, intellectual property doctrine has undergone a transition from a collectivist to an individualistic orientation. David Bollier (2002), Lawrence Lessig (2002), and Siva Vaidhyanathan (2001) have each proposed an "information commons" doctrine for revision of intellectual property practice. On their face, these information commons arguments suggest a return to collectivist principles. As seductive as the information commons may be, does it matter whether its proponents take an individualistic or collectivist route? Or, given the investment of intellectual, financial, and legislative capital in the development of intellectual property law, is it realistic that a collectivist appeal could prevail?

In the last half of the twentieth century first the Photostat and the photocopier, followed by the computer, the Internet, and the digital revolution further eased publication and reproduction not just of written text but other visual and aural media. That revolution removed institutional and structural boundaries placed on the production and distribution of intellectual materials and made possible the instantaneous communication of intellectual property in a global context. As technical constraints were removed, new institutional and legal ones were imposed.

Each technological revolution resulted in changes in practices, law, and ethics. It took less than a century for governments to seek to regulate publications through the grant of licenses to publishers but more than a century to institute protections of intellectual property. That process has in some ways not yet been fully played out, as toward the end of the twentieth century and even into the twenty-first, nation-states were becoming party to the Berne Convention and the World Intellectual Property Organization, and at the same time changing and rationalizing their national intellectual property laws to international standards.

These rights regimes have created interesting conflicts for librarians. It must be remembered that, prior to the sixteenth century, libraries sometimes owed their very existence to their ability to copy, to make reproductions of the work of others. Law to take manuscripts and to make copies for their own collections mandated the Alexandrine Library and libraries that succeeded it. Libraries and others are today barred, again by law, from much of such takings. There are certain fair use and other exceptions to the rule. Librarians may indeed be conflicted, for, on the one hand, they are expected to facilitate access to information for their patrons; yet, on the other hand, they have both legal and ethical obligations to adhere to the rules.

NOTES

1. For a copy of the Berne Convention and a list of member states, see http://www.wipo.int/treaties/en/ip/berne/

2. Helena Percas de Ponseti (2002) argues Avellaneda was Pasamonte. Others find otherwise. Pasamonte's identity is not relevant to this text.

3. Richard Carey (1972) provides two spellings of the French for libraries: *bibliotheques* and *bibliothéques*. The word was usually spelled *bibliothèque* in the eighteenth century, as it still is. It is unclear from the text whether the spelling was that of Carlenças or that of Carey.

EIGHT

Qualifications of the Librarian

The vivifying influence of personality is essential if the library is to be fruitful as a means of education. To supply it is the vital function of the library staff. This was not realized in the earlier days of modern libraries when the librarian was looked upon as a caretaker of books viewed as property.

—Ranganathan (1963b, 3)

INTRODUCTION

The training and qualifications of librarians are subjects of great interest and with major ethical implications. Of ethical issues identified in the literature and by practice, several have specific relevance with librarian training and qualifications. These include cultural diversity; diversity of opinion; equality of opportunity; faithfulness to organizational, professional, and public trust; good professional practice; preservation of the cultural record and stewardship; professional neutrality; responsiveness to social responsibilities; and skill and competence; and the roles of the information practitioner. These and all other values are included within the training library practitioners receive.

Defining qualifications is bound up with defining library science and information science. It is also bound together with our recognition of the ethics and values that practitioners embrace. Rafael Capurro (1992) has raised for us some very challenging questions at the nexus of the information professions and ethics. For example, he argues:

The question "what is information?" asks for substantial characteristics of something. But . . . information, taken as a dimension of human existence, is nothing substantial. Instead of asking: "what is information?" we can ask: "what is information (science) for?" . . . The aim of

171

information science is to thematize this con-textual dimension taking into consideration primarily all technical forms of communication as parts of other forms of life.

Taking into consideration the unity of boths [*sic*] aspects, the methodological and the pragmatic, information heuristics and information hermeneutics, information science can be considered a sub-discipline of rhetoric.

As Capurro points out for us, the intersection of Aristotelian rhetoric, politics, and ethics underpin the information professions. Capurro (1992) argues further that:

The question "what is information for?" leads to the question "what is information science for?" since information science, conceived as a hermeneutic-rhetorical discipline, studies the con-textual pragmatical dimensions within which knowledge is shared positively as information and negatively as misinformation particularly through technical forms of communication. These are not just an instrument but a "way of being." This conception of information science is important if we want information systems to become part of the background of various forms of living.

We are engaged in a new or perhaps renewed discourse on the role of information in society, colored by a changing understanding of the role and nature of information. Necessarily we must also be concerned with the place and qualifications of those who are stakeholders in information. In the early twentieth century the definition of the qualifications of librarians was left to educators who developed the curricula to train librarians. That definition was moderated by their interactions with the professionals in the field and with the accreditors seeking to ensure that whatever educators taught, they taught it well.

In Europe library studies became "documentation" under the leadership of researchers like Paul Otlet (1934). In North America, library economy became "library science" in the 1930s (Butler 1933), then "information science" in the 1970s. With the advent of the Internet and the computer, we are engaged in a debate to determine if indeed librarians and libraries are as yet still relevant; and if they are to remain relevant, in what ways must they change and not change to provide meaningful service? Will we conclude in the twenty-first century that librarians have been rendered redundant, that software and infometricians not only can perform the functions of librarians but also can do it better? Is the term "librarian" archaic, and should it be replaced with something more descriptive of the new information environment? In short, what's in a word?

In the following sections, we first consider contemporary librarian qualifications. In the second, we trace the development of librarian qualifications from Greek slaves in the private libraries of Rome to the onset

of the twentieth century. The evidence suggests that there was no perceived need for formal training for librarians until the mid-nineteenth
century, when Edward Edwards and later Melvil Dewey were to suggest
that there was more to librarianship than that which could be met by a
good undergraduate education (cf. Bak 2002; Carroll 2002). It has been
generally recognized that there exists a "core" of knowledge and skills
that should be imparted by library educators to their students. Precisely
what that core might be has been a matter of debate and discussion (for
examples, see Danton 1949; Asheim 1954; and Shera 1972). In 2009 Michalis Gerolimos published a study that documents more than fifty core
qualifications as described by library schools in three countries.

The definition of the core of library education is equally at the core of
the definition of library qualifications. In a study of librarian qualifications worldwide, Dalton and Levinson (2008, 73–81) document the curricula and training required to train librarians and demonstrate the complexity and variability of that training.

QUALIFICATIONS IN THE TWENTIETH CENTURY

Much attention has been addressed to differences among the standards
developed to define the role of librarian in the library and in the society at
large. Similarly, there is concern with the recognition of credentials and
mechanisms for certification. In the mid-twentieth century forward, in
order to be recognized as a professional librarian, one needed to graduate
from a program accredited by a national professional organization or a
national ministry of education or its equivalent. In addition, the professional librarian might be required to join a national professional association and, in some cases, successfully pass a qualifying examination.

The term "librarian" is often used to include both the professionals
and paraprofessionals employed by libraries and similar information institutions. Until the late nineteenth century librarians learned their profession on the job. There were no library schools until Melvil Dewey
founded the school at Columbia College (later University) in 1887 in New
York City. The school was later moved to Albany, New York. The number of library schools worldwide can now be numbered in the hundreds
(see e.g., American Library Association n.d.)

In Australia, Canada, New Zealand, the United Kingdom, and the
United States, an individual is considered a professional librarian if she/
he is a graduate of a professional program accredited by a specified professional association. Only in North America must one be a master's
degree graduate of a program accredited by a professional organization
to be a librarian. Ireland is an interesting variant. The Library Association
of Ireland is not a statutory organization and as such cannot compel
programs to comply. It is, however, recognized by the relevant ministry

(Department of Environment, Community and Local Government) that does have the authority to set qualifications. It should be noted that in the United States public librarians are required in some states (but not nearly all) to be licensed or certified at the state level. That certification is almost always based solely on educational criteria.

Professional Associations and Qualifications

In the history of professional organizations, the library and later information science organizations came late to the table. The American Library Association (1876) followed quickly by the Library Association in the United Kingdom (1877) and the Japan Library Association (1892) were the first of many such library associations created after the last quarter of the nineteenth century and throughout the twentieth century. At the close of the nineteenth century there were fewer than twenty national library associations and only one international organization—the International Federation for Information and Documentation (FID). By the end of the twentieth century there were more than five hundred national, regional, and international organizations. There are many reasons for this growth. George Bobinski (2000, 61) argues that much of this growth in the United States, particularly between the 1940s and the 1970s, can be attributed to "the tremendous growth of libraries and librarians." The absolute growth in the number of libraries and librarians certainly contributed to associational growth. Differentiation of function, focus, and duties within the library and information disciplines also explains part of this growth.

As the number of organizations grew in the twentieth century, there was also a differentiation among them of form and function. In some countries, library associations began to regulate the profession either by vetting library programs or by certifying practitioners. These organizations also began consideration of codes of ethics to guide practitioners (Koehler 2002a; 2002b). Some professional organizations backed away from national certification programs because of opposition from leading members of the profession (see, for example, Dana 1925); others embraced it wholeheartedly.

In many countries in Latin America, general national associations limit membership to a specific subset (for example, professional graduate librarians), as do the Asociación de Bibliotecarios Graduados de la República Argentina or the Colegio de Bibliotecarios de Chile. Their certification is not a function of accrediting a program but of assessment of the individual. The individual is licensed or certified by the national professional association through membership and examination and is usually limited to the graduate librarian. For example, see article 6 of the Argentine Statute on Professional Librarianship and Documentation (Asociación de Bibliotecarios . . . Argentina n.d.).

These organizations may be formally formed by an aggregate of an interested constituency, or they may be quasi-state-like bodies formed by national legislatures (Fernández de Zamora 2003). These latter organizations also have quasi-legislative and quasi-judicial authority to regulate and license the profession in their countries. As such, their codes of ethics and rules and regulations may have effects similar to statutes.

Similarly, librarians are defined by educational attainment in many other countries. There are programs that provide credentials, among them the certificate; diploma; and associate's, bachelor's, master's, and doctorate degrees. There are efforts to rationalize these different credentials to formal and informal standards. The European Union has initiated the Bologna Process to rationalize all credentials within its jurisdiction (see Kehm 2010; Tammaro 2012; and Johnson 2013). Informal discussions have taken place within the context of professional organizations to initiate a transnational rationalization process among African, European, and North American academicians. An important distinction needs emphasis. In common law countries, institutions and not individuals are accredited. In most countries where the legal system is based on civil codes, licensure or certification is for individuals and not their training programs (see Rochester 1994).

Qualifications Defined by Accreditation

The American Library Association (ALA) provides a definition of librarian based on education. A librarian is an individual who has graduated from an ALA-accredited school of library and information science in Canada or the United States or from a similarly recognized institution in other countries. School librarians may have their professional credentials validated by graduation from National Council for Accreditation of Teacher Education (NCATE) accredited programs.

In Canada and the United States, the accreditation process is limited to master's degree granting programs. In 1870 Ralph Waldo Emerson, noting the major increase in books and other print, recommended the creation of a professorate of books. He foresaw a need for a professional to connect information users with content. Emerson's library professor would not only maintain the collection and catalog it; he would also serve as a reference for good books for patrons and scholars. There was, however, increased pressure for professional librarians to be well versed in bibliography and classification, as the number of publications were not only increasing; so were the number of libraries. According to Jesse Shera (1972), commentators of the day were demanding not only good library skills but also good management skills of the librarian.

F. William Summers (1986) informs us that library education in the United States was chaotic between Dewey's first library school and the Williamson Report published in 1923. Librarians were trained in one of six ways: on-the-job training, apprenticeships by rotation through library departments, apprenticeships with formal training, training offered by major libraries, state library commission summer schools, and library schools (Carroll 2002). The Williamson Report (Williamson 1923), underwritten by the Carnegie Corporation, recommended establishment of library education at the graduate level. Charles Williamson advocated comprehensive national accreditation. Librarians should be trained at the graduate level according to professional standards based on sound pedagogy rather than the immediate needs of library employers.

The establishment of the Graduate Library School at the University of Chicago was a direct result of the Williamson Report. Pierce Butler (1933), a Chicago faculty member, defined library science as the "transmission of the accumulated experience of society through the instrumentality of the book." Library scientists were to be the vehicle through which that accumulated experience would be articulated. Research into the sociology and psychology of librarianship and information and their histories would help improve library service.

The American Library Association was not particularly receptive to the new library science. Neither were many working practitioners. Library experience had been an early prerequisite to library school admission. Resistance to "library science" would persist (see Houser and Schrader 1978).

The Advent of Accreditation

The American Library Association began accrediting library school programs in 1925. By 1932 twenty-five programs had been accredited. In 1933 the ALA published its minimum requirements, which recognized three program types: professional programs that required two years of college, three years of college, or a bachelor's degree for admission (Summers 1986).

The 1933 ALA *Standards for Accreditation of Master's Programs in Library and Information Studies* have undergone subsequent revision. They were first replaced in 1951, and again in 1972, 1992, 2008, and 2015. By the early 1950s, the professional-level master's degree was recognized as the preferred terminal professional degree. The 1972 standards revision for the first time placed the criteria for evaluation on individual programs and their institutional objectives together with a minimum set of expressed objectives. The 1992 standards also recognized various forms of discrimination as a standards violation. The 1992 revision added an expectation of competence with emerging technologies (Summers 1986).

In 2008 the *Standards for Accreditation* were amended to incorporate qualitative measures of program effectiveness. The assessments of effectiveness are focused on individual programs rather than on the student or graduate. It is therefore the program, and not the graduate, that is accredited. The 2015 amendments placed a requirement that library programs provide evidence-supported documentation that the program graduates had attained specified levels of professional competence. Programs were also required to provide evidence that each graduate engaged in "broad-based, systematic planning."

A key revision from the 2008 standards in 2015 was the change of standard I. The introduction to standard I in 2008 read:

> A school's mission and program goals are pursued, and its program objectives achieved, through implementation of an ongoing, broad-based, systematic planning process that involves the constituency that a program seeks to serve. Consistent with the values of the parent institution and the culture and mission of the school, program goals and objectives foster quality education.

In 2015 the introduction to standard I provides:

> A program's mission and goals, both administrative and educational, are pursued, and its program objectives achieved, through implementation of an ongoing, broad-based, systematic planning process that involves the constituencies that a program seeks to serve.

The ALA has published a number of documents to ensure that its accreditation process is well understood. The ALA (ALA Committee on Accreditation 2015) rationale is given as the following:

> Accreditation in higher education is defined as a collegial process based on self- and peer assessment for public accountability and improvement of academic quality.
> Accreditation serves to ensure educational quality, judged in terms of demonstrated results in supporting the educational development of students. Judgments are made by carefully vetted, unbiased practitioners and faculty professionals at the expert level.

An accredited library program in North America is expected to demonstrate how it meets the following educational objectives (ALA Committee on Accreditation 1992, 2008, 2015):

- the essential character of the field of library and information studies; that is, recordable information and knowledge, and the services and technologies to facilitate their management and use, encompassing information and knowledge creation, communication, identification, selection, acquisition, organization and description, storage and retrieval, preservation, analysis, interpretation, evaluation, synthesis, dissemination, and management
- the philosophy, principles, and ethics of the field
- appropriate principles of specialization identified in applicable policy statements and documents of relevant professional organizations
- the value of teaching and service to the advancement of the field

- the importance of research to the advancement of the field's knowledge base
- the importance of contributions of library and information studies to other fields of knowledge
- the importance of contributions of other fields of knowledge to library and information studies
- the role of library and information services in a rapidly changing multicultural, multiethnic, multilingual society, including the role of serving the needs of underserved groups
- the role of library and information services in a rapidly changing technological and global society
- the needs of the constituencies that a program seeks to serve

In the United Kingdom, the professional organization of librarians, the Chartered Institute of Library and Information Professionals (CILIP), specifies the professional knowledge and skills base (replacing the body of professional knowledge [BPK]) that should be mastered before being considered a librarian. There following are the twelve major professional knowledge and skills base criteria listed:

- Organising knowledge and information.
- Knowledge and information management.
- Using and exploiting knowledge and information.
- Research skills.
- Information governance and compliance.
- Records management and archiving.
- Collection management and development.
- Literacies and learning.
- Leadership and advocacy.
- Strategy, planning and management.
- Customer focus, service design and marketing. (CILIP 2013)

A professional librarian functions within an "applications environment" and attains "generic and transferable skills." The applications environment is specific to the profession and includes the "ethical framework," "legal dimension," "information policy," "information governance," and the "communications perspective" of the professional domain. Generic and transferable skills are those skills and knowledge bases outside the information domain a librarian may need to practice specialized function. CILIP also provides a means to certify library assistants as well.

CILIP serves as an accreditor of graduate and undergraduate library programs in the United Kingdom. Its accreditation process is based in large part on the ability of a program to demonstrate that it adequately imparts the body of professional knowledge.

In Canada and the United States, a number of the programs accredited to train librarians have begun to redefine their roles as producers of personnel for the information economy. Programs have begun dropping the word "library" from their titles and adding "information" in its place. These programs, known as "I-schools," have broadened their offerings to include information-related classes not part of the traditional library curriculum and therefore outside the generally accepted definition of a library qualification. One program, that at the University of California, Berkeley, voluntarily withdrew from the accreditation process as provided by the ALA in the late 1990s. The remaining two California universities that have accredited programs, San Jose State University and the University of California, Los Angeles, continue to graduate librarians. The University of Southern California is seeking ALA accreditation.

Qualifications Legally Defined

In North America and the United Kingdom, the qualifications of a librarian are defined by curriculum of the school from which he or she graduates and by guidelines for accreditation provided by professional associations. In South America, those qualifications may be defined in law. For example, article 5 of Argentina's Statute on Professional Librarianship and Documentation (*Estatuto del profesional en bibliotecologia y documentacion*) defines different skills for various professional levels:

> Artículo 5°—El profesional en bibliotecología y documentación podrá realizar las siguientes funciones, de acuerdo a su título habilitante:
>
> a. Bibliotecario, Bibliotecario Documentalista, o Bibliotecólogo:
>
> a. Planificar, organizar, administrar y dirigir y evaluar, bibliotecas, centros de información bibliográfica y departamentos, divisiones o secciones de servicios bibliotecarios, documentarios o similares, nacionales, regionales y locales, tanto generales como especializados.
>
> b. Relevar, seleccionar, procesar, almacenar, recuperar y difundir la información bibliográfica y documentaria utilizando tanto métodos manuales como sistemas automatizados.
>
> c. Capacitar y asesorar a los usuarios para el mejor uso de la información en cualquier tipo de soporte.
>
> d. Organizar, dirigir y ejecutar programas dirigidos a la promoción o prestación de servicios de difusión del libro y de las bibliotecas, centros de información bibliográfica y de documentación.
>
> e. Organizar y dirigir campañas de extensión cultural en lo referente al suministro de libros y servicios de bibliotecas, así como de centros de documentación y de información bibliográfica.

    f.   Determinar y aplicar métodos y técnicas de preservación y conservación del acervo documental.

    b.   Licenciado en Bibliotecología y Documentación, o su equivalente. Además de las funciones mencionadas en el inciso a), podrá desempeñar las siguientes:

    a.   Planificar, organizar, conducir y evaluar sistemas de bibliotecas e información nacionales, regionales y especializadas.

    b.   Asesorar en la formulación de políticas de servicios de bibliotecas e información.

    c.   Organizar servicios y recursos de información para facilitar los procesos de toma de decisión y para el apoyo de la docencia e investigación.

    d.   Planificar, asesorar, dirigir, ejecutar y evaluar proyectos de investigación en el área de la bibliotecología y documentación.

    e.   Planificar, coordinar y evaluar la preservación y conservación del acervo cultural.

    f.   Asesorar en la tasación de colecciones bibliográficas/documentales.

    g.   Realizar peritajes referidos a la autenticidad, antigüedad, procedencia y estado de materiales impresos, de interés bibliofílicos.

    h.   Asesorar en el diseño del planeamiento urbano en el aspecto bibliotecario.

    i.   Ejercer la docencia en las disciplinas de la especialidad.

    j.   Desempeñar cualquier otra actividad en forma individual o integrando equipos interdisciplinarios de trabajo o investigación en los que se requieran conocimientos y aptitudes inherentes a la bibliotecología y documentación.

    c.   Profesor en Bibliotecología y Documentación, o su equivalente:

    a.   Ejercer la docencia especializada en todos los niveles y modalidades del sistema educativo.

    b.   Planificar, conducir y evaluar el proceso de enseñanza-aprendizaje en las áreas de bibliotecología y documentación en todos los niveles del sistema educativo.

    c.   Asesorar e intervenir en la formulación y en el estudio de planes para la formación profesional en la especialidad.

Standards and the External Examiner

There is a third and somewhat more indirect method by which the qualifications of librarians are established. In the British model of higher education, each university is responsible for maintaining the quality of the education it provides. Unlike the United States, where universities as well as individual programs are accredited by various external bodies, British universities are self-policing.

In order to ensure that these universities maintain their standards, external examiners are brought in to evaluate universities as a whole and its individual programs, to include library programs. The University of Cambridge (2004), for example, defines the external examiner's role thusly:

> External Examiners are so called because they act as Examiners (alongside other examiners appointed from among the staff of the University) and, because they are from outside the University, can provide an objective view to the nature and standards of the assessment of students. They are appointed to act as independent and impartial advisors providing informed comment on the standards set and student achievement in relation to those standards and to standards of comparable institutions elsewhere.

Furthermore,

> the main duties of an External Examiner are: to verify that standards are appropriate for the course(s) concerned; to assist institutions in the comparison of academic standards across higher education degrees and parts of degrees; and to ensure that their assessment processes are fair and are fairly operated and are in line with the institution's regulations.

Many universities in the United Kingdom and its former colonies in Africa, the Americas, Asia, and Australia and New Zealand utilize external examiners as a check on program curricula. They are often requested to evaluate and critique course offerings and programs as a whole as the programs train future professionals. Thus an external examiner of a library school would have a role in defining and shaping the curriculum that graduates qualified librarians. The external examiner also often has a direct influence on who may become a librarian. She/he often sits as final authority on final examinations and theses and participates as a member of thesis defense bodies.

WHO IS A QUALIFIED LIBRARIAN?

Defining "librarian" and "librarian qualifications" is not a simple matter. As we have seen, the making of librarians in the twentieth century has evolved into a number of complex of approaches. Some definitions are ambiguous and are closely related to library school curricula and the agencies that accredited them. In most Anglophone countries, librarians are a product of experience and the curriculum provided by the professional school each attended. An accrediting body often oversees that curriculum. The accrediting agency may be a government ministry or a professional organization.

Other definitions are more specific and provide qualifications for librarians at different levels of professionalism. This is particularly true in Latin America, where the qualifications of librarians may be defined in law. While librarians are expected to be trained to professional levels through education, it is the quasi-state-like professional organization that licenses the librarian and certifies her/him as qualified.

Librarianship is, however, in the process of being redefined. First, the very concept of librarianship is being challenged as either too limiting or as anachronistic. The School of Information Management and Systems (SIMS) at the University of California, Berkeley, (1995) describes its mission as the following:

> We propose a program that will advance, through teaching and research, the organization, management and use of information and information technology, and enhance our understanding of the impact of information on individuals, institutions, and society. This mission has both a technical component, concerned with the design and use of information systems and services, and a social sciences component, concerned with understanding how people seek, obtain, evaluate, use, and categorize information.

SIMS broke from the accrediting system of the American Library Association in 1994. The school graduates information professionals whose skills include and, at least in their eyes, transcend those of librarians. Because SIMS no longer participates under the ALA accreditation program, are their graduates forever barred from being considered "librarians" if they so wish?

Second, academic libraries in the United States have begun to reconsider and reevaluate the master of library science degree as the defining professional degree. The Council on Library and Information Resources (CLIR) has created a post-doctoral fellowship program for PhD holders in the humanities interested in pursuing careers as academic librarians but bypassing the heretofore required library credential. This, the CLIR (n.d.) argues, could create a new "scholarly information professional." As might be understood, the reaction to the scholarly information professional has met with mixed reactions. John Berry III (2003), in an article interestingly titled "But Don't Call 'em Librarians," recognizes the pressures to transition PhDs to library careers. He discusses various proposed options, including library school short courses. But Berry questions whether these information professionals should be permitted to call themselves librarians. And that would be to say that one cannot be a librarian without the vetted degree.

Third, the American Library Association created the Allied Professional Association (2005) in 2001 to certify individuals with advanced skills and to support librarians and other "library workers." In the twentieth century, just as in the seventeenth century, library workers were differentiated according to role, training, and purpose. "Other library workers" generally include all other library employees who do not meet the appropriate definition for librarian. These workers may include clerical and maintenance workers, but they also include paraprofessional employees and library technicians. These paraprofessionals and technicians often hold degrees, diplomas, and certificates other than the appropriate terminal professional degree (in Canada and the United States, the master of library science or its equivalent, elsewhere the bachelor's degree), and may perform duties very similar to those of librarians. By 2015 CLIR had its postdoctoral fellowship program in place. The statement of purpose for the scholarship had been muted slightly to, "[Offers] recent PhD graduates the chance to help develop research tools, resources, and services while exploring new career opportunities" (CLIR 2015.)

And fourth, at least two major "I-schools" appointed as their deans non-information/library scientists at the onset of the twenty-first century, just suggesting that information science is perhaps less science than one might have thought, at least in the eyes of university administrations. That said, it should be recalled that many information/library science faculty have crossed over from a diverse number of disciplines into information science. One early conversion was Don Swanson, trained as a physicist, who was named dean of the Graduate Library School in 1963.

As has been shown, the definition of "librarian" varies from country to country. It would be fair to conclude that since the early twentieth century the definition of librarian has been closely tied to specialized education. How that education and the credential holder are evaluated varies, but at least some library education has been required.

As we have seen, that model is being challenged. That challenge is in part due to the increased importance of information as commodity in the global environment. It is also partly because of particular shortages in library subspecialties, particularly in academic environments. Might the ALA-APA serve to "professionalize" otherwise qualified library workers who lack the appropriate credential? What will be the end result of the Bologna Process in Europe to rationalize their various educational experiences?

LIBRARIAN QUALIFICATIONS BEFORE
ACCREDITATION AND CERTIFICATION

The definition of librarian as a function of a specialized education is relatively new. This section addresses historical concepts of library qualification in Europe and North America. Until the late nineteenth century librarians by necessity came to the profession through means other than library school education.

The definition of librarian has been the subject of interest to bibliophiles since there were libraries. Jean-Baptiste Cotton des Houssayes (1780, 34), in his Discourse on the Duties of a Librarian, found himself unable to fully expound on the character and characteristics of the librarian: "When I reflect, indeed, on the qualifications that should be united in [the librarian of the Sorbonne], they present themselves to my mind in so great a number, and in such character of perfection, that I distrust my ability not only to enumerate, but also to trace a true picture of them."

Sir Thomas Bodley on the Qualifications of the Librarian

The Bodleian Library at Oxford University was formally opened in 1603. On transfer of his collection, Sir Thomas Bodley and Oxford established statutes to govern that library. If Bodley's (1926) letters to the Bodleian's first keeper, Thomas James, are any indicator, Sir Thomas took such interest in the management of the library that he might best be described as a micromanager by post. His micromanagement was extensive and extended from book binding decisions to the cost of hired horses. For example, Bodley advised James not to mark books with catalog numbers so as to not disfigure them (letter 21, February 5, 1602, in Bodley 1926, 28–30).

The Bodleian's librarian was to be a university graduate (Bodley 1603, 68) elected by the faculty. The elected librarian was required to take the following oath (Bodley 1603, 69):

> All and every of the Statutes, Constitutions, and Decrees, either made already, or hereafter to be made that may in any wise concern the Duty of the Keeper, and good Estate of the Library, I will observe in mine own Person, and to the uttermost of my Power, will cause to be observed by all other Persons, to whom the same may belong, as I hope to be saved, by God's infinite Mercy, thro' the Merits of Christ Jesus, revealed to me by his Holy Evangelists.

A similar oath was required of those wishing to use the library (Bodley 1603, 96–97). Parenthetically, patrons of the Bodleian are still required to take the oath, as did the author in 2003.

The library keeper was to be the chief operating officer of the library. In order to avoid "notorious Abuses," Bodley (1603, 102–105) specified that the university's vice-chancellor and seven other officers, all men of "excellent Integrity" would serve as "perpetual Overseers and Visitors of the Library" to ensure that the library was well managed and that library funds were appropriately accounted for (112). The overseers had the authority under the Statutes to "admonish, remove, or reform" the library keeper.

The library keeper was to hold tenure and was not to be removed from office except for cause. Once the office fell vacant for whatever reason, a convocation was to be called to elect the successor (1603, 69–70).

The library keeper's first duty was to maintain a registry "with a special, fair, and pleasing Hand" of donors to the library of books or money (1603, 71–2). Money was to be used to secure additional books for the collection (1603, 76).

The second duty of the librarian was to arrange the collection by academic faculties and to provide catalogs for each faculty collection, listing authors alphabetically. In addition, each catalog entry was to provide the title of the work, volume number, and date and place of publication (1603, 73).

Bodley (1603, 78–80) went so far as to specify the work schedule for the library keeper, based in part on the availability of natural light. The keeper's hours were to be from 8:00 a.m. to 11:00 a.m. then 2:00 p.m. to 5:00 p.m. from Easter to the Feast of St. Michael. His hours the rest of the year were to be from 1:00 p.m. to 4:00 p.m.. The keeper was to have Sundays and Christmas fully off as well certain feast days. As the Keeper entered or left the library, a warning bell was to be rung. Everyone, including the keeper, was prohibited from entering the library at night with any form of "Fire-light, upon pain of Deprivation from his Office forever."

The keeper was not to be the sole employee of the library. In the event of the indisposition of the keeper, a deputy could be appointed. That deputy was to be a university graduate and possess skills similar to that of the keeper (Bodley 1603, 87) In addition, a daily minister was to be at hand to assist the keeper. The minister was to possess adequate skills "to seek out, and distribute any books that are demanded" (1603, 83).

The keeper was to lose twenty shillings for every unauthorized absence from his office (Bodley 1603, 80). His salary was set at twenty Nobles, plus an additional thirty-three pounds, six shillings, and eight pence half to be paid semi-annually (1603, 89). The keeper's assistant was to receive ten pounds. In addition, four pounds was to be paid to "some poor honest Scholar, or Servant of the Keeper" to serve as custodian and cleaner of books, windows and furniture (1603, 90).

The Bodleian was not established as a lending library. Materials were to be used on site. It was the keeper's duty to deliver to all comers the materials requested. Certain materials were to be chained to desks and others maintained in closed stacks.

Justus Lipsius on the Qualifications of the Librarian

Justus Lipsius's (1607) book is not an outline of the duties and qualifications of librarians. It is a history of libraries. As such, it does not speak to librarians' qualifications except parenthetically.

Lipsius noted, for example, that the Roman polymath Marcus Varro was given instructions by Julius Caesar to establish a public library. Lipsius (1607, 67) commented that Varro was an appropriate candidate for the position, for "who in the world was better fitted than Varro, most learned in Greek and Roman letters, to carry out such a scheme?" By implication, then, the early seventeenth-century librarian as well as first-century BCE librarians should have been well educated or "lettered."

Lipsius (1607, 89), commenting on a Roman private library, one assembled and owned by Epaphroditus of Chaeronea, commended the collector not for the size of his library but for "the good taste he showed in choosing them."

Gabriel Naudé on the Qualifications of the Librarian

In his masterwork *Advice on Establishing a Library*, Naudé (1627) addressed issues in library development, book selection, the ornamentation of the library, and other like issues. His remarks on the qualifications of the librarian (1627, 76) is by comparison quite terse: "But to govern public use of the library with courtesy on the one hand and with all necessary precautions on the other, in my opinion, an honorable and learned man, one who knows books, should be selected and given a commensurate salary and the rank and title of Librarian, in accordance with the practice of all the most famous libraries" — in a word, a man like Naudé himself.

John Dury on the Qualifications of the Librarian

John Dury addressed two letters to his friend Samuel Hartlib on the need for libraries and the professionalization of librarianship. Hartlib, in turn, had the letters published as well as Dury's *Supplement to the Reformed School* in 1650 (Granniss 1906, 31). Dury acquired his brief library experience as an assistant to Bulstrode Whitelock, keeper of the king's medals and books. The "drudgery" of the job fell to Dury (Granniss 1906, 28–29).

For the examination of Dury's views on the qualification of the librarian as reflected in his two letters, the 1967 reprint of John Cotton Dana and Henry W. Kent's 1906 work is referenced here. The library foremost in Dury's mind was that at Oxford. It is therefore interesting to contrast Bodley's *Statutes* with Dury's letters, the latter written almost fifty years after the former. Bodley and Dury differed in several important areas. Bodley sought to professionalize librarianship, whereas Dury described it more as an honorific. Bodley would provide a specific salary for the library keeper position; Dury was less certain. But both agreed that compensation was to be provided. Bodley was far more specific in the duties of the office and the degree to which the library keeper was to be assisted.

These differences are perhaps to be expected in that Bodley had a personal interest in the management of the library, whereas Dury did not.

Perhaps most importantly, Bodley and Dury disagreed as to general access to the library. Bodley was far more guarded on who could be admitted to use the facilities, and he provided strict criteria for its use. Dury, on the other hand, held a far more open opinion and prescribed a more general policy. Dury, arguing against restrictive policies, invoked the scriptures and exclaimed it to be *"more blessed to give then to receiv"* (Granniss 1906, 64, emphasis in the original).

John Dury did receive some of his education at Oxford, so perhaps he had some firsthand knowledge of the state of the library and its management. Whether this hypothesis is correct cannot be established through a reading of his two published letters.

In the opening of his first letter, Dury observed that the profession of library keeper was frequently looked on as one for "profit and gain . . . and not in regard to the service, which is to bee don by them unto the Common-wealth of Israël, for the advancement of Pietie and Learning." (Dury 1650b, 39)

Most library keepers of his day, Dury stated, took their positions for self-improvement, for mercenary purposes. Most looked on their positions as that of guarding the books in their custody against loss or embezzlement, "and that is all" (Dury 1650b, 40–41). Few twenty-first-century librarians would come to the profession for purely pecuniary reasons, but perhaps some do to secure a reasonably safe sinecure.

Dury (1650b, 43) suggested that library keepers come to the profession for "Honorarie" rather than "Mercenarie" purposes and to that end they be offered a "competent allowance" of two hundred pounds per annum. As two hundred pounds was then a fairly large sum, library keepers should have a greater responsibility than merely the "bare keeping of the Books."

Libraries can be more than an ornament. A "fair Librarie" can become more than an ornament; it can become a "useful commoditie" for the public. A library without spirit is but a "dead Bodie." The library can be invigorated with public spirit and can be oriented for public service. Hence, Dury (1650b, 44) suggested that only those who have demonstrated public spiritedness should be called as librarians.

> The proper charge then of the Honorarie Librarie-Keeper in an Universitie should bee thought upon, and the end of that Imploiment, in my conception, is to keep the publick stock of Learning, which is in Books and Manuscripts to increas it, and to propose it to others in the waie which may bee most useful unto all; his work then is to bee a Factor and Trader for helps to Learning, and a Treasurer to keep them, and a dispenser to applie them to use, or to see them well used, or at least not abused. (Dury 1650b, 44–45)

To that end, the library keeper must develop a catalog. Dury would have had the books first divided by subject matter—languages and sciences—or by *subjectam materiam* (that is, what they treat), then by the language in which they are written. Once divided by subject and language, they should be listed in order by title (Dury 1650b, 45–46). The catalog needs be sufficiently flexible to permit new additions. It must also provide "proper Seats" of the books; that is, their location on the shelves or elsewhere.

To increase the library stock, the keeper should correspond widely with eminent scholars to offer to trade, for profit, "that what they want and wee have." The library keeper as trader and factor should facilitate the interchange of knowledge through the exchange of knowledge. The library keeper should also acquaint himself with the expertise within his university to assist it in accessing useful literature. The library keeper should also find ways to use the university's expertise to learn of information elsewhere (Dury 1650b, 48–49).

Library keepers should be regulated to "oblige them to carefulness." To that end, the library keeper should be required annually to account for books and money entrusted to him. He should also provide evidence of his "Profit in his Trade." He should report to "the chief Doctors of each facultie" who would receive reports of the library's accounts. In sum, the library keeper should demonstrate how the stock of information increased for the year for which he reports. Each chief doctor was to suggest additions to the collections. As additions to the book were made, they were to be added to a handwritten "Catalogue of Additionals" distributed internally within the university. Every three years, the catalogs should be merged, printed, published, and distributed "abroad."

The doctors were to be required to adjudge the appropriateness of the books listed in the additionals. Those of merit were to be incorporated into the general collection. Moreover, as the library—Dury spoke here of Oxford and later Cambridge—grew from the deposits of publishers and stationers who were required to forward all books published, the doctors should evaluate that stock to determine which should be added to the general collection and which should be placed in a supplementary collection. These "supplementary" books, too, were to have their own catalogs (Dury 1650b, 53–54).

John Dury's second letter is less of a plan for a library and more of a critique of the libraries at Oxford and Heidelberg. It was also something of a plea to Parliament to provide support for the Oxford Library.

The Heidelberg University Library, Dury argued, had fallen on difficult times and was no longer a seat of great learning. The reasons were that the library had been closed to most users, had been too closely guarded, and information had not been "Traded." He equated Heidelberg to the Biblical parable of the talents. Heidelberg was the buried talent. In fact, he argued, that "the keeping of that Librarie made it an

Idol, to be respected and worshiped for a raritie by an implicit faith, without any benefit to those who did esteem of it a far off" (Dury 1650b, 62).

But the second letter was even more of a plea to support learning without regard to parochial interests within the university and the nation as well as with foreigners. The library keeper had a responsibility, through "Trade," to assist in the expansion and growth of learning. Dury closed his second letter with a particularly perceptive conclusion. If, he argued, knowledge was filtered and constrained "to deserv the contenance of a Religious State . . . the increase of knowledg will increas nothing but strife. . . . But if hee, who is to bee intrusted with the managing of this Trade, bee addressed in the waie which leadeth unto this Aim without partialitie, his negotiation will bee a blessing unto this age and to posteritie" (Dury 1650b, 70–71).

James Kirkwood on the Qualifications of the Librarian

The Reverend James Kirkwood did not address himself so much to the duties of the librarian but more to the establishment of libraries in Scotland. His work represents a shift in the theory of the role of libraries and librarians. Prior to Kirkwood's work, libraries were considered the domain of universities, monasteries, and private persons. Kirkwood widens the circle to include a more pedestrian usage at the parish level— providing for more libraries at more places for more people.

Library keepers, Kirkwood suggested, could be school masters or the reader. The keepers were answerable to the ministers and heritors. The keeper was charged with keeping the books and "preserving them from all inconveniences." The keeper was barred from lending books to any except a heretor of the parish, Presbyterian ministers, or other parish residents proven respectful of books. The keeper was to inscribe in each book the library name as well as its donor (minister, heretor, or others). When lending books, the keeper was to receive an "obligation" from the borrower that the book would be returned within a month. What form the obligation should take is not stated. Finally Kirkwood recommended a cataloging scheme (for more on this, see the classification chapter). Each keeper was to follow "the same method of ranking and placing their Books" according "to rank the books according to name and number, in the general Catalogue" (Kirkwood 1699c, 37).

In his last message on his plan to develop libraries in Scotland, Kirkwood (1699a, 83–84) specified additional duties that would fall to the library keeper. These included the preparation of lists of borrowed books, preparation of a semi-annual report on the status and condition of the books, and the preparation for an audit every two to three years by the Synod inspectors.

The library keepers were prohibited from exchanging books among themselves. They also had the responsibility for controlling book lending. No books were to be lent to those who were not library benefactors. They were to collect a deposit of 125 percent of the value of books lent in order, as Kirkwood put it, to keep libraries from becoming book sellers (Kirkwood 1699a, 80–84). Limits were placed on the period of time books could be borrowed, based in part on the distance the borrower lived from the library. Borrowers were to be fined if books were kept beyond the designated period. Moreover, books were not to be lent to individuals unless they could demonstrate that they could transport the books without damaging them (Kirkwood 1699a, 84–88).

Jean-Baptiste Cotton des Houssayes on the Qualifications of the Librarian

On December 23, 1780, the librarian of the Sorbonne, Jean-Baptiste Cotton des Houssayes, delivered an address to the Assembly of the Sorbonne in Latin titled *Oratio habita in comitiis generalibus societatis sorbonicæ*. The address, it can be deduced from the text, was made on his inauguration as the library superintendent. It was published in 1781 in French as *Discours sur les qualités et les devoirs du bibliothéquaire* and in 1839 in English as *Discourse on the Duties and Qualifications of a Librarian*. It has subsequently been republished, including the reprint of the 1906 work by John Cotton Dana and Henry W. Kent cited here.

According to John Cotton Dana and Henry W. Kent (1906 i, 10) Cotton des Houssayes's *Discourse* occupied a very important place in nineteenth century bibliographical and philological literature. Again, according to Dana and Kent (1906a i, 28–29) the abbé made a number of false starts in contributing to the library literature of his day. They assert that the *Discourse* is Cotton des Houssayes's best contribution to the genre.

To place Cotton des Houssayes's *Discourse* into context, we should recall that this is an address before a learned body of a major European university. Cotton des Houssayes sought to describe the qualifications and duties of the individual placed at the head of that university's library. He (1780, 34) reminded us of the importance of the Society of the Sorbonne, "so justly celebrated in all Europe, or, more properly throughout the world, for the depth no less than the extent of its erudition." He also reminded us that the Sorbonne was steeped in both sacred and profane learning (1780, 35). The Sorbonne's librarian, he stated, was something of an official representative of the institution. In that light, the librarian (Cotton des Houssayes 1780, 36–7) "should be, above all, a learned and profound theologian; but to this qualification, which I shall call fundamental, should be united vast literary acquisitions, an exact and precise knowledge of all the arts and sciences, great facility of expression, and, lastly, that exquisite politeness which conciliates the affection of his visitors while his merit secures their esteem."

Not only should the librarian be versed in the arts and sciences, he should be an expert in the "science of bibliography." The science of bibliography, Cotton des Houssayes argued (1780, 37–38), "is nothing more than an exact and critical acquaintance with the productions of the intellect . . . the forerunner of all [other sciences],—as their guide who is to light them with his torch."

Cotton des Houssayes (1780, 38) broadened his description of the librarian to "the superintendent of the library, whatever be its character. . . . The library superintendent . . . should be no stranger to any department of learning: sacred and profane literature, the fine arts, the exact sciences." The superintendent, should it be his desire to expand the library and its reputation, should be a public person and "receive all visitors whether scholars or the simply curious, with an assiduous attention so polite and kindly, that his reception shall appear to each one the effect of a distinction purely personal" (Cotton des Houssayes 1780, 38–39). And on leaving someone even just met, the librarian should thank the stranger for his patronage.

It is a librarian's place to anticipate the information requirements of the patron and to make available without being asked materials to facilitate the patron's work. "The custodian of a library deposit" should never hide materials from patron but rather should seek to make them widely available.

The library superintendent must also have sound administrative judgment as well as knowledge of the arts and sciences (Cotton des Houssayes 1780, 42–43). That judgment should extend to the library's selection policies. Only those books of "genuine merit and well-approved utility" have a place on the library's shelves. These materials, in turn, must be classified correctly in order to make appropriate use of them: "And if, as is said, that books are the *medicine of the soul*, what avail these intellectual pharmacopoeias, if the remedies which they contain are not disposed in order and *labelled* with care?" (Cotton des Houssayes 1780, 44, emphasis in the original).

As librarians have these characteristics, is it of any wonder, Cotton des Houssayes asked, that librarians have earned significant scholarly reputations—that is, "brilliancy in the empire of letters" (Cotton des Houssayes 1780, 45)? Cotton des Houssayes chose not to enumerate these emperors of letters but rather chose to enumerate the enumerators: Naudé, Quirini [*sic*],[1] Passioei, Muratori, and Franck (1780, 46–47).

Edward Edwards on the Qualifications of the Librarian

Edward Edwards was an assistant to Sir Anthony Panizzi of the British Museum Library. Edwards wrote at a time when librarianship was primarily a male-dominated profession, and perhaps one for the second sons of gentlemen: "Librarianship, like schoolkeeping, has, in England, too frequently been made a respectable sort of 'Refuge for the Destitute'" (Edwards 1859 ii, 1063–1064). Edwards did not advocate formal training for librarians, just as he did not recommend the formation of professional library associations in his writing. As Edwards (1859 ii, 938–939) was to suggest, a professional organization would need to provide for a more systematic study of the profession before he could support one.

Edwards was ahead of his time in several respects. The last half of his two-volume work, *Memoirs of Libraries*, is essentially a textbook on library economy titled *Economy of Libraries*. The work covers major issues of librarianship from book selection to library furniture. It includes cataloging and classification, librarian administration, and accounting. With some revision and updating, Edwards's *Economy of Libraries* might compete well as a text for a contemporary survey course in librarianship

Edwards (1859 ii, 933) is perhaps the first library theoretician to distinguish among the skills and qualifications of librarians for different types of libraries. Edwards dedicates a full chapter, "Librarianship," in his monumental two-volume *Memoirs of Libraries* to the qualifications of the librarian. Edwards (1859 ii, 933) paraphrases as he says, "An old rejoinder:—'You have convinced me that it is impossible to be a good Librarian.'"

Edwards (1859 ii, 934) refutes the idea that different libraries (the Bodleian and a "village reading room") may have different root functions and different qualifications for their librarians. In that conclusion, Edwards is also perhaps the first to suggest that there are skills specific to the librarian profession needed by all librarians to manage their libraries properly, no matter how complex or small they may be: "In truth, the root-qualities that should underlie this function, whatever the scale and the accidents of its exercise, are as necessary in the humblest Village, as in the seat of a University." A librarian must possess three qualities: "Thus he must be: (1) a lover of Books; (2) a man of methodical habits and of an organizing mind; (3) a man of genial temper and of courteous demeanor" (Edwards ii, 934). These conditions precede linguistic and bibliographical skills, which are required of an effective librarian. Furthermore, "to the common eye his duties look, and must look, much easier that they are" (Edwards 1859 ii, 935).

Edwards (1859 ii, 938) closes his chapter on librarianship with the following thought, equally relevant today:

> Meanwhile, every man who enters on this calling may give a powerful impulse to its elevation. It will never open for him a path to wealth or to popular fame. It is, and is likely to be, eminently exposed to social indifference and misconception. . . . By the enlightened and zealous discharge of its functions, a man's work may be made to carry within it the unfailing seeds of many mental harvests, only to be fully gathered in, when he shall have long lain in his grave.

Melvil Dewey on the Qualifications of the Librarian

Melvil Dewey (1898) defined the late nineteenth century as the "Library Age." The librarian, according to Dewey, as quoted in Radford and Radford (2001, 299), is a "formidable gatekeeper between order and chaos." Dewey believed that there were skills and qualifications necessary of the librarian. He (1898) also argued that other values superseded those qualifications:

> In our State Library School I give each year a course of five lectures of the qualifications of a librarian, and point out under a half-hundred different heads the things we should demand in an ideal librarian; but when we have covered the whole field of scholarship and technical knowledge and training, we must confess that overshadowing all are the qualities of the man. To my thinking, a great librarian must have a clear head, a strong hand, and above all, a great heart. He must have a head as clear as the master in diplomacy; a hand as strong as he who quells the raging mob, or leads great armies on to victory; and a heart as great as he who, to save others, will, if need be, lay down his own life. Such shall be greatest among librarians; and, when I look into the future, I am inclined to think that most of the men who will achieve this greatness will be women.

Dewey (1887) instructed in "Brief Rules for Library Handwriting" that librarians should also have a good "hand," so that when preparing catalog cards, the information would be legible.

Dewey (1989, 5) also noted that librarians were no longer mere keepers of books, protecting books from human and other damage. The librarian should also be certain that their libraries contain "the best books on the best subjects, regarding carefully the wants of his special community. Then, having the best books he must create among his people, his pupils, a desire to read those books." The librarian should teach readers how and what to select. "Such a librarian will find enough who are ready to put themselves under his influence and direction, and if competent and enthusiastic, he may soon largely shape the reading, and through it the thought, of his whole community."

Libraries and schools, Dewey (1989, 5) asserted, should work together to support literacy. The school is to teach reading; the library to supply reading material.

Ainsworth Rand Spofford on the Qualifications of the Librarian

Ainsworth Rand Spofford (1825–1908), sixth Librarian of Congress, began his career as a journalist. Abraham Lincoln appointed him Librarian of Congress. He is credited with expanding the role of the Library of Congress, its collection, and developing it into a truly national collection. His publications include *A Book for All Readers* (1900) and later editions and *The Library of Choice Literature* (1988) in ten volumes. Spofford (1900, 272–273) held that librarianship had its benefits: "Librarianship furnishes one of the widest fields for the most eminent attainments. . . . Of all the pleasures which a generous mind is capable of enjoying, that of aiding and enlightening others is one of the finest and most delightful."

As others before him, Spofford addressed the qualifications of librarians. He (1900, 242–265) was dedicated to the subject. All qualifications he indicated are important, and the order he presented them in was not an indicator of rank.

- Librarians should read only the best books. They do not have time to read them all.
- Librarians must be educated.
- Librarians need skills in foreign languages, particularly Latin and French.
- Librarians should have a wide knowledge of books.
- Librarians should have good management skills.
- Librarians should be even tempered.
- Librarians should be in good health.
- Librarians should have sound common sense.
- Librarians should love their work.
- Librarians should have a strong *esprit de corps*.
- Librarians require accuracy.
- Librarians should learn from their mistakes.
- Librarians should have a "facility for order."
- Librarians should have good time management.
- Librarians should be neat.
- Librarians need "inexhaustible patience" and "unfailing tact."
- Librarians must posses "energy and untiring industry."
- There needs to [be] mutual support among librarians and other workers.
- Librarians require a "liberal and impartial mind."
- Librarians need "a high order of talent."

The profession also had its deficits, to again quote Spofford (1900, 266–274):

- In the first place, there is very little money in it.
- There are peculiar trials and vexations connected with it. . . . The librarian must be a teacher of all sciences and literatures at once.
- There are special annoyances in the service of a public, which includes always some inconsiderate and many ignorant persons.
- The peculiar variety and great number of the calls incessantly made upon the librarian's knowledge constitute a formidable draft upon any but the strongest brain.

- Frequently the interference with his proper work by the library authorities. . . . Sometimes they are quick-sighted and intelligent persons, and recognize the importance of letting the librarian work out everything in his own way . . . but there are sometimes men on a board of library control who are self-conceited and pragmatical, thinking they know everything about how a library should be managed.

Finally to close, Spofford (1900, 274) states:

I once quoted the saying that "the librarian who reads is lost"; but it would be far truer to say that the librarian who does not read is lost; only he should read wisely and with a purpose. He should make his reading helpful in giving him a wide knowledge of facts, of thoughts, and of illustrations, which will come perpetually into play in his daily intercourse with the inquiring public.

John Cotton Dana on the Qualifications of the Librarian

John Cotton Dana (1906, 123–124) was among the first populist librarians. He argued for full and open access to the general public to public libraries: "A free public library is not a people's post-graduate school, it is the people's common school."

In his *Library Primer*, Dana (1906, 20–21) did not specify specific skills for the librarian, although he did contend that cataloging and classification skills were critical (24). He (1906, 20–23) urged libraries to hire trained librarians for both large and small libraries. The head librarian needed to have both training and experience. Library boards were advised to ignore "politics, social considerations, church sympathies, religious prejudices, family relationship" when considering someone for that post. In addition, "the librarian should have culture, scholarship, and executive ability," be a "teacher of teachers," and be able to gain the confidence of children.

Dana (1925) was opposed to librarian certification or licensure: "It is clear, I hope, that I have no faith in the theory that government interference, state or national, . . . will help library workers to become more learned, more original, wiser, or better managers; or will make librarians more highly esteemed or librarianship more like a profession."

CONCLUSIONS: THE LIBRARY AS SOCIAL ENGINE

Melvil Dewey's contributions to librarianship are legend. They are also controversial. For the most part, his contributions were for the betterment of the profession for the best of reasons—founding a library school, developing a classification scheme adopted widely, establishing the American Library Association, co-founding and editing the *Library Jour-*

nal. And in the eyes of many, he was instrumental in moving librarianship from vocation to profession. He also championed simplified spelling.

Dewey, both a bigot and a sexist, often championed progressive social policy for what we at the turn of the new millennium might interpret as the wrong reasons. It is important when criticizing historical figures to interpret them in the context of their time and not ours. He was instrumental in opening librarianship to women. He admitted women students into the library school at Columbia College in 1887, a practice that may have precipitated the school's move to Albany in 1889. Dewey was also a proponent of practical librarianship.

It has been argued that Dewey's motives for opening librarianship to women was not entirely for the betterment of women or of the profession. He was, it is suggested, seeking to depreciate the profession by making it "women's work" and thereby depressing wages in the field (Beck 1992). Moreover, according to Sarah Vann (1961, 31), without women as students, the school's enrollment would have been too small to permit its continuation.

Whatever Dewey's intention was, librarianship was metamorphosed from a male-dominated to a female-dominated profession in the twentieth century, and it was to become one with a relatively low wage structure. According to the Librarian of Congress, Herbert Putnam (1916, 880), the entry of women into the library workforce represented a "potent agency" for women at a time when female equality was largely a dream. By 1916 women had gained the right to vote in a number of countries—for example, Finland (1906), Norway (1913), and Denmark (1915). It was not until 1918 that Canadian women were granted suffrage and 1920 for their peers in the United States. The war years (World War I, 1914–1918) also marked an emergence of women into the work force of the countries involved in the conflagration. Mary Maack (1996) cites the inaugural address in 1916 by ALA president Henry Putman, in which the incoming president noted that libraries were a "potent force" for women, "bringing them into the field and admitting them on a basis of equality, thus allowing them to prove themselves." Clare Beck (1992) has called librarianship an "androgynous" profession because of the nature of the work and the people who perform it. The profession may now be "androgynous," but it certainly was not always so.

Melvil Dewey's concept for library education was soon emulated in Europe and elsewhere. Mumtaz Ali Anwar (1990/1991) describes, for example, India's first library training class at the University of the Punjab led by Asa Don Dickinson in 1915.

NOTE

1. Dana and Kent, in their endnotes, offer the correct spelling of the cardinal's name as Querini.

NINE

Love of Libraries and Advice on Library Formation

Every country has its history of great libraries and library benefactors. Libraries have often depended on and often benefited from philanthropy. In England Sir Thomas Bodley (1545–1613) participated in library creation through a bequest, just as Samuel Pepys would do ninety years later (see below). In Germany the librarians of the University of Göttingen played pivotal roles. In Spain Hernando Colón (1488–1539), one of Christopher Columbus's sons, writer, and bibliophile, established an important library. In the United States Andrew Carnegie helped build many library buildings, and the Bill and Melinda Gates Foundation has provided much computer hardware and software. The Gates Foundation also provided equipment and services to libraries in developing countries.

Others have advised their governments of the day to create libraries for the benefit of scholars, to promote their own stature and immortalization, or the public. We know that Marcus Terentius Varro (116–27 BCE) was directed by Julius Caesar to build a public library in Rome. Varro died before he could accomplish his charge. He left behind *De bibliothecis*, said to be blueprint for the design of that library. *De bibliothecis* unfortunately has not survived. Justus Lipsius (1607, 91) extols his unnamed prince to promote library creation: "Consider, O Most Illustrious Prince, how the love of books brings favour and high renown, — such favour and renown as should be granted to great men like yourself."

As is discussed in greater depth in chapter 4, our contemporary conception of public libraries differs greatly from the definition from Varro, which endured to the beginning of the twentieth century. Public libraries were "public" in part because they were usually funded from the "public purse," by a prince, government, or church. Private libraries were just that, the property of individuals like Sir Thomas Bodley, Samuel Pepys, or Thomas Jefferson, each of whom offered their libraries to "public" institutions as a gift or at a price.

Much has been made of the differences in the breadth and depth of public and private library collections. Public libraries by design and necessity are to be balanced and broad in their collection policies. Private libraries reflect the tastes and interests of their owners and are therefore far more selective.

Sir Thomas Bodley

Sir Thomas Bodley was both a true bibliophile and a grateful son of Oxford University. Bodley did not discuss his love of books in his autobiographical sketch *Reliquiæ Bodleianæ* (Bodley 1609). He stated his wish to leave public service and to retire to a quieter life, he concluded to "set up my Staff at the Library-Door at Oxon" to rebuild a library at Oxford to the benefit of its students. He made great provision for the restoration, maintenance, and enlargement of that library (Bodley 1609, 57–59). To govern that library, an extensive set of statutes was promulgated (Bodley 1603). Bodley's statutes are discussed in detail in chapter 8 on the librarian qualifications.

Gabriel Naudé

Gabriel Naudé (1627) was not the first to write a treatise on library formation, but his *Avis pour dresser une bibliothèque présenté à Monseigneur le Président de Mesme*[1] first published in 1627 is by far the best known and perhaps the most frequently copied. Naudé's work was translated into several languages soon after its publication, including Latin, making it available to scholars throughout Europe very quickly. The book has been retranslated and updated into the twentieth century, to include an American translation published in 1950. Each chapter of *Avis* addresses a different aspect of library establishment. The first two chapters are a justification of library establishment.

The third chapter lays out a strategy by which to begin. Naudé (1627, 4) recognized that attaching one's name to a library might serve to perpetuate the memory of the name. The Mesmes name did not so last. Naudé was more successful later in his career with the Mazarine Library. Libraries, by maintaining the works of great minds, also help to maintain the memory of those great minds (Naudé 1627, 6). Naudé would have those who seek to build great libraries to emulate those who have done so or those who have studied the process. Of the former, he cites Fontney, Hallé, and others; of the latter Juan Bautista Cardona, Richard de Bury, Vincenzo Pinelli, and Antonio Possevino[2] (Naudé 1627, 10–11). He would then copy the catalogs of both public and private libraries, not to imitate them but to learn from them and to infer from the collections what a good collection is. A collection of catalogs also aids one in finding items of interest (Naudé 1627, 12–13).

The fourth chapter addresses the size of the collection. A good library is not judged by the quantity of books it contains but by the quality of the books. Libraries created for private use or merely for show may be designed by interests or esthetics. A library for public use must have a more general collection of the " principal authors who have written upon the great diversity of particular subjects and chiefly upon all of the arts and sciences" (Naudé 1627, 16). "It must be said also that there is nothing more to the credit of a library than that every man finds in it what he seeks . . . since it may be said that there is no book whatsoever, be it never so bad or disparaged, but may in time be sought for by someone" (Naudé 1627, 17). Naudé would have a library err on the side of size when all else is taken into consideration; for the greater the number of books, the greater the likelihood that there will be quality among the rest.

The fifth chapter focuses on selection. According to Naudé (1627, 20):

> The prime rule . . . is . . . to furnish a library with all the first and principal authors, both ancient and modern, chosen from the best editions (collected works or single books), along with the best and most learned interpreters and communicators that are to be found in every field of learning, not forgetting those that are least common and consequently more interesting.

Naudé's second rule is to collect materials in their original languages and idioms. Third, collect the experts in each discipline. Fourth, collect the best commentaries. Fifth, collect dissertations on "any particular subject, general or specific." Sixth, collect those who argue against any particular subject or thesis. Seventh, collect innovators and those who propound new theories. Eighth, collect the first authors to express an idea, as these ideas are the purest. Ninth, collect works on little-known, little-treated, and new subjects. Tenth, collect contrarians and heretics as well as those "that hate us." Eleventh, sets or collections of different writers on the same subject should be collected. Twelfth, libraries need to collect from among the popular literature of the day so as not to miss the gem among the dross. Thirteenth, dictionaries and the like are needed. And fourteenth, collect literatures in vogue in different places and in different times so as not to be out of touch with popular tastes (Naudé 1627, 21–35). One might hasten to point out that Naudé did not have in mind popular fiction but rather different schools of philosophy, law, history, or polemics. Perhaps it is meaningful that Naudé mentions Boccaccio's (1313–1375) *De casibus* but not the *Decameron.* No references are made either to Chaucer (1343–1400) or to Cervantes (1547–1616).

Juan Páez de Castro

Juan Páez de Castro's (1512–1570) earlier and more obscure work the *Memorial sobre la utilidad de juntar una buena biblioteca* was addressed to Felipe II of Spain and urged the establishment of a royal library. Naudé (1627, 1) himself cites Bishop Juan Bautista Cardona as having published counsel on the establishment of the Royal Library of El Escorial, a work he damned with faint praise. Ambrosio de Morales is also credited with preparation of a memorandum supporting establishment of the library. That said, none of the three, Páez de Castro, Cardona, nor Morales developed a theory of practice (López de Prado 2000). They were successful in their counsel to Felipe II, who established the Biblioteca de El Escorial. Felipe II ascended the Spanish throne in 1529 at the age of two and reigned until 1598. He began building the palace at El Escorial in 1563.

Johann Christian Koch

Ninety years after Naudé published his *Avis,* Johann Christian Koch (1678–1738) wrote a work as obscure as that of Juan Páez de Castro. That work, *Schediasma de ordinanda bibliotheca,* dated 1713, describes how to order a library. It, too, is dedicated and directed to a ranking official, in this case to the elector of Saxony (Prideux 1904). Koch was recognized as an important library advocate in his day (Prideux 1904).

ON THE LOVE OF BOOKS

Expressions of love for libraries and of books have a long history. The literature distinguishes four types of individuals "afflicted" with book or library passion—the bibliophile, the bibliomaniac, bibliomane, and the book collector. According to Rabinowitz and Kaplan (1999, 134) a bibliophile is "one who loves books," a bibliomaniac is "a book lover gone mad," and a bibliomane is "one who collects books indiscriminately." Bibliomania has been with us a long time and has been defined in a variety of related ways. Bibliomania comes in two extreme forms. The first is a monomania for rare books without discernment to quality or purpose. The second is to follow the cultural currents of the day and collect what is *à la mode* to collect.

Bibliophiles, bibliomanes, and bibliomaniacs have been among us forever. Justus Lipsius (1607, 91) cites Lucius Annaeus Seneca. Book collecting was commonplace in Seneca's day (3 BCE–65 CE). But Seneca did not particularly approve of it, as most collectors collected for show rather than use. In 1345 Richard de Bury equated the love of books with the love of God. The *Dictionnaire universel* of 1708 defined bibliomania as *"folie, manie d'amasser des livres"* (folly, a mania for amassing books). Gustave Flaubert's short book *Bibliomania: A Tale,* first published in 1836, recounts the fictional trials and tribulations of the bookseller Giacomo, a former monk who had been willing to kill in search of the *Mystery of St. Michael*.

Édouard Rouveyre (1899 i, 24), quoting A. Claudin, offers further enlightenment on bibliomania. Nicholas Basbanes (1995, 12) differentiates between the bibliophile and the bibliomane. He cites Hanns Bohatta: "The bibliophile is the master of his books, the bibliomaniac their slave." Basbanes (1995, 27–28) also borrows a psychoanalytic definition from Dr. Norman Weiner. Bibliomania is "'an inordinate desire' for books . . . [it is] 'a problem-solving complex of activities that relieves anxiety or directly gratifies certain instinctual drives.'" Bibliomania is therefore Freudian in its manifestations.

Not infrequently each of the three—bibliophile, the bibliomane, and the collector—are found in the one. A bibliophile is one who loves books and what they represent. A bibliomane is one with an obsessive compulsion to collect books; the book collector has the means to satisfy that compulsion. Further distinctions may be drawn. A bibliophile loves books for their content. A book collector may collect for reasons of "external" esthetics rather than "internal" knowledge. Such a collector opts for the well-bound book rather than the well-written book. Some (e.g., Sorel 1664) are disdainful of those who treat books like tapestries, something to hang from their shelves. But others recognize that books are collected for any number of reasons, some more intellectual than others.

Bibliophiles, or at least those who write about bibliophiles, have an interesting sense of humor. Jules Richard (1883, 100–101) recounts that a certain Chalon of Mons, Belgium, published a small catalog of the books lost in a fire by Count T. N. A. de Fortsas. But it was a catalog of imaginary books. Moreover, the account was republished several times. Then there is the story on the library of the apocryphal abbot of Pouponville, yet another library stocked with imaginary books.

Holbrook Jackson (2001), writing in 1930, described bibliomania as an essentially masculine undertaking. He was to claim that women and books were at odds with one another (1932). Women collectors were not to be taken seriously unless they collected in a "masculine way." There were, however, important women collectors and commentators on female bibliophiles. Among them were Marjorie Wiggin Prescott (1932, cited in Hastings 2014) and Genevieve B. Earle (1933, cited in Hastings 2014). Prescott's work was privately published. For additional detail, see Emi Hasting's web-posted article (2014) "Women Collectors in Their Own Words." Hasting's post documents the importance of women as book collectors and bibliophiles.

Christian Galantaris (1998) presents us with a history of the book, of bibliophiles, and of bibliomanes, as well as numerous humorous anecdotes and stories. Galantaris discusses in two volumes all aspects of bibliophilia and bibliomania in a historic and contemporary context. The focus is primarily on the French experience.

Both Rabinowitz and Kaplan (1999) and Basbanes (1995) are more than a little droll. Rabinowitz and Kaplan (1999) present a great variety of material on the book, as indicated by their subtitle: *A Book Lover's Treasury of Stories, Essays, Humor, Lore, and Lists on Collecting, Reading, Borrowing, Lending, Caring for, and Appreciating Books.* This is truly a subtitle in the old style and syntax. The book is a collection of essays by book lovers and ranges in subject matter from "Ten Memorable Books That Never Existed" to "Benjamin Franklin's Epitaph."

Nicholas Basbanes (1995) is something of a collector of collectors. He recounts histories of famous bibliophiles, bibliomanes, and bibliokleptos (book thieves). His emphasis is on twentieth-century American collectors, but he does provide a history in the first few chapters. In chapter eight (1995, 275), Basbanes informs us that "we are what we read." As proof, he cites several prominent collectors—among them Maurice Robert, Erastothenes of Alexandria, and Charles Lamb. We conclude from his work that there are any number of kinds of bibliophiles and bibliomanes. Fortunately for the world of libraries there are far fewer bibliokleptos. One valuable contribution made by Basbanes (1995) is his discussions on the disposition of personal libraries when, inevitably, the collectors die or are otherwise forced to be divested of the collection. Some make bequests to universities. Others allow their collections to go to auction. Some do not wait for death and either choose to sell or are forced by circumstances to sell their collections. Basbanes repeatedly reminds us that personal libraries that can be retained intact and are gifted or purchased by universities are in and of themselves major contributions to scholarship and are, implicitly, a social good. And as we shall see at the end of this chapter, William Blades (1888), who wrote on library disasters, had his moments as well.

Perhaps the best known of these love affairs with books is that of Richard de Bury as expressed in his *Philobiblon*, dating from the fourteenth century. The book was written in 1345, about one hundred years before Gutenberg and the invention of printing in the West; but it was first published in Cologne in 1473. As we appreciate de Bury's love of books, we must also appreciate that by "books" he meant holographic writings, handwritten manuscripts. And not quite seven hundred years later, we have digital online access to his and other works. Thus the fourteenth-century context in which de Bury loved his books is very different from that of the sixteenth and subsequent centuries.

Books in the fourteenth century were expensive. The production of books was extremely labor intensive, with monks in scriptoria, copying one book from another, the imagery brought to us by Umberto Eco in his novel *The Name of the Rose.*

De Bury[3] puts his love of books thusly:

To this end, most acceptable in the sight of God, our attention has long been unweariedly devoted. This ecstatic love has carried us away so powerfully, that we have resigned all thoughts of other earthly things, and have given ourselves up to a passion for acquiring books. That our intent and purpose, therefore, may be known to posterity as well as to our contemporaries, and that we may for ever stop the perverse tongues of gossipers as far as we are concerned, we have published a little treatise written in the lightest style of the moderns; for it is ridiculous to find a slight matter treated of in a pompous style. And this treatise (divided into twenty chapters) will clear the love we have had for books from the charge of excess, will expound the purpose of our intense devotion, and will narrate more clearly than light all the circumstances of our undertaking. And because it principally treats of the love of books, we have chosen, after the fashion of the ancient Romans, fondly to name it by a Greek word, *Philobiblon*. (De Bury 1909, preface)

The *Philobiblon* is available in numerous translations and editions. Originally published in Latin, the electronic edition of the 1909 English translation by E. C. Thomas is referenced here. Thomas noted and rejected claims in his introduction that the *Philobiblon* had been written by Robert Holkot rather than by de Bury.

Books for de Bury (1909, 10) preserve knowledge and truth:

Truth that triumphs over all things, which overcomes the king, wine, and women, which it is reckoned holy to honour before friendship, which is the way without turning and the life without end, which holy Boethius considers to be threefold in thought, speech, and writing, seems to remain more usefully and to fructify to greater profit in books.

. . . that nothing is better than wisdom: wherefore no prize could be assigned for wisdom. (1909, 15)

Moreover, since books are the aptest teachers, as the previous chapter assumes, it is fitting to bestow on them the honour and the affection that we owe to our teachers. . . . Whoever therefore claims to be zealous of truth, of happiness, of wisdom or knowledge, aye, even of the faith, must needs become a lover of books. (1909, 17–18)

In chapter 7 de Bury addresses the woes of war and the destruction of books. It is only in chapter 8 that he begins to explain his book acquisitions. It must be recalled that de Bury, a bishop and nobleman, had ample opportunity to explore both public and private libraries. His love of books came to him early. As his position in society improved, so did his access to books. He had opportunities to travel widely as a diplomat. While abroad he spent his time well searching for books. He reports that he would uncover book caches and free the books. And as his love of books became more widely known, the number of books he received as gifts increased: "But in truth we wanted manuscripts not moneyscripts;

we loved codices more than florins, and preferred slender pamphlets to pampered palfreys" (1909, 56).

In chapter 9 de Bury expressed a preference for the "works of the ancients," but by no means did he eschew more contemporary manuscripts. He built further on this in chapter 10. He noted that later scholars drew on the wisdom of earlier writers, that without the earlier knowledge, new discoveries were not possible. Thus, as de Bury described it, books improved through that process. In this he anticipated Sir Isaac Newton (c. 1642–1727), who observed that his discoveries were the result of the standing on the shoulders of giants.

In chapter 11 de Bury stated his preference for "books of liberal learning" over law books. His explanation is as timely today perhaps as it was in his day:

> But in truth, as the [law] deals with contraries, and the power of reason can be used to opposite ends, and at the same the human mind is more inclined to evil, it happens with the practisers of this science that they usually devote themselves to promoting contention rather than peace, and instead of quoting laws according to the intent of the legislator, violently strain the language thereof to effect their own purposes.

Unlike many others of his day, de Bury did not reject poets and writers of fables. Poetry and fables serve well to inform and to enlighten. As he wrote:

> Taking this salutary instruction to heart, let the detractors of those who study the poets henceforth hold their peace, and let not those who are ignorant of these things require that others should be as ignorant as themselves, for this is the consolation of the wretched. (De Bury 1909, ch. 13)

De Bury paid particular care to the meaning of words. It was his practice to annotate and update older texts to reflect the meanings of foreign and archaic terms. Rhetoric and grammar were important to him. He was also protective of books. Books were to be cared for, looked after, mended, and repaired. Books were to be treated with great care. De Bury was as disdainful of students and their disregard for books and knowledge, as was H. G. Wells in an essay in *World Brain* (1938), or many twenty-first-century observers. He was equally critical of ill-bred scholars:

> You may happen to see some headstrong youth lazily lounging over his studies, and when the winter's frost is sharp, his nose running from the nipping cold drips down, nor does he think of wiping it with his pocket-handkerchief until he has bedewed the book before him with the ugly moisture. Would that he had before him no book, but a cobbler's apron! His nails are stuffed with fetid filth as black as jet, with which he marks any passage that pleases him. He distributes a multitude of straws, which he inserts to stick out in different places, so that

the halm may remind him of what his memory cannot retain. These straws, because the book has no stomach to digest them, and no one takes them out, first distend the book from its wonted closing, and at length, being carelessly abandoned to oblivion, go to decay. He does not fear to eat fruit or cheese over an open book, or carelessly to carry a cup to and from his mouth; and because he has no wallet at hand he drops into books the fragments that are left. Continually chattering, he is never weary of disputing with his companions, and while he alleges a crowd of senseless arguments, he wets the book lying half open in his lap with sputtering showers. Aye, and then hastily folding his arms he leans forward on the book, and by a brief spell of study invites a prolonged nap; and then, by way of mending the wrinkles, he folds back the margin of the leaves, to the no small injury of the book. Now the rain is over and gone, and the flowers have appeared in our land. Then the scholar we are speaking of, a neglecter rather than an inspecter [*sic*] of books, will stuff his volume with violets, and primroses, with roses and quatrefoil. Then he will use his wet and perspiring hands to turn over the volumes; then he will thump the white vellum with gloves covered with all kinds of dust, and with his finger clad in long-used leather will hunt line by line through the page; then at the sting of the biting flea the sacred book is flung. (De Bury 1909, ch. 17)

In chapters 18 and 19 de Bury addressed more administrative questions—the use of his collection by scholars and the means of lending books to students. In chapter 18 he indicated his wish that his books be given to Oxford University. Anticipating Bodley, de Bury prescribed that five scholars be appointed to oversee his library. By permission only, books could be loaned for study or "inspection" away from the library. And this was only permitted where duplicate copies existed; an exception was to be made for Oxford dons. Borrowers were required to leave a pledge. If for any reason the book could not be returned, borrowers were required to repay the value of the lost materials. Copying or transcription had to be done on the premises. The keepers (librarians) were to account for all books on an annual basis.

De Bury's books were sent to Durham College, Oxford. When Henry VIII dissolved Durham College, parts of the de Bury collection were distributed to other Oxford libraries and a portion into private hands.

Samuel Pepys (1633–1703) is often cited as the epitome of the bibliophile. Pepys maintained a very well-ordered and cataloged library, said to include some three thousand volumes at his death. The library was given to Magdalene College of Cambridge University by bequest. Like Sir Thomas Bodley before him, Pepys left his library to one of England's premier universities. Unlike Bodley, Pepys did not leave extensive instructions on the use and management of his library. Pepys did direct that the library be named the "Bibliotheca Pepysiana" and that no one but the master of Magdalene College be allowed to physically remove books from the library and that he be limited to no more than ten at a time. In addition, some of Pepys's manuscripts found their way to Oxford's Bodleian Library.

Samuel Pepys may not have left specific instructions on developing libraries, but he was familiar with Gabriel Naudé's instructions. Pepys noted in his diary for October 1665:

> I abroad to the office and thence to the Duke of Albemarle, all my way reading a book of Mr. Evelyn's translating [of Naudé's (1627) *Advice on Establishing a Library*] and sending me as a present, about directions for gathering a Library; but the book is above my reach. (Pepys 1659)

Thus not only had Naudé's *Advice* spread; it had fallen into the hands of noted bibliophiles.

Charles Sorel (1664), a novelist and satirist, informs us that the criteria for the selection of books in French should begin with an analysis of the purity of the language, the very roots of the Académie française:

> Comme les paroles sont les principales marques de la pensée et des intentions, il faut que ce qui sert à les exprimer soit entierement pur et sans obscurité. (Sorel 1664, 1)

Moreover,

> pour bien sçavoir la langue françoise, on doit s'adresser d'abord aux livres qui en rapportent tousles mots. Cela est absolument necessaire aux estrangers, et mesmes les naturels françois, en ont quelquefois besoin pour terminer leurs doutestouchant quelques façons de parler extraordinaires. (Sorel 1664, 2)

Once the purity of language criterion is satisfied, one should then collect the classic and modern rhetoric texts. The second chapter provides a list of the classics as well as French rhetoricians (Sorel 1664). Each subsequent chapter addresses a specific genre: chapter 3, philosophical works; chapter 4, Christian instruction; chapter 5, what we might today call sociology; chapter 6, the art of speaking; chapter 7, the belles-lettres; chapter 8, histories; chapter 9, fables and allegories; chapter 10, poetry; chapter 11, translated works; and chapter 12, the evolution of the language. Sorel, with perhaps a bit of his famed satire, recommends the acquisition of four copies of important books. The first copy is for display. It should be the most handsome of choices. The second copy is for use. And the third is to be set aside to lend to friends. The fourth is to replace the third.

According to John Cotton Dana and Henry W. Kent (1906a, 9), Pierre-Alexander Gratet-Duplessis was responsible in 1781 for the French translation of the Abbé Jean-Baptiste Cotton des Houssayes's address *Oratio habita in comitiis generalibus societatis sorbonicæ* before the Assembly of the Sorbonne. Gratet-Duplessis was also responsible for making the document public, where it was published under the title *Discours sur les qualities et les devoirs du bibliothéquaire*.[4]

By the nineteenth century, bibliophilia had been differentiated into bibliomania and bibliophilia. Authors like Etienne-Gabriel Peignot (1823), Jacques-Charles Brunet (1860), Édouard Rouveyre (1899), and Émile Henriot (1928) wrote at length (some at greater length than others) on the creation of libraries. While not limited to home libraries, their texts were generally directed to the individual seeking to develop the well-rounded home library. While Brunet (1860) purports to offer an international survey, the work is limited to European works, with an emphasis on the French. It does provide an extensive bibliography of fifteenth- to nineteenth-century European publications. The work is selective rather than exhaustive, suggesting the relative value of authors and their writing as well as the works of individual authors.

Etienne-Gabriel Peignot's (1823) *Manuel du bibliophile* describes itself as a treatise on the selection of books. Peignot also made something of a name for himself as a librarian by labeling pornographic works as immoral. He was also author of a work, published in 1806, of disapproved books: *Dictionnaire critique, littéraire et bibliographique des principeaux livres condamnés au feu, supprimés ou censurés, précédé d'un discours sur ces sortes d'ouvrages.*

Édouard Rouveyre's *Connaissances nécessaires à un bibliophile* was published in multiple editions and in four volumes. Perhaps it helped that Rouveyre was a prodigious author and also a publisher. The first of the four volumes begins with a brief history of libraries, of books, and of writing. Rouveyre first published his study in 1877. Citing P. Namur, librarian at the University of Liège in 1834, Rouveyre (1899 i, xi) acknowledges that his reasons for writing and publishing *Connaissances nécessaires* derive from a need to both know and classify books. In keeping with most writers on establishing libraries and on bibliophilia, Rouveyre (1899, ch. 1) begins *Connaissances nécessaires* with a history of the book and of the library. The work is aimed at the amateur collector. It is printed on beautiful and heavy paper stock (*papier velin teinté*), and it is well illustrated with engravings.

Rouveyre (1899 iii, 23) held books in extraordinary esteem. Books serve different purposes at different times and in different circumstances:

> Les livres sont un guide dans la jeunesse, et une distraction dans l'âge avancé. Ils nous soutiennent dans la solitude, et nous empêchent de devinir à charge à nous-mêmes. Ils nous aident à oublier la malice des hommes et des choses, ils calment nos soucis et nos passions, et ils endorment nos chagrins.

Rouveyre's love of books and of libraries is borne out in the following:

> Le livre pouvant être compare à une créature vivante, animée de sensibilité, de caprice, ou d'originalité, exige une manipulation habile, une conservation soignée, une solicitude de tous les instants. (Rouveyre 1899 i , 21)

The work in its four volumes covers virtually everything from the history of the book to choices of binding. There is a section on library furniture and on papers and their watermarks. Rouveyre discusses common abbreviations and printing layout. In sum, it is an encyclopedic exploration of the book and everything related to it.

Rouveyre (1899 iii, 3–11) is almost poetic in his discussion of the books that should be found in the library of an amateur. By using the term "amateur," Rouveyre is by no means denigrating book seeking. An amateur should collect to his/her taste.

Rouveyre acknowledges that all cultures have a rich literature. The independent man of free spirit (1899 iii, 4) should nevertheless collect major poets; literature of the first order; and major religious, philosophical, and scientific theoreticians. These works, he continues, represent the intellectual patrimony of mankind. In sum, "pa là, une bibliothèque est un bagage que traîne l'humanité dans son incessante transformation, et les beautés, les trésors qui l'emplissent servent trop souvant à ralentir, voire à relantir, voire à détourner les faibles qui s'y attardent." (1899 iii, 4–5). Rouveyre acknowledges the impossibility that most amateurs can develop a truly comprehensive library—too many books, too small the storage, and too expensive the undertaking (1899 iii, 11–12). Because of these limits, public libraries are, he argues, treasure houses one should not ignore (1899 iii, 13). Rouveyre acknowledges that one cannot read all the great books, nor can they be read in their original languages. One must turn to translations for that purpose. He warns, however, that translations introduce error into the interpretation of the text (1899 iii, 14–15). Usually he has found that translations of scholars and scientists are well done. Such is not the case for other works, at least not in France.

Émile Henriot's (1928) *L'art de former une bibliothèque* is no less valuable than the others but significantly thinner, at less than 170 pages. The library, to paraphrase Henriot, should reflect the human spirit. In its self-reflection, the human spirit oscillates between two poles. Henriot (1928, 117) would have us inscribe the names of those two poles in gold letters at the entrance of all libraries: *la poésie et la vérité*—poetry and truth. That said, Henriot (1928, 10–11) recognizes the impossibility of any one individual to build an all-comprehensive library, one can but build a library that reflects one's needs.

Henriot's work addresses books in their variety of formats—the novel, foreign literature, poetry, histories, bibliographies, and so on. Each type is explored in its own chapter by century. His chapter 10 carries an interesting title that translates to "On the Choice of Books and How to Read Them—Preferred Editions." In order to develop a balanced personal library, Henriot (1928, ch. 11) offers his *conseil de dix*, or rule of ten. One should possess ten poets, ten novelists, ten major foreign works, ten books of verse, ten moralists, and so on. He provides recommendations under each of his fifteen classifications. With but a few exceptions and as one might expect, Henriot's (1928, 110–12) recommendations are for the French classics. Recommended foreign authors are limited to Homer, Virgil, Dante, *A Thousand and One Nights*, Shakespeare, Goethe, Byron, Dickens, Kipling, and Tolstoy.

Henriot (1928, 107–108) prescribes the collection of three copies of each of the classics for the bibliophile. First, acquire a first edition. Second, acquire the most recent edition if the author still lives or the first edition after the death of the author. And third, a critical edition of the author's collected works. Finally, there are certain works that a comprehensive library should hold.

On leaving the nineteenth century, perhaps we can end on a different note: William Blades's (1888) *The Enemy of Books.* Blades lists all the calamities that can befall books, each with its own chapter: fire, water, gas and heat, dust and neglect, ignorance and bigotry, the bookworm, other vermin, bookbinders, collectors, and servants and children. Blades discusses in some detail, with much humor and through anecdotes, each of those calamities. He offers a number of remedies to protect books. He is also not oblivious to technological change. For example, he offers the following on the merits of electric lights, an innovation of his day:

> The electric light has been in use for some months in the Reading Room of the British Museum, and is a great boon to the readers. The light is not quite equally diffused, and you must choose particular positions if you want to work happily. There is a great objection, too, in the humming fizz which accompanies the action of the electricity. There is a still greater objection when small pieces of hot chalk fall on your bald head, an annoyance which has been lately (1880) entirely removed by placing a receptacle beneath each burner. (Blades 1888, ch. 3)

Blades's conclusion is as follows:

> It is a great pity that there should be so many distinct enemies at work for the destruction of literature, and that they should so often be allowed to work out their sad end. Looked at rightly, the possession of any old book is a sacred trust, which a conscientious owner or guardian would as soon think of ignoring as a parent would of neglecting his child. An old book, whatever its subject or internal merits, is truly a portion of the national history; we may imitate it and print it in facsimile, but we can never exactly reproduce it; and as an historical document it should be carefully preserved.
>
> I do not envy any man that absence of sentiment which makes some people careless of the memorials of their ancestors, and whose blood can be warmed up only by talking of horses or the price of hops. To them solitude means *ennui*, and anybody's company is preferable to their own. What an immense amount of calm enjoyment and mental renovation do such men miss. Even a millionaire will ease his toils, lengthen his life, and add a hundred per cent. to his daily pleasures if he becomes a bibliophile; while to the man of business with a taste for

books, who through the day has struggled in the battle of life with all its irritating rebuffs and anxieties, what a blessed season of pleasurable repose opens upon him as he enters his sanctum, where every article wafts to him a welcome, and every book is a personal friend! (Blades 1888, conclusion)

CONCLUSION

There has been no end of additions to the genre. Examples include Nicholas Basbanes's (1995) *A Gentle Madness: Bibliophiles, Bibliomanes, and the Eternal Passion for Books*, his (2003) *Patience and Fortitude: Wherein a Colorful Cast of Determined Book Collectors, Dealers, and Librarians Go About the Quixotic Task of Preserving a Legacy*, Christian Galantaris's (1998) *Manuel de bibliophilie*, and Harold Rabinowitz and Rob Kaplan's (1999) *A Passion for Books*.

NOTES

1. Henri de Mesme (or Mesmes), premier président de Parlement de Paris, assumed office February 6, 1627.
2. Jesuit Antonio Possevino, author of *Bibliotheca selecta* (1593), a text and science bibliography.
3. http://www.philobiblon.com/philobiblon.shtml
4. Cotton des Houssayes's address was later translated into English as *Discourse on the Duties and Qualifications of a Librarian*.

TEN

New Conditions and New Principles

Today's global age has the technological sophistication dialectically to
destroy all humanity while simultaneously binding all nations into a
worldwide information network.

—Clifford Christians (1991, 3–4)

Nietzsche pragmatically argued that by right was meant that which
produced the next stage of evolution, what Nietzsche called the super-
man. That makes ethics easy to define for ourselves, because ethics
then becomes whatever one wants it to be, from conclusions one has
already reached.

—Herbert White (1991, 32)

INTRODUCTION

For most of its history, librarianship was none too concerned with its own
ethics. Robert Hauptman (1991, 83) finds that there was little published
on the subject before the 1980s, and that which was published before the
1980s was largely "etiquette and decorum rather than ethics." It is not
inconsequential that librarians and other information professionals have
begun to address ethical issues with more than a little enthusiasm. Stephen Almagno (Rockenback and Mendina 2001), Rafael Capurro (2006),
and Luciano Floridi (2001, 2014) have played important roles in placing
information ethics in a larger philosophical context. This interest has been
fueled both by the technological changes that have so impacted the information professions but also by the growing awareness of the importance
of information and the infosphere.

It has been suggested in more than one context and as a basic premise
of this work that changing circumstances and changing social constructs

change professional ethics. We find ourselves in a period of major changes in the basic fabric of global society, changes that are reflected in the library and in library education. Some suggest that these changes (e.g., Morrison 1991) have precipitated our enhanced interest in information ethics and professional ethics. Yet Morgan and Reynolds (1997) suggest that a preoccupation with ethics signals a greater interest in appearances than substance.

We can arbitrarily pick a starting point for the emergence of the new conditions and principles that guide contemporary practice. For example, the establishment of the first rate-based public libraries in the 1850s, the acceptance of women as patrons and librarians in the late nineteenth century, the introduction of "riff-raff" literature into public libraries at the beginning of the twentieth century, or the introduction of computers into libraries in the last quarter of the twentieth century might all represent an appropriate point of departure.

We can also look to the writings of celebrated librarians and bibliophiles. The volume of library and information science literature has increased dramatically in the last century. We can also look to the date when professional codes of ethics became important to the profession. The American Library Association was first to promulgate an associational code of ethics in the late 1930s. Many other library associations followed, but most not until much later (Koehler 2004).

The computer has, of course, had a significant impact on our recent ethical thinking. Computer scientists and computer users, the library community among them, are deeply concerned with the influence a set of technologies has and will continue to have on our professional practice. No hyperbole intended, the computer has contributed significantly to the redefinition of librarianship and its ethics. The computer has exacerbated issues of privacy and patron confidentiality (Mathiesen 2004). It has redefined information access and use behavior. Intellectual property rights and individual uses of intellectual property are in flux (Floridi 2013). Is document digitization prompting a return to a more fluid use of the works of others? Is it changing the way we acknowledge authorship in its broadest sense? Soraj Hongladarom (2004, 85) puts the issue thusly: "Information and communication technologies (ICTs) have pervaded very deeply in the lives of an increasingly greater number of people, especially in the poorer countries."

As a global culture, we are also far more sensitive to relative economic disparities and cultural differences among peoples both within and across countries. Some suggest (e.g., Rogerson and Beckett 2003) that information technologies have forced a redefinition of individual rights, as information technologies have reduced the ability of national authorities to regulate transnational interactions.

The obviation of distance is a result of the new information technologies. This ability to virtually research whatever one might wish from wherever one might wish at little cost has magnified our concern with privacy rights. It has always been possible to uncover much about whomever one might want to investigate. Because records were physically distributed and maintained under a variety of regulations and formats, assembling comprehensive dossiers was time consuming and expensive. Relational databases and the Internet have eased the process. The barriers of cost and distance that once protected individuals from all but the most persistent investigator can no longer so function. If privacy is still a right, then new methods must be employed to re-erect those protective barriers.

This chapter is necessarily more speculative than those that precede it. Our concern here is with emerging norms rather than those that are rooted in more distant practices. That said, newly emergent principles often have their antecedents in library practice and, at a minimum, in the expressed concerns of different constituencies.

Finally, there is the concern that information, particularly information in its new formats, will come to replace what we understand to be reality. Albert Borgmann (1999) has argued that information has historically been related to the human understanding of the natural environment and our level of sophistication in understanding and managing that natural environment. The computer and other digital manifestations have the power to replace that reality. Information, for Borgmann, may be "primitive" or "cultural." Primitive information is based on direct environmental observations and "natural" conclusions reached from those observations—dark clouds signal rain, animal spoor suggest the presence of beasts, and even Sherlock Holmes's dog that did not bark in the night suggest natural causal relationships. Cultural information, on the other hand, is both descriptive and predictive. It also moves our perception of reality into what Luciano Floridi (2014) has called the *infosphere.* Cultural information cannot only create reality within the infosphere context; it can also form it. Borgmann (1999) defines a third type of information— technological information. Technological information both moderates reality and can also replace it. If and as technological information becomes more pervasive, it will inevitably displace or replace primitive information.

The rise of a new information form must necessarily give rise to new ethical principles and a redefinition of older ones. Technological information is also not alone in its ability to replace the primitive. Recall that Karl Marx and Frederick Engels once described religion as the opiate of the masses. Fiction, literature in its various forms, truly cultural information, may both color and obfuscate our perceptions of reality. It can be suggested that a new digital literature, perhaps as virtual reality, will come to replace our conceptions of reality in ways heretofore only imagined. The use and misuse of information and the technology used to manage and manipulate that information fall well within the scope of a new consideration of information ethics.

LIBRARY LITERACY

Libraries, by their very purpose, require literate patrons. In Europe library patrons as well as librarians could read Greek, Latin, and several vulgate languages—French, German, Spanish—until the eighteenth century, when "universal" language competencies gave way to nationalistic impulses. Until the mid-nineteenth century, patrons came to the library with reading skills in hand. Public libraries began to focus on reading skills when their doors were opened to the *general* public in the 1850s onward.

As the rate-supported public library was introduced throughout Europe and North America and as the movement in support of universal public education grew, public and school libraries were reoriented to address the expanded patron base. The expanded patron base included and continues to include children, illiterate adults, and immigrants. As the patron base of the library expanded, so did the role of the library.

In recent years, literacy has taken on a new meaning: technological literacy. As Koehler et al. (2000) have shown, most librarians, as part of their ethical mandate, recognize both literacy and technical literacy. Robert Burnheim (1992) describes information literacy as a core competency.

DIGITAL DIVIDE

In the fourth quarter of the twentieth century, new technology placed new literacy responsibilities on libraries. By the beginning of the twenty-first century, many libraries in both the developing and developed world had accepted responsibility as one of the, if not the primary, public portals to the Internet. The advent of the microcomputer, and more particularly the Internet, has prompted a new socio-technical ethical concern—the digital divide.

The digital divide, as both a concept and as a term, came into use in the 1990s. According to David Gunkel (2003, 501–502), the term was perhaps first used in 1995 to distinguish between technology advocates and detractors, the rich and the poor, those who embrace technology and those neo-Luddites who are suspicious, and most recently the technology-adept and those who are not. It has also been used to describe "technical incompatibilities" and access to or ownership of information technology (Gunkel 2003, 502). It is only in 1999, according to Gunkel (2003, 503), that "digital divide" had come to mean those with technology or access to technology and those without. Under this definition, the digital divide may take on racial, class, gender, age, and transnational overtones. Gunkel (2003, 507) is rightly critical of those arguments in strictly binary ways—haves, have-nots; technically sophisticated, technically ignorant (e.g., Hargittai 2002); over-privileged, under-privileged; and so on. The digital topography has far more gradation than digital divide arguments allow. More nuanced or more demographically based studies in recent years have found other variations in digital usage patterns (e.g., Brandtzæg, Heim, and Karahasanović 2011).

The digital divide is usually identified in two dimensions—the intra-national and international divides (see Hongladarom 2004). In both the intra-national and international contexts, the digital divide concept is defined in terms of explanatory theory. For example, Jeremy Moss (2002) places it in the context of information and power as described by Michel Foucault. The digital divide may also be construed in economic, perhaps in *dependencia* and interdependence theory. The digital divide has also been addressed as a pedagogical issue and as one of social relevance. The digitally adept may, it is posited, be more competent in the establishment and maintenance of virtual communities that support both positive and negative ends. The point I am trying to make here is that the digital divide, however defined, can be used to support and exploit any number of socially relevant theories.

Luciano Floridi (2001) has suggested an additional dimension: the horizontal and vertical digital divides. For Floridi (2001, 1), the vertical digital divide is a temporal one:

> The vertical gap separates ours from past generations. In less than a century, we have moved from a state of submission to nature, through a state power of potential total destruction, to the present state, in which we have the means and tools to engineer new realities, tailor them to our needs and even invent the future.

"The vertical gap," according to Floridi (2001, 2) "signals the end of modernity." Infospace is, for Floridi (2001, 2) the new post-modern environment. A horizontal digital divide can be identified. Its occupants can be segregated and sometimes self-segregated as *netizens* and everyone else. The netizen, wherever she/he may be found, is both technologically capable and technologically active. Thus "the [digital divide] abolishes space and time constraints but creates new technological barriers between insiders and outsiders." The post-modern horizontal digital divide is, according to Floridi (2003, 3), a pernicious presence, as it "disempowers, discriminates, and generates dependency." Floridi argues that information ethics is a response to this new manifestation of the horizontal digital divide. He calls for a "new ecological model" to develop ethical norms to bridge and abolish the digital divide.

MARKETING AND MANAGEMENT

Should libraries market their services? Darlene Weingand (1999, xi), in her library marketing text, makes it clear that librarians are often reluctant to market because it is something librarians (and other not-for-profit entities) simply do not do. It is incumbent on libraries, if they are to thrive rather than just survive, to market their services (Weingand 1999, xii). Weingand (1999, 2) is careful to define marketing as "an *exchange* relationship" between library and customer/patron. Marketing, she continues, "is a [process] that reflects the identified needs of the target populations."

In an interesting paper published in 1991, Kathleen Heim (now McCook) raises the question of ethics in personnel management. Heim sought to identify ethical issues specific to library administrators within the context of personnel management in general. She notes that the library profession is generally perceived as a service profession; that a sense of that service motivates its practitioners more than in some other professions. Heim was writing at a time when the pool of potential librarians (and other service professionals) was predicted to be in decline. Administrators in such an environment need to pay particular heed to the rights and privileges of employees and potential employees. Heim (1991, 112) aptly summarizes her argument with these words:

> Technology will need to be tempered by moral commitment to individual rights and worth. Legal and technical environments may change but at the heart of the matter, untouched by shifting background, must lie [*sic*] a reasoned and humane commitment to a just society.

We would agree, but would argue that the definitions for "reasoned and humane" and "just society" have undergone redefinition over time as well.

LIBRARIANSHIP AND THE NEW RIGHTS

The mid- to late twentieth century was an era of major cultural, social, and political changes. These changes ranged from the dismantling of formal colonialism to the onset and end of the Cold War and the emergence of China as a world economic power. It was also an era of significant shifts in racial, gender, and sexual preference issues as social tropes. We now include equality and equity as the standard of what Kathleen Heim (1991, 112) has called a "just society," but the definition of a just society has undergone and continues to undergo redefinition. During the eighteenth century, the slavery trade was accepted social practice. Women were considered chattel. Children were little adults without rights. In the nineteenth century, the Industrial Revolution tolerated child labor;

women remained chattel. Slavery was condemned in Europe but accepted in the Americas. It took a civil war and constitutional amendments in the United States to reverse accepted, legal, and institutional-
ized discrimination against persons of African descent. The Constitution
of the United States, to take one example, ratified in 1789, stipulated that
for purposes of apportionment for elections to the US Congress, free
persons were to be counted as one. Un-taxed Indians were not to be
counted. All other persons—which is to say Negro slaves—were only to
be counted individually as three-fifths of a person. The Fifteenth Amendment extended suffrage to African American men in 1870 but not to
women until 1920 by the Nineteenth Amendment. In the eyes of the
American Founding Fathers, discrimination against women, children,
and peoples of color was both legal and just.

Discrimination extended to persons with disabilities. With the advent
of new technologies, libraries have expanded their services to persons
with varying disabilities. Books published with large print are among the
earlier adaptations. Recorded books and Braille publications for the vision impaired were published. Library technologies have proliferated to
a point where some commentators have urged that libraries "keep it
simple" but effective (Green and Blair 2011).

Women as Patrons and Librarians

For much of the history of libraries, women have had but a very small
presence, both as librarians and as patrons. It has only been since the
middle of the nineteenth century that women were admitted as patrons
in public libraries, and then, often, they were segregated into separate
reading rooms. Public library careers for women began as matrons of the
women's reading rooms. After all, women patrons might be scandalized
if men serviced their library needs.

It needs also to be remembered that Melvil Dewey scandalized the
dons of Columbia College in New York City by insisting that women be
admitted as students in their library school. This affront to Columbia's
dignity was so great that Dewey was forced to move the program to
Albany, New York.

For all his good works, Melvil Dewey was, it seems, a racist, an anti-
Semite (see Wiegand 1995), and a misogynist (see Beck 1996). To his
credit, perhaps, he was no worse in these regards than the standards of
his time. He was also something of a cad and a roué. For the definitive
Dewey biography, see Wayne Wiegand's (1996) *Irrepressible Reformer: A
Biography of Melvil Dewey*.

It has also been suggested that Dewey promoted women as librarians
as a means to drive down the cost of labor—a qualified female librarian
would command a lower salary than a male one, and the resulting overall
costs would then be reduced. If indeed that was his purpose, he was

largely successful. Or perhaps those professions that were to become dominated by women in the late nineteenth and twentieth centuries— secretarial, nursing, teaching, and librarianship were all subject to an overall depression of wages for practitioners of women-dominated professions. Sidney Ditzion (1947), for example, lauds the library profession for its acceptance of women into its ranks as equals to men.

It was only toward the middle of the twentieth century that wage discrimination was first acknowledged and then accepted as a social wrong. The American Library Association's Feminist Task Force, established in 1970, followed by the Women Library Workers in 1975, and the Committee on the Status in Librarianship increased awareness of the status of women in libraries. For all that, at the beginning of the twenty-first century, there was some but not adequate readjustment of wage levels for all librarians in general and women in particular.

There is an interesting and informative literature on women and libraries in both "mainstream" (masculine?) and feminist writing. Suzanne Hildenbrand (2000) has argued that the history of women in libraries is rooted in "library feminist activism." She acknowledges the conventional wisdom that women in libraries translates into "low status and salaries." Despite gains in the profession after Dewey's "revolutionary" ideas, Hildenbrand (2000, 52) provides evidence in the literature to the decline of women's status and salaries in the years following World War II. Alison Adam (2000) has offered a critique and review of the limited feminist literature on ethics in computer science.

The image of the female librarian remains problematic. Marie Radford and Gary Radford (1997) offer an image of American popular culture within the context of Foucaultian power analysis and feminist theory. Radford and Radford (1997, 251) remind us that the stereotypical image of the librarian has shifted from the "mousey" male of the nineteenth century to the "shushing spinster complete with bun" of the twentieth.

While Hildenbrand (2000) does not use the term "ethics" in her paper, she closes with a speculation as to the state of the discipline, should gender as well as class, racial, and sexual preference issues become more central in the library profession's central thought—and particularly if the focus on these groups were to be joined.

Race and Ethnicity

If gender was the concern of the late nineteenth and early twentieth century, race and ethnicity followed soon thereafter. In the United States many public facilities, including public libraries (and academic libraries at segregated universities), restricted or prohibited access to people of color, particularly to African Americans. These restrictions covered both employment in and use of libraries.

Again in the United States, prospective African American students were denied admission to many library schools until after the 1954 US Supreme Court decision in *Brown v. Board of Education of Topeka, Kansas*. To provide training to African Americans, the Hampton Institute began library education in 1924. This endeavor was undertaken with support from the American Library Association and Carnegie Foundation funding (Martin and Shiflett 1996).

The Hampton program was moved to what was to become Clark-Atlanta University in 1941. The library school was closed in 2005. One library school, that at the second program at a historically black college or university, North Carolina Central University, continues to provide library instruction. After the *Brown v. Board of Education* decision in the 1950s, library schools began integrating their programs.

PRIVACY, CONFIDENTIALITY, AND DATA PROTECTION

Privacy is a well-recognized concern of libraries (see, for example, Gorman 2000; Koehler and Pemberton 2000; Rubin and Froehlich 1996). Privacy covers a multitude of issues and concerns. June Lester and Wallace Koehler (2007, 350) argue that librarian concerns with privacy and confidentiality are largely twentieth-century phenomena. However, as late as 1986, commentators were to conclude that information policy and, by implication, privacy were ill defined (Burger 4). Nevertheless, privacy is now considered an important component of other principles, including freedom of access and of expression (Falk 2004). Following the events of September 11, 2001, and the subsequent passage of the USA PATRIOT Act, there has been increasing concern over the rights and obligations of libraries, librarians, and patrons to guard or share patron information. That concern includes the status of patron borrowing practices and other library usages both online and face-to-face. The advent of new technology has enhanced those concerns. The International Federation of Library Associations and Institutions (IFLA) initiated a study in 2013 to address the impact of new technologies on practice. The IFLA's *Trend Report* (2013) is concerned with a wide range of possible implications of technology, to include privacy concerns. As such, the *Trend Report* can also alert us to possible new ethical concerns.

Librarians have a concern with privacy concerns, chiefly with patron records. The digital era has brought new concerns not necessarily specific to the librarian. Patrons (and librarians) may now access a wide variety of personal information from the comfort of the public access library-based computer or from their home machines. We recognize that much of that information might well have been available before the advent of online databases, but access to that information was then more expensive (in time and money) and more difficult to acquire.

The privacy concerns of librarians (and others) now extend well beyond guarding records. Jeroen van den Hoven (2004) recognizes several public good–related phenomena: information-based harm, informational inequality, informational injustice, spheres of access, and encroachments on moral autonomy.

Appearance Ethics

Peter Morgan and Glenn Reynolds (1997), in their book *The Appearance of Impropriety*, document the emergence of a new ethical phenomenon: appearance as a measure of ethical behavior rather than actual behavior. Their focus is, of course, not librarians but rather "high" government officials and business leaders in the United States. They argue that the great urge dating from the Watergate scandal of the Nixon Administration has been to implement complex ethical rules in order to ensure the public that appropriate behaviors have been adopted or at least policed to enforce ethical behavior (Morgan and Reynolds 1997, 1– 6).

One of the problems Morgan and Reynolds (1997) lament is that when complex ethical environments are created, those affected by them become more concerned with the appearance of adherence to the rules rather than with "doing the right thing." We adopt postures for appearance's sake rather than taking stands for the right reasons.

This last statement begs the question somewhat, what are "right reasons"? Within the context of this argument, it is less important to know the right reasons in some absolute way. Rather, we should act from what we individually and collectively conclude to be the right reasons rather than from how our actions and inactions will be perceived to measure up against those right reasons.

Malpractice

Malpractice is a knowing, and even if unknowing, unacceptable behavior on part of a professional. Librarians and other information professionals have not for most of their history been subject to malpractice concerns. Malpractice, as such, is not, strictly speaking, an ethical concern; it is, rather, a legal matter. Appropriate professional practice, on the other hand, falls well within the scope of professional ethics.

Robert Hauptman's (1976) now famous (perhaps infamous) experiment in professional ethics and bomb-making information illustrates the ambiguousness of determining appropriate professional practice. Library school students were instructed to approach reference librarians with a request for bomb building instructions. Most reference librarians complied without objection.

INFORMATION AND ENTROPY

Timothy Ferris (1997, 90–96), writing a layman's account of astrophysics, offers an interesting discussion that connects information decay to the second law of thermodynamics. Drawing on the work of Claude Shannon, Ferris (1997, 98) asserts that information undergoes entropy: "The concept of entropy is related to that of *information*." Ferris (1997, 94) defines the second law as follows: "A system left to itself will tend toward a state of maximum entropy." Furthermore, Ferris asserts (1997, 92), "The statement of the second law of thermodynamics—that entropy increases unless energy is exerted to decrease it—therefore also means that information tends always to decrease."

Just as Shannon's concept of information theory and of noise has been adopted and modified across information disciplines, so can Ferris's marriage of information and entropy. A corollary to the second law of thermodynamics might be that work (the expenditure of energy) is required in order to overcome entropy. Ferris is concerned with cosmic black holes, not the so pedestrian library. Or perhaps his interest also extends to libraries as well (Ferris, 322, n. 20):

> One might go so far as to say that the excitement generated by life, art, science, and the spectacle of a bustling city with its libraries and theaters is at its root the excitement of seeing the law of entropy being defeated—in one place at least, for a while.

The library might then be said to be one of many social institutions that serve to moderate information entropy. It might be described as the library's social deontology—a duty, a requirement to bring order to what would otherwise be chaos. Perhaps, then, all other functions of information systems can be derived from this first duty. And as we can see, overcoming entropy for the library is in fact first the preservation function. But it is also the library's information sharing function. In order to "defeat" entropy in the larger social space, information inputs are required. The library, to avoid its own inherent entropy, must balance preservation with access and information dissemination.

This balance can be demonstrated in the digital library. Digital documents are like medieval manuscripts. To be preserved and to protect their content, they must be copied or reproduced from time to time and from medium to medium. However efficient digital documents may be as a mechanism for information dissemination and however inefficient were medieval manuscripts, both need replacement if content is to be preserved. Digital documents have to be renewed, reproduced, and upmigrated at least every decade, whereas medieval manuscript replacement was measured in centuries.

It has been implicit to library practice that documents be preserved. It must now be recognized that the preservation function be formally recognized as an imperative of the profession. While the digitization movement holds great promise as a vehicle for access and information distribution, it also offers significant challenges for the long-term preservation of content and meaning.

GLOBALIZATION

Internet-based technologies are global. The distribution by country of that penetration varies widely by country and by region. The website Internet World Stats (http://www.internetworldstats.com/stats.htm) provides current data on the degree of Internet penetration in detail. At the time of writing, Internet penetration and use in Africa, for example, lags other regions. There are several reasons given for varying degrees of penetration, including technological sophistical of the population, economic development and political will (e.g., Nisbet, Stoycheff, and Pearce 2012; Cruz-Jesus, Oliveira, and Bacao 2012).

According to Simon Rogerson and Robert Beckett (2003), technological changes have outstripped the ability of social institutions, particularly governments, to regulate and moderate those changes and their implications for society. These information technologies have global reach. For Rogerson and Beckett (2003, 18), the computer is at the heart of these changes. These technologies transcend national boundaries, and as a consequence it's difficult or impossible for individual legal systems to address these changes. Rogerson and Beckett look to the UN Declaration on Human Rights for guidance in the development of global e-rights.

The World Summit on the Information Society (WSIS), an intergovernmental conference, was convened in two phases in 2003 and 2005. There was participation from a number of non-governmental organizations as well. The WSIS sought to find common ground and to develop mechanisms to address new information technologies, particularly the Internet. The WSIS "Tunis Commitment" (2005), the product of the 2005 meeting in Tunis, Tunisia, reaffirmed the intentions of the member governments to support international information rights, with attention to digital divide concerns.

There have been non-governmental organizations formed to support information rights, particularly in developing counties. The African Network for Information Ethics is one such group. It has convened a series of meetings to support information ethics in the region and to support the Tshwane Declaration (2007), the product of the first conference in South Africa in 2007. Particular focus is placed on the protection of indigenous knowledge and its exploitation.

Indigenous Knowledge

Indigenous knowledge is a concept concerned with knowledge developed by individual cultures (e.g., Sillitoe 1998). The ethics of treatment of indigenous knowledge is shifting toward recognition of the rights of the creators of the knowledge against unwanted exploitation or profit taking by outside agencies. There is a growing library and information science literature to analyze and support those rights (see Brush and Stabinsky 1996; Britz and Lipinski 2001; Britz and Lor 2003 and 2004; Kawooya 2006 and 2013; Sturges 2005). Indigenous knowledge is now considered to be the intellectual property of the culture that created it, be that knowledge folk art, folk stories, medical knowledge, and so on. The general consensus is now that in order to exploit that knowledge, the permission of its holder must be acquired.

Censorship

Censorship and control of information flows have a deep history, as is documented elsewhere in this work. A number of countries, the People's Republic of China among them, regulate domestic access to the Internet (e.g., Xu, Mao, and Halderman 2011). Barney Warf (2011) has documented the extent of Internet regulation in various forms to include the web and various social media technologies. Thus, from an international perspective, the variation in regulation and control of the Internet creates pockets of inequality of access.

CONCLUSION

Since the middle of the twentieth century, there have been many changes and new concerns brought to library and information science practice. John Budd (2001; 2003) has discussed many of these changes in terms of library and information science philosophy.

The scope of the change is broad. These include a focus on equality in the practice for women and members of minority groups. They include the rights of access to information and to the support of literacy. These rights include promotion and protection of indigenous knowledge rights. They also include the concept of rights of access to information technology, especially since the advent of the Internet in the 1960s and the World Wide Web in the 1990s.

These new ideas and new technologies are at times in conflict with one another. The right of access to information and protections of indigenous knowledge have contradictory elements. Can societies like the People's Republic of China or the Democratic People's Republic of Korea control access to information technologies? Is it legitimate to censor? Is there a balance between the freedom of expression and guarding of cultural and religious mores?

These new conditions pose interesting questions for Ranganathan's five laws. Clearly new conditions are consistent with the fifth law: the library is a growing organism. Libraries become defined more broadly than brick and mortar. The digital environment expands the boundaries of libraries well beyond what once they were.

Concerns for new users and new providers expand the second law: every reader, her/his book. Expanding the reach of information provision and reducing the digital divide expand both the first and second laws— books are for use; every reader, a book. That said, concern for and protection of indigenous knowledge place limits on all five laws.

I once encountered a situation where an African university library purposely chose not to support digitization of the theses the university students produced. The reason given was that anyone wishing to access those materials should need to access the physical object in situ. Given the state of digital technology, that policy would appear to contravene Ranganathan's fourth law: save the time of the user. New conditions require new solutions, new solutions interpreted within the scope of existing traditions. And yet, libraries must also take into account how and where they distribute their collections and compliance with local practice, mores, and laws.

ELEVEN

Concluding Chapter

Osymandyas of Egypt was of all kings the first, as far as history shows, to have a library of any note. Along with other famous deeds he established, says Diodorus, a library of sacred literature, and placed over the entrance the inscription: "Here is Medicine for the Mind."

—Justus Lipsius (1607, 33)

I suspect that the human species—the *only* species—teeters at the verge of extinction, yet that the library—enlightened, solitary, infinite, perfectly unmoving, armed with precious volumes, pointless, incorruptible, and secret—will endure.

—Jorge Luis Borges (2000, 36)

ICTs are not mere tools but rather environmental forces that are increasingly affecting:

1. our self-conception (who we are);
2. our mutual interactions (how we socialise);
3. our conception of reality (our metaphysics); and
4. our interactions with reality (our agency).

In each case, ICTs have a huge ethical, legal, and political significance, yet one with which we have begun to come to terms only recently.

We are also convinced that the aforementioned impact exercised by ICTs is due to at least four major transformations:

1. the blurring of the distinction between reality and virtuality;
2. the blurring of the distinction between human, machine and nature;
3. the reversal from information scarcity to information abundance; and

4. the shift from the primacy of stand-alone things, properties, and binary relations, to the primacy of interactions, processes and networks.

—Luciano Floridi (2015, 2)

INTRODUCTION

The ethics of the library and librarianship have been implicit but not explicit until the twentieth century. Librarianship has not been perceived as a profession as such, and even today it has been identified as a "pseudo-profession." Profession or pseudo-profession, librarianship has a rich history of both theory and practice—more practice than theory. Because there is a history of practice, I suggested at the onset of this work that theory could be derived from a description of the practice.

I came to this research with a focus on information ethics and its roots. Information ethics has been an interest of mine for some time. I am not a historian. This book only incidentally contributes to the literature on the role of the fall of Rome, the Enlightenment, the Reformation, the Counter-Reformation, and the Renaissance on library theory. Other social phenomena, for example, the emergence of nationalism and the nation-state have left their marks as well. I leave the history and political science theory to others as well.

Yet even a non-historian such as myself cannot ignore the breakpoints between, say, Richard de Bury (c. 1287–1345) or Gregory of Rimini (c. 1300–1358) on the one hand and Gabriel Naudé (1600–1653) or James Kirkwood (c. 1650–1708) on the other. Nor can we ignore differences in library theory that occur before and after the great publishing watershed event—Gutenberg's moveable type and the advent of printing.

Of course, there were other technological changes that have affected librarianship. The influences these have had on library theory can also be explored. These include the inventions of paper, the codex, cheap paper, improvements in literacy, and most recently the digital revolution.

The digital revolution has created a new set of ethical challenges. It is my belief that examining library practice and theory over the centuries can throw light on current conundrums. For example, James Kirkwood, a Scot and a Presbyterian minister, sought to create libraries in every parish in Scotland. Kirkwood proposed buying books from throughout Europe and republishing them in Scotland. In a copyright environment, Kirkwood would probably have been vilified and prosecuted by intellectual property owners of his day. Perhaps fortunately for Kirkwood, he died two years before the passage of the Statute of Anne of 1710 by the English Parliament. The Statute of Anne was, of course, the first ever attempt at copyright regulation. Print created a need for copyright; the digital revolution has exacerbated the stresses on traditional copyright jurisprudence. Dick Kawooya (2008) is exploring the copy and reproduction industry in the informal sector of third world economies. His work brings to mind James Kirkwood's ideas to stimulate printing and thereby the economy of seventeenth-century Scotland. Kawooya (e.g., 2013) is also active in documenting information ethics in Africa.

Ruth Granniss (1906, 26), in her brief biography of Gabriel Naudé, informs us that before the creation of the Mazarine Library in Paris in the mid-seventeenth century, only three major public libraries had been successfully initiated in Europe after the collapse of the Roman Empire. These three were the Bodleian at Oxford in 1603, the Angélique in Rome in 1604, and the Ambrosian in Milan in 1609. Perhaps we might add to this list the El Escorial in Spain, begun in 1563.

Libraries were to suffer from a variety of plagues, man made and natural. Earlier libraries were particularly vulnerable. Sir Thomas Bodley did not endow the first library at Oxford. According to Granniss (1906, 14–16), Oxford's first library came with a bequest from Bishop Cobham in 1367. Richard de Bury, Bishop of Durham presented Durham College, Oxford with his collection. That library was further augmented by gifts from others. Henry VIII dissolved Durham College and its library. Some books were lost through attrition and theft, others by censorship. By the time Bodley arrived at Oxford, the library was a library in name only. The Mazarine Library would also suffer from politics and the economic ruin of its patron but was to reopen in part because of the prodigious efforts of Gabriel Naudé, its librarian.

If the sixteenth century in Europe was the century of the printing revolution, the seventeenth century was the century of the library evolution. Libraries and even public libraries, as we have seen, had come into existence well before the collapse of Rome, in both Greece and Rome. There were certainly many fine private, church, and monastery libraries but no public libraries in medieval Europe. The public library as an enduring institution was the product of the convergence of two great forces, one social and the other technological. The printing press and the advent of inexpensive paper had greatly expanded the availability of books, the "basic building blocks" of libraries. The Renaissance had taken root, and the Protestant Reformation was well underway.

The eighteenth century witnessed the beginnings of the redefinition of intellectual property and its regulation. The Statute of Anne of 1710, much amended and ultimately superseded, was landmark legislation designed to protect the intellectual property of printers and stationers, the publishers of their day. In eighteenth-century Europe the entrenchment of the nation-state, the sweep of nationalism, and political and philosophical redefinition created new pressures on libraries and their social and academic roles. Both the American and French Revolutions in the latter quarter of the eighteenth century were precursors of revolution and political realignment in Europe and its colonies in the nineteenth century. It was also a time of realignment among the social and intellectual elites from a Pan-European community of interests based on Latin as a means of communication to a fractionalized and factionalized redefinition of allegiances to the state. The Tower of Babel was once again deconstructed, and Latin was to be eclipsed by regional and national languages.

The nineteenth century was a century of invention. There was an extraordinary expansion in the transport and communications infrastructure (see, for example, Lester and Koehler 2007). The steam engine came into its own at the beginning of the century, to be eclipsed by the petroleum-based internal combustion engine at the end of the century. While no one was to succeed in developing heavier-than-air flight, balloons had come into their own, and great strides were being made in aviation technology. Railroads were a nineteenth-century phenomenon, as was the macadam roadway. The ship under sail yielded to self-powered craft capable of greater speed, comfort, and cargo.

The nineteenth century was also the century of the library and of an increasing use of libraries by ever-broader social groups (Battles 2003, 117–155). In Matthew Battles's words (2003, 128), "The mass produced book flourished." This explosion of books placed increased pressures on libraries to manage their collections. These pressures gave rise to the great catalogers of their time, Anthony Panizzi, Melvil Dewey, Charles Ammi Cutter, Charles Coffin Jewett, and others and the invention of more sophisticated cataloging schemes, among them the Dewey Decimal, the Prussian Principles, and Panizzi's Rules.

Communications infrastructure was revolutionized. The telegraph and the telephone came into their own. For the first time images and sound could be directly but not quite exactly recorded.

The nineteenth century was also an era of the popularization of fiction and the popularization of newspapers and magazines. Libraries therefore had to respond to an ever-increasing volume of materials and began to redefine selection policies to respond to those changes. It was also a time when analysis of bibliophilia and bibliomania, a trend not unabated into the twentieth and twenty-first centuries.

The twentieth century was also marked by major changes in technology and in political and social thought. While the first professional organizations for librarians came into existence in the last fifth of the nineteenth century (in the United States, the United Kingdom, and Japan, for example), most new professional organizations emerged in the twentieth century (Koehler 2004). The first formal treatment of professional ethics in library science and related fields also emerged in the twentieth century.

It was during the first quarter of the twentieth century that public libraries began to seriously reexamine their collection policies. Books and other materials, once considered (by Sir Thomas Bodley) riff raff and excluded from public libraries not only were added to library collections but often became the mainstay of circulation. As we have seen, John Cotton Dana was very much at the forefront in the movement to redefine public libraries in the United States.

However, as riff raff was being added to libraries, libraries were under attack. In a very real sense the twentieth century was, for libraries and books, a bipolar era. Battles (2003, 156) opens his sixth chapter of *Library: An Unquiet History* thusly: "If the nineteenth century was about the building of libraries, the twentieth was about their destruction. . . . It was in the twentieth century that new ways of destroying books, and of exploiting their destruction, were tested and refined."

Books and libraries, of course, have been destroyed across history through man-made and natural disasters, but perhaps never on the same scale, Battles suggests (2003, 156–191), as in the twentieth century. This claim may be challenged. One can cite the loss of the Library of Alexandria and argue that it was more cataclysmic than any other set of events in library or book history. There were so few libraries during the ascendancy of the Alexandrine Library. The loss of one library, even one book in that era, was of far greater consequence than the loss of libraries and books in the twentieth century. After all, there were many other libraries and many other copies of most of the material then destroyed (Polastron 2007; Báez and Mac Adam 2008).

This argument begs the following question: The twentieth century was witness to so many challenges to books and libraries over so many years in so many cultures, can we ever truly appreciate the consequences of those collective events? The challenge to books is a challenge to our collective psyche and to our sense of self. These destructions of books have been a part of concerted efforts to erase cultures. And again, while not unique to the twentieth century, it was the intensity of the effort that astounds us. Worse, perhaps we have grown inured. Nazi desecrations were decried. More recent cultural atrocities, like the destruction of the stone Buddhas by the Afghani Taliban in 2001 or the ruin of the Iraqi National Library in 2002 or the Timbuktu Library in 2013, have been treated almost as historical footnotes.

Our dialog and its context keep changing. *Library* keeping becomes *librarianship* and *library economy*. These in turn became *documentation* and *library science*. *Documentation* and *library science*, in their turn, have become *information science*.

To quote Douglas Adams (1996, 6), "The Hitchhiker's Guide has already supplanted the great Encyclopedia Galactica as the standard repository of all knowledge and wisdom, for though it has many omissions and contains much that is apocryphal, or at least widely inaccurate it scores over the older, more pedestrian work in two important respects: (1) It is slightly cheaper. (2) It has the words DON'T PANIC inscribed in large friendly letters on its cover." I suspect that Adams presaged *Wikipedia* as a precursor to the *Hitchhiker's Guide* and the *Encyclopedia Galactica*.

THE PUBLIC LIBRARY

There was very little public about public libraries until the mid-nineteenth century. Library access certainly broadened from the first *public* libraries of Greece and Rome. But until the establishment of the mechanics' and miners' libraries, followed by the American and British public libraries in the 1850s, libraries were the reserve of scholars and other elites. Until the nineteenth century the term "public library" was synonymous with research facility. Many such libraries did not lend materials from their collections, and almost all maintained closed collections.

The public libraries of the last half of the nineteenth century were designed with the enrichment and uplifting of its patrons in mind. These libraries also slowly reinvented themselves or were invented anew as lending libraries. Some experimented with open stacks.

It was not until library reformers like John Cotton Dana were to become influential that the public library began to add popular materials to their collections, designed not to uplift their patrons but to entertain them. These libraries tended to resist acceptance of alternative media such as audio and video recordings, but by the close of the twentieth century these objects were deemed appropriate as well. In fact, some libraries so redefined themselves that they began lending toys and tools as well.

The ethical practice of public librarians has undergone a significant shift. The ideal library was once considered a repository, an archive of knowledge to be tended and guarded with great care. While special collections, archives, and research libraries continue the tradition of collection protection, public libraries underwent a major metamorphosis in the twentieth century. These libraries now actively promote the lending and circulation of their collections and seek ways to market their wares and to draw an ever-wider circle of patrons through their doors. The public librarian is no longer a "protector" of the civic culture; she/he is more a "promoter" of the popular culture.

This shift in purpose has necessarily meant a shift in the underlying philosophy in collection development. The "public" librarian in the eighteenth century was concerned with building a comprehensive collection of "good" books in theology and religion, philosophy, the sciences and mathematics, and literature. The public librarian of the nineteenth century sought the same good books as well as books that taught social graces, educated the reader, and uplifted the user. The public librarian of the twentieth century sought to find a balance between good books and artifacts (books and other media) that could amuse, distract, and entertain the patron. The public librarian of the twenty-first century not only entertains the patron through collection development; she/he also is expected to serve as a facilitator for access to the web and as a software and hardware teacher. This function tends to remove the librarian from his or her historical function as information manager and intermediary to an often-reluctant custodian of the machine.

INTELLECTUAL PROPERTY

Based on the history of intellectual property doctrine in the West, librarians are ethically required to provide and promote access to information in its various formats. This obligation is constrained by an increasing accretion of rights and privileges granted to intellectual property owners. These rights and privileges have served to circumscribe the ability of the librarian to provide free use. Free use has become a much more limited "fair use."

Librarians are among the most challenged and conflicted of professionals in the interpretation and application of intellectual property issues. Librarians are required to interpret and apply copyright law. At the same time, they are required by profession and often by inclination to make resources available to their various patron bases.

As application of ethical principles, intellectual property has evolved. Before the eighteenth century there was, with certain license exceptions, no intellectual property protection for authors and publishers. Fair use might best have been described as "any use." Because intellectual property practice has undergone significant changes in the West and because there are significant philosophical differences among cultures as to the definition and source of intellectual property, both legal and professional canon may conflict or result in ambiguity of practice.

It should be noted first that global protection of intellectual property is a very recent phenomenon. National copyright protection was first conceived in 1710. It was not until 1886 that multilateral copyright protection came into existence, a regime not partially accepted by the United States until 1952 and more fully in 1988.

In the United States, for example, a "rule of five" has been accepted by some as the maximum number of copies of articles or parts of books that may be made in a reasonable period of time (every other semester, perhaps) for educational purposes.

In Europe and, by association, North America, there were no intellectual property rights that adhered to authors or publishers until the sixteenth century. Until the sixteenth century any rights that existed were the rights of the state to take and copy the intellectual products of others. Between the sixteenth and early eighteenth centuries, licenses and patents were awarded to publishers as a means to control and censor publications. As a byproduct of these controls, certain stationers and printers gained monopolistic privileges to certain documents (state papers, for example) and books. Copyright as a right of author or publisher was first conceived in England in 1710.

There are ample variations in the way in which one country sought to implement intellectual property protection and in others. Countries on the European continent, by the eighteenth century adherents of civil law (an outgrowth of Roman law), had developed concepts of the rights of authors or creators. The common law countries—the United Kingdom, the United States, Australia, Canada, and other former British colonies—evolved their own approaches, some more formalistic than others.

The nineteenth century and particularly the twentieth century, with their growth in the concept of nationalism as well as the technological advances in communications, witnessed a greater requirement for an international rather than national or local management of intellectual property. By the mid-twentieth and now twenty-first centuries, large multinational interests have come to dominate both popular and scholarly publishing and other communications media. The Berne Convention and the two international organizations (the World Intellectual Property Organization and the World Trade Organization) have served to standardize and rationalize intellectual property practices. And some would claim that WIPO and the WTO serve the large economic enterprise to the disadvantage of the state and the individual.

The changes in the law require librarians to make changes in practice. Librarians have both ethical and legal obligation to be professionally responsive to the norms and mores of the society in which they live. They also have an ethical and professional responsibility to help meet the information needs of their patrons. At times their legal, social, and professional obligations may conflict.

Second, changing legal norms and practices may change an appropriate professional practice from one that is legitimate and acceptable to one that is, at least from a legal perspective, no longer legitimate. Interestingly, these have not historically been matters of much concern to librarians.

Librarians and library theoreticians warned against plagiarism, and some outright advocated the copying of the work of others. But it has only been since the introduction of efficient and inexpensive reproduction technologies that copyright and other questions of intellectual property have intruded into the library.

Technology has changed our ability to make "true" copies of digital materials and "nearly true" copies of the non-digital. The challenges brought to the professional ethics of librarians through changes in intellectual property doctrine are of very recent etiology. Technology, combined with the concentration of economic power, has created a situation within which much of the sharing of intellectual products is deemed to be unlawful. Librarians, promoting these transfers as a manifestation of the principle of intellectual freedom, have had to try to make accommodation with the new technological and economic reality. This forced accommodation has understandably left many librarians with a sense of intellectual discomfort and a sense that the status quo is less than perfect.

CLASSIFICATION

I have already suggested that library classification is a form of code. Jorge Luis Borges (2000) took an even more imaginative approach to language in his *The Library of Babel*. He posited an alphabet consisting of twenty-two imaginary letters and three orthographic signs for a total of twenty-five characters. "That discovery enabled mankind, three hundred years ago, to formulate a general theory of the Library and therefore satisfactorily solve the riddle that no conjecture had been able to divine—the formless and chaotic nature of virtually all books" (Borges 2000, 20–22). And moreover, Borges (2000, 23) continues:

> This philosopher observed that all books, however different from one another they might be, consist of identical elements: the space, the period, the comma, and twenty-two letters of the alphabet. He also posited a fact which all travelers have since confirmed: *In all the Library, there are no two identical books.*

More to the point, somewhat more than twenty-five orthographic symbols are used to describe to a lesser or greater degree all of the content of all of the books of the Library. These orthographic symbols are combined as alphanumerics or numerics behaving as alphanumerics to describe "aboutness" and "place" in absolute, relative, and abstract terms.

Classification is, as Bowker and Starr (2000) demonstrate, an essential human characteristic. Simple constructs require simple classification and description. The more complex the construct, the more complex are the classification and description. The way in which societies define constructs and therefore the way in which classification and description are invented are inter-related and culturally bound.

Because classification has its social boundaries, it has its ethical implications as well. While seemingly circular and tautological, how we classify an object, an artifact, or a thing, a human being defines the relationship of the classified objects to other objects in the environment. In turn, that environmental relationship prompts definition and classification. Sanford Berman spent much of his career as a cataloger, critiquing, redefining, and promoting change to the terms of the Library of Congress Subject Headings (LCSH). His efforts were not quixotic; they were well grounded in an understanding of the importance and implications a specific taxonomic construct—LCSH—has on the perception not only of librarians but the general public as well. His efforts also increased the awareness and sensitivity of the library community to the importance of terminology.

Perhaps second to the preservation impulse, classification has always been recognized as a primary librarian function. The classification requirement has endured. The way in which classification is to be done, and to some degree the reason why classification is performed as it has been performed, has undergone change to a lesser or greater degree. In the library, classification has always served as a finding and retrieval aid. While the sense of meaning in classification was usually implicit, it was not always well defined or understood. The fact that any given book was found in a nineteenth-century public library, for example, was proof that the work was considered by someone to have merit. The book might educate, edify, or uplift. It most certainly was not meant to amuse or titillate. Hence the very act of acquisition was and remains a classification function.

It has also been suggested that the extent of classification has increased as the complexity and scope of information has grown. The more complex and the greater the size of the information pool, the greater and more complex must be the means to organize that pool (see Taylor 2004). There has also been recognized a need to catalog information across repositories rather than solely within repositories. The classification mechanism should also be somewhat standardized across those repositories. Library classification began as an ad hoc and particular experience. Each library adopted whatever system the librarian might propose. Juan Páez de Castro recommended three rooms, each housing a different set of subjects, broadly defined. Gabriel Naudé sought to arrange the books of his library by a more complex subject structure. Authority, while of interest to Páez de Castro and Naudé, would not become a major classification characteristic until the eighteenth century. In the nineteenth century Antonio Panizzi, Melvil Dewey, and S. R. Ranganathan developed systems that were based not only on subject, title, and author but also on other specific bibliographic characteristics.

FREEDOM OF EXPRESSION, INTELLECTUAL FREEDOM, AND CENSORSHIP

Freedom of expression, intellectual freedom, and censorship are addressed at length in chapter 5. There have been and continue to be tensions and challenges that mold our ethics and thinking. There are many dualities of concern that influence our thinking. Intellectual property rights and intellectual freedom have an inherent tension. The history of copyright points toward the increasing value and commodification of information (see e.g., Porsdam 2006). What is legitimate and illegitimate taking of the work of others remains in flux (Koehler 2008).

I believe our professional ethics constantly evolve. Information workers have forever been conflicted by freedom of expression and censorship (e.g., Sturges 2005; 2006). In the last fifty years, a number of works have been challenged as sacrilegious. These include *The Last Temptation of Christ*, by Nikos Kazantzakis. The Kazantzakis work suggests both the humanity and the human fallibility of Jesus. Salman Rushdie published his novel *Satanic Verses* in 1988. Some have interpreted this work as blasphemous. In 1988 the Iranian Ayatollah Khomeini announced a fatwa or death sentence against Rushdie. In 2005, the Danish newspaper *Jyllands Posten* published a series of cartoons critical of the Prophet Mohammed. These cartoons led to demonstrations in many parts of the Muslim world, acts of terrorism, and threats against the newspaper and the cartoonists. In another instance the satirical French magazine *Charlie Hebdo* published many cartoons and articles critical of many institutions, including Christian, Islamic, and Jewish institutions and icons. In January 2015, the editorial offices of *Charlie Hebdo* in Paris were attacked by Islamic fundamentalists, leaving twelve employees of the magazine dead (see Sturges 2006).

Since the advent of the web in the mid-1990s, "harmful to children" has been employed to justify various forms of censorship, particularly of online pornography. Management of pornography and obscenity has long been a concern for libraries. Through the end of the nineteenth century, librarians interpreted their function as ensuring that collections were free of "riff raff," that the collection was wholesome. Riff raff meant any material that was not "wholesome" or informative. Non riff raff materials were also factual and led to self-improvement. In historical terms it is only recently (in the last hundred years or so) that it is has been accepted that public library collections should include popular fiction. John Budd (2003) reminds us of the symbolic power of libraries. Perhaps the standards that define the acceptable in libraries have been relaxed; both social standards and, more specifically, library standards are evolving (see Etzioni 2003).

In the United States in particular, the use of racial epithets and similar language has moved from accepted and common as late as 1960 to unacceptable and subject to significant sanctions today. Use of racial taunts has moved beyond freedom of expression to generally prohibited. Helen Bannerman's children's book *Little Black Sambo*, first published in 1899, was once considered a classic and is now seen as insulting to people of color. Mark Twain's *Huckleberry Finn* uses the "n" word. *Little Black Sambo* cannot be found in many libraries. *Huckleberry Finn* is frequently bowdlerized. The use of racial epithets has also become the cause of sanctions, particularly of persons in the public eye. For example, Marge Schott, once the owner of a professional baseball team, was sanctioned in

1993 and again in 1996 for using racial slurs. In 2013 Paula Deen, a television chef, found her career significantly diminished after she admitted to using the "n" word. And in 2014 Donald Sterling, owner of a professional basketball team, was banned from the sport for the same reasons. Sanctions may extend beyond the famous. In 2015 a fraternity was closed and two students expelled at the University of Oklahoma after a racist chant was revealed. The question has been raised, does freedom of expression need to yield to a group's right not to be insulted? For an interesting constitutional discussion in Canadian and US contexts, see Kent Greenawalt (1992).

TOPOGRAPHY OF ETHICAL SPACE IN THE INFOSPHERE

After a historical exploration of selected principles of librarianship and information practice, some interesting generalizations can be derived. Certain ethical principles can be paired. The dyads within each pair are reflections (from a mathematical perspective) of one another. For example, stewardship and access are two closely related concepts, two concepts at odds with one another in both a historical as well as a professional context. If, as Peter Brophy (2001, 89, emphasis in the original) has posited, the common purpose of libraries in the twenty-first century is "*to enable users to gain access to and use information that they need,*" then all other library functions should accommodate this first purpose. Yet, as we have seen, libraries have not always upheld the access principle as the first principle. In fact, the access principle as universally applied to the broad spectrum of the population is, as a first principle, a recent development. Moreover, this first principle, as broadly applied, does not today guide archival or records management practice or, for that matter, access to most proprietary databases.

The "universal" access principle is moderated by at least four other library practices. The first, the oldest, and in many ways the most important of these is stewardship. The intellectual integrity and continuity of the collection is to be protected. Public and many academic libraries may have relaxed their stewardship impulse to facilitate access, but they have only done so in the last century. Other information organizations have either not relaxed stewardship but have erected additional barriers to protect the integrity and security of their collections, be they electronic or paper.

It might be argued that libraries, museums, archives, records management facilities, digital databases, and so on have always supported and continue to support unfettered use and access to "their" information to *certain defined populations*. What is important to remember is that the criteria, which define the authorized user pool, have tended to expand or contract as political, social, technological, and economic conditions change. Even in the twenty-first century public library user privileges often have a jurisdictional or territorial basis. Only those members of a specified community, however defined, may be granted full access to all library services.

Access is limited by intellectual property concerns. As we have seen, the regulations governing the use of intellectual property have changed and will continue to change. Intellectual property rules establish the conditions under which patrons and libraries may legally exploit information. It was once considered appropriate for the state to appropriate and copy any manuscript it could to augment the library and to increase the pool of knowledge. It was once deemed necessary and prudent to copy and recopy manuscripts to preserve their content. It was common practice for scholars and authors to freely copy and arrogate as their own large portions of the works of others without attribution. These practices no longer meet the legal or ethical standards of our day. Yet it is equally true that the current intellectual property legal and ethical principles are continuing to undergo redefinition and restructuring in response to social, economic, technological, and political considerations.

The following is a partial list of major shifts of the library trope and paradigm. Each change in technology, practice, or perception has led to a change in the philosophical perception of the information professions.

- Bodley—library as information source (others)
- Lipsius—vulgate languages, library history as field of study
- Dury—freer access to libraries
- Kirkwood—wider distribution of libraries to a wider population
- Cotton des Houssayes—librarians to have bibliographical expertise
- Panizzi—public access to "research library"
- Edwards—skills requirement (cataloging)
- Blades—planning for and managing disasters
- Dewey—formal library education, women as librarians
- Dana—full public access, "riff raff" books, foreign language books
- Public libraries as repositories of quality, uplifting, to entertainment
- Librarians from guardians of the treasury to advocate of free access
- Diderot, Otlet, Welles, and Burners-Lee—central knowledge repository
- Otlet and Briet—defined "document"
- Butler—defined "library science"
- Intellectual property—evolution from none to some to much
- The catalog as linear inventory to code to descriptor of content to intellectual decline, despite its technical sophistication, with DC, semantic web, and so forth
- The digital revolution, the Internet and the web (1960s onward)

There have been other important political, social, and economic changes that have been important for library and information ethics. These include changes in literacy rates, the broadening of access to education, not to mention political and economic shifts.

FUTURE LIBRARIES, FUTURE OF INFORMATION

Aristotle (384–322 BCE) or Marcus Terentius Varro (116–27 BCE) could probably have more easily predicted the shape of the library world in 1950 than we now are able to anticipate developments in the infosphere in 2150. Information and the communication of information have shifted from the prevailing paradigm of 1950, resulting in a state of uncertainty for the foreseeable future.

Luciano Floridi has spent much of his professional life seeking to understand ethics in the infosphere. The infosphere he defines as the aggregate of human knowledge; it is, if you will, a self-contained environment of the mind (Floridi 1999). That said, there is an important interrelationship between the infosphere and the individual mind (Floridi 1999, 98):

> In search of its own individuality, autonomy and stability, the single mind can firmly establish itself at the crossroads of Being and Culture only by epistemically emancipating itself both from the world of things surrounding it and the infosphere it inherits from the past. However, in thus establishing its own individual autonomy, each single mind cannot help contributing to the growth of the infosphere, thus also generating new knowledge, to which future generations will need to react

Floridi has as his point of departure the technology of computer science as it contributes to human volition and conscience. Information and its application become a "game" in a deontological environment. Floridi (1998) has written, for example:

> Because of the remoteness of the process, the immaterial nature of information and the virtual interaction with faceless individuals, the infosphere is easily conceived of as a magical, political, social, financial dream-like environment, and anything but a real world, so a person may wrongly infer that her actions are as unreal and insignificant as the killing of enemies in a virtual game. The consequence is that not only does the person not feel responsible for her actions (no one has ever been charged with murder for having killed some monsters in a video game), but she may be perfectly willing to accept the universal maxim, and to extend the rules of the game to all agents. The hacker can be a perfect Kantian because universality without any concern for the actual consequences of an action is ethically powerless in a moral game.

Technological distance may therefore remove us from the "virtual" as well as the real-world consequences of the interpretation and application of information. There has always been a distance between information and its creation and consequences. Floridi would have us appreciate that the distance have both increased and become more anonymous by some order of magnitude. It is also *different*. Moreover, as Floridi (1998) suggests:

> Virtue Ethics is intrinsically anthropocentric and individualistic. Nothing would prevent it from being applicable to non-individual agents, like political parties, companies or teams, yet this is not usually the way in which Virtue Ethics is developed, partly because of a historical limitation, which has Greek roots in the individualist conception of the agent in question and the metaphysical interpretation of his functional development, and partly because of a contemporary empiricist bias, which consists in an anti-realist conception of non-individual entities — paradoxically, we live in a materialist culture based on ICT but we do not treat data or information as real objects — and in a pre-theoretical refusal to conceive of moral virtues also as holistic properties of complex systems. We shall see later that the removal of such limitations has interesting consequences for the foundation of [computer ethics].

Floridi (1998) has prescribed a wider definition for information ethics, an ethics that incorporates computer ethics:

> [Information ethics] takes as its fundamental value information, and describes entropy as evil, so that moral prescriptivity becomes (at least also) an intrinsic property of information: some features of the infosphere are descriptive and action-guiding and generate reasons for action independently of any motives or desires that agents may actually have.

From the perspective of library ethics, "entropy is evil." Stewardship is the prescription against entropy. In "library ethics" anything that contributes to entropy, including ever-expanding services to users, represents destabilization, the relaxation of constraints on entropy, and therefore an injury to the collection. Computer management of information resources, because of its inherent ability to conserve and share resources, may offer a technological solution to the inherent conflict, the yin and yang of stewardship and access.

But the computer carries with it its own costs. While computers may hold the evils of entropy at bay, social and technological forces inevitably lead to a different entropy. Digital libraries are inherently centralized and inherently proprietary. The historical social role of the library was to provide a highly distributed and redundant repository for information, for certain cultural artifacts. Technology, particularly the press and transport, significantly augmented that role. While electronic networks make distribution universal and instantaneous, they have reduced the role of redundancy in stewardship. Moreover, as information ceases to be perceived or defined as "real objects"—books and other solids—it loses a consequentialist quality. Information becomes no longer real. And as it is no longer real, its manipulation or application is therefore inconsequential.

There are broader consequences. A depersonalization of information and the use of information may also result in a social and ethical desensitization of the consequences of the use and management of information. As Floridi suggests, information becomes game. As game, the consequences may be Orwellian.

The library profession has witnessed a spate of predictions over the last half-century on the fate of the library, ranging from its immediate demise to its metamorphosis into sometimes recognizable and sometimes not-so-recognizable forms (Sapp 2002). We frequently point to Vannevar Bush (1945) as having had the first vision of the "digital future." Perhaps we were first made aware of impending and radical change by F. W. Lancaster's (1978) famous "Whither Libraries? Or, Wither Libraries?" article that brought to our attention, among other things, the emergence of libraries in an electronic world.

Our definitions of information are changing. Ronald Day (2001, 2) documents changing definitions for information and looks to three major movements and meanings in the twentieth century: European documentation, US information theory and cybernetics, and the "virtual" information of the present. Another observer concludes that information science has begun a transition from "little" to "big" science based on Price's classic 1963 definitions (Koehler 2001). New fields have emerged from computer science in the early 1950s to information architecture in the late 1990s. US library school programs have begun realignment from autonomous units to incorporation into wider programs (Hildreth and Koenig 2002). They have either moved away from "library" to an "information concentration" or they have expanded their definitions of domain. As the currency has changed, so has the practice. Prior to World War II perhaps one could distinguish between the European and American schools of documentation. In the post-war period information theory and cybernetics gained adherents. Certainly in the current era the "virtual" era, practice follows theory. That is to say, as theory has become globalized, so has practice.

A group of computational ethicists (Floridi 2015, 7) are suggesting a need "to launch an open debate on the impacts of the computational era on public spaces, politics, and societal expectations toward policymaking in the Digital Agenda." The group (Floridi 2015, 10) posits that distinctions between public and private are being blurred and that this blurring applies to public libraries as well. The new "hyperconnected," "onlife" reality has fundamental implications for human interactions, for human society. Consequentially, it also impacts our institutions to include libraries and their keepers. In so doing, information ethics are also undergoing metamorphosis. This metamorphosis is beginning to be documented in education (see Bottery 2000) and in society in general (Castells 2010).

RETHINKING LIBRARIES

Libraries are under stress. A recent report from the United Kingdom Department of Media, Culture, and Sport (2014) finds English libraries under significant economic stress. In the United States many library systems have or have contemplated closing branches or curtailing services (e.g., Mantel 2011). Library systems are being asked to do far more with far less. The digital revolution has also brought both challenges and opportunities to libraries.

According to some, the future of the library is in doubt (see Inayatullah 2014) or that that future will see major changes (Maness 2006). It is the year e^xy42. The library as we knew it has long ceased to exist from lack of need or want. The human race has ceased to exist. Or the human race has de-evolved into what H. G. Wells named the Eloi and Morlocks, in his 1895 novel *The Time Machine*. According to Wells, neither group would have had any use of the written word, not to mention the library or the museum. Or perhaps human beings have merged with machines: we have become cyborgs. *YaJoogle* has long since developed the perfect virtual question-and-answer engine.

Finally, information workers have a responsibility to maintain the cultural record. I close with a paraphrase from twentieth-century polymath Isaac Asimov's *Prelude to Foundation* (1991, 150), both mathematician and science fiction author. Asimov's protagonist in the distant future, Dors Venabili, will observe that everything erodes over time and is eventually dissolved into the background noise. The librarian has a cultural mandate to seek to conserve memories, information from that erosion.

Bibliography

A&M Records Inc. v. Napster Inc. 2001. 239 F.3d 1004 (9th Cir.).

Adam, Alison. 2000. "Gender and Computer Ethics." *Computers and Society* 30: 17–24.

Adams, Douglas. 1996. *The Ultimate Hitchhikers Guide.* New York: Wings Books.

African Network for Information Ethics. 2007. "Tshwane Declaration." Accessed February 23, 2015: http://www.africainfoethics.org/tshwanedeclaration.html

Ali Anwar, Mumtaz. 1990/1991. "The Pioneers: Asa Don Dickinson." *World Libraries* 1. Accessed February 10, 2015: http://cybra.p.lodz.pl/Content/1175/vol01no2/anwar_v01n2.html

Allen, David. 2001. "Eighteenth-Century Private Subscription Libraries and Provincial Urban Culture: The Amicable Society of Lancaster, 1769–c. 1820." *Library History* 17: 57–76.

Allied Professional Association. 2005. "ALA-APA Guiding Principles." Accessed February 10, 2015: http://ala-apa.org/about-ala-apa/governing-documents/guiding-principles/

Alstad, Colleen, and Ann Curry. 2003. "Public Space, Public Discourse, and Public Libraries." *Libres* 13. Accessed February 20, 2015: http://libres-ejournal.info/wp-content/uploads/2014/06/Vol13_I1_pub_space.pdf

Altair, Octaevius. 2011. *The Violators: No Human Rights for You (Canada).* Toronto: Lulu.com.

Altick, Richard. 1957. *The English Common Reader: A Social History of the Mass Reading Public, 1800–1900.* Chicago: University of Chicago Press.

Amegatcher, O. Andrew. 2002. "Protection of Folklore by Copyright—A Contradiction in Terms." *Copyright Bulletin* 2: 33–42.

American Geophysical Union v. Texaco Inc. 1995. 37 F.2d 881 (2d Cir. 1994), modified, 60 F.3d 913 (1995). http://www.ala.org/advocacy/intfreedom/librarybill/

American Library Association. n.d. "World List." Accessed February 10, 2015: http://www.ala.org/educationcareers/employment/foreigncredentialing/worldlist

American Library Association. *Library Bill of Rights 1948.* Accessed June 9, 2015: http://www.ala.org/advocacy/intfreedom/librarybill

American Library Association Committee on Accreditation. 1992. "Standards for Accreditation of Master's Programs in Library and Information Studies 1992." Accessed February 10, 2015: http://www.ala.org/accreditedprograms/standards/standards

American Library Association Committee on Accreditation. 2008. *Standards for Accreditation of Master's Programs in Library and Information Studies 2008.* Accessed February 10, 2015: http://www.ala.org/accreditedprograms/sites/ala.org.accreditedprograms/files/content/standards/standards_2008.pdf

American Library Association Committee on Accreditation. 2015. *Revised Standards for Accreditation of Master's Programs in Library and Information Studies.* Accessed February 10, 2015: http://www.ala.org/accreditedprograms/sites/ala.org.accreditedprograms/files/content/COA-approved_Revised_Standards_23Jan2015_final.pdf

American Library Association Committee on Education. 2008. *Core Competencies of Librarianship.* Accessed February 10, 2015: http://www.ala.org/educationcareers/sites/ala.org.educationcareers/files/content/careers/corecomp/corecompetences/finalcorecompstat09.pdf

American Library Association Office for Intellectual Freedom. 2006. *Intellectual Freedom Manual*, 7th ed. Chicago: American Library Association.

Anderson, Benedict. 1991. *Imagined Communities: Reflections on the Origin and Spread of Nationalism*, rev. ed. London: Verso.

Arendt, Hanna. 1951. *The Origins of Totalitarianism*. New York: Harcourt.

Aristotle. (350 BCE) 2000. *The Categories*. E. M. Edghill, trans. Project Gutenburg. Accessed February 23, 2015: http://www.gutenberg.org/dirs/etext00/arist10.txt

Arms, William. 2000. *Digital Libraries*. Cambridge, MA: MIT Press.

Arnold, Richard. 2014. "Harmonization by Degrees." Book review. *Journal of Intellectual Property Law and Practice*. Accessed February 13, 2015: http://jiplp.oxfordjournals.org/content/early/2014/07/08/jiplp.jpu122.extract

Asheim, Lester, ed. 1954. *The Core of Librarianship*. A report of a workshop held under the auspices of the Graduate Library School of the University of Chicago, August 10–15, 1953. Chicago: American Library Association.

Asheim, Lester. 1992. "Ethics in Academic Librarianship: The Need for Values." In Geraldene Walker, ed., *The Information Environment: A Reader*. New York: G.K. Hal.

Asimov, Isaac. 1991. *Prelude to Foundation*. New York: Bantam Reissue.

Asociación de Bibliotecarios Graduados de la República Argentina. n.d. "Estatuto del profesional en bibliotecologia y documentacion." Accessed February 10, 2015: http://www.abgra.org.ar/estatutoprof.htm

Association des bibliothécaires de France. 2003. *Code de déontologie du bibliothécaire. adopté lors du conseil national de l'Association des Bibliothécaires Français le 23 mars 2003.* Accessed February 20, 2015: http://www.abf.asso.fr/fichiers/file/ABF/textes_reference/code_deontologie_bibliothecaire.pdf

Australian Government, Office of Film and Literature Classification. 2005. *Guidelines for the Classification of Publications*. Accessed February 1, 2015, http://www.oflc.gov.au/resource.html?resource=63&filename=63.pdf

Ayala, John L., and Salvador Güereña. 2012. *Pathways to Progress Issues and Advances in Latino Librarianship*. Santa Barbara, CA: Libraries Unlimited.

Báez, Fernando, and Alfred Mac Adam. 2008. *A Universal History of the Destruction of Books: From Ancient Sumer to Modern-day Iraq*. New York: Atlas.

Bak, Greg. 2002. "The Greatest Librarians of the World Were Not Graduates of Library School." *Libraries and Culture* 37: 363–378.

Baker, Sharon. 1992. "Needed: An Ethical Code for Library Administrators." *Journal of Library Administration* 16: 1–17.

Baruchson-Arbib, Shifra, and Eti Yaari. 2005. "Printed versus Internet Plagiarism: A Study of Students' Perception." *International Review of Information Ethics* 1. Accessed February 13, 2015: http://www.i-r-i-e.net/inhalt/001/ijie_001_05_baruchson.pdf

Basbanes, Nicholas. 1995. *A Gentle Madness: Bibliophiles, Bibliomanes, and the Eternal Passion for Books*. New York: Owl Books.

Basbanes, Nicholas. 2003. *Patience and Fortitude: Wherein a Colorful Cast of Determined Book Collectors, Dealers, and Librarians Go About the Quixotic Task of Preserving a Legacy*. New York: Perennial.

Basic Books Inc. v. Kinko's Graphics Corp. 1991. 758 F.Supp. 1522 (S.D.N.Y.).

Batambuze, Charles, and Dick Kawooya, 2002. "Librarianship and Professional Ethics: The case for the Uganda Library Association." In Robert Vaagan, ed., *The Ethics of Librarianship: An International Survey*. Munich: IFLA/K.G.Saur Verlag.

Battles, Mathew. 2003. *Library: An Unquiet History* New York: WW Norton.

Bawden, David. 2007. "Towards Curriculum 2.0: Library/Information Education for a Web 2.0 World." *Library and Information Research* 31. Accessed February 14, 2015: http://www.lirgjournal.org.uk/lir/ojs/index.php/lir/article/view/49

Bawden, David. 2008. "Smoother Pebbles and the Shoulders of Giants: The Developing Foundations of Information Science." *Journal of Information Science* 34: 415–426.

Bearman, Toni Carbo. 1987. "Educating the Future Information Professional." *Library Hi Tech* 5: 27–40.

Beck, Clare. 1992. "Fear of Women in Suits: Dealing with Gender Roles in Librarianship." *Canadian Journal of Information Science* 17: 29–39.

Beck, Clare. 1996. "A 'Private' Grievance against Dewey." *American Libraries* 27: 62–64.

Beghtol, Clare. 2004. "Exploring New Approaches to the Organization of Knowledge: The Subject Classification of James Duff Brown." *Library Trends* 52: 702–718.

Beghtol, Clare. 2005. "Ethical Decision-Making for Knowledge Representation and Organization Systems for Global Use." *Journal of the American Society for Information Science and Technology* 56: 903–912.

Beghtol, Clare. 2008. "Professional Values and Ethics in Knowledge Organization and Cataloging." *Journal of Information Ethics* 17: 12–19.

Belton, Benjamin. 2003. *Orinoco Flow: Culture, Narrative, and the Political Economy of Information.* Lanham, MD: Scarecrow.

Bender and Hyperlaw v. West Publishing. 1998. 94 Civ. 0589, U.S.D.C. S.D.N.Y, 158 F.3d 693 (2d Cir.).

Bently, Lionel, and Brad Sherma. 2014. *Intellectual Property Law.* Oxford: Oxford University Press.

Berlin, Isaiah. 1991. *The Crooked Timber of Humanity: Chapters in the History of Ideas.* Henry Hardy, ed. New York: Alfred A. Knopf.

Berlin, Isaiah. 1996. *The Sense of Reality: Studies in Ideas and their History.* Henry Hardy, ed. New York: Farrar, Straus and Giroux.

Berlin, Isaiah. 2001. *Against the Current: Essays in the History of Ideas.* Henry Hardy, ed. Princeton, NJ: Princeton University Press.

Berlin Declaration. 2003. Conference on Open Access to Knowledge in the Sciences and Humanities in Berlin. Accessed February 13, 2015: http://openaccess.mpg.de

Berman, Sanford. 1971. *Prejudices and Antipathies: A Tract on the LC Subject Heads Concerning People.* Jefferson, NC: McFarland.

Berners-Lee, Tim, James Hendler, and Ora Lassila. 2001. "The Semantic Web." *Scientific American* 284(5): 34–43. Accessed February 14, 2015: http://www.scientificamerican.com/article.cfm?articleID=00048144–10D2–1C70–84A9809EC588EF21&catID=2

Berry III, John. 2003. "But Don't Call 'em Librarians." *Library Journal.* November 1. Accessed February 10, 2015: http://lj.libraryjournal.com/2003/11/library-education/but-dont-call-em-librarians/

Bertot, John Carlo, Paul T. Jaeger, Charles R. McClure, eds. 2011. *Public Libraries and the Internet: Roles, Perspectives, and Implications.* Santa Barbara: ABC-CLIO.

Besnoy, Amy, ed. 2009. *Ethics and Integrity in Libraries.* London: Routledge.

Bettig, V. Ronald. 1996. *Copyrighting Culture: The Political Economy of Intellectual Property.* Boulder, CO: Westview.

Birkerts, Sven. 1994. *The Gutenberg Elegies: The Fate of Reading in an Electronic Age.* Boston: Faber and Faber.

Bivens-Tatum, Wayne. 2012. *Libraries and the Enlightenment.* Sacramento, CA: Library Juice.

Blades, William. 1888. *The Enemy of Books,* 2nd ed. London: Elliot Stock. Project Gutenberg online edition. Accessed February 20, 2015: http://www.gutenberg.org/etext/1302.

Blair, Ann. 2003. "Reading Strategies for Coping with Information Overload ca. 1550–1700." *Journal of the History of Ideas* 64: 11–28.

Bliss, Henry E. 1935. *A System of Bibliographic Classification.* New York: H.W. Wilson.

BMG Canada Inc. v. John Doe. 2005. Canadian Federal Court of Appeals, Toronto. FCA 193. Accessed February 14, 2015: http://decisions.fca-caf.gc.ca/fca-caf/decisions/en/item/32246/index.do?r=AAAAAQAbQk1HIENhbmFkYSBJbmMuIHYuIEpvaG4gRG9lAAAAAAE

Bobinski, George. 1969. *Carnegie Libraries: Their History and Impact on American Public Library Development.* Chicago: American Library Association.

Bobinski, George. 2000. "Is the Library Profession Over Organized?" *American Libraries* 31: 58–61.

Bodley, Sir Thomas. (1603) (1906) 1967. "First Draught of the Statutes of the Publick Library at Oxon Transcribed from the Original Copy, Written by His Own Hand, and Reposited in the Archives of the Said Library, 1603." In John Cotton Dana and Henry W. Kent, eds. *Literature of Libraries in the Seventeenth and Eighteenth Centuries.* Chicago: A.C. McClurg, 1906. Reprint as vol. 4 of 6: 63–116, Metuchen, NJ: Scarecrow Reprint Corp.

Bodley, Sir Thomas. (1609) (1906) 1967. "*Reliquiæ Bodleianæ* or Sir Thomas Bodley's Remains, 1609." In John Cotton Dana and Henry W. Kent, *Literature of Libraries in the Seventeenth and Eighteenth Centuries.* Chicago: A.C. McClurg, 1906. Reprint as vol. 4 of 6: 33–59, Metuchen, NJ: Scarecrow Reprint Corp.

Bodley, Sir Thomas. 1926. *Letters of Sir Thomas Bodley to Thomas James, First Keeper of the Bodleian Library.* G. W. Wheeler, ed. Oxford: Clarendon.

Bollier, David. 2002. *Silent Theft: The Private Plunder of Our Common Wealth.* New York: Routledge.

Borges, Jorge Luis. 2000. *The Library of Babel.* Andrew Hurley, trans. Boston: David R. Godine.

Borgman, Christine. 2000. *From Gutenberg to the Global Information Infrastructure: Access to Information in the Networked World.* Cambridge, MA: MIT Press.

Borgmann, Albert. 1999. *Holding Onto Reality: The Nature of Information at the Turn of the Millennium.* Chicago: University of Chicago Press.

Bottery, Mike. 2000. *Education, Policy and Ethics.* London: A&C Black.

Bowker, Geoffrey, and Susan Leigh Star, eds. 1998. "How Classifications Work: Problems and Challenges in an Electronic Age." *Library Trends* 47: 1–3.

Bowker, Geoffrey, and Susan Leigh Star. 2000. *Sorting Things Out: Classification and Its Consequences.* Cambridge, MA: MIT Press.

Brabazon, Tara. 2008. *The University of Google: Education in the (Post) Information Age.* Farnham, UK: Ashgate.

Branch, Katherine. 1998. "Librarians Value Service Most." *College and Research Libraries News* 59: 176–177.

Bridgeport Music Inc. v. Dimension Films. 2004. 230 F. Supp.2d at 841.

Brandtzæg, Petter Bae, Jan Heim, and Amela Karahasanović. 2011. "Understanding the New Digital Divide—A Typology of Internet Users in Europe." *International Journal of Human-Computer Studies* 69: 123–138.

Briet, Suzanne. 1951. *Qu'est-ce que la documentation.* Paris: Éditions Documentaires Industrielle et Techniques.

Britz, Johannes, and Tomas Lipinski. 2001. "A Moral Reflection on Current Legal Concepts of Intellectual Property." *Libri* 51: 234–247.

Britz, Johannes, and Peter Lor. 2003. "A Moral Reflection on the Information Flow From South to North: An African Perspective." *Libri* 53: 160–173.

Britz, Johannes, and Peter Lor. 2004. "A Moral Reflection on the Digitization of Africa's Documentary Heritage." *IFLA Journal* 30: 216–223.

Brophy, Peter. 2001. *The Library in the Twenty-First Century: New Services for the Information Age.* London: London Association.

Brown v. Board of Education of Topeka. 1954. 347 U.S. 483.

Brunet, Jacques-Charles. (1860) 1964. *Manuel du libraire et de l'amateur de livres,* 5th ed. 6 vols. Paris: Firmin Didot. Reprint, Paris: Maisonneuve et Larose.

Brush, Stephen, and Doreen Stabinsky, eds. 1996. *Valuing Local Knowledge: Indigenous People and Intellectual Property Rights.* Washington, DC: Island Press.

Buckland, Michael. 1997. "What Is a 'Document'?" *Journal of the American Society of Information Science* 48: 804–809.

Budd, John M. 2001. *Knowledge and Knowing in Library and Information Science: A Philosophical Framework.* Metuchen, NJ: Scarecrow.

Budd, John M. 2003. "The Library, Praxis, and Symbolic Power." *Library Quarterly: Information, Community, Policy* 73: 19–32

Budd, John M., and Douglas Raber. 1996. "Discourse Analysis: Method and Application in the Study of Information." *Information Processing and Management* 32: 217–226.

Budge, E. A. Wallis. 1929. *Babylonian Story of the Deluge and the Epic of Gilgamesh with an Account of the Royal Libraries at Nineveh*. Reprint, Whitefish, MT: Kessinger.

Bundy, Alan. 2001. "The 21st Century Profession: Collectors, Managers or Educators?" Professional Perspectives Series Address to Information Studies Program Students. University of Canberra, August 29. Accessed February 14, 2015: http://ura.unisa.edu.au/R/?func=dbin-jump-full&object_id=unisa28344

Burger, Robert. 1986. "Introduction." *Library Trends* 35: 3–6. Accessed March 4, 2015: https://www.ideals.illinois.edu/bitstream/handle/2142/7466/library-trendsv35i1_opt.pdf?sequence=3

Burke, Susan. 2008. "Use of Public Libraries by Immigrants." *Library Reference and User Services* 48: 164–174.

Burnheim, Robert. 1992. "Information Literacy—A Core Competency." *Australian Academic and Research Libraries* 23: 188–196.

Burt, Eleanor and John Taylor. 2001. "When 'Virtual' meets Values: Insights from the Voluntary Sector.'" *Information, Communication & Society* 4:54–73.

Bury, Richard de. 1909. *The Love of Books: The Philobiblon of Richard de Bury, 1473*. E. C. Thomas, trans. London: Chatto & Windus. Electronic Text Center, University of Virginia Library Online. Accessed February 10, 2015: http://etext.lib.virginia.edu/toc/modeng/public/BurLove.html

Buschman, John. 2003. *Dismantling the Public Sphere: Situating and Sustaining Librarianship in the Age of the New Public Philosophy*. Westport, CT: Libraries Unlimited.

Bush, Vannevar. 1945. "As We May Think." *Atlantic Monthly* 176: 101–108.

Butler, Pierce. 1933. *An Introduction to Library Science*. Chicago: University of Chicago Press.

Buzás, Ladislaus. 1986. *German Library History, 800–1945*. William Boyd, trans. Jefferson, NC: McFarland.

Byrne, Alex. 2002. "Information Ethics for a New Millennium."

Caidi, Nadia. 2003. "Cooperation in Context: Library Developments in Central and Eastern Europe." *Libri* 53: 103–117.

Campbell, aka Skyywalker, et al. v. Acuff Rose Music Inc. 1994. (92–1292), 510 U.S. 569.

Canadian Library Association. 1974. "Executive Council Statement on Intellectual Freedom." Approved June 1974, revised 1983 and 1985. Accessed February 16, 2015: http://www.cla.ca/AM/Template.cfm?Section=Position_Statements&Template=/CM/ContentDisplay.cfm&ContentID=3047

Capurro, Rafael. 1992. "Foundations of Information Science Review and Perspectives." Accessed February 16, 2015: http://www.capurro.de/tampere91.htm. Originally published as "What Is Information Science For? A Philosophical Reflection." In Pertti Vakkari and Blaise Cronin, eds., *Conceptions of Library and Information Science. Historical, Empirical and Theoretical Perspectives*, 82–98. London: Taylor Graham.

Capurro, R.: 1996. "Information Technology and Technologies of the Self." *Journal of Information Ethics*, Vol. 5 (2): 19–28.

Capurro, Rafael. 2006. "Towards an Ontological Foundation of Information Ethics." *Ethics and Information Technology* 8: 175–186.

Capurro, Rafael, Johannes Britz, Thomas Hausmanninger, Makoto Nakada, Felix Weil, and Michael Nagenborg, eds. 2007. "African Information Ethics in the Context of the global Information Society." *International Review of Information Ethics* 7.

Carbo, Toni. 2004. "Models for Ethical Decision-Making for Use in Teaching Information Ethics: Challenges for Educating Diverse Information Professionals." *International Review of Information Ethics* 2. Accessed February 20, 2015: http://container.zkm.de/ijie/ijie/no002/ijie_002_08_carbo.pdf

Carbo, Toni. 2007. "Information Rights: Trust and Human Dignity in e-Government." *International Review of Information Ethics* 7. Accessed February 20, 2015: http://fiz1.fh-potsdam.de/volltext/ijie/08093.pdf

Carbo, Toni. 2008. "Ethics Education for Information Professionals." *Journal of Library Administration* 47: 5–25.

Carbo, Toni, and Martha M. Smith. 2008. "Global Information Ethics: Intercultural Perspectives on Past and Future Research." *Journal of the American Society for Information Science and Technology* 59: 1111–1123.

Cardona, Juan Baptista. 1889a. "De Regia S. Lavrentii Biblioteca, De la Real Biblioteca de San Lorenzo." In *Juan Páez de Castro*, 97–192. Madrid: E. de la Riva.

Cardona, Juan Baptista. 1889b. "Traza de la Librería de San Lorenzo el Real." In *Juan Páez de Castro*, 53–95. Madrid: E. de la Riva.

Carey, Richard. 1972. "'Bibliotheques': An Extract from Essais sur l'histoire des belles letters et des art of Felixe de Juvenal de Carlencas (1697–1760) with translation and annotation by Richard J. Carey." *Journal of Library History* 7: 208–250.

Carr, Ronnie, Paul Light, and Martin Lighthead. 2014. *Growing Up in a Changing Society*. New York: Routledge.

Carroll, Mary. 2002. "The Well-Worn Path." *Australian Library Journal* 50: 117–126.

Carter, Jimmy. 2005. *Our Endangered Values*. New York: Simon & Schuster.

Casson, Lionel. 2001. *Libraries in the Ancient World*. New Haven, CT: Yale University Press.

Castells, Manuel. 2010. *The Rise of the Network Society*, 2nd ed. Chichester, UK: John Wiley & Sons.

CCH Canadian Ltd. v. Law Society of Upper Canada. 2004. Supreme Court of Canada. 1 S.C.R. 339, 2004 SCC 13 (CanLII).

Chako, Mary. 2008. *Portable Communities: The Social Dynamics of Online and Mobile Connectedness* Albany: SUNY Press.

Chan, Lois Mai. 2007. *Cataloging and Classification: An Introduction*. Lanham, MD: Scarecrow.

Chandel, A. S., and Rai Vijay Prasad. 2013. "Journey of Catalogue from Panizzi's Principles to Resource Description and Access." *DESIDOC Journal of Library and Information Technology* 33: 314–322. Accessed February 5, 2015: http://publications.drdo.gov.in/ojs/index.php/djlit/article/viewFile/5007/2913

Chaplain, Heather, and Aaron Ruby. 2005. *Smartbomb: The Quest for Art, Entertainment, and Big Bucks in the Videogame Revolution*. Chapel Hill, NC: Algonquin Books.

Chartered Institute of Library and Information Professionals. 2013. "What Is the Professional Knowledge and Skills Base?" May 13. Last updated January 30, 2014. Accessed February 10, 2015 http://www.cilip.org.uk/cilip/jobs-and-careers/professional-knowledge-and-skills-base/what-professional-knowledge-and-skills

Christ, Karl. 1984. *The Handbook of Medieval Library History*. Theophil Otto, trans. and ed. Metuchen, NJ: Scarecrow.

Christians, Clifford. 1991. "Information Ethics in a Complicated Age." In F. W. Lancaster, ed., *Ethics and the Librarian*, 3–17. Urbana-Champaign: University of Illinois Press.

Chugani, Reema "Semantic Web" 2013. Accessed June 10, 2015: http://www.reemachugani.com/blog/2013/jul/04/semantic-web/

Churchland, Paul. 1984. *Matter and Consciousness*. Cambridge, MA: MIT Press.

Chute, Adrienne, Elaine Kroe, Patricia O'Shea, Maria Polcari, and Cynthia Jo Ramsey. 2003. *Public Libraries in the United States: Fiscal Year 2001—E.D. TAB*. NCES 2003-399. Washington, DC: National Center for Education Statistics. Accessed February 8, 2015: http://nces.ed.gov/pubsearch/pubsinfo.asp?pubid=2003399

Comerford, Kathleen. 1999. "What Did Early Modern Priests Read? The Library of the Seminary of Fiesole, 1646–1721." *Libraries and Culture* 34: 203–221.

Commission on Online Child Protection. 2000. *Final Report of the COPA Commission*. Presented to Congress, October 20. Accessed February 5, 2015: http://www.copacommission.org/report/

Computer Science and Telecommunications Board, National Academy of Sciences. 2002. "Youth, Pornography, and the Internet." Dick Thornburgh and Herbert Lin, eds. Washington, DC: National Academy Press. Accessed February 9, 2015: http://www.nap.edu/books/0309082749/html/R1.html

Cornog, Martha, and Timothy Perper. 1996. *For Sex Education, See Librarian: A Guide to Issues and Resources*. Westport, CT: Greenwood.

Cotton des Houssayes, Jean-Baptiste. (1780) 1967. "Discourse on the Duties and Qualifications of a Librarian 1780." In John Cotton Dana and Henry W. Kent, eds., *Literature of Libraries in the Seventeenth and Eighteenth Centuries*. Reprint as vol. 1 of 6: 33–55, Metuchen, NJ: Scarecrow Reprint Corp.

Council of Europe. 1950. Convention for the Protection of Human Rights and Fundamental Freedoms of 1950. Accessed February 5, 2015: http://conventions.coe.int/Treaty/EN/Treaties/Html/005.htm

Council on Library and Information Resources. n.d. "Postdoctoral Fellowship in Scholarly Information Resources." Accessed February 15, 2015: http://www.clir.org/fellowships; http://www.clir.org/fellowships/postdoc

Cox, Richard, Mary Biagini, Toni Carbo, Tony Debons, Ellen Detlefsen, Jose Marie Griffiths, Don King, David Robins, Richard Thompson, Chris Tomer, and Martin Weiss. 2001. "The Day the World Changed: Implications for Archival, Library, and Information Science Education." *FirstMonday* 6. Accessed February 20, 2015: http://journals.uic.edu/ojs/index.php/fm/article/view/908/817

Crawford, Walt, and Michael Gorman. 1995. *Future Libraries: Dreams, Madness, and Reality*. Chicago: American Library Association.

Cruz-Jesus, Frederico, Tiago Oliveira, and Fernando Bacao. 2012. "Digital Divide across the European Union." *Information and Management* 49: 276–291.

Dalton, Kate and Pete Levinson. 2008. "An Investigation of LIS Qualifications Throughout the World" 73–81 in Lan Quan Liu and Xiaojun Cheng, eds. *International and Comparative Studies in Information and Library Science: A Focus on the United States and Asian Countries*. Lanham, MD: Scarecrow Press.

Damien, Robert. 1995. *Bibliothèque et état: Naissance d'une raison politique dans la France du XVIIe siècle*. Paris: Presses Universitaires de France.

McClurg. Reprint as vol. 1 of 6: 25–29, Metuchen, NJ: Scarecrow Reprint Corp.

Dana, John Cotton. 1906. *A Library Primer*, 4th ed. Chicago: Library Bureau.

Dana, John Cotton. 1920. *A Library Primer*, 1920 ed. Boston: Library Bureau.

Dana, John Cotton. (1925) 1991. "Standardization in Libraries." *Wilson Bulletin* 2: 1925: 452–453. Reprint in Carl Hanson, ed. *Librarian at Large: Selected Writings of John Cotton Dana*, 125–126. Washington, DC: Special Libraries Association.

Dana, John Cotton, and Henry W. Kent. (1906a) 1967a. "Bibliographical Note [Cotton des Houssayes]." In *Literature of Libraries in the Seventeenth and Eighteenth Centuries*. Chicago: A.C. McClurg. Reprint as vol. 1 of 6: 9–14, Metuchen, NJ: Scarecrow Reprint Corp.

Dana, John Cotton, and Henry W. Kent. (1906b) 1967b. "Introduction [Cotton des Houssayes]." In *Literature of Libraries in the Seventeenth and Eighteenth Centuries*. Chicago: A.C.

Danton, Jeriam, 1949. *Education for Librarianship*. Reprint, Paris: United Nations Educational, Scientific, and Cultural Organisation.

Darwin, Charles. 1859. *The Origin of Species by Means of Natural Selection or the Preservation of Favored Races in the Struggle for Life*. Reprint from the 6th London ed., New York: Hurst.

Davison, Robert, Doug Vogel, Roger Harris, and Noel Jones. 2000. "Technology Leapfrogging in Developing Countries—An Inevitable Luxury?" *Electronic Journal of Information Systems in Developing Countries* 1: 1–10. Accessed February 25, 2015: http://www.ejisdc.org/ojs2/index.php/ejisdc/article/view/5/5

Day, Ronald. 2001. *The Modern Invention of Information: Discourse, History and Power*. Carbondale: Southern Illinois University Press.

Delicostopolou, A. 1992. "Copyright Works: Who Owns Them?" *Managing Intellectual Property*: 28–33.

Desktop Marketing Systems Pty Ltd v. Telstra Corporation Ltd. 2002. FCAFC 112 (May 15).

Devlin, M., and H. Miller. 1995. "Ethics in Action: The Vendor's Perspective." *Serials Librarian* 25, 1995: 295–300.

Dewey, Melvil. (1876) 1989. "The Profession." *Library Journal* 114. Reprint from *American Library Journal*, 1.

Dewey, Melvil. 1887. "Brief Rules for Library Handwriting." *Library Notes* 1: 281.

Dewey, Melvil. 1898. "Relation of State to Public Library." *Transactions and Proceedings of the Second International Library Conference.* Accessed February 10, 2015: https://archive.org/details/transactionsand00unkngoog

Dewey, Melvil. 1975. "Relations of State to Public Library." Reprinted in Barbara McCrimmon, ed., American Library Philosophy: An Anthology. Hamden, CT: Shoe String.

Ditzion, Sidney Herbert. 1947. *Arsenals of a Democratic Culture: A Social History of the American Public Library Movement in New England and the Middle States from 1850 to 1900.* Chicago: American Library Association.

Dix, T. Keith. 1994. "Public Libraries in Ancient Rome: Ideology and Reality." *Libraries and Culture* 29: 282–296.

Dole, Wanda, Jitka M. Hurych, and Wallace Koehler. 2000. "Values for Librarians in the Information Age: An Expanded Examination." *Library Management* 21: 285–297.

Donaldson v. Beckett. 1774. United Kingdom, House of Lords. 4 Burr 2408, 98 Eng Rep 257; 2 Bro PC 129, 1 Eng Rep 837.

Douglas, J. Y. 2001. *The End of Books—or Books without End? Reading Interactive Narratives.* Ann Arbor: University of Michigan Press.

Drassinower, Abraham. 2003/2004. "Sweat of the Brow, Creativity and Authorship: On Originality in Canadian Copyright Law." *University of Ottawa Law and Technology Journal* 1: 105–123. Accessed February 14, 2015: http://ssrn.com/abstract=621184

Drzewieniecki, Walter, and Joanna Drzewieniecki-Abugattas. 1974. "Public Library Service to American Ethnics: The Polish Community on the Niagara Frontier, New York." *Journal of Library History* 9: 120–137.

Durán Guardeño, Antonio. 2003. "Los manuscritos griegos de Arquímedes en la Biblioteca del Real Monesterio de El Escorial." In José Luis Montesinos, ed., *Proceedings Symposium Arquímedes*, 5–20. Fundación Canaria Ortotava de Historia de la Ciencia. Max-Planck-Institut für Wissenschaftsgeschichte.

Durrance, Joan, Karen Pettigrew, Michael Jourdan, and Karen Scheuerer. 2001. "Libraries and Civil Society." In Nancy Kranich, ed., *Libraries and Democracy: The Cornerstones of Liberty*, 49–59. Chicago: American Library Association.

Dury, John. (1650a) (1906a) 1967a. "The Reformed Librarie-Keeper or Two Copies of Letters Concerning the Place and Office of the Librarie-Keeper by John Dury, 1650." In John Cotton Dana and Henry W. Kent, eds., *Literature of Libraries in the Seventeenth and Eighteenth Centuries.* Chicago: A.C. McClurg, 1906. Reprint as vol. 2 of 6: 9–36 Metuchen, NJ: Scarecrow Reprint Corp.

Dury, John. (1650b) (1906b) 1967b. "The Reformed Librarie-Keeper or Two Copies of Letters [to Samuel Hartlib] Concerning the Place and Office of a Librarie-Keeper, 1650." In John Cotton Dana and Henry W. Kent, eds., *Literature of Libraries in the Seventeenth and Eighteenth Centuries.* Chicago: A.C. McClurg, 1906. Reprint as vol. 2 of 6: 39–71 Metuchen, NJ: Scarecrow Reprint Corp.

Earle, Genevieve. 1933. "Pandora Buys a Book: A Collector in Search of an Author." *American Book Collector.* Cited in Hastings 2014.

Eco, Umberto. 1989. *The Open Work.* Cambridge, MA: Harvard University Press.

Eco, Umberto. 1995. *The Search for the Perfect Language: The Making of Europe.* James Fentress, trans. London: Blackwell.

Eco, Umberto. 1998. *Serendipities: Languages and Lunacy.* William Weaver, trans. New York: Columbia University Press.

Eco, Umberto, ed. 2004. *History of Beauty.* Alastair McEwen, trans. New York: Rizzoli.

Edwards, Chloë. 2013. "The Social Role of Public Library Classifications." *NASKO* 4: 40–52.

Edwards, Edward. 1859. *Memoirs of Libraries.* 2 vols. London: Trübner.

Edwards, Edward. 1864. *Libraries and the Founders of Libraries*. London: Trübner.

Edwards, Julie Biando, and Stephan P. Edwards. 2010. *Beyond Article 19 Libraries and Social and Cultural Rights*. Duluth, MN: Library Juice.

Eisenstein, Elizabeth. 1979. *The Printing Press as an Agent of Change: Communications and Cultural Transformations in Early-Modern Europe*, vol 1. Cambridge: Cambridge University Press.

Eisenstein, Elizabeth. 1983. *The Printing Revolution in Early Modern Europe*. Cambridge: Cambridge University Press.

Emerson, Ralph Waldo. 1870. "Books." In *Society and Solitude*, 189–221. Boston: Houghton Mifflin.

Encyclopaedia Britannica Educational Corp. v. Crooks. 1982. 542 F.Supp. 1156 (W.D.N.Y.).

Eskildsen, Kaspar. 2005. "How Germany Left the Republic of Letters." *Journal of the History of Ideas* 65: 421–432.

Etzioni, Amitai. 1993. *The Spirit of Community*. New York: Crown.

Etzioni, Amitai. 2003. "On Protecting Children from Speech." *Chicago-Kent Law Review* 79. Accessed February 10, 2015: http://www2.gwu.edu/~ccps/etzioni/A315.pdf

European RDA Interest Group (EURIG). 2011. *EURIG—Cooperative Agreement*. Accessed February 5, 2015: http://www.slainte.org.uk/eurig/docs/EURIG_cooperation_agreement_2011.pdf

Falk, Howard. 2004. "Privacy in Libraries." *Electronic Library* 22: 281–284.

Fattahi, Rahmatollah. 1997. *Recycling the Past: Historical Development of Modern Catalogues and Cataloging Codes*. PhD dissertation. Accessed February 10, 2015: http://profsite.um.ac.ir/~fattahi/thesis1.htm

Fauchart, Emmanuelle, and Eric von Hippel. 2008. "Norms-Based Intellectual Property Systems: The Case of French Chefs." *Organization Science* 19: 187–201.

Feather, John. 1980. "The Book Trade in Politics: The Making of the Copyright Act of 1710." *Publishing History* 19: 25–45.

Feather, John. 1994. *Publishing, Piracy, and Politics: An Historical Study of Copyright in Britain*. London: Mansell.

Feist Publications v. Rural Telephone Services Co. 1991. 499 U.S. 340.

Felski, Rita. 1989. *Beyond Feminist Aesthetics: Feminist Literature and Social Change*. Cambridge, MA: Harvard University Press.

Fernández de Zamora, Rosa María. 2003. *Los Códigos de Ética en América Latina*. World Library and Information Congress: 69th IFLA General Conference and Council, Berlin, August 1–9. Accessed February 10, 2015: http://www.ifla.org/IV/ifla69/papers/087s_trans-Fernandez-de-Zamora.pdf

Ferris, Timothy. 1997. *The Whole Shebang: A State of the Universe(s) Report*. New York: Simon & Schuster.

Finegan, Jack. 1974. *Encountering New Testament Manuscripts: A Working Introduction to Textual Criticism*. Grand Rapids, MI: Eerdmans.

Fiske, Marjorie. 1959. *Book Selection and Censorship: A Study of School and Public Libraries in California*. Berkeley: University of California Press.

Fleming, Samantha. 2002. "Information and Communication Technologies (ICTs) and Democracy Development in the South: Potential and Current Reality." *Electronic Journal of Information Systems in Developing Countries* 10: 1–10. Accessed February 16, 2015: http://www.ejisdc.org/ojs2/index.php/ejisdc/article/view/56

Floridi, Luciano. 1998. *Information Ethics: On the Philosophical Foundation of Computer Ethics*. Originally presented at ETHICOMP 98, updated version. Accessed February 10, 2015: http://www.philosophyofinformation.net/publications/pdf/ieotpfoce2.pdf

Floridi, Luciano. 1999. *Philosophy and Computing: An Introduction*. London: Routledge.

Floridi, Luciano. 2001. "Information Ethics: An Environmental Approach to the Digital Divide." *Philosophy in the Contemporary World* 9: 1–7.

Floridi, Luciano. 2013. *The Ethics of Information*. Oxford: Oxford University Press.

Floridi, Luciano. 2014. *The Fourth Revolution: How the Infosphere Is Reshaping Human Reality*. Oxford: Oxford University Press.

Floridi, Luciano. 2015. "Introduction." In Luciano Floridi, ed., *The Onlife Manifesto: Being Human in a Hyperconnected Era.* Cham: Springer. Accessed February 11, 2015: http://download.springer.com/static/pdf/470/bok%253A978-3-319-04093-6.pdf?auth66=1423656722_d0f242d3c8e25e47363fdf545aeb64ed&ext=.pdf

Foerstel, Herbert. 2002. *Banned in the U.S.A: A Reference Guide to Book Censorship in Schools and Public Libraries,* revised and expanded ed. Westport, CT: Greenwood.

Folsom v. Marsh. 1841. 9 F.Cas. 342.

Ford, Barbara. 1998. "ALA President's Message: Visions, Values, and Opportunities." *American Libraries* 29: 54.

Foucault, Michel. 1977. "What Is an Author?" Donald F. Bouchard and Sherry Simon, trans. In Donald F. Bouchard, ed. *Language, Counter-Memory, Practice.* Ithaca, NY: Cornell University Press.

Franklin, Benjamin. 1944. *The Autobiography of Benjamin Franklin.* New York: Carlton House.

Friedman, Thomas. 2005. *The World Is Flat: A Brief History of the Twenty-first Century.* New York: Farrar, Straus and Giroux.

Froehlich, Thomas. 1992. "Ethical Considerations of Information Professionals." *Annual Review of Information Science and Technology* 27: 291–324.

Froehlich, Thomas. 2000. "Intellectual Freedom, Ethical Deliberation, and Codes of Ethics." *IFLA Journal* 26: 264–272.

Galantaris, Christian. 1998. *Manuel de bibliophilie* , 2 vols. Paris: Éditions des Cendres.

Garcia Cuadrado, Amparo. 2001. "Un proceso de impression: La 'Censura de historias fabulosas' de Nicolás Antonio." *Boletin de la Asociatión de Bibliotecarios* 64: 89–122.

Garnier, Jean. 1678. *Systema bibliothecae collegii Parisiensis S.J.* Paris: Sebastianus Mabre-Cramoisy. Accessed February 14, 2015: http://alfama.sim.ucm.es/dioscorides/consulta_libro.asp?ref=B2137367X

Garrison, Dee. 1972/1973. "The Tender Technicians: The Feminization of Public Librarianship." *Journal of Social History* 6: 131–156.

Gates, J. K. 1979. *Guide to the Use of Books and Libraries,* 4th ed. New York: McGraw-Hill.

Gerolimos, Michalis. 2009. "Skills Developed through Library and Information Science Education." *Library Review* 58: 527–540.

Goldstein, Daniel. 2003. "The Spirit of an Age: Iowa Public Libraries and Professional Librarians as Solutions to Society's Problems, 1890–1940." *Libraries and Culture* 38: 214–235.

Gorbatov, Inna. 2006. *Catherine the Great and the French Philosophers of the Enlightenment: Montesquieu, Voltaire, Rousseau, Diderot and Grim.* Bethesda, MD: Academica.

Gorman, Michael. 1990. "A Bogus and Dismal Science; or the Eggplant that ate Library Schools." *American Libraries* 21: 462–463.

Gorman, Michael. 2000. *Our Enduring Values: Librarianship in the 21st Century.* Chicago: American Library Association.

Gorman, Michael. 2003. *The Enduring Library: Technology, Tradition, and the Quest for Balance.* Chicago: American Library Association.

Gough, Cal, and Ellen Greenblatt. 2011. "Barriers to Selecting Materials about Sexual and Gender Diversity." In Ellen Greenblatt, ed., *Serving LGBTIQ Library and Archives Users: Essays on Outreach, Service, Collaboration and Access,* 163–175. Jefferson, NC: McFarland.

Grand Upright Music, Ltd v. Warner Brothers Records Inc. 1991. 780 F.Supp. 182 (S.D.N.Y.).

Granniss, Ruth. (1906) 1967. "Biographical Sketch [of Dury]." In John Cotton Dana and Henry W. Kent, eds., *Literature of Libraries in the Seventeenth and Eighteenth Centuries.* Chicago: A.C. McClurg. Reprint as vol. 2 of 6: 9–36, Metuchen, NJ: Scarecrow Reprint Corp.

Green, Ravonne, and Vera Blair. 2011. *Keep It Simple: A Guide to Assistive Technologies.* Santa Barbara: ABC-CLIO.

Greenawalt, Kent. 1992. "Free Speech in the United States and Canada." *Law and Contemporary Problems* 55: 5–33. Accessed March 12, 2015: http://scholar-ship.law.duke.edu/cgi/viewcontent.cgi?article=4120&context=lcp

Greenhalgh, Liz, and Ken Worpole, with Charles Landry. 1995. *Libraries in a World of Cultural Change.* London: University College London Press.

Griswold v. Connecticut. 1965. 381 U.S. 479.

Gruber, Tom. n.d. "What Is an Ontology?" Accessed February 14, 2015: http://www.ksl.stanford.edu/kst/what-is-an-ontology.html

Gunkel, David. 2003. "Second Thoughts: Toward a Critique of the Digital Divide." *New Media and Society* 5: 499–522.

Gurevich, Konstantin. 1990. "Russian/Soviet History in Library Classifications." *Cataloging and Classification Quarterly* 12: 63–85.

Habermas, Jürgen. 1989. *The Structural Transformation of the Public Sphere: An Inquiry into a Category of Bourgeois Society.* Thomas Burger, trans. Cambridge: MIT Press.

Habermas, Jürgen. 1995. "Institutions of the Public Sphere." In Oliver Boyd-Barrett and Chris Newbold, eds., *Approaches to Media: A Reader,* 235–244. London: Arnold.

Hackel, Heidi. 1997. "'Rowme' of Its Own: Printed Drama in Early Libraries." In John Cox and David Kastan, eds. *A New History of Early English Drama.* New York: Columbia University Press.

Hafner, Arthur, and Jennifer Sterling-Folker. 1993. "Democratic Ideals and the American Public Library." In Arthur W. Hafner, ed., *Democracy and the Public Library.* Westport, CT: Greenwood.

Hague v. Congress of Industrial Organizations. 1939. 307 U.S. 496.

Hansen, Debra. 2004. "Professionalizing Library Education, the California Connection: James Gillis, Everett Perry, and Joseph Daniels." *Library Trends* 52: 963–987.

Hargittai, Eszter. 2002. "Second-Level Digital Divide: Differences in People's Online Skills." *FirstMonday* 7. Accessed February 12, 2015: http://firstmonday.org/ojs/index.php/fm/article/view/942

Harloe, Bart, and John M. Budd. 1994. "Collection Development and Scholarly Communication in the Era of Electronic Access." *Journal of Academic Librarianship* 20: 83–87.

Harper & Row, Publishers Inc. v. Nation Enters. 1985. 471 U.S. 539.

Harris, Michael. 1973. "The Purpose of the American Public Library: A Revisionist Interpretation of History—the Continuing Debate." *Literary Journal* 98: 2509–2514.

Harris, Michael. 1995. *History of Libraries in the Western World,* 4th ed. Lanham, MD: Scarecrow.

Harris, Michael, and Stan Hannah. 1993. *Into the Future: The Foundations of Library and Information Services in the Post-Industrial Era.* Norwood, NJ: Ablex.

Hartley, John. 1992. *The Politics of Pictures: The Creation of the Public in the Age of Popular Media.* New York: Routledge.

Hastings, Emi. 2014. "Women Collectors in Their Own Words." *Adventures in Book Collecting.* Posted September 16. Accessed February 23, 2015: https://librarianofba-bel.wordpress.com/2014/09/16/women-collectors-in-their-own-words/

Hauptman, Robert. 1976. "Professionalism or Culpability? An Experiment in Ethics." *Wilson Library Bulletin* 5: 626–627.

Hauptman, Robert. 1988. *Ethical Challenges in Librarianship.* Phoenix, AZ: Oryx.

Hauptman, Robert. 1991. "Five Assaults on Our Integrity." In F. W. Lancaster, ed., *Ethics and the Librarian,* 83–91. Urbana-Champaign: University of Illinois Press.

Hawking, Stephen. 1998. *A Brief History of Time: Updated and Expanded Tenth Anniversary Edition.* New York: Bantam Books.

Heim, Kathleen. 1991. "Human Resources Management: Ethics in Personnel." In F. W. Lancaster, ed., *Ethics and the* Librarian, 101–113. Urbana-Champaign: University of Illinois Press.

Heins, Marjorie. 2001. *Not in Front of the Children: "Indecency," Censorship, and the Innocence of Youth.* New York: Hill & Wang.

Henriot, Émile. 1928. *L'art de former une bibliothèque,* Paris: Librarie Delagrave.

Hernon, Peter, and Ellen Altman. 2010. *Assessing Service Quality: Satisfying the Expectations of Library Customers*, 2nd ed. Chicago: American Library Association.

Hesse, Carla. 1996. "Books in Time." In Geoffrey Nunberg, ed., *The Future of the Book*, 21–36. Berkeley: University of California Press.

Hewitt, Martin. 2000. "Confronting the Modern City: The Manchester Free Public Library, 1850–80." *Urban History* 27: 62–88.

Hildenbrand, Suzanne. 1996. *Reclaiming the American Library Past: Writing the Women In.* Norwood, NJ: Ablex.

Hildenbrand, Suzanne. 2000. "Library Feminism and Library Women's History: Activism and Scholarship, Equity, and Culture." *Libraries and Culture* 35: 51–66.

Hildreth, Charles, and Michael Koenig. 2002. "Organizational Realignment of US Programs in Academia: From Independent Standalone Units to Incorporated Programs." *Journal of Education for Library and Information Science* 43: 126–33.

Hill, Heather, and Marni Harrington. 2014. "Beyond Obscenity: An Analysis of Sexual Discourse in LIS Educational Texts." *Journal of Documentation*, 70: 62–73.

Hisle, W. Lee. 1998. "Values for the Electronic Age: Crossroads of Profession." *College and Research Libraries News* 59: 504–505.

Hjørland, Birger. 1997. *Information Seeking and Subject Representation. An Activity-Theoretical Approach to Information Science.* Westport, CT: Greenwood.

Hjørland, Birger. 2011. "The Importance of Theories of Knowledge: Indexing and Information Retrieval as an Example." *Journal of the American Society for Information Science and Technology* 62: 72–77.

Hohne, Herbert. 1978. "Zur Durchsetzung der Einheitsklassifikation im wissenschaftlichen Bibliothekswesen der DDR." *Zentralblatt für Bibliothekswesen* 92: 18–22.

Hongladarom, Soraj. 2004. "Making Information Transparent as a Means to Close the Global Digital Divide." *Minds and Machines* 14: 85–99.

Houser, L., and A. Schrader. 1978. *The Search for a Scientific Profession: Library Science Education in the US and Canada.* Metuchen, NJ: Scarecrow.

Houston, George. 2002. "The Slave and Freedman Personnel of Public Libraries in Ancient Rome." *Transactions of the American Philological Association* 132: 139–176.

Inayatullah, Sohail. 2014. "Library Futures: From Knowledge Keepers to Creators." *Futurist* 48. Accessed February 10, 2015: http://www.wfs.org/futurist/2014–issues-futurist/november-december-2014–vol-48–no-6/library-futures-knowledge-keepers-c

International Federation of Information Associations and Institutions. 1999. "Statement on Libraries and Intellectual Freedom." Accessed February 10, 2015: http://www.ifla.org/publications/ifla-statement-on-libraries-and-intellectual-freedom

International Federation of Information Associations and Institutions. 2009. *Statement on International Cataloguing Principles.* Accessed February 5, 2015: http://www.ifla.org/files/assets/cataloguing/icp/icp_2009–en.pdf

International Federation of Information Associations and Institutions. 2013. *Trend Report: Riding the Waves or Caught in the Tide? Navigating the Evolving Information Environment.* Accessed March 4, 2015: http://trends.ifla.org/insights-document

International Federation of Information Associations and Institutions. n.d. "Committee on Free Access to Information and Freedom of Expression." Accessed February 10, 2015: http://www.ifla.org/faife

Intner, Shiela, and Jorge Reina Schement. 1998. "The Ethic of Free Service." *Library Journal* 112: 50–52.

Jackson, Holbrook. 1932. *The Fear of Books.* London: Soncino.

Jackson, Holbrook. 2001. *Anatomy of Bibliomania.* Urbana-Champagne: University of Illinois Press.

Jaeger, Paul T., Ursula Gorham, John Carlo Bertot, and Lindsay C. Sarin. 2013. "Democracy, Neutrality, and Value Demonstration in the Age of Austerity." *Library Quarterly* 83: 368–382.

Janke, Terri, and Livia Iacovino. 2012. "Keeping Cultures Alive: Archives and Indigenous Cultural and Intellectual Property Rights." *Archival Science* 12: 151–171.

Jefcoate, Graham. 1998. "Christian Gottlob Heyne and the University Library at Göttingen as 'Universalbibliothek' of the Eighteenth Century." *Library History* 14: 111–116.

Jefferson, Renée, and Sylvia Contreras. 2006. "Ethical Perspectives of Library and Information Science Graduate Students in the United States." *New Library World* 106: 58–66.

Jochum, Uwe. 1998. "Die Bibliothek als Locus Communis."*Deutsche Vierteljahrsschrift fürft und Geistesgeschichte* 72: 14–30.

Joeckel, Carleton. 1935. *The Government of the American Public Library.* Chicago: University of Chicago Press.

Johnson, Ian. 2013. "The Impact on Education for Librarianship and Information Studies of the Bologna Process and Related European Commission Programmes—and Some Outstanding Issues in Europe and Beyond." *Education for Information* 30: 63–92.

Johnson, W. G. 1994. "The Need for a Value Based Reference Policy: John Rawls at the Reference Desk." *Reference Librarian* 47 1994: 201–211.

Jones, Barbara. 1999. *Libraries, Access, and Intellectual Freedom: Developing Policies for Public and Academic Libraries.* Chicago: American Library Association.

Josey, E. J., ed. 1970. *The Black Librarian in America.* Metuchen, NJ: Scarecrow.

Josey, E. J., and Ismael Abdullahi. 2002. "Why Diversity in American Libraries?" *Library Management* 23: 10–16.

Joyce, Michael. 1996. "(Re)placing the Author: 'A Book in the Ruins'." In Geoffrey Nunberg, ed., *The Future of the Book*, 273–293. Berkeley: University of California Press.

Kahani, Mohsen. 2005. "Experiencing Small-Scale E-Democracy in Iran. "*Electronic Journal of Information Systems in Developing Countries* 22: 1–9. Accessed February 9, 2015: http://www.ejisdc.org/

Kawooya, Dick. 2006. *Copyright, Indigenous Knowledge and Africa's University Libraries: The Case of Uganda.* World Library and Information Congress: 72nd IFLA General Conference and Council, August 20–24, Seoul, Korea. Accessed February 20, 2015: http://193.5.93.80/export/sites/www/tk/en/databases/creative_heritage/docs/dick_kawooya_uganda.pdf

Kawooya, Dick. 2008. "An Examination of Institutional Policy on Copyright and Access to Research Resources in Uganda." *International Information and Library Review* 40: 226–235.

Kawooya, Dick. 2013. "Ethical Implications of Intellectual Property in Africa." In Dennis Ocholla, Johannes Britz, Rafael Capurro, and C. Bester, eds., *A Handbook for Information Ethics in Africa: Cross Cutting Themes*, 43–57. Pretoria: African Centre of Excellence for Information Ethics, University of Pretoria.

Keen, Paul. 1999. *The Crisis of Literature in the 1790s: Print Culture and the Public Sphere.* Cambridge: Cambridge University Press.

Kehm, Barbara. 2010. "Quality in European Higher Education: The Influence of the Bologna Process." *Change: The Magazine of Higher Learning* 42: 40–6.

Kent, Susan. 2002. "The Public Library Director in the Dot (.) World." *New Library World* 103: 48–54.

Kilgour, Frederick. 1998. *The Evolution of the Book.* New York: Oxford University Press.

Kincaid, James. 1998. *Erotic Innocence: The Culture of Child Molesting.* Durham, NC: Duke University Press.

Kirkwood, James. (1669a) (1906a) 1967a. "An Account of a Design about Erecting Some Libraries in the Highlands of Scotland for the use chiefly of Ministers and Probationers, 1699." In John Cotton Dana and Henry W. Kent, eds., *Literature of Libraries in the Seventeenth and Eighteenth Centuries.* Chicago: A.C. McClurg, 1906. Reprint as vol. 3 of 6: 73–89, Metuchen, NJ: Scarecrow Reprint Corp.

Kirkwood, James. (1699b) (1906b) 1967b. "A Copy of a Letter Anent a Project, for Erecting a Library in Every Presbytery, or at least County, in the Highlands, 1699." In John Cotton Dana and Henry W. Kent, eds., *Literature of Libraries in the Seven-*

teenth and Eighteenth Centuries. Chicago: A.C. McClurg, 1906. Reprint as vol. 3 of 6: 61–72, Metuchen, NJ: Scarecrow Reprint Corp.

Kirkwood, James. (1699c) (1906c) 1967c. "An Overture for Establishing of Bibliothecks in Every Paroch throughout this Kingdom, 1699." In John Cotton Dana and Henry W. Kent, eds., *Literature of Libraries in the Seventeenth and Eighteenth Centuries*. Chicago: A.C. McClurg. 1906. Reprint as vol. 3 of 6: 18–60, Metuchen, NJ: Scarecrow Reprint Corp.

Kirkwood, James. (1703) (1906) 1967. "A Copy of a Letter Anent a Project, for Erecting a Library in Every Presbytery, or at Least County, in the Highlands 1703?" In John Cotton Dana and Henry W. Kent, eds., *Literature of Libraries in the Seventeenth and Eighteenth Centuries*. Chicago: A.C. McClurg. 1906. Reprint as vol. 4 of 6: 61–89, Metuchen, NJ: Scarecrow Reprint Corp.

Knox, Emily. 2014. "'The Books Will Still Be in the Library': Narrow Definitions of Censorship in the Discourse of Challengers." *Library Trends* 62: 740–749.

Kochen, Manfred. 1987. "Ethics and Information Science." *American Journal of Information Science* 38: 206–210.

Koehler, Wallace. 1981. "Canadian Foreign Policy Politics under Trudeau: 'From Colony to Nation' Again." *American Review of Canadian Studies* 11.

Koehler, Wallace. 1999a. "An Analysis of Web Page and Web Site Constancy and Permanence." *Journal of the American Society for Information Science* 50: 162–180.

Koehler, Wallace. 1999b. "Digital Libraries and World Wide Web Sites and Page Persistence." *Information Research* 4: Accessed February 5, 2015: http://InformationR.net/ir/4–4/paper60.html

Koehler, Wallace. 2001. "Information Science as 'Little Science': The Implications of a Bibliometric Analysis of the Journal of the American Society for Information Science." *Scientometrics* 51: 117–132.

Koehler, Wallace. 2002a. "The Organizations That Represent Information Professionals: Form, Function and Professional Ethics." In Barbara Rockenbach and Tom Mendina, eds., *Ethics and Electronic Information: A Festschrift for Stephen Almagno*, 59–73. Jefferson City, NC: McFarland.

Koehler, Wallace. 2002b. "Trends of Library Associations and Ethics in the US." In Robert Vaagan, ed., *The Ethics of Librarianship: An International Survey*, 323–337. Munich: K.G. Saur.

Koehler, Wallace. 2003. "Professional Values and Ethics as Defined by 'The LIS Discipline.'" *Journal of Education for Library and Information Science* 44: 99–119.

Koehler, Wallace. 2004. "Professional Organizations and Their Ethics Codes: A Quantitative Review." In Tom Mendina and Johannes Britz, eds., *Information Ethics in the Electronic Age: Current Issues in Africa and the World*, 65–72. Jefferson, NC: McFarland.

Koehler, Wallace. 2006. *Public Libraries as Institutional Repositories and Stewards in an Historical and Ethical Context*. World Library and Information Congress: 72nd IFLA General Conference and Council. Accessed February 5, 2015: http://archive.ifla.org/IV/ifla72/papers/151–Koehler-en.pdf

Koehler, Wallace. 2008. "In the Matter of Plagiarism . . . Practice Makes Imperfect." *Journal of Library Administration* 47: 111–124.

Koehler, Wallace, Jitka Hurych, Wanda Dole, and Joanna Wall. 2000. "Ethical Values of Information and Library Professionals—an Expanded Analysis." *International Information and Library Review* 32: 485–506.

Koehler, Wallace, and J. Michael Pemberton. 2000. "A Search for Core Values: Towards a Model Code of Ethics for Information Professionals." *Journal of Information Ethics* 9: 26–54.

Köhler, Johann David. 1728. *Scriptorum de bene ordinanda et ornanda bibliotheca*.

Köhler, Johann David. 1973. *Anweisung für reisende Gelerte, Bibliothecken, Münz-Cabinette, Antiquitäten-Zimmer, Bilder-Sale, Naturalien-und Kunst-Kammern, u.m.b. mit Ruken zu befeben*. Bonn: Bouvier Verlag Herbert Grundmann.

Kranich, Nancy, ed. 2001. *Libraries and Democracy: The Cornerstones of Liberty*. Chicago: American Library Association.

Kranich, Nancy. 2002. "Libraries: The Information Commons of Civil Society." Accessed February 16, 2015: http://dlc.dlib.indiana.edu/dlc/handle/10535/4085

Kreimer v. Bureau of Police for the Town of Morristown. 1991. 765 Suppl. 181 (DNJ).

Krupskaya, Nadezhda. 2002. "On Communist Ethics." Transcribed and HTML markup by Sally Ryan. Accessed February 16, 2015: http://www.marxists.org/archive/krupskaya/works/ethics.htm

Kunitz, Stanley. 1939. "That Library Serves Best. . . ." *Wilson Library Bulletin* 4: 314.

Kuruk, Paul. 2002. "African Customary Law and the Protection of Folklore." *Copyright Bulletin* 2: 4–32.

Lancaster, F. W. 1978. "Whither Libraries? Or, Wither Libraries?" *College and Research Libraries* 39: 345–357.

Lankes, R. David. 2011. *The Atlas of New Librarianship*. Cambridge, MA: MIT Press.

LaPélerie, François. 1998. "La qualité essentielle du bibliothécaire." *Bulletin des bibliothèques de France* 43: 68–73.

Laskova, Ekaterina. 1984. "Die Sowjetische Bibliothekarisch-Bibliographische Klassifikation (BBK) in Bulgarien." *Zentralblatt für Bibliothekswesen* 98: 496–503.

Lea, Gary. 1993. "Databases and Copyright." *Computer Law and Security Report* 9: 68, 127.

Le Gallois, Pierre. 1680. *Traitté historique des plus belles bibliothèques de l'Europe: Des premiers Livres qui ont été faits. De l'invention de l'imprimerie. Des Imprimeurs. De plusieurs Livres qui ont été perdus et recouvrez par les soins des sçavans. Avec une Methode pour dresser une Bebliotheque*. Paris: Michallet.

Lee, Earl. 1998. *Libraries in the Age of Mediocrity*. Jefferson, NC: McFarland.

Leigh, Robert. 1950. *The Public Library in the United States: The General Report of the Public Library Inquiry*. New York: Columbia University Press.

Le Roy-Ladurie, Emmanuel. 1995. *Les 1000 années de la bibliothèque et du livre*. Conference proceedings, Collège de France.

Lessig, Lawrence. 2002. *The Future of Idea: The Fate of the Commons in a Connected World*. New York: Random House.

Lester, June, and Wallace Koehler. 2007. *Fundamentals of Information Studies: Understanding Information and Its Environment*, 2nd ed. New York: Neal-Schuman.

Lester, June, and Connie Van Feet. 2008. "Use of Professional Competencies and Standards Documents for Curriculum Planning in Schools of Library and Information Studies Education." *Journal of Education for Library and Information Science* 49: 43–69.

Levine, Judith. 2002. *Harmful to Minors: The Perils of Protecting Children from Sex*. Minneapolis: University of Minnesota Press.

Lévi-Strauss, Claude. 1969. *The Elementary Structures of Kinship*. Boston: Beacon Press.

Library Association. 1904. *The Library Association Record*. London: Library Association. Available from: https://books.google.com/books?id=U0pFAAAAYAAJ&pg=PA129&lpg=PA129&dq=Johann+Christian+Koch+libraries&source=bl&ots=epLc4yOST4&sig=hufkEYgOxIGIVTCCyfXyL9XgxP0&hl=en&sa=X&ei=LofbVO-tMYGvogTv8oBY&ved=0CEwQ6AEwCQ#v=onepage&q=Johann%20Christian%20Koch%20libraries&f=false

Lin Ming, Qui Weiquing, and Lian Zhang. 2014. "Traditional Chinese Book and Document Preservation: Brief History And Essential Techniques and Their Contemporary Applications." *Preservation, Digital Technology and Culture* 43: 142–161.

Lipinski, Tomas. 2003. "The Myth of Technological Neutrality in Copyright and the Rights of Institutional Users: Recent Legal Challenges to the Information Organization as Mediator and the Impact of the DMCA, WIPO, And TEACH." *Journal of the American Society for Information Science and Technology* 54: 824–835.

Lipinski, Tomas, and Johannes Britz. 2000. "Rethinking the ownership of information in the 21st century: Ethical implications." *Ethics and Information Technology* 2: 49–71.

Lipsius, Justus. (1607) 1967. *A Brief Outline of the History of Libraries.* John Cotton Dana, trans. John Cotton Dana and Henry Kent, eds. Reprinted as vol. 5 of 6, 31–121. Metuchen, NJ: Scarecrow.

López de Prado, Rosario. 2000. *La biblioteconomía y la Formación profesional del bibliotecario en la actualidad.* Accessed February 16, 2015: http://www.oocities.org/zaguan2000/301.html

Lor, Peter. 2011. "Is a Knowledge Society Possible without Freedom of Access to Information?" *Journal of Information Science* 37: 555–569.

Lowenthal, Leo, and Marjorie Fiske. 1957. "The Controversy over Art and Popular Culture in Eighteenth Century England." In Mirra Komatovsky, ed., *Common Frontiers of the Social Sciences.* Glencoe, IL: Free Press.

Maack, Mary Niles. 1996. "Women's Values, Vision and Culture in the Transformation of American Librarianship, 1890–1920." Libraries and Reading in Times of Cultural Change. Moscow: Ministry of Culture of the Russian Federation. Accessed February 10, 2015: http://www.gseis.ucla.edu/faculty/maack/Values.htm

MacKinnon, Catharine, and Andrea Dworkin, eds. 1998. *The Pornography Civil Rights Hearings.* Cambridge, MA: Harvard University Press.

Mai, Jens-Eric. 2013. "Values and Morality in Contemporary Library Classifications." *Knowledge Organization* 40: 242–253.

Mäkinen Ilkka. 1996. "Widow's Mite, or Crumbs from the Rich Man's Table: Popular Support for Public Libraries in Finland during the Nineteenth Century." *Libraries and Culture* 31: 394–408.

Malone, Cheryl. 2000. "Toward a Multicultural American Public Library History." *Libraries and Culture* 35: 77–87.

Maness, Jack. 2006. "Library 2.0 Theory: Web 2.0 and Its Implications for Libraries." *Webology* 3. Accessed February 11, 2015: http://www.webology.org/2006/v3n2/a25.html

Mantel, Barbara. 2011. "Future of Libraries. Can They Survive Budget Cuts and Digitization?" *CQ Researcher* 21. Accessed March 4, 2015: http://www.interamericano.com.br/site/imagens/file/Future%20of%20Libraries.pdf

Martin, Robert Sidney, and Orvin Lee Shiflett. 1996. "Hampton, Fisk, and Atlanta: The Foundations, the American Library Association, and Library Education for Blacks, 1925–1941." *Libraries and Culture* 31: 299–325. Accessed February 12, 2015: http://libres.uncg.edu/ir/uncg/f/O_Shiflett_Hampton_1996.pdf

Mathiesen, Kay. 2004. "What Is Information Ethics?" *Computers and Society* 32. Accessed February 16, 2015: http://papers.ssrn.com/sol3/papers.cfm?abstract_id=2081302

In the Matter of Patent Applications Gb 0226884.3 and 0419317.3 by Cfph L.L.C. 2005. United Kingdom, High Court of Justice, Chancery Division, Patent Court. EWHC 1589 (Pat). Available: http://www.bailii.org/ew/cases/EWHC/Patents/2005/1589.html

Maxtone-Graham v. Burtchaell. 1986. 803 F.2d 1253 (2d Cir.), cert. denied, 481 U.S. 1059 (1987).

McCook, Kathleen de la Peña. 1999. "Using Ockham's Razor: Cutting to the Center." Professional Concerns Committee of the Congress on Professional Education. Accessed February 5, 2015: http://archive.ala.org/congress/mccook_print.htm

McCook, Kathleen de la Peña. 2000. *A Place at the Table: Participating in Community Building.* Chicago: American Library Association.

McCook, Kathleen de la Peña. 2004. *Introduction to Public Librarianship.* New York: Neal-Schuman.

McCook, Kathleen de la Peña. 2011. *Introduction to Public Librarianship,* 2nd ed. New York: Neal-Schuman.

McDonnell, Janice, Wallace Koehler, and Bonnie Carroll. 1999. "Cataloging Challenges in an Area Studies Virtual Library Catalog (ASVLC): Results of a Case Study." *Journal of Internet Cataloging,* 2: 15–42.

Mcilwaine, I. C. 2000. *The Universal Decimal Classification: Guide to Its Use.* The Hague: UDC Consortium.

McPheeters, Annie. 1988. *Library Service in Black and White.* Metuchen, NJ: Scarecrow.

Merrill, Andrea, ed. 2003. "The Strategic Stewardship of Cultural Resources: To Preserve and Protect." Library of Congress Symposium. *Journal of Library Administration* 38.

Meyrowitz, Joshua. 1985. *No Sense of Place: The Impact of Electronic Media on Social Behavior.* New York: Oxford University Press.

MGM v. Grokster. 2005. 545 U.S. 913.

Mirchin, David. 2005. "Israeli Court Rules on Help Wanted Case." *Information Today* 22: 1ff.

Mitchell, Sydney. 1939. "The Public Library in the Defense of Democracy." *Library Journal,* March 15: 209.

Moeck, Pat. 2002. "Academic Dishonesty: Cheating among Community College Students." *Community College Journal of Research and Practice* 26: 479–491.

Moll, Jaime. 1994. *De la imprenta al lector: Estudios Sobre El Libro Español de los Siglos XVI al XVIII.* Madrid: Arco/Libros.

Montgomery, John. 1962. *A Seventeenth-Century View of European Libraries: Lomeier's De Bibliothecis, Chapter X.* John Warwick Montgomery, trans. University of California Publications in Librarianship, vol. 5. Berkeley: University of California Press.

Morgan, Peter, and Glenn Reynolds. 1997. *The Appearance of Impropriety: How the Ethics Wars Have Undermined American Government, Business, and Society.* New York: Free Press.

Morrison, Samuel. 1991. "The Ethics of Access: Towards an Equal Slice of the Pie." In F. W. Lancaster, ed., *Ethics and the Librarian,* 93–100. Urbana-Champaign: University of Illinois Press.

Morristown v. Kreimer. 1992. US Court of Appeals, Second Circuit. 958 F. 2d1242 (2d Cir.).

Moss, Jeremy. 2002. "Power and the Digital Divide." *Ethics and Information Technology* 4: 159–165.

Myrvold, Barbara. 1986. "The First Hundred Years: Toronto Public Library." In Peter McNally, ed., *Readings in Canadian Library History,* 65–79. Ottawa: Canadian Library Association.

Naudé, Gabriel. (1627) 1950. *Advice on Establishing a Library.* Berkeley: University of California Press.

Naudé, Gabriel. (1652) 1967. "News from France or a Description of the Library of Cardinal Mazarin before It Was Utterly Ruined, Sent in a Letter from Monsieur G. Naudaeus, Keeper of the Publick Library 1652." In John Cotton Dana and Henry W. Kent, eds., *Literature of Libraries in the Seventeenth and Eighteenth Centuries.* Reprint as vol. 1 of 6: 61–75, Metuchen, NJ: Scarecrow Reprint Corp.

Nautical Solutions Mktg. Inc. v. Boats.com. 2004. Case No. 8:02-CV780–T-23TGW (MDFla. April 1).

Negroponte, Nicholas. 1996. *Being Digital.* New York: Knopf.

Newman, Simon, and Wallace Koehler. 2004. "Copyright: Moral Rights, Fair Use, and the Online Environment." *Journal of Information Ethics* 13: 38–57.

Nisbet, Eric, Elizabeth Stoycheff, and Katy Pearce. 2012. "Internet Use and Democratic Demands: A Multinational, Multilevel Model of Internet Use and Citizen Attitudes about Democracy." *Journal of Communication* 62: 249–265.

Nunberg, Geoffrey, ed. 1996. *The Future of the Book.* Berkeley: University of California Press.

Ó Baoill, Andrew. 2000. "Slashdot and the Public Sphere." *First Monday* 5: 9. Accessed February 9, 2015: http://journals.uic.edu/ojs/index.php/fm/article/view/790

Obasaki, Tony. 2010. "Automated Indexing: The Key to Information Retrieval in the 21st Century." *Library Practice and Philosophy 2010.* Accessed February 5, 2015: http://www.webpages.uidaho.edu/~mbolin/obaseki.htm

Oliver, Bette. 1999. "Safeguarding the Nation's Past: Chamfort's Brief Career at the Bibliothèque Nationale." *Libraries and Culture* 34: 373–379.

Ontario Film Review Board. 2005. "Our Mission." Accessed February 14, 2015: http://www.ofrb.gov.on.ca/english/page2.htm

Ontario Film Review Board. 2011. "Our History." Accessed February 14, 2015: http://www.ofrb.gov.on.ca/english/page4.htm

Ontario Film Review Board. 2012. "Classification Categories." Accessed February 14, 2015: http://www.ofrb.gov.on.ca/english/page6.htm

Otlet, Paul. 1934. *Traité de documentation: Le livre sur le livre—théorie et pratique.* Brussels: Éditiones Mundaneum.

Otlet, Paul. 1935. *Monde: Essai d'universalisme: Connaissance du monde, sentiment du monde, action organisée et plan du monde.* Brussels: Éditiones Mundaneum.

Páez de Castro, Juan. 1889. "Memorial." In *Juan Páez de Castro,* 9–50. Madrid: E. de la Riva.

Paine, Thomas. 1915. *The Rights of Man.* London: J.M. Dent & Sons.

Panizzi, Anthony. 1841. *Rules for the Compilation of the Catalogue.* London: Nichols and Son.

Park, Bruce. 1992. "Libraries without Walls; or, Librarians without a Profession." *American Libraries* 23(9): 746–747.

Patry, William. 1994. *Copyright Law and Practice.* Rockville, MD: Bureau of National Affairs Books.

Patterson, Lyman. 1968. *Copyright in Historical Perspective.* Nashville: Vanderbilt University Press.

Peignot, Etienne-Gabriel. 1806. *Dictionnaire critique, littéraire et bibliographique des principeaux livres condamnés au feu, supprimés ou censurés, précédé d'un discours sur ces sortes d'ouvrages.* Paris: Allais.

Peignot, Etienne-Gabriel. 1823. *Manuel du bibliophile ou traité du choix des livres.* Dijon: V. Lagier.

Pepys, Samuel. *Diary of Samuel Pepys, Complete.* 1863. Project Gutenberg. Transcription by Minors Bright. Accessed February 10, 2015: http://www.gutenberg.org/dirs/4/2/0/4200/4200.txt

Percas de Ponseti, Helena. 2002. "Un misterio dilucidado: Pasamonta fue Avellaneda." *Cervantes* 22: 127–154.

Perry Educational Association v. Perry Local Educators' Association. 1983. 460 U.S. 37.

Phinazee, Annette. 1980. *The Black Librarian in America.* Metuchen, NJ: Scarecrow.

Plessy v. *Ferguson.* 1896. 163 U.S. 537.

Polastron, Lucien. 2007. *Books on Fire: The Destruction of Libraries throughout History.* Rochester, VT: Inner Traditions.

Porsdam, Helle, ed. 2006. *Copyright and Other Fairy Tales: Hans Christian Andersen and the Commodification of Creativity.* Cheltenham, UK: Edward Elgar.

Pourciau, Lester, ed. 2001. *Ethics and Electronic Information in the Twenty-First Century.* West Lafayette, IN: Purdue University Press.

Pratt, Vernon. 1987. *Thinking Machines: The Evolution of Artificial Intelligence.* Oxford: Basil Blackwell.

Prescott, Marjorie Wiggin. 1932. *Stray Thoughts of a Book Collector.* Greenwich, CT: MWP. Cited in Hastings 2014.

Prideux, W. R. B. 1904. "Library Economy (Chiefly Continental) at the End of the Seventeenth Century." *Library Association Record* 6. Accessed February 10, 2015: https://books.google.com/books?id=U0pFAAAAYAAJ&pg=PA129&lpg=PA129&dq=Johann+Christian+Koch+libraries&source=bl&ots=epLc4yOST4&sig=hufkEYgOxIGIVTCCyfXyL9XgxP0&hl=en&sa=X&ei=LofbVO-tMYG-vogTv8oBY&ved=0CEwQ6AEwCQ#v=onepage&q=Johann%20Christian%20Koch%20libraries&f=false

Publius [James Madison or Alexander Hamilton]. 1788. "The Structure of the Government Must Furnish the Proper Checks and Balances between the Different Departments." *Independent Journal.* Available: http://etext.lib.virginia.edu/etcbin/toccernew2?id=HMJFedr.sgm&images=images/modeng&data=/texts/english/modeng/parsed&tag=public&part=51&division=div1

Putnam, Herbert. 1916. "The Woman in the Library." *Library Journal* 41: 880.

Raber, Douglas. 1997. *Librarianship and Legitimacy: The Ideology of the Public Library Inquiry.* Westport, CT: Greenwood.

Rabinowitz, Harold, and Rob Kaplan, eds. 1999. *A Passion for Books: A Book Lover's Treasury of Stories, Essays, Humor, Lore, and Lists on Collecting, Reading, Borrowing, Lending, Caring for, and Appreciating Books.* New York: Times Books.

Radford, G. P., and Radford, M. L. 2001. "Libraries, Librarians, and the Discourse of Fear." *Library Quarterly* 71: 299–329.

Radford, Marie, and Gary Radford. 1997. "Power, Knowledge, and Fear: Feminism, Foucault, and the Stereotype of the Female Librarian." *Library Quarterly* 67: 250–266.

Ranganathan, S. R. 1957. *The Five Laws of Library Science.* Madras: Madras Library Association. Publication series. 2.

Ranganathan, S. R. 1960. *Colon Classification*, 6th ed. Bangalore: Sarada Ranganathan Endowment for Library Science.

Ranganathan, S. R. 1963a. *The Five Laws of Library Science*, 2nd ed. Bombay: Asia Publishing House.

Ranganathan, S. R. 1963b. *The Organization of Libraries*, 3rd ed. Bombay: Oxford University Press.

Rawls, John. 1993. *Political Liberalism: The John Dewey Essays in Philosophy, #4.* New York: Columbia University Press.

Reinsfelder, T. L. 2014. "E-books and Ethical Dilemmas for the Academic Reference Librarian" *Reference Librarian* 55: 151–62.

Reno v. ACLU. 1997. 117 S. Ct. 2329.

Richard, Jules. 1883. *L'Art de former une bibliothèque.* Paris: Éd. Rouveyre & G. Blond.

Robbins, Louise. 1996. *Censorship and the American Library: The American Library Association's Response to Threats to Intellectual Freedom, 1939–1969.* Westport, CT: Greenwood.

Robbins, Louise. 2000. *The Dismissal of Miss Ruth Brown: Civil Rights, Censorship and the American Library.* Norman: University of Oklahoma Press.

Rochester, Maxine. 1994. "Equivalency of Qualifications in Anglo/American Countries." Sixtieth IFLA General Conference—Conference Proceedings, August 21–27. Accessed February 15, 2015: http://www.ifla.org/IV/ifla60/60–rocm.htm

Rockenback, Barbara, and Tom Mendina, eds. 2001. *Ethics and Electronic Information: A Festschrift for Stephen Almagno.* Jefferson City, NC: McFarland.

Roe v. Wade. 1973. 410 U.S. 113.

Rogerson, Simon, and Robert Beckett. 2003. "E-Democracy, Rights and Privacy in the Age of Information." *Intermedia* 31: 18–27.

Rokeach, Milton. 1973. *The Nature of Human Values.* New York: Free Press.

Rostgaard, Frederic. 1698. *Project d'une nouvelle methode pour dresser le catalogue d'une bibliotheque*, 2nd ed. Paris: n.p.

Roszak, Theodore. 1994. *The Cult of Information: A Neo-Luddite Treatise on High Tech, Artificial Intelligence, and the True Art of Thinking*, 2nd ed. Berkeley: University of California Press.

Rouveyre, Édouard. 1899. *Connaissances nécessaires à un bibliophile*, 5th ed. 4 vols. Paris: Édouard Rouveyre.

Rovelstad, Mathilde. 2000. "Two Seventeenth Century Library Handbooks, Two Different Library Theories." *Libraries and Culture* 35: 540–556.

Rubin, Richard. 1991. "Ethical Issues in Library Personnel Management." *Journal of Library Administration* 14: 1–16.

Rubin, Richard. 2004. *Fundamentals of Library and Information Science*, 2nd ed. New York: Neal-Schuman.

Rubin, Richard, and Thomas Froehlich. 1996. "Ethical Aspects of Library and Information Science." In A. Kent and C. Halls, eds., *Encyclopedia of Library and Information Science.* Vol. 58, supplement 21, 33–52. New York: Marcel Dekker.

Rudinow, Joel, and Anthony Graybosch. 2002. *Ethics and Values in the Information Age*. New York: Wadsworth.

Samek, Toni. 2001. *Intellectual Freedom and Social Responsibility in American Librarianship, 1967–1974*. Jefferson, NC: McFarland.

Samek, Toni. 2002. "Ethics and the Canadian Library Association: Building on a Philosophical Framework of Intellectual Freedom." In Robert Vaagan, ed., *The Ethics of Librarianship: An International Survey*. München: K.G. Saur. 35–58.

Samek, Toni. 2003. "*Synergy*, Social Responsibilities and the Sixties: Pivotal Points in the Evolution of American Outreach Library Service." In Robert S. Freeman and David M. Hovde, eds., *Libraries to the People: Histories of Library Outreach*, 203–218. Jefferson, NC: McFarland.

Samek, Toni. 2007. *Librarianship and Human Rights: A Twenty-First Century Guide*. Oxford: CHANDOS (Oxford) Publishing.

Samek, Toni. 2012. "'I Guess We'll Just Have to Wait for the Movie to Come Out': A Protracted First Stand for Teaching Information Ethics." *Journal of Information Ethics* 21: 33–51.

Sapp, Gregg. 2002. *A Brief History of the Future of Libraries: An Annotated Bibliography*. Lanham, MD: Scarecrow.

Schechter, Stephen. 1990. "The Library as a Source of Civic Literacy." *Bookmark* 48: 176–182.

School of Information Management and Systems at the University of California, Berkeley. 1995. "History Proposal for SIMS: Original Proposal for the Creation of the School Issued in 1993." Last updated April 8, 2015. Accessed February 10, 2015: http://www.sims.berkeley.edu/about/history/

Schulz, Hannelore. 1984. "BBK-Arbeitswoche in Gotha 1983." *Zentralblatt für Bibliothekswesen* 98: 27–30.

Select Committee on Public Libraries. 1849. *Report from the Select Committee on Public Libraries Together with the Proceedings of the Committee, minutes of evidence, and appendix*.

Seymour, Whitney. 1981. "The Public Library in a Free Enterprise Society." *Wilson Library Bulletin* 56: 27–31.

Shah, Aakash Kaushik, Jonathan Warsh, and Aaron S. Kesselheim. 2013. "The Ethics of Intellectual Property Rights in an Era of Globalization." *Journal of Law, Medicine and Ethics* 41: 841–851.

Shannon, Claude. 1948. "A Mathematical Theory for Communication." *Bell System Technical Journal* 27: 379–423, 623–636.

Shera, Jesse. 1949. *Foundations of the Public Library: The Origins of the Public Library Movement in New England, 1629–1855*. Chicago: University of Chicago Press.

Shera, Jesse. 1965. *Libraries and the Organization of Knowledge*. D. J. Foskett, ed. Hamden, CT: Archon Books.

Shera, Jesse. 1972. *The Foundations of Education for Librarianship*. New York: Wiley.

Shimanoff, Susan. 1980. *Communication Rules: Theory and Research*. Beverly Hills, CA: Sage.

Smith, David. 2005. "Artist Hits at Tate 'Cowards' over Ban." *Guardian*, September 25. Accessed February 16, 2015: http://www.theguardian.com/uk/2005/sep/25/arts.religion

Smith, Eldred, and Peggy Johnson. 1993. "How to Survive the Present while Preparing for the Future: A Research Library Strategy." *College and Research Libraries* 54: 389–396.

Smith, Martha M. 1993. "Educating for Information Ethics: Information Ethics 101: Sources for Faculty and Students." *Journal of Information Ethics* 2: 5–10.

Smith, Martha M. 1997a. "Information Ethics." *Annual Review of Information Science and Technology* 32: 339–366.

Smith, Martha M. 1997b. "Information Ethics." Martha E. Williams, ed. *Annual Review of Information Science and Technology* 32: 339–366.

Smith, Martha M. 2001. "Global Information Justice: Rights, Responsibilities, and Caring Connections." *Library Trends* 49: 519–537

Sorel, Charles. 1664. *La bibliothèque Françoise de M. C. Sorel, ou le choix et l'examen des livres François qui traitent de l'eloquence, de la philosophie, de la dévotion et de la conduite des moeurs.* Accessed February 10, 2015: https://books.google.com/books?id=GW4_9uGEQ9MC&pg=PP5&lpg=PP5&dq=La+bibliothèque+françoise+de+M.+C.+Sorel,+ou+Le+choix+et+l%27examen+des+livres+françois+qui+traitent+de+l%27éloquence,+de+la+philosophie,+de+la+dévotion+et+de+la+conduite+des+moeurs&source=bl&ots=fQpTp-258v&sig=x0q7zDzwsrA0SY2CnCiylMkp13c&hl=en&sa=X&ei=R4TbVPXECY6nyAT04ICQAw&ved=0CC8Q6AEwAg#v=onepage&q=La%20bibliothèque%20françoise%20de%20M.%20C.%20Sorel%2C%20ou%20Le%20choix%20et%20l'examen%20des%20livres%20françois%20qui%20traitent%20de%20l'éloquence%2C%20de%20la%20philosophie%2C%20de%20la%20dévotion%20et%20de%20la%20conduite%20des%20moeurs&f=false

Sorel, Charles. 1974. *De la connoissance des bons livres ou examen de plusiers auteurs.* Rome: Bulzoni.

Spinello, Richard, and Herman T. Tavani, eds. 2001. *Readings in CyberEthics.* Sudbury, MA: Jones and Bartlett.

Spofford, Ainsworth Rand. 1900. *A Book for All Readers: Designed as an Aid to the Collection, Use, and Preservation of Books, and the Formation of Public and Private Libraries.* New York: Putnam.

State Intellectual Property Office of the People's Republic of China. 2003. "Report on the Protection of Intellectual Property Rights in China in 2003 (Abstract)." Accessed February 14, 2015: http://english.sipo.gov.cn/news/official/200904/t20090417_453539.html

State Street Bank & Trust Co. v. Signature Financial Group. 1998. 149 F3d 1368 (Fed Cir 1998), cert. denied, 525 US 1093.

Stichler, Richard, and Robert Hauptman, eds. 1988. *Ethics, Information and Technology[:] Readings.* Jefferson, NC: McFarland.

St. Jorre, John de. 1994. *Venus Bound: The Erotic Voyage of the Olympia Press and Its Writers.* New York: Random House.

Sillitoe, Paul. 1998. "The Development of Indigenous Knowledge: A New Applied Anthropology." *Current Anthropology* 39: 223–252.

Sony Corp. of America v. Universal City Studio. 1984. 464 U.S. 417.

Sturges, Paul. 2005. "Understanding Cultures, and IFLA's Freedom of Access to Information and Freedom of Expression (FAIFE) Core Activity." *Journal of Documentation* 61: 296–305.

Sturges, Paul. 2006. "Limits to Freedom of Expression? Considerations Arising from the Danish Cartoons Affair." *IFLA Journal* 32: 181–188: Accessed February 10, 2015: http://www.ifla.org/files/assets/faife/publications/sturges/cartoons.pdf

Sturges, Paul. 2014. "Some Structuring Principles for Planning LIS Qualifications in Developing Countries." *Information Development* 30: 378–381.

Sturges, Paul, and Almuth Gastinge. 2010. "Information Literacy as a Human Right." *Libri* 60: 195–202.

Sudnow, David. 1972. *Studies of Social Interaction.* New York: Free Press.

Sukiasyan, E. R. 1988. "Classification Practice in the USSR: Current Status and Development Trends." *International Classification* 15: 69–72.

Summers, F. William. 1986. *Role of the Association for Library and Information Science Education in Library and Information Science Education.* Accessed February 10, 2015: https://www.ideals.illinois.edu/bitstream/handle/2142/7453/library-trendsv34i4i_opt.pdf?sequence=1

Suntrust Bank v. Houghton Mifflin Co. 2001. N.D. GA., Civil Action Number 1:01-CV-701-CAP, April 19.

Swan, Deann. W., Justin Grimes, Timothy Owens, Kim Miller, J. Andrea Arroyo, Terri Craig, Suzanne Dorinski, Michael Freeman, Natasha Isaac, Patricia O'Shea, Regina Padgett, and Peter Schilling. 2014. *Public Libraries in the United States Survey: Fiscal Year 2012* (IMLS-2015–PLS-01). Washington, DC: Institute of Museum and Library Services. Accessed February 20, 2015: http://www.imls.gov/assets/1/AssetManager/PLS_FY2012.pdf

Symons, Ann, and Carla Stoffle. 1998. "When Values Conflict." *American Libraries* 29: 56–58.

Tammaro, Anna Maria. 2012. "The Bologna Process Impact on Library and Information Science Education: Towards Europeisation of the Curriculum." In Amanda Spink, Jannica Heinström, ed. *Library and Information Science Trends and Research.* Vol. 6, *Europe*, 195–215. Emerald Group.

Taylor, Arlene. 1995. "On the Subject of Subjects." *Journal of American Librarianship* 21: 484–491.

Taylor, Arlene. 2004. *The Organization of Information*, 2nd ed. Westport, CT: Libraries Unlimited.

Tele-Direct (Publications) Inc. v. American Business Information Inc. 1997. Supreme Court of Canada. 2 F.C. 22; (1997) 76 C.P.R. (3d) 296, 310 (F.C.A.); Leave to appeal to S.C.C. denied [1998] 1 S.C.R. xv; (1998) 78 C.P.R. (3d) v.

Tenopir, Carol. 1999. "Human or Automated, Indexing is Important." *Library Journal* 124: 34–38.

Thimbleby, Harold. 1998. "Personal boundaries/global stage." *First Monday* 3:3. Accessed June 9, 2015: http://journals.uic.edu/ojs/index.php/fm/article/view/582/503

Thomas, Alan. 1997. "Bibliographical Classification: The Ideas and Achievements of Henry E. Bliss." *Cataloging and Classification Quarterly* 25: 51–104.

Time Inc. v. Bernard Geis Associates. 1968. 293 F. Supp. 130 (S.D.N.Y.).

Tocqueville, Alexis de. 1835. *Democracy in America.* Vol. 1. Accessed February 16, 2015: http://xroads.virginia.edu/~HYPER/DETOC/toc_indx.html

Tocqueville, Alexis de. 1840. *Democracy in America.* Vol. 2. Accessed February 16, 2015: http://xroads.virginia.edu/~HYPER/DETOC/toc_indx.html

Turner, Dale. 2006. *This Is Not a Peace Pipe: Towards a Critical Indigenous Philosophy.* Toronto: University of Toronto Press.

United Kingdom Department of Media, Culture and Sport. 2014. *Independent Library Report for England.* December 18.

United Nations. 1948. "Universal Declaration of Human Rights." Accessed February 10, 2015: http://www.un.org/Overview/rights.html

United Nations. 2006. "Convention on the Rights of Persons with Disabilities." Accessed March 3, 2015: http://www.un.org/disabilities/convention/conventionfull.shtml

United States Copyright Act of 1976. 17 U.S.C. §107.

United States Department of Education. 2001. Regulations, The No Child Left Behind Act of 2001. PL 107–110. Available from: http://www.ed.gov/policy/elsec/leg/esea02/pg37.html#sec2441

United States Department of the Interior, Bureau of Education. (1876) 1967. *Public Libraries in the United States of America: Their History, Condition, and Management— Special Report.* Washington, DC: US Government Printing Office. Reprint, Monograph Series, no. 4, Urbana-Champagne: Graduate School of Library Science, University of Illinois Press.

United States Library of Congress. 2014. *National Agenda for Digital Stewardship.* Accessed February 5, 2015: http://www.digitalpreservation.gov/ndsa/documents/2014NationalAgenda.pdf

United States Library of Congress. 1999. *Stewardship Report, Heritage Assets, Library Collections.* September 30. Accessed February 5, 2015: http://www.loc.gov/fsd/fin/pdfs/fy9904.pdf

United States v. One Package of Japanese Pessaries. 1936. 86 F.2d 737 (2d Cir.).

United States v. One Book Named Ulysess by James Joyce. 1934. 72 F.2d 705 (2d Cir.).

University of Cambridge. 2004. "External Examiner." Accessed February 10, 2015: http://www.admin.cam.ac.uk/offices/education/examiners/external.html

Vaagan, Robert, ed. 2002. *The Ethics of Librarianship: An International Survey*, Munich: K. G. Saur.

Vaagan, Robert, and Wallace Koehler. 2005. "Intellectual Property Rights vs. Public Access Rights: Ethical Aspects of The DeCSS Decryptation Program." Information Research 10, paper 230. Accessed February 14, 2015: http://InformationR.net/ir/10–3/paper230.html

Vaidhyanathan, Siva. 2001. *Copyrights and Copywrongs: The Rise of Intellectual Property and How It Threatens Creativity*. New York: New York University Press.

Valentine, Patrick. 2012. *A Social History of Books and Libraries from Cuneiform to Bytes*. Lanham, MD: Scarecrow.

van den Hoven, Jeroen. 2004. "Privacy and the Varieties of Informational Wrongdoing." In Richard Spinello and Herman Tavani, eds., *Readings in Cyberethics*, 2nd ed. Sudbury, MA: Jones and Bartlett.

Vann, Sarah. 1961. *Training for Librarianship before 1923*. Chicago: American Library Association.

Vitz, Paul. 1986. *Censorship: Evidence of Bias in our Children's Textbooks*. Ann Arbor, MI: Servant Books.

Vivant, Michel. 1991. "Protection of Raw Data and Databanks in France." In E. J. Dommering and P. B. Hugenholz, eds., *Protecting Works of Fact*. Boston: Kluwer Law and Taxation.

W3C. 1999. "Resource Description Framework (RDF) Schema Specification, W3C Proposed Recommendation," March 3. Accessed February 16, 2015: http://www.w3.org/TR/1998/WD-rdf-schema/

Wadsworth, Sarah, and Wayne Wiegand. 2012. *"Right Here I See My Own Books": The Woman's Building Library at the World's Columbian Exposition*. Amherst: University of Massachusetts Press.

Warf, Barney. 2011. "Geographies of Global Internet Censorship." *GeoJournal* 76: 1–23.

Warrior, Robert. 1995. *Tribal Secrets: Recovering American Indian Intellectual Traditions*. Minneapolis: University of Minnesota Press.

Weibel, Kathleen, and Kathleen Heim, eds. 1979. *The Role of Women in Librarianship, 1876–1976: The Entry, Advancement, and Struggle for Equalization in One Profession*. Phoenix, AZ: Oryx.

Weinberg, Bella Hass. 1988. "Why Indexing Fails the Researcher." *Indexer* 16: 3–6.

Weinberg, Bella Hass. 1991. *Cataloging Heresies: Challenging the Standard Bibliographic Product—Proceedings of the Congress for Librarians, February 18, 1991 St. John's University, Jamaica, New York, with Additional Contributed Papers*. Medford, NJ: Learned Information, 1991.

Weingand, Darlene. 1999. *Marketing/Planning Library and Information Services*, 2nd ed. Englewood, CO: Libraries Unlimited.

Wells, H. G. 1938. *World Brain*. London: Methuen.

Wells, H. G. (1923) 2003. *Men Like Gods*. Online Project Gutenberg of Australia. Accessed February 12, 2015: http://gutenberg.net.au/ebooks02/0200221.txt

West Publishing Co. v. Mead Data Cent. Inc. 1986. 616 F. Supp. 1571 (D. Minn. 1985), aff'd, 799 F.2d 1219 (8th Circ.), cert. denied, 479 U.S. 1070.

Wheaton v. Peters. 1834. 33 U.S. (8 Pet.) 591.

Wheeler, Maurice B. 2005. *Unfinished Business: Race, Equity, and Diversity in Library and Information Science Education*. Lanham, MD: Scarecrow.

White, Herbert. 1991. "Teaching Professional Ethics to Students of Library and Information Science." In F. W. Lancaster, ed., *Ethics and the Librarian*, 31–43. Urbana-Champaign: University of Illinois Press.

Wiegand, Shirley, and Wayne Wiegand. 2007. *Books on Trial: Red Scare in the Heartland*. Norman: University of Oklahoma Press.

Wiegand, Wayne. 1968. "The 'Amherst Method': The Origins of the Dewey Decimal Classification Scheme." *Libraries and Culture* 33: 175–194.

Wiegand, Wayne. 1986. *The Politics of an Emerging Profession: The American Library Association, 1876–1917*. New York: Greenwood.

Wiegand, Wayne. 1989. *An Active Instrument for Propaganda:" The American Public Library During World War I*. New York: Greenwood.

Wiegand, Wayne. 1995 "'Jew Attack': The Story behind Melvil Dewey's Resignation as New York State Librarian in 1905." *American Jewish History* 83: 359–379.

Wiegand, Wayne. 1996. *Irrepressible Reformer: A Biography of Melvil Dewey*. Chicago: American Library Association.

Wiegand, Wayne. 1998. "Main Street Public Library: The Availability of Controversial Materials in the Rural Heartland, 1890–1956." *Libraries and Culture* 31: 127–133.

Wilkinson, L[ane]. 2014. "Principles and Ethics in Librarianship" *Reference Librarian* 55: 1–25.

Williamson, Charles. 1971. Training for Library Work. In S. K. Vann ed., *The Williamson Reports of 1921 and 1923, Including Training for Library Work and Training for Library Service*, 1–276. Metuchen, NJ: Scarecrow.

Wong, Tzen, and Graham Dutfield, eds. 2010. *Intellectual Property and Human Development: Current Trends and Future Scenarios*. New York: Cambridge University Press.

World International Property Organization. 2013. "Marrakesh Treaty to Facilitate Access to Published Works for Persons Who Are Blind, Visually Impaired or Otherwise Print Disabled." Accessed March 3, 2015: http://www.wipo.int/treaties/en/ip/marrakesh/

World Summit on the Information Society. 2005. "Tunis Commitment." WSIS-05/TUNIS/DOC/7–E. Accessed February 20, 2015: http://www.itu.int/wsis/docs2/tunis/off/7.html

Xu, Xueyang, Z. Morley Mao, and Alex Halderman. 2011. "Internet Censorship in China: Where Does the Filtering Occur?" *Lecture Notes in Computer Science* 6579: 133–142.

Yu, Peter. 2006. "Five Disharmonizing Trends in the International Intellectual Property Regime." Accessed February 16, 2015: http://infojustice.org/download/gcongress/waysandmeansdevelopment/yu%20article%203.pdf

Zeng, Marcia Lei, and Lois Mai Chan. 2003. "Trends and Issues in Establishing Interoperability among Knowledge Organization Systems." *Journal of the Association for Information Science and Technology* 55: 377–395.

Index

AACR. *See* Anglo-American Cataloging Rules

AACR2. *See* Anglo-American Cataloging Rules, second edition

accreditation, 178–179, 179, 180, 181, 182

ALA accreditation, 182

ALA Black Caucus, 3

African Network for Information Ethics, 224; Tshwane Declaration, 224

African Americans, 117

Agreement on Trade-Related Aspects of Intellectual Property Rights, 158

ALA COA. *See* ALA Committee on Accreditation

ALA Committee on Accreditation, 182

ALA Committee on Education, 3

ALA Committee on the Status in Librarianship, 220

ALA Core Competencies, 3

ALA Gay, Lesbian, Bisexual, and Transgender Round Table, 3

ALA. *See* American Library Association

Allied Professional Association ALA, 182, 183

American Indian Librarian Association, 3

American Library Association, 3

American Library Association Office for Intellectual Freedom, 103, 123

Anglo-American Cataloging Rules, 73

Anglo-American Cataloging Rules, second edition, 15, 73

antelope in the zoo, 11

appearance ethics, 222

archival mark-up, 67–68

Argentina, 179

art, 117–118

code of ethics, 32; Association des Bibliothécaires de France, 32; American Library Association, 22, 214

Asian Pacific American Librarians Association, 3

associations, professional, 13

Author, 15

Banned books, 104–105

Basbanes, Nicholas, 204

BBK. *See* Bibliotechnobibliograficheskaíà klassifikatsiíà

Beauty, 5

Berlin, Isaiah, 4, 5

Berman, Sanford, 44, 46, 74, 235

Berne Convention, 145, 147, 162, 163

Biblioéconomie , 75

Bibliomane, 202–205

Bibliomaniac, 202–205

Bibliophile, 202–205

Bibliotechnobibliograficheskaíà klassifikatsiíà, 15, 47, 72, 134

Bill and Melinda Gates Foundation, 97, 199

Bill of Rights, United States, 23

Blades, William, 204, 211

Bliss classification, 46

Bodleian Library, Oxford University, 36

Bodley, Sir Thomas, 36, 40, 52, 125, 127, 150, 173–175, 200

Bologna Process, 175, 183

Bolsheviks, 4

Book deposit, 150, 151

Boston Public Library, 92, 95

Briet, Suzanne, 10, 11

British Board of Film Classification, 113

British Museum cataloging rules, 56
Brown v. Board of Education, 136
Brown, James Duff, 57
Brown, Ruth, 136
Buckland, Michael, 10

Canadian Library Association, 111, 132
Capurro, Rafeal, 3, 171–172, 213
Cardona, Juan Bautista, 39
Carnegie, Andrew, 95, 199
Catalog, 49–50
Catherine the Great, 134
Catholic Index of Forbidden Books, 117
censorship, 112, 149, 225
Cervantes, Miguel de, 148
Charlie Hebdo, 116
Child Online Protection Act, 84
Children, 84–85, 115
Children's Internet Protection Act, 84
China, Peoples Republic of, 8, 142, 162, 163
Chinese American Librarians Association, 3
Churchill, Winston, 136
CILIP. *See* Chartered Institute of Library and Information Professionals, 178
CIPA. *See* Children's Internet Protection Act
circulating libraries, 93
Civic culture, 134
Civil law, 154
CLA. *See* Canadian Library Association
Classes of literature, 1
Classification, 43, 49; As language, 43, 48; As social activity, 43; Defined, 44; Cultural phenomenon, 46, 72; Linguistic aspects, 47; Political aspects, 47; Meaning, 49; Early historical, 51–52; Sources, 52–54; Technology, 71
Classification Board, Australia, 113
Clément, Claude, 23
CLIR. *See* Council on Library and Information Resources
Codex, 19
Collectivist ethos, 154
Colon classification, 46, 61–62

Commission on Online Child Protection, 103
Committee on Free Access to Information and Freedom of Expression, IFLA, 109–110
commodification of information, 22
common law, 154
commons initiatives, 164
Communications technology, 7, 104
Community building, 140
Community information, 140
Computer, 214
Computer algorithms, 75
Comstock Law, 118
Conference on Open Access to Knowledge in the Sciences and Humanities, 164–166
COPA. *See* Child Online Protection Act
Council on Library and Information Resources, 182
Convention for the Protection of Human Rights and Fundamental Freedoms of 1950, 107; Article 9, 107; Article 10, 107–108; Article 11, 108
Constitution, United States, xii, 84, 85, 103, 106, 112, 118, 137, 149, 218
copy tax, 149
copyright, 20, 146
Copyright Designs and Patents Act of 1988, UK, 145
corporatism, 139
Cotton des Houssayes, Jean-Baptiste, 41, 130, 184, 190–191
Cuba, 142
cultural bias, 74
cultural determinants, 34, 82
cyberspace, 135

Dana, John Cotton, 81, 95, 195
Darwin, Charles, 50
DDC. See Dewey Decimal Classification
De Bury, Richard, 88, 124, 125, 200, 202, 204, 205–206, 207, 228, 229
Declaration of the Rights of Man and the Citizen of 1789, 106
democracy, 133; catalyst, 134
democratization of libraries, 95

de-selection, 120
Desktop Marketing Systems Pty Ltd. v. Telstra Corporation Ltd., 156
Dewey Decimal Classification, 15, 46, 56
Dewey, Melvil, 23, 28, 56, 96, 123, 132, 192–193, 195
Dialog, 73
Diderot, Denis, 134
digital divide, 216–217
Digital Millennium Copyright Act of 1998, US, 145
Digital Rights Management, 146
digital technologies, 20
disadvantaged, 2
discourse, 14
document, 15
documentation, 10, 11, 172, 231, 242
Donaldson v. Beckett, 1774, 147, 155
DRM. *See* Digital Rights Management
Dublin Core, 15, 66–67
Dürer, Albrecht, 149
Dury, John, 40, 41, 128, 186–189

economic environment, 138
e-democracy, 141
e-rights, 224
e-vote, 142
Eco, Umberto, 5, 13, 14, 36, 48, 49, 71; *The Name of the Rose*, 36; *Search for a Perfect Language*, 49
Edwards, Edward, 2, 23, 45, 45–46, 57, 87, 88, 93–94, 191–192; access, 93–94
El Escorial, 38, 39
elites, social, 10
encyclopedism, 21
Enlightenment, 7, 105, 134
entropy, 223
ERIC, 63
Estatuto del profesional en bibliotecologia y documentacion (Argentina), 179–180
ethical precepts, 24–25
European government, 6
existentialism, 8, 9
external examiner, 180–181

Fabius-Gayssot Law, 117
fairness and originality, 153

fair use, 154, 159–161; Purpose and character, 159–160; Nature of the work, 160; Amount taken, 160–161; Market impact, 161
Federalist Papers, 136–137
Feist Publications, Inc., v. Rural Telephone Service Co , 156
Feminist Task Force, ALA, 220
Finland, Grand Duchy of, 95
Finnish language, 71
Five Laws of Library Science, 11, 12, 18
Franklin, Benjamin, 92
freedom of expression, 103
FRBR. *See* Functional Requirements for Bibliographic Records
FAIFE. *See* Committee on Free Access to Information and Freedom of Expression, IFLA
Floridi, Luciano, 3, 213, 215, 228
Foucault, Michel, 9, 10, 14
Functional Requirements for Bibliographic Records, 73

global individual rights, 142
globalization, 224
God Is Great, 117
Google Books, 22, 32
Gorman, Michael, 1, 2, 17, 23, 133, 134; Stewardship, 32
graphic works, 14
Gutenberg, 149

Habermas, Jürgen, 5, 6, 141
harmful to minors, 115, 119–120
Harris, Michael, 6, 10, 21, 96
Harvard Library, 91
Hauptman, Robert, 22, 213
Henriot, Émile, 210
Heyne, Christian Gottlob, 131
homelessness, 139–211
HTML-based search and retrieval systems, 64–66
human communication, 6

I-school, 179, 183
IFLA. *See* International Federation of Library Associations and Institutions
imprimatur, 150

indexing, 74
indigenous knowledge, 3, 225
individualist ethos, 154
information commons, 97, 166
information ethics, 22
infosphere, 215
ICT. *See* Information Communication Technology
informal sector, 228
Information Communication Technology, 142
information ethics researchers, 2
intellectual freedom, 103
intellectual property, 19, 145; Defined, 146–147
International Federation of Library Associations and Institutions, 13, 132; Paris Declaration, 73; Lyons Declaration, 110
Internet, 64, 73–74, 81, 83–84, 141
Iowa Library Movement, 95

Joeckel, Carleton, 80
junto, 92
Jyllands Posten , 116

Kirkwood, James, 2, 40, 90–91, 129–130, 151–152, 189–190, 228
Koch, Johann Christian, 202
Koehler, Wallace, 17, 147, 167, 216, 221
Köhler, Johann David, 23, 40, 50, 73, 91, 131, 152
Kraemer v. Morristown. See Morristown v. Kraemer
Kranich, Nancy, 134, 136
Krupskaya, Nadezhda K., 134, 140–141
Ku Klux Klan, 117

language, perfect, 48
LCCS. *See* Library of Congress Classification System
Le Gallois, Pierre, 2
Lévi-Strauss, Claude, 9, 10
librarian defined, 15, 83
librarian qualifications, 171
librarianship defined, 15
Library of Alexandria, 35, 148
Library Bill of Rights, ALA, 110
library destruction, 35

Library, digital, 32
Library economy, 75
library feminist activism, 220
Library of Congress Classification System, 15, 46, 58–59, 73, 74
Library of Congress, United States, 35, 36
library, public historical definitions, 87–96
library iconography, 23
library science, 172, 176
Licenses, 19, 149, 150
Licensing Act of 1662, UK, 150
limited public forum, 86
limits, social, 104
Linnaeus, Carl, 48, 52, 54, 89
Lipsius, Justus, 3, 23, 122, 185
Lomeier, Johannes, 90

Ma'arv-Modiin Publishers Ltd., v. All You Need Ltd., 156
Machine Readable Cataloging Standards, 15, 62; MARC variants, 62
Magna Carta, 23
Manchester Free Library, 94
Mao Zedong, 140
marketing, 218
malpractice, 222
McCook, Kathleen de la Peña, 37, 81, 96, 140
MARC. *See* Machine Readable Cataloging Standards
Mazarine Library, 38
MLIS. *See* master of library science degree
MS (IS). *See* master of library science degree
MIS. *See* master of library science degree
master of library science degree, 182
Marxism-Leninism, 4, 47, 134
miners and mechanics libraries, 93
minority rights, 3
Mitchell, Sydney, 141
modernism, 5, 6, 7
morals, 18
moral rights of the author, 147, 163
Morristown v. Kraemer , 86

Multilingualism, 48

National Association to Promote Library and Information to Latinos and the Spanish-Speaking, 3
nationalism, 5
natural environment, 215
Naudé, Gabriel, 23, 38, 125, 128, 186, 200–201, 208
NCIPA. *See* Neighborhood Children's Internet Protection Act
Neighborhood Children's Internet Protection Act, 84
Newspaper Program, US, 36
non-linear, 13

one legal copy, 164
Online Computer Library Center, 73
Ontario Free Libraries Act, 95
Ontario Film Review Board, 114
Ohio College Library Center. *See* Online Computer Library Center
OCLC. *See* Online Computer Library Center
Otlet, Paul, 10, 21, 172

P2P. *See* peer-2-peer
Panizzi, Sir Anthony, 23, 56, 72; *91 Rules for Compilation of the Catalogue*, 72
paper manufacture, 19
patents, 157–158
peer-2-peer, 156, 161, 164
Pepys, Samuel, 199, 207–208
Peter the Great, 134
Philobiblon, 204, 205, 208
philosophy, library, 31
pornography, 74, 114–115
post-modernism, 5, 6, 7
Pourciau, Lester, 13
power, 9
power symbols, 10
plagiarism, 152
pluralism, 139
pre-modern, 6
printing patent, 150, 151
propaganda, 141

Páez de Castro, Juan, 38, 39, 202; Memorial, 39
preservation, 35, 36, 38
preservation, digital, 38
privacy, 221–222
Project Gutenberg, 22, 32
Prussian Principles, 15, 47, 73
public forum doctrine, 85–86
public library definition, 81
Public Library Inquiry, 97
public library theory, 18, 80
public sphere, 5, 6, 7, 28, 104–105, 140, 141

race and ethnicity, 96–97, 99, 220–221
Ranganathan, S.R., 1, 2, 11, 12, 33, 42, 44, 132, 171; Library history, 32; Library future, 32; First law, 12, 19, 33, 44, 132, 226; Second Law, 19, 132, 226; Third Law, 19, 33, 104, 132; Fourth Law, 19, 44, 226; Fifth Law, xi, 11–12, 44, 132, 226
RAK. *See* Regeln fur die alphabetische Katalogisierung
RDF. *See* Resource Description Framework
REFORMA. *See* National Association to Promote Library and Information to Latinos and the Spanish-Speaking
Regeln fur die alphabetische Katalogisierung, 73
Resource Description Framework, 68–69, 73
Richard, Jules, 131
riff-raff books, 104, 127, 214
Rights of minorities, 3
Rouveyre, Édouard, 203, 209–210

Samek, Toni, 3
samizdat, 122
secondary and derivative social body, 79
second law of thermodynamics, 223
segregation, 139
self-censorship, 112, 116, 117
selection, 120
Semantic Web, 15, 22, 69–71
service, 2, 31, 40

Shera, Jesse, 79, 80, 98, 133
social factors, 21
social institutions, 9, 79
social paradigm shift, 5
society, authoritarian, 7
society, civil, 8, 224
society, liberal, 7
Sorel, Charles, 128
Soviet Union. *See* Union of Soviet
    Socialist Republics
Spofford, Ainsworth Rand, 193–195
standard of originality, 155
standards of practice, 4
state sponsored taking, 148
Statement on Intellectual Freedom
    Canadian Library Association, 111
Statement on Libraries and Intellectual
    Freedom, IFLA, 108–109
Statute of Anne, 149, 150, 153, 155, 228
sweat of the brow, 156
stewardship, 2, 31
stone tablets, 19
structuralism, 8, 9
subject heading, 46
subscription library, 139

Tate Britain Museum, 117
TEACH Act. *See* Technology,
    Education, and Copyright
    Harmonization Act
*Tele-Direct (Publications) Inc. v.
    American Business Information Inc.*,
    156
Technology, Education, and Copyright
    Harmonization Act, 161
technology changes, 19, 32, 141, 169,
    224
technological literacy, 216
thesaurus, 47
time, place, manner rule, 86
Tocqueville, Alexis de, 7, 9, 28
Toronto Public Library, 95
TRIPS. *See* Agreement on Trade-
    Related Aspects of Intellectual
    Property Rights
tropes, 218
type, moveable, 19

Uganda, 111

UDC. *See* Universal Decimal
    Classification
United Kingdom, 13, 104
Universal Declaration of Human
    Rights, 23, 106–107, 111, 142
Universal Decimal Classification, 46,
    60–61, 73
Universal Copyright Convention of
    1952, 162
USSR. *See* Union of Soviet Socialist
    Republics
union catalog, 73–74
Union of Soviet Socialist Republics, 47,
    162
University of Cambridge Library, 94

Varro, Marcus Terentius, 22, 186, 199
Voltaire, 134
vital principle, 12
virtual community, 140

Web documents, native, 64
weeding. *See* de-selection
Weinberg, Bella Hass, 74
Wells, H. G., 21
Wheaton v. Peters (1834), 155
WIPO. *See* World Intellectual Property
    Organization
WSIS. *See* World Summit on the
    Information Society
World Intellectual Property
    Organization, 145, 147, 162, 163
WTO. *See* World Trade Organization
World Summit on the Information
    Society, 224; Tunis Commitment,
    224
World Trade Organization, 145, 147,
    158
Women, 2, 96, 114, 219–220
Women's library, 96
Women Library Workers, 220
World Wide Web, 99, 121, 225
work in movement, 13
working class libraries, 93
World Brain, 21
WorldCat, 73
World Wide Web, 22, 135

XML Markup, 15

About the Author

Wallace C. Koehler Jr. retired in July 2014 from Valdosta State University, where he is now professor emeritus. He was director of the Master of Library and Information Science Program at VSU from 2001 until retirement. Dr. Koehler led the program through its initial ALA accreditation in 2007 and its reaccreditation in 2014. He holds a PhD from Cornell University and an MS in information science from the University of Tennessee.

Dr. Koehler is author of numerous articles that address library and information science ethics; bibliometrics; and information policy. He is co-author of *Fundamentals of Information Studies*, in two editions.

Lightning Source UK Ltd.
Milton Keynes UK
UKOW03n1506240317

297454UK00001B/28/P

9 781442 254268